D1083890

The Rise of the
French Communist Party
1920–1947

THE RISE OF THE
French Communist Party

1920–1947

EDWARD MORTIMER

faber and faber
LONDON · BOSTON

First published in 1984
by Faber and Faber Limited
3 Queen Square London WC1N 3AU
Filmset by Wilmaset Birkenhead Merseyside
Printed in Great Britain by
Redwood Burn Ltd
Trowbridge Wiltshire

British Library Cataloguing in Publication Data

Mortimer, Edward
The rise of the French Communist Party
1. Parti Communiste Français. *History*
I. Title
324.22′44′075   JN3007.C6

ISBN 0–571–09754–5

TO RICHARD COBB,
a constant source of inspiration
but in no sense responsible

Contents

Contents

Glossary of Abbreviations

AEAR *Association des Ecrivains et Artistes Révolutionnaires* (fellow-travelling intellectuals' group, founded 1932)

AMGOT Allied Military Government in Occupied Territory (World War II)

ARAC *Association Républicaine des Anciens Combattants* (pacifist war veterans' group, founded 1917 by Henri Barbusse, later Communist-controlled)

AS *Armée Secrète* (wartime resistance movement, non-Communist)

BCRA *Bureau Central de Renseignements et d'Action* (Gaullist intelligence network, World War II)

CCN *Comité Confédéral National* (governing body of the CGT)

CDS *Comité de Défense Syndicaliste* (anti-war trade unionists' group, founded 1917)

CERM *Centre d'Etudes et de Recherches Marxistes* (PCF research institute, post World War II)

CFTC *Confédération Française des Travailleurs Chrétiens* (Catholic trade union movement)

CFDT *Confédération Française Démocratique du Travail* (socialist trade union movement, formed by majority of CFTC in 1964)

CGT *Confédération Générale du Travail* (the largest French trade union movement, founded in 1895, PCF-dominated since 1945)

CGTSR *Confédération Générale du Travail Syndicaliste Révolutionnaire* (anarcho-syndicalist split from CGTU, 1926)

CGTU *Confédération Générale du Travail Unitaire* (revolutionary split from CGT, 1922, which soon came under PCF control; reunited with CGT in 1935)

CI Comintern (Communist International)

COMAC *Comité Militaire d'Action* (internally appointed command of French Resistance, 1944; under PCF control)

CP Communist Party

CPSU Communist Party of the Soviet Union

CPY Communist Party of Yugoslavia

CRRI *Comité pour la Reprise des Relations Internationales* (French component of the 'Zimmerwald movement', 1916–19)

CRS *Compagnies Républicaines de Sécurité* (French riot police)

CSRs *Comités Syndicalistes Révolutionnaires* (revolutionary opposition within CGT, 1920–2)

ECCI Executive Committee of the Communist International

EEC European Economic Community

11

Glossary of Abbreviations

FFI *Forces Françaises de l'Intérieur* (unified French Resistance forces, 1944)

FTP *Francs-Tireurs et Partisans* (Communist Resistance forces, 1941–4)

IFTU International Federation of Trade Unions (non-Communist, pre-World War II)

ILP Independent Labour Party

JC *Jeunesses Communistes* (PCF youth movement)

KMT *Kuomintang* (Chinese Nationalist Party)

KPD *Kommunistische Partei Deutschlands*

MRG *Mouvement des Radicaux de Gauche* (section of Radical Party which split off and signed Socialist-Communist joint programme, 1972)

MRP *Mouvement Républicain Populaire* (Christian Democrat party, 1944–67)

MUR *Mouvement Unifié de la Résistance* (fellow-travelling group, founded 1945)

NATO North Atlantic Treaty Organization

ORA *Organisation de Résistance de l'Armée* (wartime resistance movement, non-Communist, composed mainly of army officers)

OS *Organisation Spéciale* (Communist self-defence body, 1940–1)

PC *Parti Communiste*

PCE *Partido Comunista de España*

PCF *Parti Communiste Français*

PCI *Partito Comunista Italiano*

PCP *Partido Comunista Português*

Profintern: Red International of Labour Unions

PS *Parti Socialiste*

PSU *Parti Socialiste Unifié* (name used by the SFIO before 1920; since 1960, an independent far-left party)

PTT *Postes, Télégraphe et Téléphone* (the French Post Office)

PUP *Parti d'Unité Prolétarienne* (party formed by dissident communists in early 1930s)

SFIC *Section Française de l'Internationale Communiste* (original title of the PCF, 1920–1)

SFIO *Section Française de l'Internationale Ouvrière* (the main French Socialist party from 1905 to 1969)

SPD *Sozialdemokratische Partei Deutschlands*

UDSR *Union Démocratique et Socialiste de la Résistance* (non-Communist political group, founded 1945)

USPD *Unabhängige Sozialdemokratische Partei Deutschlands* (left splinter from SPD, 1916–22)

WFTU World Federation of Trade Unions (successor to Profintern, founded 1945)

VO *La Vie Ouvrière* (syndicalist review, edited by Pierre Monatte until 1922; then the organ of the CGTU, and later of the CGT)

Introduction

The greater part of this book was researched and written during 1971 and 1972. It was originally intended to be a complete history of the French Communist Party up to that time. The project grew out of my experience as Assistant Paris Correspondent of *The Times* from 1967 to 1970, and more especially from reflection on the events of 1968. Reporting from Paris at that time one inevitably paid a lot of attention to groups and movements on the left of the Communist Party. They were 'news' because they were new, and because they went in for spectacular activities and pronouncements. By contrast there was relatively little to say in a daily newspaper about the PCF itself—an organization which was determinedly *un*spectacular, cautious and slow-moving. Its leaders were elderly and anything but flamboyant, carefully concealing their debates and decision-making processes, and expressing themselves in leaden prose which was studiously imitated by the younger party cadres. The PCF was not 'good copy'.

And yet, the more one struggled to explain to British newspaper readers what was going on in France, and particularly what the new left (*gauchistes*) were up to, the more one realized that one could do so only in terms of the peculiar position in French politics occupied by the PCF, and its role in contemporary French history. I was increasingly struck by the fact that, while the PCF itself claimed to be the principal force for change in the country, virtually everyone else, whether on its left or on its right, regarded it as the principal obstacle to change. Reforming technocrats constantly found it in the front rank of those protesting against any specific innovation, whether in industry, agriculture, education or social security, leading the resistance of this or that social category to any real or supposed infringement of its 'acquired rights'. Liberals argued that the 'totalitarian' and 'undemocratic' character of the largest opposition party (as the PCF then was) distorted the political system as a whole, making impossible a healthy 'alternation' of government and opposition (on the British model) and thus encouraging the existing regime to become illiberal, immobilist and complacent. Socialists or social democrats felt that the PCF had neutralized the hard core of working-class votes on which a democratic socialist party, strong enough and moderate enough to win elections (as in neighbouring countries to the north and east), should have been based. 'The left cannot win without the Communist Party,' the saying went, 'and it cannot win with it.' But revolutionary leftists equally felt that the PCF was abusing the trust of the most class-conscious section of the working class, using its influence to render strikes and protest movements politically harmless, in the interests of an electoral strategy which in the last resort was equivalent to that of social democracy.

The PCF had thus become 'objectively' (as its own jargon would put it) a conservative party. Assuredly its leaders did not see themselves as conservatives. In fact some of them (notably at that time Waldeck Rochet) were seeking, according to their lights, to adapt the party's policies to the changed conditions of late twentieth-century western Europe. But the process of adaptation, even compared to that of other French political parties, or to that of a comparable Communist Party—the PCI—was painfully slow. The more I thought about it the more it seemed to me anomalous that a party of this type should occupy such an important position in French politics and society. The explanation for it could not be found in the present: it had to be sought in the past.

This book is an attempt at such an explanation. It is not, for the most part, a work of original research, but a work of analysis based on what I hope was a fairly thorough examination of the available secondary sources. I do not think its conclusions are significantly affected by the studies which have come out since most of it was written, such as Philippe Robrieux's excellent biography of Thorez.

I have to apologize for the lateness with which it appears, and also for its incompleteness. I found it impossible to contain my original project within the bounds of space and time that I had set for it. I allowed myself two years and one volume for a history of the PCF. By the end of the two years I had written enough for a fair-sized volume, but had only just reached the Second World War. My fellowship at All Souls College, Oxford, had meanwhile expired, and I was due to resume full-time employment on *The Times*. In any case, I felt that a second volume devoted mainly to the period after 1947 would not be of great interest, since the most striking feature of the PCF during that period was its stability, not to say immobility. By 1947 the PCF had already achieved the position it was to hold in France for the next thirty years, and its attempt to use that position to establish itself in power had already come to grief. I therefore decided to end my detailed narrative with the party's ejection from government by

Ramadier in May 1947, and to content myself with a short epilogue tracing its subsequent history.

That, essentially, is the form of the book as now presented. But for a long time it failed to get finished at all, as various journalistic preoccupations drew me away from it. I was drawn back to it in the late 1970s mainly by the appearance of what is called 'Euro-communism', which lent a new interest to the subject and enabled us to see it in a new light. 'Eurocommunism' was in fact an attempt to resolve those very contradictions which I perceived in the position of the PCF in the late 1960s, and which affected other western Communist Parties in more or less equal measure. It seems doubtful now (1982) whether 'Eurocommunism' was the right label to hang on the various changes which occurred in the PCF during the 1970s. Certainly if it is used it should not be taken to imply that the French, Italian and Spanish parties converged on a common position. In the case of the PCF it rather took the form of an attempt to reinforce the specifically French identity of the party, and that, on many issues, meant taking positions opposite to those of its Italian and Spanish counterparts (PCI and PCE).* And in this respect at least there is continuity between the party's attitude in 1976–7 (the high point of 'Eurocommunism') and its return to self-isolation in 1978–81.

What was striking was that the themes of the PCF in its 'Eurocommunist' incarnation—imperfect and incomplete as that was—were echoes of themes belonging to its earlier history, and precisely those which coincided with its periods of greatest growth and dynamism. The central argument of this book (most fully developed in the concluding sections of Chapters Six and Seven) is that there is an organic connection between the two senses in which the PCF can be called a 'national' party—the fact that it fosters French national pride and the fact that it enjoys nationwide support and plays a key role in national politics—and that this national role, which it acquired almost by accident as a by-product of certain phases of Stalin's foreign policy, has become central to its identity and its image of itself: so that there is a contradiction between the PCF as it is and its original *raison d'être*, which (as indicated in Chapters One to Three) was to compensate for the inadequacy of

---

* Jean Elleinstein has coined the word 'gallo-communism' to describe this phe-nomenon (*Maintenant*, no. 9, 7 May 1979, p. 4).

French national solutions to the problem of working-class emancipation by imposing an imported solution and subjecting the French labour movement to the tightest international discipline.

My thanks are due, in the first place, to All Souls College, which welcomed me back like a prodigal son three years after I had officially renounced academic status; and secondly to *The Times*, which showed a similar tolerance in finding new employment for me two years after I resigned. Had either of these two ancient English institutions been less flexible I could never have written this book. I must also thank Faber and Faber Ltd for agreeing to publish a book which is not the one they originally commissioned, and which was not delivered until nearly six years after the original deadline.

The book was to have been published in 1980, and the epilogue was updated to cover the party's Twenty-Third Congress, held in May 1979. Events beyond my control have delayed publication for another three years, during which the PCF's fortunes and policies have undergone further dramatic transformations, which are only briefly summarized in the concluding pages. It is noted there that the party has returned to government in 1981 in a much weaker position than it enjoyed in the governments of the Liberation (1944–7). Yet it remains a striking fact that in France, alone among West European countries, the Communist Party is at present a party of government. Its importance is sufficient, in other words, for the Socialists to have thought it politically necessary to include it in the government, even though it was not necessary arithmetically. At the same time the behaviour of the party and its leaders remains, to many people, an enigma. I hope that these facts will add to, rather than detract from, the interest of an account of the party's rise to influence, if not power, and of the processes by which its self-image was formed.

Professor Max (now Lord) Beloff read each chapter as I produced it, and made many helpful comments in spite of the difference in our political outlooks. Many other friends and colleagues on both sides of the Channel gave help and advice, but none more so than the members of the former *Groupe Unir*. They more than anyone helped me to appreciate the decency and courage of thousands of French men and women for whom, at different times, the PCF has been a source of hope and inspiration. They deserved a better party than they got.

EDWARD MORTIMER
September 1982

PART ONE

A Party of a New Type
1920 – 1934

1

The Problem

1914–1920

The French Communist Party came into existence on 29 December 1920, at ten o'clock in the evening, in the Salle du Manège at Tours. The occasion was the Eighteenth Congress of the Unified Socialist Party. A motion for the party to join the Communist International was passed by 3,208 votes to 1,022.[1]

These 3,208 mandates represented some 120,000 Socialist militants, out of a total party membership of nearly 180,000.* Nor was this representation purely formal, since the motion had been debated and voted on at the local level throughout France before the congress met, and delegates cast their votes at the congress in accordance with the instructions given them by their local federations. And enthusiasm for the Communist International in France at this time was, as we shall see, by no means confined to members of the Socialist Party.

The Communist International had been founded less than two years before, in Moscow in March 1919. At its founding congress, France was 'represented' by two Frenchmen living in Moscow, neither of whom had any mandate from any organization in France. At its second congress, in July and August 1920, the International laid down twenty-one conditions for membership, conditions of great stringency, many of which were entirely foreign to the traditions of the French labour movement. Why then this great enthusiasm in France

---

* Party membership was 178,372 on 1 October 1920. There seems to have been roughly one mandate for every thirty-eight members, but it is not known how the exact number of mandates per federation was worked out. See *Parti Socialiste* (SFIO), *18e Congrès National, Tours, 25–31 décembre 1920, Compte-rendu sténographié* (Paris, 1920), pp. vi, x; and A. Kriegel, *Aux Origines du Communisme français* (Paris and The Hague, 1964), vol. II, p. 828n.

in 1920 for the Communist International? What was the problem of the French labour movement, that it required so new and so foreign a solution?

Socialism and Revolutionary Syndicalism

Of course France was not alone in feeling the pull of communism in 1920. The very creation of a Communist International was only made possible by two events which affected the whole of Europe, the first directly and the second indirectly. These were, of course, the First World War and the Russian Revolution. But if we compare the impact of these events on the labour movement in France with their impact on it in Germany and Britain, we quickly perceive that it was very different in each case, and that the difference has to do, among other things, with the great differences that existed between the labour movements in these three countries before the First World War began.

What do we mean by a labour movement? A movement, in the words of the *Oxford English Dictionary*, 'claiming to further the interests of the labouring or wage-earning classes'. What forms of organization can such a movement take? In a non-revolutionary situation there are in practice two: the trade union and the political party. In Western European labour movements of the last hundred years, at any rate, the two have almost invariably co-existed, but the relationship between them has varied. In Germany before 1914 there was a political party, the SPD, which had a strong and united trade union movement firmly under its control. In Britain there was a political party, the Labour Party, which had been created by the trade unions and remained largely dependent on them. And in France there was a trade union movement, the *Confédération Générale du Travail* (CGT), whose leaders professed hostility to all political parties, including the Socialist Party.

I think this point is crucial. It is possible to say about Britain and Germany, and about a number of other north European countries, that by 1914 there was a political party which a majority of the politically conscious, class-conscious working class regarded as *their* party, whatever criticisms they might make of its policies or its leaders—and this surely hinges on the connection between that party and the trade unions, which are working-class organizations *par excellence*. This was emphatically not true of the French Socialist Party.

The *Parti Socialiste Unifié* was, as its name suggests, a composite party, formed in 1905 by the union of two rival socialist parties,

20

themselves resulting from mergers between some half-dozen groups four years earlier. The final unification was achieved by the arbitration of the Second International, to which both rival parties belonged, and hence the unified party was known sometimes by its title (PSU) and sometimes by its subtitle, *Section française de l'Internationale ouvrière* (SFIO). The dominating figures in it were Jules Guesde, who since the late 1870s had been the most assiduous apostle of Marxism in France, and Jean Jaurès, a parliamentary orator of great prestige who had started his career as a follower of Gambetta, announced his conversion to socialism in 1892, and continued to view the bourgeois Republic as a stage on the road to socialism rather than an obstacle to be smashed. Party membership, which started at under 35,000 in 1905, was still short of 100,000 at the outbreak of war— whereas the German SPD had over a million members. Party activity and recruitment became increasingly geared to electioneering and tended to flourish as much in rural areas as in industrial ones. There was also a vigorous party press, including four daily newspapers of which one, *L'Humanité*, had an estimated readership of 200,000—but again, this has to be compared with seventy socialist dailies and over two million readers in Germany.[2]

Undoubtedly the party's most conspicuous successes were electoral: in the elections of 1914 it won 1.4 million votes (17%) and 103 seats out of 586.[3] But 'much of the Socialist vote came not from workers, but from small proprietors, businessmen, government employees, and professional men'—and peasants. 'The Socialists, it seemed, were steadily encroaching on the electoral fiefs that had been the Radicals' preserve in the early years of the Third Republic.'[4] Not only were nearly all the party leaders of bourgeois origin—this has been true of most socialist parties at most times, and is even true of the Italian Communist Party today—but so were many of the rank-and-file militants. And party propaganda, taking its tone from Jaurès, tended increasingly to bracket specifically working-class grievances with those of all the 'petites gens' who felt themselves oppressed or exploited—including shopkeepers and small farmers, teachers and civil servants.

The CGT was also a composite body. Founded in 1895 as a federation of national trade unions (one for each industry or craft), it merged in 1902 with the *Fédération Nationale des Bourses du Travail*. The *bourses du travail* were labour exchanges, subsidized by law out of municipal funds but controlled and administered by workers, so that they brought together workers of different crafts on the local level. After 1902 the two types of organization were represented in strict parity on the confederate bodies, but the confederate leadership had no authority over either. Each trade union, or *syndicat*, and each *bourse* enjoyed a jealously guarded independence and could not be obliged to carry out any confederal decision.

All this is, of course, quite contrary to Marxist ideas on organization. The structure and principles of the CGT were in part a reaction against Marxist ideas in the form which Guesde and his followers had attempted, very clumsily, to impose on the nascent French trade union movement in the 1880s and early 1890s. The first trade union federation had in fact been formed in 1886 by the Guesdists, who attempted, on the German model, to keep it under the close supervision of their party, the *Parti Ouvrier*. But by the 1890s an increasing number of trade unionists were coming under anarchist influence. Ideas derived directly or indirectly from Proudhon were in the air: the workers must organize their own society of free producers; they must emancipate themselves from capitalism directly, and not waste time trying to capture the state or to set up a 'socialist' government which would only turn out as oppressive as its predecessor. The division of the Socialists into mutually hostile groups, the high-handed methods of the Guesdists, the ease with which Socialist parliamentarians and municipal councillors fitted into the bourgeois system: all these helped to turn trade union leaders away from politics and towards direct, economic action. And the form which such action should take they deduced easily from their own experience: the general strike. These ideas were associated especially with the *Fédération Nationale des Bourses du Travail*, which was founded in 1892. It was contact with this body which led to the collapse of the Guesdist *Fédération Nationale des Syndicats* (the Guesdists refused to accept the general strike) and so to the foundation of the CGT in 1895. The most effective exponent of the new ideas was Fernand Pelloutier, secretary of the *Fédération des Bourses* from 1895 until his death in 1900. He is generally regarded as the founder of revolutionary syndicalism, which is the name given to the principles and practice of the CGT after 1902. But whereas Pelloutier himself emphasized the task of educating the working class and building, through the *bourses du travail*, an alternative set of institutions ready to replace capitalism when the moment came, after his death the syndicalists came to lay more emphasis on the violent conflict between workers and capitalists

The Problem

here and now; and the vision of the general strike changed from one in which the workers simply folded their arms and watched capitalism collapse of its own accord to one involving violent insurrection. This was partly the fruit of experience: strikes in practice were most often accompanied by violence against blacklegs or employers, and even when the workers themselves refrained from violence, it was used against them. Simply to ignore the state was not possible, since the state provided the repressive forces which protected capitalism against the workers. What syndicalists particularly resented was that workers themselves were conscripted into the armed forces and then used to repress their brothers who were on strike. Anti-militarism was consequently one of the main themes of syndicalist propaganda, and no doubt the one which most frequently brought syndicalist propagandists before the courts.

The emphasis shifted also from the *bourse*—a constructive, self-help institution which did not in itself threaten the established order—to the *syndicat*, which was the instrument of combat, directly aimed at the employer. But there was still no place in the syndicalist scheme of things for the political party. The slogan was: 'le syndicat suffit à tout'. It was both the instrument which would destroy the existing society, and the institution on which the new society would be based. Through their *syndicats* the workers would freely organize production, and all other forms of organization would be superfluous.

For Socialists, the existence of revolutionary syndicalism was, of course, highly embarrassing. Guesde remained implacably hostile to it on orthodox Marxist grounds, arguing that by ignoring the problem of state power the syndicalists were in fact renouncing any real hope of changing the economic order. He continued to advocate penetration of the unions by the Socialists in order to bring them back to their true role in the struggle. But other Socialists, and notably Jaurès, saw that to proclaim such a policy would merely exacerbate the conflict between the party and the CGT. At the Socialist congresses of 1906 and 1907 Jaurès joined forces with the veteran revolutionary Edouard Vaillant, who had held office during the 1871 Paris Commune. Vaillant, of course, did not share Jaurès's parliamentary and electoralist outlook, but he did share his admiration for the revolutionary *élan* of the syndicalist leaders, some of whom were, like himself, former disciples of the great nineteenth-century conspirator, Auguste Blanqui. Together Jaurès and Vaillant presented motions calling upon party members 'to work to the best of their ability to

23

dispel any misunderstanding between the CGT and the SFIO', and suggested that the basic harmony of the proletariat's political and economic aims must eventually lead to 'free co-operation between the two bodies'. These motions passed, though by quite narrow majorities.[5]

The result in practice was that Socialists habitually defended syndicalist strikes in their speeches and newspapers, but increasingly avoided any direct interference. The CGT leaders came grudgingly to accept that Socialist support could be useful in certain limited circumstances, until in July 1914, immediately before the outbreak of war, they were even willing to form a joint action committee with the Socialists. But the syndicalist press continued to pour scorn on the faction-fighting and empty rhetoric of Socialist congresses, on the dishonesty and ineffectiveness of Socialist parliamentary activity— for instance the party's failure to propose the repeal of the three-year conscription law in the summer of 1914 once its campaign on the issue had produced the desired electoral results.[6] At the same time, by tacitly abandoning all industrial action to the CGT, the party had in effect increased the distance between itself and the working class, of which it thus appeared less the representative than the bourgeois ally.

Does this imply that, while the SFIO was not the party of the working class, the CGT was so in all but name, that the French working class had rejected socialism in favour of revolutionary syndicalism? Hardly. In the first place, although revolutionary syndicalism was the doctrine of the leaders of the CGT, it is by no means sure that their outlook was shared by the majority of CGT members. A number of the biggest and best-organized unions in the CGT were in fact controlled by people who opposed the policies of the confederal leadership—either Guesdists (among the textile-workers, for example), or 'reformists', as was the case with the printing and mechanics' unions, and the railwaymen. The revolutionaries were able to maintain their control of the confederal leadership—except for a brief episode in 1909—mainly because of the rule of one *syndicat*, one vote, which enabled tiny unions with only a handful of members to outvote others whose membership was reckoned in tens of thousands. The 'reformists' tolerated this situation, since the confederal leadership could not in any case interfere with their running of their own unions, but the danger of a split was always present. It was to avoid this that after 1909 the revolutionaries agreed to send representatives to the conferences organized by the Berlin International

Trade Union Secretariat, despite their hostility to this very tame organization which was completely under the thumb of the German Social Democrats.[7]

But if the revolutionary syndicalists were unrepresentative of the CGT, the CGT itself was even less representative of the French working class. For one thing, it was far from having a monopoly of organized workers. Even if we discount the 'yellow' unions backed by the employers, there were also Catholic unions, which in 1913 formed the *Fédération des syndicats d'employés catholiques*, and many independent unions owing allegiance to no national federation. But in any case the vast majority of workers were not organized at all. It has been calculated that there were about 5,700,000 industrial and commercial wage-earners in France in 1906,[8] of whom only 836,000 belonged to unions. CGT membership was nominally about 300,000, but probably not more than two thirds of these were paid-up members (not that this worried the revolutionary leaders, who regarded large union funds as a disadvantage, because likely to encourage cautious and bureaucratic tendencies). By 1914 CGT membership had risen to 600,000, and the total number of organized workers to over a million,[9] but one of its most recent historians concludes: 'It is clear that the C.G.T. never officially represented more than half the organized workers in France and at best one-tenth of the industrial wage-earners (to say nothing of the agricultural workers).'[10]

In short, the CGT of 1914 was no more comparable in size and strength to the British and German trade-union federations than was the SFIO to the German SPD. The French working class, unlike that of Britain or Germany, had not found an organization to express its consciousness. The most likely explanation for this is that it was not yet fully conscious—which is likely enough, for the good reason that it did not yet fully exist. In 1906 one-third of the wage-earners in industry and commerce worked in firms employing less than ten people.[11] Industry employed only 38.6% of the working population, while 44.2% made their living by farming.[12] 58% of the population lived in villages of less than 2,000 inhabitants.[13] And these figures hardly changed at all between 1906 and 1913; the bourgeoisie increased from six to seven million, at the expense of the 'popular classes', while the total population went up by only half a million, remaining just short of forty million.[14]

On such a France—increasingly bourgeois but still rural—and on such a working class—immature, imperfectly conscious, divided—fell the catastrophe of 1914: 'the Great War, the one which broke history in two'.[15]

The War

Up to now I have emphasized the differences between Socialists and revolutionary syndicalists. But these differences should not disguise the fact that they had a number of sentiments and ideas in common. Among these were internationalism and hostility to war. Both groups regarded themselves as the allies of the working class in foreign countries, and regarded national rivalries as a bourgeois device for diverting attention from class conflicts and recruiting working-class enthusiasm into the service of capitalist acquisitiveness. They regarded war as the expression of capitalism in its purest and most detestable form, since it obliged workers to kill each other in the service of capitalist interests; and they regarded the threat of war as a pretext for maintaining large standing armies which could be used for the repression of striking or demonstrating workers. Both CGT and SFIO, therefore, were consistently hostile to nationalism, militarism and long-term conscription; and they saw it as their task to prevent the outbreak of war by whatever means were at their disposal. The only point of disagreement—not so much between the two organizations as within the SFIO—was, what means were in fact at their disposal. Vaillant and Jaurès followed the CGT in proclaiming the insurrectional general strike as the ultimate recourse against war, while Guesde and others argued that this tactic was unrealistic, and insofar as it succeeded would defeat its purpose because 'the most socialist nation will put itself at a disadvantage *vis-à-vis* the least socialist one, and then it's the most socialist nation which, disarming itself by insurrection, will be beaten by the most backward one.'[16]

Guesde borrowed this argument from the German Socialist leader, Wilhelm Liebknecht. In 1914 it was to be used by German Socialists to justify the defence of Germany against Russia, and by French Socialists to justify the defence of France against Germany. It certainly seems paradoxical that anyone could regard the France of 1914 as a 'more socialist' country than Germany, given the relative strengths of the two Socialist Parties. But here we touch on another characteristic which seems to have been common to all French

26

Socialists and to almost all French syndicalists: attachment to a French revolutionary tradition. For the Jauressien Socialists, of course, this is obvious enough. Their attachment to the Republic was straightforward, and when they opposed militarism, revanchism and nationalism they did so in the name of 'the defence of the Republic', and often in alliance with the Radicals. But even those who professed to have no illusions about the bourgeois nature of this particular Republic could not forget that they were the heirs of men for whom the Republic had been a revolutionary ideal, for which many of them had given their lives. Both Socialists and syndicalists derived their ideas and their inspiration from the Communards of 1871, whom Marx had glorified but who were mostly followers of Proudhon or Blanqui. Yet the Commune was an insurrection that had broken out not against war but against a dishonourable peace. Its leaders were the advocates of a last-ditch struggle against the Prussian invader, looking back in their turn to the revolutionary patriotism of 1792.

In short, there were two possible types of war. The war which everyone expected, and against which Socialist and syndicalist congresses passed resolutions, was a capitalist war for territorial and financial gain, in which there would be nothing to choose between the sides. The war which actually happened was one in which the French Republic was attacked and invaded, apparently without provocation, by the forces of the German Empire. In such circumstances the fact that German social legislation was well in advance of French ceased to be relevant. It became self-evident which country was the backward, aggressive tyranny and which, for all its faults, was the democratic Republic, homeland of revolution. 'If France were attacked she would have no more ardent defenders than the socialists of the Parti Ouvrier, who are convinced of the great role reserved for her in the approaching social Revolution.' Such had been the resolution of the Guesdist congress in 1894, and such was the attitude of Guesde and his followers in 1914.[17] And, as it turned out, the attitude of most revolutionary syndicalists was remarkably similar. The crime of German imperialism seemed so blatant in August 1914 that the shortcomings of the Republic were temporarily forgotten. 'This monstrous crime that is going to plunge all Europe into barbarousness, into the abyss of mourning, and into ruins, let it be punished!' wrote the CGT newspaper *La Bataille Syndicaliste* on 2 August. 'Let thrones be overthrown, let crowns break! . . . And let the name of the old Emperor Franz Joseph be cursed.'[18] Earlier CGT literature had often taunted the Republic with breaking her promises,[19] but this after all implied some kind of belief in a republican ideal. As Léon Jouhaux, the CGT's general secretary, wrote when explaining his apparent *volte-face* to an uncomprehending colleague: 'I cannot forget that my grandfather died for the Republic, on the barricades of 1848. . . . The only thing that matters for me is that imperialism is threatening the Republic.'[20]

And what of the danger of delivering 'German Socialist civilization to the hordes of the Russian autocracy's army', which was worrying Guesde as late as mid-July 1914?[21] The Russian autocracy was certainly an embarrassing ally for French Socialists, and some of them felt later that France could and should have averted the German attack by denouncing her Russian alliance. In 1915 it was alleged by opponents of the war—and hotly denied by its supporters—that Jaurès, on the day of his assassination, 31 July 1914, had said that he was going to write an article 'on the necessity of tearing up the Franco-Russian alliance'.[22] However that may be, the notion of 'German Socialist civilization' was quickly forgotten after the SPD deputies had voted for the German war credits in the Reichstag, on 4 August. If the German Socialists had opposed the war, no doubt the French Socialists would have claimed to be fighting against German imperialism in the name of German socialism. As it was, they had no hesitation in branding the German Socialists as traitors to internationalism and accomplices of imperialist aggression. And here we touch on a third characteristic which Socialists shared with syndicalists in pre-war France: an inferiority complex about German Social Democracy. Within the Second International, the SFIO came under the unchallenged hegemony of the SPD. The very terms of its unification had been dictated by the Germans in 1904 at the Congress of Amsterdam, which had imposed on France the Dresden Resolution, condemning the revisionist heresy, and had thereby committed the French party in word if not in deed to the Marxist principles of class struggle and total opposition to the bourgeois state. This hegemony the French Socialists accepted respectfully from a party obviously so much stronger and maturer than their own; but not without growing irritation at the ponderousness of German conference manners ('Genossen, Genossen! J'en ai mare de toutes ces genosseries!' exclaimed Jaurès at the Congress of Basle in 1912), and not without growing doubts about the sincerity of German internationalism. A considerable stir was caused in 1913 when

Charles Andler, one of the leading Germanists in the SFIO, published two articles on the theme of 'Socialisme impérialiste dans l'Allemagne contemporaine'. And significantly these articles were published in the syndicalist review *La Vie Ouvrière*—for the revolutionary syndicalists were exasperated by the SPD's complete domination of the German trade unions and the German domination of the International Trade Union Secretariat. They at least would have no special difficulty in reconciling themselves to the collapse of 'German Socialist civilization'.

But although the decision of both Socialist and syndicalist leaders to support the war was less surprising than it seems at first sight, the war was nonetheless catastrophic for both organizations. Both were the children of a forty-year peace, of an optimistic world in which class differences appeared to have become more important than national ones. It could be said they were also the victims of this world, which condemned them to isolation as the representatives of a minority class. In this sense the war came as a release, enabling them to integrate themselves into the national community, enabling their leaders to play the role to which they felt themselves entitled in guiding the nation. Two Socialists, Guesde and Marcel Sembat, joined the government in August 1914, and they were joined the following year by a third, Albert Thomas. Jouhaux, meanwhile, became a 'commissioner for the nation', and the government rapidly formed the habit of consulting him and other CGT leaders about all kinds of labour problems during the war. The CGT was transformed overnight from a revolutionary sect into a national institution playing its part in the war effort. At the same time the syndicalists forgot their hostility towards the Socialist Party, with which they set up a permanent action committee.

It is tempting, but futile, to speculate what would have been the result of these decisions if the war had been 'over by Christmas', as everyone expected at the time when they were taken. With the Socialists freed from their international ties and the syndicalists from their prejudice against party politics, with both sharing the credit for having stood by the nation in its hour of peril, it is conceivable that they would have joined forces in a reformist Labour Party—not unlike the British one, although no doubt using a more revolutionary phraseology. Or would they have wound up war socialism as quickly as the war itself and returned to square one, each preparing for revolution in their own way, with more or less conviction?

Anyway, the war was not over by Christmas. It lasted for four years. It mobilized nearly eight million Frenchmen between the ages of eighteen and fifty-one: one fifth of the total population. It cost 1.3 million of them their lives: 10% of the male working population, and including 27% of all men between the ages of eighteen and twenty-seven. 700,000 more were mutilated, and three million wounded.[23] The birthrate plummeted, and though France recovered Alsace-Lorraine with nearly two million inhabitants she was left with a lower population in 1921 than she had had in 1913.[24]

The two classes proportionally worst affected by the bloodletting were the intellectuals and the peasantry, and undoubtedly it was on the latter that the impact of the war was greatest. Peasants whose peacetime military service had been confined to their own region, or who reached military age only after the war began, now got their first glimpse of a France beyond the borders of their own *département* and found themselves for the first time in close contact with compatriots from other regions. A national event, a political event, intruded brutally into their everyday lives, broke up and decimated their families, obliged women to undertake tasks and responsibilities hitherto reserved for men, and left the male survivors with the memory of four hellish years in the trenches, often with painful or unsightly wounds as a reminder. Small wonder that the war was followed by a sharpening of peasant political consciousness.

The industrial working class did not escape these sacrifices, even though proportionally it was less badly hit. More than 350,000 workers lost their lives, and those who were not mobilized bore the brunt of the food shortage and the soaring inflation: the cost of living more than doubled during the four years of war, while wages went up on average by only 75%. At the beginning of the war factory legislation protecting workers was swept away, and in the momentary enthusiasm of the 'Sacred Union' they did not protest. But by the third year of war they were becoming keenly aware of the hardships it had brought them, and noticing that these hardships were not shared by their employers. They also discovered that the constant drain of manpower to the front and the pressure on arms production had created an intense demand for labour, especially female labour. Predictably, this combination of circumstances led to a wave of very militant strikes in the spring of 1917, centring on the munitions industry and coinciding with a wave of mutinies at the front.

To some extent the Socialist and syndicalist leaders who had joined the war effort were able to use their bargaining position to secure advantages for the workers: a law of 1915 gave women working at home a minimum wage, and one of 1917 stipulated that all working women should have Saturday afternoon off. But such trifles did not begin to compensate the workers for the sacrifices which the war effort had required of them. The longer the war lasted, the more intolerable was the spectacle of men who claimed to be working-class leaders sitting in the government, making speeches in support of the war and proposing toasts at employers' banquets. When they joined the Sacred Union in 1914, the leaders of both CGT and SFIO undoubtedly had the support of the overwhelming majority of their followers. But thereafter the logic of events carried them further and further from their rank-and-file. The leaders could only justify their position, in the light of their previous anti-war statements, by maximizing the difference between wars in general and this war in particular; and consequently they became as passionate and extreme in their defence of the war as any nationalist. The purity and nobility of France's war aims, the utter iniquity of German imperialism and the appalling treachery of the German Socialists were nowhere more fanatically exposed than in the speeches of the working-class leaders. Yet at the same time it was increasingly obvious to the ordinary working man that things were not so simple: it became clear that the Allied governments, even if they had not started the war, had their own interests in going on with it, interests which were not necessarily those of the working class, and so even if it was necessary to go on fighting for the time being, working-class leaders would be better employed seeking a basis for peace and trying to re-establish contact with their colleagues in enemy countries than in proclaiming the absolute necessity of victory and denouncing any sign of moderation as treachery.

Those who expressed these views, both in the Socialist Party and in the trade unions, were known as the *minoritaires*, because, until the last year of the war, they remained a minority within their respective organizations. Rapidly the distinction between *majoritaires* and *minoritaires* took on a greater immediate importance than that between Socialists and syndicalists. While the *majoritaires* of both organizations were thrown together in the action committee and in numerous governmental activities, the *minoritaires*, finding themselves subject to the same persecution and the same censorship, inevitably made common cause. Some of the leading *minoritaires* were in fact members of both organizations. For instance Albert Bourderon, secretary of the barrel-makers' union and a self-proclaimed disciple of Pelloutier, was nonetheless a card-holding member of the Socialist Party; and Fernand Loriot, who was to emerge as the leader of the extreme left within the Socialist Party, was also an active member of the primary-school teachers' union. Such personal overlaps were common enough, but their political significance should not be exaggerated. Ludovic-Oscar Frossard, a Socialist *minoritaire* who had himself been active in the CGT before the war, later wrote—no doubt with some exaggeration—that 'the same militants whom he met in socialist assemblies, when he came across them in trade union meetings were the most violent in denouncing the "politicians" and, with their party card and often their town councillor's mandate in their pocket, in proclaiming that "Syndicalism was sufficient unto itself".'[25] Such behaviour could not disguise the fundamental choice that had to be made between two philosophies. It was quite normal for Socialists to feel that they had a role to play in the unions as well as in the party; it was not impossible for revolutionary syndicalists to feel that it was worth taking out a party card; but it was clearly impossible to accept the claims made by both organizations to leadership of the revolutionary movement.

In consequence, it was not one minority that grew out of the opposition to the war but two; and their policies and methods were quite distinct, even though they maintained contact with each other. The syndicalists were the more radical, being led by a small group of men who had the consistency and the courage to oppose the war from the very start: Alphonse Merrheim, leader of the metal-workers' federation, Pierre Monatte, editor of *La Vie Ouvrière*, his close friend Alfred Griot, better known by his pen-name Rosmer, the miner Georges Dumoulin and the writer Marcel Martinet. This group rapidly made contact with the Russian exiles in Paris who opposed the war, including Trotsky and the Menshevik Yulii Martov. The French syndicalists found it easier to work with these Russian socialists than with French ones, although by the end of 1914 a few individual members of the French Socialist Party were coming to their meetings at the *Vie Ouvrière* offices on the Quai de Jemmapes. The main opposition within the Socialist Party was much more moderate in tone, being led by the deputies Jean Longuet (grandson of Karl Marx) and Adrien Pressemane, and by Paul Faure, editor of

Le Populaire du Centre. Both Faure and Pressemane belonged to the dynamic Guesdist federation of the Haute-Vienne, which they rapidly made a stronghold of pacifism. But their pacifism was only relative: they opposed the 'jusqu'au-boutisme' of the party leadership and demanded a more positive attitude towards peace proposals, especially those emanating from foreign socialist parties, but they accepted the need for national defence and voted for the war credits. Above all, they were terrified of splitting the party whose unity had been achieved with so much difficulty only ten years before. This made them an easy prey in the first years of the war to the very strong moral pressure put on them by the majority, and twice in 1915—at a national council in July and at a full party congress in December — they allowed themselves to be bullied into voting for a compromise resolution. For the same reason they could not bring themselves to accept the invitation of the Swiss and Italian Socialist Parties to a conference of 'all the parties, working-class organizations, and groups known to have remained faithful to the former principles and resolutions of the Labour International'. They thus missed the chance to be present in September 1915 at the historic conference of Zimmerwald, which was later to be seen as the origin of the Third International.

The syndicalist minority did accept the invitation, however, with the result that Merrheim and Bourderon met Lenin. Contact was thus established between revolutionary syndicalism and Bolshevism. But these two syndicalists, neither of whom was in fact to become a Communist, were not prepared to follow Lenin in calling for a Third International (since in any case they had never belonged to the Second) nor in turning the imperialist war into a class war, which they knew to be a totally unrealistic aim in the existing French climate. What they wanted was an uncompromising call for peace, and they were glad enough to sign the compromise resolution drafted by Trotsky which put all the emphasis on this. They also signed a joint declaration with the German delegates (the Socialist deputies Hoffmann and Ledebour), promising to 'work untiringly in our respective countries until the peace movement is strong enough to impose on our governors the cessation of this slaughter'.[26]

Back in Paris, Merrheim and Bourderon gave an account of the conference to two separate meetings, one of syndicalists and one of Socialists. Out of the syndicalist meeting grew an International Action Committee, which in January 1916 became the *Comité pour la*

Reprise des Relations Internationales (CRRI), with Merrheim as secretary. Although composed mainly of syndicalists, it also included a number of Socialists, as well as anarchists, and it was soon divided into two sections, the Socialists and syndicalists working separately in their respective milieux and each publishing their own tracts.

Who were the Socialists involved? Besides Bourderon and Loriot there were Charles Rappoport, a scholar and journalist of Russian Jewish origin, Louise Saumoneau, founder of the review *La Femme Socialiste* and secretary of the needle-workers' union, and the schoolteacher François Mayoux (as well as the Russians Trotsky and Lozovsky). These were the nucleus of the 'Zimmerwaldian' opposition which from then on formed the extreme left of the party, acting as a kind of gadfly to the minority led by Longuet, from which, however, it was always careful to distinguish itself. This policy soon produced its first fruits: in April 1916 at a national council of the SFIO, Longuet and Pressemane for the first time pushed their motion demanding the re-establishment of relations with foreign socialist parties to a vote—and won the support of one third of the delegates. Later the same month a second international conference was held by the Zimmerwald movement at Kienthal (also in Switzerland), and three deputies belonging to Longuet's group attended it: Pierre Brizon, Alexandre Blanc and Jean Raffin-Dugens. (The CRRI's own representatives were unable to attend because the government refused them passports.) At Kienthal the three deputies came under heavy pressure from the other delegates (Poles and Italians as well as Russians), and promised that in future they would vote against war credits. This promise they kept, but they were not joined in doing so by their fellow *minoritaires*.

By the end of 1916 both syndicalist and Socialist minorities had gathered strength, and the majority in both organizations felt the need to play down their association with the government. In December both the SFIO party congress and the CGT national conference voted almost unanimously to ask the Allied governments to accept an offer of mediation in the war by President Wilson—then still a neutral—and in the SFIO the minority won eleven out of twenty-four places on the *Comité Administratif Permanent*, the party's governing body. Both organizations acclaimed Wilson's 'peace without victory' speech of 22 January 1917. These were essentially successes for the moderates, and they undermined the unity of the Zimmerwaldians. In early 1917 there was a crisis in the CRRI which

ended in the departure of its more moderate members: Brizon and
Raffin-Dugens returned to the Longuet minority, taking with them
Bourderon, while Merrheim withdrew to concentrate on trade union
activity. Meanwhile the syndicalist section of the CRRI had become
an independent body under the name of *Comité de Défense Syndicaliste*
(CDS) and chiefly under the influence of anarchist trade unionists,
especially Raymond Péricat of the stonemasons' union, though it was
also supported by the more radical revolutionary syndicalists such as
Rosmer and Monatte. Trotsky had been expelled from France in
September 1916, but the CRRI was left in the hands of those whom he
had most influenced among the French Socialists—Loriot, Rappoport, Louise Saumoneau and François Mayoux. Trotsky's violent
denunciations of Longuet had helped to hold this small faction to its
intransigent Zimmerwaldian line, and thereby to preserve the
nucleus which after the war would push the French Socialist Party
towards the Communist International. Lenin too had tried to
influence them from Switzerland, through his emissary Inessa
Armand who visited France at the end of 1915. In April 1917, just
before his departure for Petrograd, Lenin met Loriot in
Switzerland.[27] The meeting must have had a considerable impact on
both men. Loriot became Lenin's leading admirer and disciple in
France, while Lenin looked to Loriot as the man around whom the
French section of the new revolutionary International should be built.

The Russian Revolution

From April 1917 onwards, of course, Lenin had to judge events in
France at a much greater distance, and had many more urgent things
to think about. At the same time large numbers of Frenchmen began
to take a passionate interest in events in Russia—about which,
however, they were quite as ill-informed as Lenin was about events in
France.

The two Russian Revolutions of March and November 1917 could
not, indeed, have occurred at a time when they would have had a
greater impact on France. France was war-weary, and Russia was her
ally in the war. French Republicans were embarrassed at being the
allies of the most reactionary and despotic monarchy in Europe: and
the Russians rose, overthrew their autocrat and proclaimed a
Republic. Frenchmen wanted peace, and the Petrograd Soviet called
for peace, with 'neither annexations nor indemnities'. French

Socialists were ashamed and embittered at the failure of their International either to prevent or to end the war: and now Russian Socialists enthusiastically supported the International Socialist Conference in Stockholm, which had been proposed by the neutrals and at first rejected by the French *majoritaires*. France's working-class organizations were discredited and divided by their failure to live up to their revolutionary ideals, and by their leaders' support of the war: yet in November 1917 a Russian working-class party actually carried out a revolution and proclaimed the dictatorship of the proletariat, and in March 1918 it took Russia out of the war. French workers and peasants, in the factories and in the trenches, struck and mutinied in May and June 1917, often with the cry of 'Down with war! Long live the Russian Revolution!' They met with firm repression, and the war went on; but workers, peasants and soldiers were less and less willing to hear of the crimes of German imperialism. More and more of them could see only the crime of the government, the regime, the system which had sent them to war; and how should they not be stimulated by the news that, in Russia, workers, peasants and soldiers had formed their own councils, had revolted against the war, had overthrown the government and the regime and had set about destroying the system?

Their sense of solidarity was sharpened in the summer of 1918 when the French government began to intervene directly in the Russian civil war, on the side of counter-revolution. Of course, the government justified this policy by arguments of national defence: the Bolsheviks, by making the separate peace of Brest-Litovsk, had enabled the Germans to launch their May offensive on the western front and had brought France within inches of defeat. The restoration of a Russian government willing to continue the struggle was therefore a legitimate French war aim. But to many Frenchmen such arguments merely helped to illuminate the nature of the war itself, and to convince them that the slogan of national defence had been a sham all along. Such suspicions were strengthened by the attitude of the Clemenceau government, which was responsible for the intervention, in home affairs. Clemenceau had come to power in November 1917 proclaiming 'l'unique pensée d'une guerre intégrale'. Already in June his predecessors, on the advice of the commander-in-chief, had refused passports to the Socialist delegation for the Stockholm Conference. Now Clemenceau, who had already won a solid reputation as a strike-breaking prime minister before the war, declared a reign of terror against pacifism, sweeping aside all social questions and any suggestion of a negotiated peace: 'Ma politique étrangère et ma politique intérieure, c'est tout un. Politique intérieure: je fais la guerre. Politique extérieure: je fais la guerre. Je fais toujours la guerre!' Louis Malvy, the former Minister of the Interior, was impeached for having shown too much tolerance towards pacifists, and in August 1918 he was condemned to exile by the Senate sitting as High Court. Left-wing circles saw this as an attack on the working class, since Malvy's main crime was his kid-glove treatment of working-class organizations—a policy which had in fact worked remarkably well from the government's point of view, especially in August 1914 when his decision not to arrest the working-class militants listed in 'Carnet B' (i.e. earmarked for immediate arrest on mobilization) had paid off handsomely.

Intervention in Russia and repression at home were clearly part of the same policy. Up to November 1918 this could be presented as a war policy. After the armistice its class basis became transparent. The war had been won. Now workers and peasants expected to reap the fruits of their four-year sacrifice. At the very least they expected to have done with fighting and return to their homes and families. But the pace of demobilization was painfully slow, and one obvious reason for this was that the government, instead of withdrawing its troops from Russia, sent more to join them. To the detachment in Archangel and the military mission in eastern Siberia was added an expeditionary force which, in December 1918, occupied part of the Crimea and invaded the Ukraine, with the support of a naval squadron anchored off Odessa. The men composing these forces could see no good reason for being there, and were an easy prey for the 'very active and insidious Bolshevik propaganda' which was soon reported by the British War Office.[28] Among the French troops occupying Odessa this propaganda was carried out by Jeanne Labourbe, a French-woman who had been working in Russia as a governess and had become a convinced Bolshevik. She had founded the 'Groupe communiste français de Moscou' in August 1918, and had come to work in Odessa because she could not bear the idea that 'the sons of the Communards of 71, the descendants of the revolutionaries of 93, should come and smother the great Russian Revolution'.[29] Arrested by the French military authorities, she was shot on the night of 1 March 1919, thus becoming the first French Communist martyr. On the same day there was a mutiny on the Archangel front among

French troops ordered to go up to the line.[30] Early in April Odessa had to be evacuated because the French troops there refused to march against the Bolsheviks; and then naval mutinies in the Black Sea squadron, led by the 'officier-mécanicien' André Marty, persuaded the French government to withdraw its expeditionary force altogether.

Meanwhile prices in France continued to rise, and the franc fell rapidly on the foreign exchange market after the lapsing of the wartime financial agreements with Britain and the United States. At the same time speculation in 'real values'—gold, real estate, commodities, foreign stocks—led to a stock exchange boom.[31] On 29 March Raoul Villain, the murderer of Jaurès, was acquitted 'in the name of victory', whereas soon afterwards the anarchist Emile Cottin, who had tried unsuccessfully to murder Clemenceau in February, was condemned to death.[32] And at the peace conference Clemenceau was taking an intransigent line, opposing Wilson's doctrine of self-determination and insisting that France should have her full pound of flesh from Germany. All the illusions that had seemed to justify the Sacred Union were shattered—the idea that France was fighting a war to end war, an unselfish, defensive war in the name of freedom, a war that was as much in the interests of the workers as of the bourgeoisie; the idea that a French victory would be, as Guesde put it, 'the beginning as well as the precondition of a Socialist victory tomorrow'; and even the alternative idea that by supporting the war the working class had put the bourgeois parties in its debt and would be able to claim payment once it was over.[33] Instead the bourgeoisie had emerged triumphant, apparently eager to spit on the working class at home and to prolong the fighting abroad even while stuffing its pockets with the fruits of victory. In these circumstances the hysteria of the bourgeois press in denouncing the Bolshevik 'bandits' could only help to prejudice working-class militants in their favour. Even the right-wing Socialist leaders, who made no secret of their hostility to the Bolsheviks, were embittered and disillusioned by the government's attitude and felt obliged to protest against the intervention in Russia. In December 1918 Pierre Renaudel, who as editor of *L'Humanité* from 1914 to 1918 had been the effective leader of the SFIO during the Sacred Union, delivered a long speech in the Chamber of Deputies on the right of the Russian people to self-determination.[34] At the end of March 1919, just when the news of the first mutinies had begun to filter through the French censorship, the government's demand for further military credits led to a further debate on intervention in the Chamber. Again Renaudel attacked the government: 'The state of mind of the soldiers is deeply saddened at the thought of going on with the war since the armistice,' he said, and threatened to read out secret documents revealing the degree of discontent among the troops.[35] When the news of the mutinies was confirmed there were enthusiastic demonstrations of support, followed by protests against the sentences handed out to the mutineers by courts martial: five death sentences (though none were in fact carried out) and 630 years of prison shared between twenty-eight soldiers and 102 sailors.[36] Marty, who was sentenced to twenty years' forced labour, was to be built up by the campaigns for his release into a kind of folk hero.

Anger at the French intervention and sympathy with the mutineers inevitably led working-class militants in France to identify with the Bolsheviks, the brave revolutionaries who were suffering the assault of French imperialism and gloriously repulsing it. 'The workers understood,' as Marty later put it, 'that the Russian revolution was their revolution.'[37] But how much did they know about the actual nature of that revolution? Very little. Except in a few groups on the extreme left, such as the CRRI, the names of Lenin and Trotsky had been unknown before 1917. Between 1917 and 1920 communications between Russia and France were very difficult, because of the war and then the allied blockade. Personal letters were occasionally exchanged between Trotsky and his former friends in the CRRI, and also between the members of the 'Groupe communiste français de Moscou' and their friends in France, but nothing like a regular correspondence could be kept up, since there were no normal postal services. Running the blockade between Russia and the West was a risky business, and letters were often intercepted by the police even between France and the Western countries from which the blockade could be run (most often Sweden, Norway, or, after 1918, Germany). After the creation of the Communist International in March 1919 the French labour movement was bombarded with wireless messages and telegrams from Moscow; but these were of limited value since they were not ciphered, they could only be received through French official services (with all the opportunities for censorship and police supervision that that implied), and the recipients had no means of replying. As for the 'bourgeois' press, it too was subject to censorship, its prejudice against the Bolsheviks was evident, and its reports of terror and dictatorship were discounted by most working-class militants. In any case it had few sources of information after the withdrawal of the Allied representatives from Petrograd in February 1918 and the arrest of *Le Temps*'s correspondent in Russia, Ludovic Naudeau.

The result of this general ignorance about events in Russia was that each faction of the French labour movement tended to read between the lines of the news bulletins the fulfilment of its own revolutionary desires. The *majoritaires* hailed the February Revolution as the triumph of democratic institutions, likely to make Russia a more trustworthy and valuable ally for the Western democracies and at the same time to hasten an upheaval in Germany,[38] while the CRRI, without waiting for October, assumed that it was already *the* Revolution and called on French workers 'to transform the Russian revolution into an international revolution': 'The Russian revolution is the signal for universal revolution. And the universal revolution will ensure the final success of the Russian revolution; and the reply to world war must be world revolution.'[39] In between, the Socialist *minoritaires* and the moderate syndicalists led by Merrheim seized on the appeals for peace of the Petrograd Soviet.

The October Revolution brought an even wider range of interpretations. Although in moderate circles the first reaction to the seizure of power by the 'maximalists' (as the Bolsheviks were at first known in France) was one of shock and bewildered disapproval, many *majoritaires* came later, especially after the end of the war, to accept the Bolshevik regime as a valid system for Russia, resulting from Russian self-determination. They insisted on its specifically Russian character, the better to argue that its methods were not applicable to the very different problems and circumstances of France. This interpretation was also that of the 'centre' of the Socialist Party, composed mainly of former *minoritaires*, who tended however to believe that it was possible and necessary for French Socialists to join forces with the Bolsheviks internationally without adopting all their methods in France.

Socialists were influenced especially by the attitude of two former *majoritaires* who were in Russia during 1917. Marcel Cachin was one of a delegation sent to Russia in May to encourage Russian Socialists to go on supporting the war. Instead, he was infected with the prevailing pacifism in Petrograd and moved rapidly towards the minority of his own party. In October 1918, when the *minoritaires* at last won control of the party, he replaced Renaudel as editor of *L'Humanité*. At this period he was far from being a Bolshevik, but that only made him more effective as a propagandist in defence of Russia and against French intervention. Jacques Sadoul, a member of the French military mission, was won over by the Bolsheviks after the October Revolution and remained in Russia when the mission was withdrawn. His letters praising the Bolshevik regime and castigating intervention were circulated widely in the SFIO and on occasion even read out at party congresses.

Again Merrheim was close to the Longuet line in defending the Bolsheviks against the French government without approving all their methods—but for him, as a syndicalist, the problem of international relations with Russian Socialists did not arise. Among the more radical syndicalists, however, there was a feeling that the war and the Bolshevik Revolution had invalidated the distinction between Socialists and syndicalists, and 'established a new classification. On one side the traitors, the Socialist defaulters, who, when faced with revolution, become aware of the fact that they are only simple democrats; on the other side, the revolutionaries.'[40] They accepted the need for a new International which would bring together all the revolutionaries, whether of syndicalist or Socialist origin, and so carry on the work begun by Zimmerwald and Kienthal. They accepted, too, that the trade union was not, after all, a sufficient instrument of revolution by itself, and that the problem of state power could not simply be ignored. But in spite of this, they managed to interpret the Russian Revolution as essentially syndicalist. 'Is the Soviet something so different from the local federation of unions?' they asked. 'Is the federal Republic of Soviets something so different from what a federal syndicalist Republic might be?'[41] One even went so far as to assert that the Russian Revolution 'derives its inspiration from Proudhon'![42] And they also noted that the Russian Revolution had begun with a strike of textile workers, developing into a general strike of all the workers in Petrograd.[43] This was the interpretation expounded by *La Vie Ouvrière*, which reappeared in 1919 as a weekly, edited by Monatte and Rosmer, and became the standard-bearer of the post-war minority in the CGT. (By 1919 the more moderate leaders of the wartime minority—Merrheim, Bourderon and Dumoulin—had made their peace with Jouhaux and rejoined the confederal leadership.)

Another interpretation, that of the 'ultra-left', was really more a European phenomenon than a French one: it consisted in taking seriously the slogan 'all power to the soviets' and believing that this meant the destruction of the state and the abolition of all authority except that of spontaneously formed workers' councils. In Holland, Germany and Britain this interpretation was put forward by extreme left-wing Socialists who lumped together trade unions and parliament as incurably bureaucratic and reformist institutions from which true revolutionaries should dissociate themselves completely. In France it was put forward mainly by anarchists and mainly within the trade union movement—the leading figure being Raymond Péricat, secretary of the *Comité de Défense Syndicaliste*. This group formed, in May 1919, a 'Parti communiste, rattaché à la IIIe Internationale de Moscou', which seems never to have had more than about 1,500 members.

Amidst all this confusion Loriot, who had gone to Switzerland in April 1917 and met Lenin on the eve of the latter's departure for Petrograd, was virtually alone in both understanding and accepting the principles of the Bolshevik Revolution. Even he did not accept the doctrine of revolutionary defeatism, but he did recognize the importance of a well-organized, uncompromising revolutionary party, and the need for a new International whose decisions would be binding on its national sections. He believed that the Socialist Party must be split, and that no more was to be hoped for from wishy-washy 'centrists' like Longuet than from hard-line right-wingers like Renaudel and Albert Thomas. But he came to accept that the moment for the split must be carefully chosen so that the maximum of mass support could be brought to the revolutionary cause. For this reason he agreed to support the *minoritaires* when they finally defeated the *majoritaires* at a party congress in October 1918, and he even accepted the post of party treasurer, so as to have a better platform from which to criticize the new party leadership. For the same reason in 1919 he refused flatly to merge his group with the 'Parti Communiste'. He knew that the time was not yet ripe, that the mass of Socialist militants still had confidence in their new leaders and that to split the party now would mean isolation. But he was convinced that the popularity of the *minoritaires* would not last. They were glad enough now to win applause by proclaiming their support for the Russian Revolution: disillusionment would be all the greater when the contrast between their behaviour and that of the Russian

42

revolutionary leaders became apparent. Accordingly he decided to remain within the SFIO and agitate for it to join the new International, while co-ordinating his action with that of the revolutionary elements outside the party. For this purpose the CRRI was kept in existence, changing its name in May 1919 to 'Committee for the Third International'. Its four secretaries were Rosmer for the *Vie Ouvrière* group, Péricat for the anarchistic Communists, Loriot himself and Louise Saumoneau for the left-wing Socialists.

The French Non-Revolution

To sum up: by 1919 there was widespread enthusiasm in France for the Russian Revolution, but great ignorance about what was actually happening in Russia. Many people were inspired and encouraged by the Bolsheviks' example, but few thought it necessary to imitate Bolshevik methods in France, and even fewer had any precise idea of what Bolshevik methods were. In any case, events would hardly wait on any detailed discussion of the Russian experience, for the revolutionary tide was sweeping across Europe and seemed likely to engulf France at any moment. The defeat of the Central Powers and the ending of hostilities seemed to let loose a whirlwind of pent-up forces which swept away the old map of Europe and threatened to bring down every established institution and principle. New nations, and old ones long buried, sprang suddenly into the daylight: Yugoslavia, Czechoslovakia, Poland. Austria and Hungary, shorn of their subject territories, broke apart. The Austrian and German monarchies were overthrown. In both countries the Socialist Parties found themselves propelled into power, and at once in danger of being outflanked on their left. Even in peaceful Switzerland, November 1918 brought a general strike.

In Germany the situation developed with bewildering rapidity. Soldiers' and workers' councils sprang up all over the country and the one in Berlin stepped into the vacuum when the Kaiser abdicated and appointed a provisional government of six members: three from the majority SPD and three from the 'Independent Socialist Party' (USPD), created in 1916 by the equivalent of the French *minoritaires*. This government, which pursued a policy of placating the Western powers, seemed to be the equivalent of the 'Kerensky period' in Russia; and by the end of December the next stage of the German revolution seemed imminent: the USPD ministers resigned, under pressure from their more militant supporters, especially the 'revolutionary shop-stewards', while the extreme left of their party, the *Spartakusbund*, split off to form a German Communist Party (KPD). In January 1919 came the inevitable clash between the revolutionaries and the government. The government won and the two outstanding leaders of the new Communist Party were murdered, but at the time this did not by any means seem a final conclusion. If anything the episode appeared to further the cause of revolution by showing social democracy in its true colours. In March came the proclamation of the Third International in Moscow, and of a Soviet republic in Hungary; in April it was the turn of Bavaria. After that the tide ebbed: Munich fell to the counter-revolution on 1 May, a Communist putsch failed in Vienna on 15 June, and in August the Hungarian Soviet Republic was suppressed with the help of French troops while a second general strike in Switzerland fizzled out. But for another three years the supposed imminence of proletarian revolution in central Europe was to be the subject of many hopes and fears.

The victor countries were not, of course, shaken to the same extent. But nor were they immune to the revolutionary upsurge. In France both workers and peasants emerged from the war full of anger and bitterness at the regime which had imposed such sacrifices on them. Seeking a constructive outlet for their passions they flocked into the two mass organizations which since before the war had been promising a new and different world: the trade union movement and the Socialist Party. Both the CGT and the SFIO had suffered a drastic fall in membership at the beginning of the war. In 1915 the CGT distributed less than one fifth of the number of membership stamps it had sent out the previous year, and in August 1916 the SFIO had just over a quarter the number of members it had had two years before. This was due mainly to the disorganization provoked by the call-up, but no doubt partly also to the psychological effect of the Sacred Union. After 1916 both organizations began to revive, but the CGT much the faster of the two. Already during the strike wave of 1917 membership had overtaken the pre-war peak; in 1918 it was well over twice as high and by January 1920 it had had reached nearly two million, more than three times the 1914 figure. In the SFIO the big influx did not come until after the war had ended. At the end of 1918, when the *minoritaires* took over the party leadership, the party still had under 36,000 members, compared to over 90,000 in July 1914. A year later membership had nearly quadrupled, to 133,000, and by the Congress of Tours in December 1920 it was nearly 180,000.

It is perhaps dangerous to overstress the parallel between these two sets of figures. The growth of the Socialist Party was by no means confined to the industrial working class. The most striking increases in membership were not in the most heavily industrialized areas: some of them were even in distinctly rural and backward *départements*: the Corrèze, the Cantal, the Lot-et-Garonne, the Basses-Alpes. The growth of the trade unions, on the other hand, was obviously a specifically working-class phenomenon: and it reflected a new stage in the development of the French working class. The war had had a profound effect on the French economy, an effect which has even been called a 'second industrial revolution'. Paris had become a major industrial centre. Its suburbs had filled with big factories and working-class slums—the 'Red Belt' of future electoral politics. Wartime needs had brought a shift from textile production—which was most often organized in small workshops, or even on the putting-out system—to metal industries (arms, aeroplanes, motor vehicles) which brought large numbers of workers together under one roof. The Federation of Metalworkers, led by Merrheim, was one of the groups of unions whose membership increased most spectacularly—from 7,500 in 1912 to 204,000 at the end of 1918—a fact which may help to explain Merrheim's own development from the isolated revolutionary pacifist of 1915 to the cautious, moderate trade union boss of 1918. At the same time, to make up the labour shortage caused by mobilization, new labour had to be recruited from every possible source. Full employment was reached in March 1917. Efforts to increase individual productivity by improved work-procedures aroused trade union protests from 1915 onwards. Women, boys and foreign immigrants were brought into the factories; peasants were attracted to the towns. Factories were grouped together to ensure higher yield, or rebuilt further away from the battlefields (thus providing France with extra productive capacity at the end of the war when the old plant was made safe again or recaptured from the enemy). All this helped to break down the artisan-craftsman traditions which had still dominated so much of pre-war French industry, and to create a true proletariat—mobile, vulnerable, aware of its own need for organization.

This was the soil on which the great, organized labour movements of Britain and Germany had grown. But they had not grown overnight, and they had not grown in the heady atmosphere of national and international crisis which prevailed in 1919. Indeed in Germany the crisis was of such proportions that it almost shattered the powerful labour movement that already existed there. 1919 was not a moment for patient and methodical organization. It was a time for passionate political conflict, for heated argument, for action: a time, many people felt, for revolution.

How many people wanted revolution, and what they understood by the word, it is hard to say. Contemporaries, especially those who had belonged to the CGT or the Socialist Party before 1918, often had the impression that the new members flooding into their organizations were boiling over with revolutionary impatience and pushing them rapidly to the left, and there must be some truth in this. But a modern historian, Annie Kriegel, has shown that there is no clear correlation between the trade unions or socialist federations that had the greatest increases in membership and those that voted for the most revolutionary motions at national congresses. In the Socialist Party, at least, the correlation seems to be rather the other way about, the most revolutionary federations being often ones with a relatively small increase in membership. Yet to a certain extent such analyses can only be made by pre-judging the issue. For the trade unions, Mme Kriegel takes as her yardstick of revolutionary fervour the votes cast against the confederal majority, whereas elsewhere she argues at some length that the majority was no less committed than the minority to revolution as an ideal and a goal. For the Socialist Party, her criterion is the proportion of votes cast in favour of joining the Third International. But how much does this help us, when what we are trying to discover is, *how* did French Socialists come to identify the prospects of revolution in France with those of the Third International? Of those who opposed joining the new International, very few were explicitly opposed to the idea of revolution as such: Léon Blum, the main spokesman of this opposition, disagreed with the Bolsheviks not about the need for revolution but about the timing of it, about the objective conditions which were required for it to succeed.

By 1920 that at least was clear: the *minoritaires* in the CGT, and the partisans of the Third International in the Socialist Party, were those who believed in revolution as an immediate objective, a chance to be seized here and now. But even that was not clear in the spring of 1919. There was a general feeling then that the situation was fluid, that great things were possible, that something was going to happen to make the world new and better, and better especially for the working man. People went into the trade unions and the Socialist Party with great hopes, but it seems unlikely that in most cases these hopes were at all precise.

Whatever they were, these hopes were disappointed. The revolution of 1919 did not happen, and nor did the revolution of 1920. Almost the only concrete achievement was the eight-hour-day law—a constant theme of strikes and demonstrations before 1914, now pushed through by a frightened Chamber of Deputies in April 1919 after a demonstration by over 100,000 people against the acquittal of Jaurès's murderer, and in the middle of a new wave of militant strikes. The hope was to forestall a major upheaval on 1 May, the traditional date for labour demonstrations, for which the CGT had called a general work stoppage. In the event, 1 May 1919 did have something of the atmosphere of a revolutionary *journée* in Paris. Thousands of workers took to the streets at the call of the local trade union leadership, which was *minoritaire*, in defiance of both a government ban and the advice of the confederal leadership, which was to stay calm and avoid incidents. There were numerous and violent clashes between demonstrators and police. Jouhaux himself and a Socialist deputy were the victims of police violence, and a nineteen-year-old electrician was shot dead. But the provinces remained calm and the CGT leaders, including some of the *minoritaires*, feared that if they called a general strike they would fall into a government trap. Throughout May and June the strikes continued, including a strike of militant metalworkers who completely repudiated the moderate leadership of Merrheim and his colleagues. But somehow nothing came of it all, and on 14 July the massive turnout for the victory parade of the French army showed that the regime was by no means crumbling and that France—including many French workers—was not prepared to repudiate her victory. On 20 July came the first serious setback for the labour movement when the CGT leaders decided to call off a one-day protest strike against Allied intervention in Russia and Hungary. The *majoritaires* claimed that consultation with member unions had shown the strike had little chance of success. Also, Clemenceau had promised certain minor concessions if it did not take place—but that only made the betrayal worse, and it was a particularly grave betrayal in that the planned strike was an international one, agreed in advance with the Italian trade unions. The episode led to prolonged recriminations and made the gap between *majoritaires* and *minoritaires* hard to bridge.

A similar effect was produced in the Socialist Party by the election of November 1919. The increase in party membership and the general atmosphere of discontent, turbulence and thirst for change encouraged the Socialists to believe they would make big gains in the elections. But they too were sharply reminded that these revolutionary enthusiasms affected only a minority of the population, and that the bourgeoisie, far from disintegrating, was united as never before and giving nothing away. A new electoral law replaced the old single-member constituencies with a system of voting by lists, which gave a built-in advantage to parties fighting the election in alliance. To take advantage of this the bourgeois parties banded together in a *Bloc National*, which in more than half the constituencies included the Radicals, pre-war allies of the Socialists. The *Bloc National* fought the election on an anti-Bolshevik platform, using a famous election poster which depicted the Bolshevik as a man with a knife between his teeth. The Socialists, who themselves were deeply divided on the issue of the Russian Revolution, adopted a programme which neither proclaimed nor repudiated solidarity with it, but agreed to fight the election as the party of revolution *tout court* and therefore to eschew all electoral alliances. Local federations were left to choose for themselves what line they would take about Russia. Most tried to play down the issue, but in the Paris region it was played up and Sadoul, who had just been sentenced to death *in absentia* for desertion, was run as a candidate.

In the event the Socialist vote went up: 1.7 million or 23% compared to 1.4 million and 17% in 1914. But this was far less than had been hoped for, and the electoral system turned it into a loss of thirty-five seats, to which must be added those formerly held by the SPD in Alsace-Lorraine. A particularly hard blow was the defeat of the Socialist list in the Paris suburbs, a working-class area where the party expected to do extra well. The list included three of its most important leaders: Longuet, Paul Faure, and the general secretary, L.-O. Frossard. The party was left with only sixty-eight deputies in a Chamber of 610. And this was the 'Chambre Bleu-Horizon', with the most right-wing majority France had seen since the 1870s. Any hope of sweeping social and economic reforms to alleviate the lot of the workers now while undermining the system of capitalist exploitation and so paving the way for revolution in the future, any hope that the working class could find salvation through parliamentary democracy, now seemed to be vain. The Jauressian vision of a

48

republic belonging to all Frenchmen, in which the working class would progressively conquer its rightful place, seemed to recede into the far distance.

Right and left of the party fell to quarrelling more bitterly than ever about the responsibility for the defeat, and the issue which divided them—the Russian Revolution—took on greater importance. The right maintained that the country had voted against Bolshevism and that the party had paid the penalty for not dissociating itself clearly from the Man with the Knife Between His Teeth. The left, led by Loriot, replied that it was not surprising if workers had failed to rally to a party which had not given them a clear lead, which continued to talk of revolution as an abstraction while doing nothing to put it into practice, and which did not even give unqualified support to the one country where revolution had actually occurred.*

This polarization of opinion in the party made life increasingly difficult for the leadership, which was drawn from the centre. The centrist thesis that the party should support the Bolsheviks and seek to establish links with them, but not endorse all their methods and still less apply them in France, was becoming untenable.

The debate centred on the problem of the International. Since March there had been two competing Internationals in existence. Indeed one reason for the haste with which the first congress of the Third International had been summoned was to reply to the February meeting in Berne at which the old socialist parties had begun to piece together the fragments of the Second. The revival of the old International had been the central plank of the *minoritaire* platform throughout the war; so it was logical enough that Longuet went to Berne at the head of a strong SFIO delegation. But when he got there he found that the Zimmerwaldian parties—the ones that had resolutely and consistently opposed the war—were boycotting the conference so as not to sit down with the 'social-patriots' and the murderers of Karl Liebknecht and Rosa Luxemburg. In their absence the conference was dominated by the right: the British and Belgians, most of the Scandinavians, the French ex-*majoritaires* and the German

---

* This view finds some corroboration in Mme Kriegel's analysis of the voting at party congresses: electoral success, as opposed to increase in membership, does correlate positively to a significant extent with the federations voting in favour of the Third International at the Congress of Strasbourg in February 1920. Presumably these federations would be the ones which emphasized solidarity with the Russian Revolution in their election campaigns.

SPD sank their differences over German war-guilt and joined with remarkable alacrity in condemning the Bolshevik Revolution.

This was not at all what Longuet and his friends wanted. Even after the foundation of the Communist International (or Comintern) they clung to the hope that the two bodies could be reconciled, and they were supported in this 'centrist' position by the German USPD and by the Austrians. At a second conference in Lucerne in September they tried to clear the way for reconciliation by getting the old International to repudiate formally the policies which its members had followed during the war. This failed, and the 'centrists' were forced to look round for a new opening.

It came from the Swiss, whose leadership had voted in favour of joining the Comintern only to have their decision reversed by a referendum of party members after the failure of the Swiss general strike. Robert Grimm, the leader of the Swiss Socialist Party, then suggested to the centrists that they make a new attempt at 'reconstructing' the International, this time specifically excluding parties that would not condemn 'social-patriotism'. On this basis, it was hoped, the parties that had joined the Third International could be reclaimed and the responsibility for schism could be placed squarely on the right. The leaders of both SFIO and USPD seized on this idea eagerly. From now on Longuet and his group would identify themselves with 'Reconstruction'. In December the USPD congress at Leipzig voted to leave the Second International and declared that 'an effective proletarian International should be formed by uniting our party with the Third International and with social-revolutionary parties of other countries.' In February 1920 the SFIO congress at Strasbourg followed suit and passed a motion, presented by Longuet's Committee for the Reconstruction of the International, which demanded that the party leave the Second International and instructed the leadership to enter into negotiations with the Third International, the USPD and the Swiss and Italian Socialist Parties, in order to prepare a conference for a final regrouping of 'all those parties resolved to continue to act on the basis of the traditional principles of Socialism'. But the voting at Strasbourg showed that the centre was now losing ground rapidly to the left: against 3,000 votes for Longuet's motion there were 1,621 votes for Loriot's, which called for immediate adherence to the Third International. Loriot's 'Committee for the Third International' could no longer justify its refusal to break with the party by arguing that it did not yet have enough support: instead it concluded that schism was no longer necessary, since its support was growing so fast that it would soon be in a position to take the party over.[44]

There remains one episode to be described to complete the picture of the situation of the French labour movement, but it is a very important one: the failure of the great railway strike of May 1920. All the events of the previous year can be seen as merely skirmishes, but May 1920 was a crushing and conclusive defeat from which the labour movement would not recover for many years.

The Railwaymen's Federation was one of the unions whose growth at the end of the war had been most spectacular: from 65,000 members at the beginning of 1917 to 352,000 at the beginning of 1920, the highest figure ever reached by any French trade union up to that time. It was also one of the unions where the battle between *majoritaires* and *minoritaires* was fiercest. In the spring of 1920 the *majoritaire* leadership discredited itself by settling a dispute with the railway companies and calling off a general railway strike at the very moment when the CGT had been persuaded to support it and a general transport strike was about to start. The settlement included wage increases and other advantages, but the companies interpreted it in such a way that a number of strikers lost their jobs. Exploiting the railwaymen's anger at this, the *minoritaires* succeeded in winning control of the federation at its national congress in the last week of April. The new leader, Gaston Monmousseau, was an ardent revolutionary, close to the *Vie Ouvrière* group, and a member of the Committee for the Third International. He persuaded the congress to call a general strike if the dismissed workers were not immediately reinstated, and then manoeuvred the confederal leadership of the CGT into supporting him, despite their grave doubts about the timing of the strike. The strike began on 1 May. Its official objective was the nationalization of the railways, the mines and the electrical industry. But both the *minoritaires* and the employers believed that the situation was potentially revolutionary. So did a good many other people less directly involved, among them Anatole France.[45]

The CGT's tactic was to call out successive categories of workers in support of the railwaymen in a series of 'waves of assault': first the miners, seamen and dockers—to deprive industry of raw materials—then the metalworkers, builders, transport workers, the automobile and aircraft industries and the bargees. But the government fought back: by arresting the railwaymen's leaders along with several members of the Committee for the Third International (Monatte, Loriot, Boris Souvarine) and of the ultra-left splinter groups (the 'Parti Communiste' and its offshoot the 'Fédération Communiste des Soviets'), it succeeded in persuading the press and a large section of public opinion that the strike was really a diabolical Bolshevik plot to starve out Paris, planned in Moscow. It also obtained a court order dissolving the CGT. This was never enforced, but it helped to convince the confederal leadership that the prime minister, Millerand, was not as irresolute as they thought, and that the government had greater staying power than the strikers. It was ready with forces of strike-breakers wherever they were needed: students from the *Grandes Écoles*, naval ratings, Chinese immigrants, even metalworkers who went on strike in their own jobs but worked as blacklegs on the Paris Metro. Solidarity between professions was far from perfect, and the railway strike itself was both incomplete and ineffective: the railwaymen of the north and east networks failed to join in, and over the whole country traffic never fell below 52% of normal.

On 21 May an extraordinary meeting of the confederate committee voted to call off the strike. The next day the great majority of workers went back to their jobs. The railwaymen carried on grimly for another week before admitting defeat.

The defeat was total and abject: 22,000 railwaymen lost their jobs, one eighth of all those who had gone on strike. The results were summed up as follows by one of the moderate railwaymen's leaders: 'Loss of wages, months of poverty in the families, imprisonment, dismissals, sackings, punishments. . . . The result of your mistake has even been loss of reason for some union members who are now leading a miserable existence in asylums. . . . The result of your mistakes is the corpses that have lately been fished out of the Garonne.'[46] Some of those dismissed were prepared to cringe to their employers to get their jobs back, promising to forswear all union activity in future. Others remained unemployed for years, savouring their pride and their anger, and among these the Communist Party was to find many of its local leaders.

But the defeat did not affect only railwaymen. It had a shattering effect on the whole of the CGT. The Confederation had claimed 2,500,000 members at the beginning of 1920. By the end of the year it had only half that number, and by the spring of 1921 it was down to 650,000. For fifteen years government and employers would no longer need to take the trade unions seriously. Jouhaux and his colleagues could no longer hope to bargain with ministers as equals, while employers could cut wages and ignore the eight-hour-day law with impunity. The new trade unionism born of the war had suffered a very severe setback. But the old revolutionary syndicalism had suffered a mortal blow. It was hardly possible any longer to believe in the myth of the general strike, of the trade union as the sole agent of revolution. In the immediate aftermath, the *minoritaires* blamed the *majoritaires* for betraying the movement and failing to launch a revolutionary general strike, just as the *majoritaires* blamed *them* for provoking the disaster by their irresponsible extremism. So the defeat led straight to the split in the CGT which at last came about the following year. But its implications went beyond that. It would not be enough for the revolutionaries to separate themselves from the *majoritaires*: they were driven also to admit—some sooner than others—that a new recipe for revolution was needed.

That was the problem of the French labour movement in 1920. Twice in six years these two rival working-class organizations, the Socialist Party and the CGT, had failed to achieve what was expected of them. They had neither been able to avert war, nor to answer war with revolution; and when the war ended they had been able to offer the working class only defeat and humiliation. Their failure contrasted glaringly with the success of the Bolsheviks in Russia. And so it was to Russia, and to Bolshevism, that the French labour movement looked for a solution.

2

The Solution

1920–1924

The Split in the Socialist Party (1920)

Let us now look at the French situation in 1920 from the point of view of the Bolsheviks themselves. In the short term, it was discouraging. The post-war revolution had failed to materialize, and this failure had left the working-class leaders demoralized and bitterly divided amongst themselves. The world revolution on which Lenin and Trotsky counted to ensure the success of the Russian Revolution, and to justify it historically, was clearly not going to start in France. But that did not surprise them, and they continued to pin their hopes on Germany. They knew the weaknesses of the French labour movement, and they saw that in the slightly longer term the present difficulties offered them a chance: in its present state of demoralization the French Socialist Party could be won to the Third International and purged of its opportunist leaders; and in their present state of demoralization the revolutionary syndicalists, who much more than the existing Socialist Party represented the genuinely revolutionary elements in French society, could be persuaded of the need for direct political action, and especially a political party. The ingredients for a 'party of a new type' were there. The task was nonetheless a complicated one, and by the time it was completed, in 1924, Lenin would be dead and Trotsky deprived of direct influence on the making of Russian policy. A new set of priorities would have been introduced, with world revolution no longer at the head of the list.

The first stage of the operation was the simplest: the split in the Socialist Party, carried through at the end of 1920. It was part of an operation not confined to France, but planned and executed on a European scale so that the Third International could reap maximum advantage from the disintegration of the Second.

The Solution

The Bolsheviks were well aware that there was a certain unreality about the Third International as constituted in the first year of its existence. The founding congress, in March 1919, had been little more than an act of bravado by the Bolsheviks themselves, then under acute military pressure, and by the handful of foreign revolutionaries who had managed to get through the Allied blockade to proclaim their solidarity. The highly unstable situation in Europe, especially central Europe, at the time had, it is true, ensured a greater impact on world opinion than such a gathering might normally have made. But the groups and individuals in western Europe who had, in the weeks following the congress, announced their allegiance to the new International were a mixed bag; they included some with whom the Bolsheviks knew that they had little in common, but did not include others whose support they were desperately anxious to attract. In the former category were the various 'ultra-left' groups whose communism was closely akin to anarchism and who wished to eschew all parliamentary and trade union activity: but also some moderate leaders whose parties adhered to the Comintern as much out of pacifism as out of revolutionary spirit—the most important example being the Italian Socialist Party which had opposed Italy's entry into the war in 1915 and represented the moderate wing of the Zimmerwaldian movement. In the second category were the parties representing the organized working classes of the major western European countries: France, Britain and Germany. On the workers of these countries depended the chances of world revolution, but they could only be influenced through the parties in which they had confidence, and these parties were led at the moment by men whom Lenin regarded as opportunists. If the masses were to be won to communism, the parties would have to be split and their leaders forced to make a clear choice. This applied as much to the pacifist parties nominally within the Comintern—like the Italian one—as to those which had so far remained outside it, like the SFIO in France, the Independent Labour Party in Britain, and the USPD in Germany.

The defeat of the pacifists within the Second International in 1919, and the ensuing proposal for 'Reconstruction' gave the Bolsheviks their chance. In February 1920 the Executive Committee of the Communist International (ECCI) responded to the USPD's overtures by inviting all the parties which had broken with the Second International to send delegates to Moscow for negotiations, while at the same time warning the workers in the USPD that they would have to break with their right-wing leaders who 'hold the same fatal views as the leaders of the majority of the French Socialist Party, of the American Socialist Party and the British ILP'.[1] The lines of the proposed split were thus clearly laid even before the SFIO took its decision to leave the Second International at the Congress of Strasbourg, and the leaders of the majority at that congress— Longuet and his friends—should have realized that by proposing an approach to the Third International they were setting the party on a path which led logically to their own expulsion. If they were in any doubt on this point, it should have been resolved by the telegram from the Comintern's president, Zinoviev, which was read out at the congress: 'We reject any collaboration with the leaders of the right wing of the USPD and with the Longuettistes, who are dragging the movement down again into the bourgeois morass of the yellow Second International.'[2] But as yet they were reluctant to believe that the Russians really meant what they said (in January Longuet had written to assure Lenin that he did not hold him responsible for the language he had used about him because he realized it had been based on inadequate information about French affairs);[3] and in any case they thought it right to make direct contact with the Russian Bolsheviks and to obtain first-hand information about the nature of the Russian Revolution before taking any final decision.

It was hardly likely that the Bolsheviks would wait passively for the delegates of western socialist parties to come and visit them. In the spring of 1920 they were just emerging victorious from the long and desperate civil war, and more than ever convinced that revolution was imminent in Germany and the rest of Europe. The Kapp Putsch of March 1920 was immediately identified as the 'German Kornilov affair', which meant that the calendar of the German revolution had now reached August 1917.[4] In May Zinoviev announced the impending convocation of the Second Congress of the Comintern, which was to be 'a demonstration of the political forces of the world proletariat marching to victory'. The main task of this congress would be 'to determine in a clear and precise fashion the practical policy of the Comintern, and to consolidate in it a real organization of party members supplied with *one* programme and *one* tactic'.[5] As he was to put it at the congress itself, from now on the Comintern would no longer be 'a propaganda association, but a fighting organ of the international proletariat'.[6] This implied a closing of ranks, and

56

extension to the International of Lenin's ideas on party organization and discipline. In preparation, Lenin himself wrote his pamphlet *'Left-Wing' Communism: An Infantile Disorder*, in which he condemned the heresies of the ultra-left and explained that it was necessary to work within reformist trade unions and parliamentary socialist parties in order to reach the masses and demonstrate to them the treachery of their reformist leaders.

By the time that the delegates of the SFIO at last arrived in Moscow, in mid-June, the preparations for the Comintern Congress were already in full swing. The two delegates were Marcel Cachin, the editor of *L'Humanité*, and L.-O. Frossard, the party's general secretary, who had been chosen to go instead of Longuet more or less at the last minute. Both belonged to the centre of the party, which favoured 'Reconstruction' of the International, rather than to the left, which wanted a straightforward adhesion to the Comintern. But the Reconstruction formula had made little progress since February, for it turned out that the Italians had as little intention of leaving the Third International as the British had of leaving the Second, while the USPD declined to make any further moves until the result of the negotiations with Moscow was known. It was increasingly obvious that the choice for or against the Third International had only been postponed, not avoided. Frossard at least seems to have decided in favour of adhesion before he left Paris.[7] Cachin may have been more reticent initially, but as in 1917 he was quickly affected by the revolutionary atmosphere once he arrived in Russia.

In Moscow the two men were subjected to a kind of hot-and-cold treatment, being received with courtesy, taken on conducted tours of Moscow and the Volga valley, supplied with all the facts and figures they could wish, but at the same time given clearly to understand that they had come not only to examine but to be examined. In a series of interviews with the ECCI they were questioned at length by the Bolshevik leaders—and by fellow-foreigners already in the Comintern, including their countryman Sadoul—about the attitudes and behaviour of the French party, whose parliamentarianism and generally bourgeois outlook were unsparingly criticized. At the same time they found themselves pressingly invited to stay in Moscow for the Comintern Congress, which they could attend 'in a consultative capacity'. They were not inclined to refuse, although they realized that the invitation was intended to force their hand. 'As for our personal adhesion to the Comintern,' wrote Frossard in his diary on

26 June, 'it is now only a matter of hours. We're being carried away by the current.'[8] Next day they sent a telegram to the National Council of the SFIO, requesting permission to attend the congress. The Council met in Paris on 14 July and agreed, by 2,735 votes against 1,632 abstentions, to authorize them to attend.

The USPD was also invited to attend the congress, on the same basis, and it sent four delegates: two in favour of affiliation to the Comintern and two against. In this way both German and French 'centrists' found themselves appearing before the congress half as observers, half as accused; while the delegates with full voting rights included representatives of smaller and more extreme groups from their own countries: from Germany the KPD and from France the Committee for the Third International, whose delegation included a member of the left wing of the SFIO, Raymond Lefebvre, as well as three members of the CGT Minority. One of these, Rosmer, had arrived in June as the Committee's permanent delegate in Moscow, and thanks to his friendship with Trotsky was at once made a member of ECCI and of the mandates commission for the congress. He was also elected to the presiding bureau of the congress and afterwards remained in Moscow as the permanent representative in the Comintern of France, Belgium and Switzerland.[9] The other two, Marcel Vergeat and Jules Lepetit, were delegated by the committee of the *minoritaire* trade unions and had come with Lefebvre specifically for the congress and for the trade union conference which was to follow it. The better-known leaders of the Committee for the Third International—Loriot, Souvarine and Monatte—were unable to come since they were still in prison awaiting trial for their part in the alleged 'conspiracy' during the May strike. Even the delegates who did get through had a hazardous journey across Europe, and on the return journey Lefebvre, Lepetit and Vergeat were to disappear on the White Sea while trying to reach Norway in a small sailing vessel. (The inevitable rumours that they had been murdered by the Bolsheviks seem not to be supported by any strong evidence.) This contrasted strongly with the conditions in which Frossard and Cachin made the journey, being protected as far as the Russian frontier by their status as the representatives of an important French parliamentary party (Cachin indeed being actually a member of parliament).

A fifth member of the French delegation, named Goldenberg, appears to have been the representative of a revolutionary student group.[10] In addition, Sadoul and Henri Guilbeaux, the only

Frenchmen who had participated in the founding congress the year before, were again present as representatives of the 'Groupe communiste français de Moscou', though only in a consultative capacity. But the delegate of the ultra-left 'Parti Communiste', Mauricius, was arrested as soon as he arrived in Moscow on suspicion of being a French government spy; and a French Socialist deputy who had come on his own initiative, Ernest Lafont, was expelled from Russia for the same reason.[11]

Frossard and Cachin were thus heavily outnumbered even among the Frenchmen present at the congress. Their position was weakened by their isolation in Moscow and the competition of the French extreme left within the congress. Hinting that they would be quite happy to wash their hands of the SFIO and fall back on Rosmer, the Russians skilfully manoeuvred them into sending a telegram to Paris which cut the ground from under their own feet: 'We have thought it necessary to inform the Party of the state of our inquiry and the conclusions we had reached. We have done this after a month of negotiations, with the conviction that agreement was possible with the Communist International.' After sending this it was virtually impossible for them to break off the negotiations without making fools of themselves and ensuring the triumph of the party's right wing. Zinoviev roundly abused them in the congress, while negotiating with them behind the scenes. The main point which they were anxious to impress on the Russians was that their party could not accept conditions which required it to expel named persons, and especially not Longuet who was now its effective leader. At first, therefore, they had reacted very strongly to the Russians' demands, which included the expulsion of Longuet as well as the change of the party's name from Socialist to Communist and the granting of two-thirds of the places on the *Comité Administratif Permanent* to the left group headed by Loriot. But they were obliged to accept verbal assurances from Zinoviev: the demand for Longuet's expulsion was purely symbolic —'if citizen Longuet is willing to adopt the standpoint of the Third International, we shall be happy to welcome him among us.'[12] As for the proposal to give two-thirds of the places in the party leadership to the left, that could be treated as a suggestion rather than a demand. On this basis they drew up a joint statement which Cachin read to the congress on the morning of their departure, announcing that they accepted the conditions of admission, and enumerating what they understood to be the 'guiding ideas' of these conditions:

—that the party must break in word and deed with reformism and opportunism;

—that as a result of this, each militant must choose personally between reformism and revolution;

—that they must act as socialists in the trade unions and 'work fraternally with the revolutionary militants of the trade union organization who admit the need for political action';

—that in peacetime as in wartime, no duty can come before class duty and therefore it is never legitimate to vote credits or to join the government;

—that the party programme must be revised and a rigorous discipline established, in particular by a strict control of socialist journalists and parliamentarians;

—that support for the Soviet republics requires that the French proletariat be called on to refuse the transport of weapons and munitions. . . .

With that Cachin and Frossard went home to report to the French people; and the immense enthusiasm which greeted their account of Russian achievements at a series of public meetings all over France soon made their doubts about the terms of admission to the Comintern seem quite academic. Frossard evidently foresaw the difficulties ahead, for he quickly provided an idiosyncratic interpretation of the issue which Lenin and Zinoviev would certainly not have accepted: 'Comrade workers,' he told a crowd of over 10,000 in Paris on the day after his arrival, 'it is not a question of asking you to make a revolution tomorrow, nor, if you make it, of slavishly copying the Russian soviets. It's a question of demonstrating in some way other than in words, our solidarity with the Russian proletariat.'[13] Cachin adopted a humbler attitude towards the Bolsheviks, asserting that since they had actually made a revolution it was not for French Socialists, who had failed to make one, to criticize their methods. 'When a French Socialist meets such men,' Cachin wrote in *L'Humanité*, 'he has everything to learn from them. He has lessons to take; he has none to give.'[14] Thus were sown the seeds of French subservience to Russian leadership.

In Moscow, however, Cachin's speech accepting the conditions of admission had enraged the left in the congress and provoked a spate of attacks on the SFIO. It was denounced for its flabby opportunism first by one of its own members (Lefebvre), then by a man who had been outside France for five years (Guilbeaux), then by an unknown student (Goldenberg). All three of these insisted on the bankruptcy of the French Socialist Party and the need for a real Communist Party which would include the revolutionary syndicalists. The same point was made by representatives of the left in other European countries and by Lozovsky, who at least had a first-hand knowledge of the French labour movement. All these speakers opposed admitting the USPD and the French party into the International. But Zinoviev took a more balanced line: 'We do not ask you to welcome the French Socialist Party into the Third International as it is. We simply ask you to instruct the Executive Committee to establish, after the Congress, whether the conditions fixed have been carried out.' This was the conclusion which the congress eventually accepted. But Cachin and Frossard were spared the embarrassment of listening to this debate, which took place on the day they left for home.

In the congress-hall hung a huge map on which the delegates could follow the daily advance of the Red Army towards Warsaw.[15] They expected any day to hear news of revolution in Poland, which was regarded as the last bulwark of world imperialism against the Bolsheviks.[16] The victory of communism throughout Europe seemed so close that there was no need for compromise with opportunists like Cachin and the parties they represented; and though Zinoviev managed to avert any absolute veto on the admission of the SFIO and USPD, there was general agreement to make the conditions of admission as stringent as possible. The Twenty-One Conditions finally adopted by the congress went well beyond the understanding given by Cachin and Frossard in their deliberately rather imprecise statement, and on at least two points they went beyond the more precise Russian drafts which Cachin and Frossard had seen and on which their understanding had been based. These two last-minute conditions were number Eighteen, obliging all party organs to publish all important official documents issued by ECCI, and number Twenty-One—much more drastic—which stipulated that party members who voted against the Conditions at the party congress must be expelled from the party. In addition, all the points to which Cachin and Frossard had objected in their discussions with Zinoviev were retained. Condition number Seven named Longuet as one of the 'notorious opportunists' whose presence in the Third International could not be tolerated (the others being Kautsky and Hilferding of the USPD, MacDonald of the ILP and the Italian moderates Turati and Modigliani—which showed that the Conditions applied as much to parties already in the Comintern as to those now wishing to join). Condition number Seventeen obliged all parties wishing to join to take the title 'Communist Party', and added that this was no mere formality since 'the Communist International has declared war on the entire bourgeois world and on all yellow social-democratic parties'. Condition Twenty insisted that parties now joining the Comintern 'must see to it that, before entering the Communist International, not less than two-thirds of the members of their central committee and of all their leading central bodies consist of comrades who publicly and unambiguously advocated the entry of their party into the Communist International before its second congress'. Here, however, it was added that exceptions might be made with the approval of the ECCI, which also—a last chance for Longuet—'has the right to make exceptions in the case of representatives of the centre mentioned in paragraph 7'.

Almost every one of the Conditions involved a sharp break with the traditions of the SFIO. Number Three stated that it was the duty of Communists 'everywhere to create a parallel illegal organization which at the decisive moment will help the party to do its duty to the revolution'. Number Eight laid down that each party was obliged 'to support every colonial liberation movement not merely in words but deeds, to demand the expulsion of their own imperialists from these colonies . . . and to carry on systematic agitation among the troops of their own country against any oppression of the colonial peoples'. Number Nine dealt with the trade unions and other mass workers' organizations: 'Communist cells must be organized which shall by persistent and unflagging work win the trade unions, etc., for the Communist cause. . . . The Communist cells must be completely subordinate to the party as a whole.' Number Eleven called for the complete subjection of the parliamentary fractions to the party presidium and 'to the real interests of genuinely revolutionary propaganda and agitation', while Number Twelve prescribed the introduction of 'democratic centralism' in the internal organization of the party: 'In the present epoch of acute civil war, the communist party will be able to fulfil its duty only if its organization is as centralized as possible, iron discipline prevails, and if the party centre, upheld by the confidence of the party membership, has strength and authority and is equipped with the most comprehensive powers.' Further, under Condition number Thirteen all parties in countries where legal activity was possible were to undertake periodic purges of their membership. Party programmes were subject to confirmation by ECCI (Condition Fifteen) and all decisions of Comintern congresses and of ECCI were mandatory for all affiliated parties (Condition Sixteen).[17]

The Comintern Congress ended on 7 August, but the details of the Conditions were not known in France until 2 September, when a text of them translated from the German paper *Die Freiheit* was printed in Paul Faure's newspaper *Le Populaire*. (By that time, incidentally, a dramatic change had come over the international situation with the victorious counter-offensive of the Polish army. But the implication of this—that the workers of Europe would not rise to join the advancing Red Army and that Russia would therefore remain for a long time the only socialist state—was not immediately realized.)

Inevitably, the publication of the Conditions led to the disintegration of the centre which had led the French Socialist Party since 1918. Paul Faure immediately pronounced that the conditions relating to the unions, the expulsion of Longuet, and the predominance of the left in the central organs of the party were unacceptable. Ten days later Longuet himself agreed that the Conditions were 'absolutely unacceptable'.[18] Rapidly Longuet's Committee for the Reconstruction of the International became the rallying point for resistance, not to the Third International itself—that role was reserved for the right-wing *Comité socialiste de résistance à l'adhésion* led by Blum and Renaudel—but to the conditions of admission. Longuet and his friends claimed to be in favour of the principle of joining the Third International, but unwilling to sacrifice the unity and independence of their party. For Cachin and Frossard this position was no longer tenable. In fact it was no longer tenable for anyone who really wanted to join the Third International, since it was quite obvious that ECCI would make the greatest difficulty about accepting Longuet at all, and would certainly not allow him to join on his own terms. Cachin and Frossard were in an awkward position, for they had been asserting since their return from Moscow that there were only nine conditions, and at first they suggested that the Twenty-One were not meant to apply to France. When this proved not to be the case, Frossard fell back on the view that they were only a general guide to revolutionary activity, to be followed to the extent circumstances permitted.[19] There thus emerged a left-centre under Cachin and Frossard's leadership, which argued not so much *for* the Conditions as for joining the Comintern in spite of the Conditions, the importance of membership being too important for quibbles over this or that Condition to stand in its way. The members of this left-centre resigned from the Committee for the Reconstruction of the International on 23 September.

The outlook of these men was, of course, still a long way from Bolshevism. But it was to them that fell the task of leading the majority of the SFIO into the Third International. The left wing of the party, which had favoured joining the Third International all along, was far from enthusiastic about this prospect. But it was ill placed to take the lead itself since its leaders, Loriot and Souvarine, were still in prison, and its own delegate to the Comintern Congress, Lefebvre, had not returned. In any case, if Lenin and Zinoviev had been willing to negotiate with Cachin and Frossard, the would-be French Bolsheviks could hardly refuse all contact with them; and if these two men who held the most important posts in the party now accepted the main point of the Left's programme, there was little point in splitting the pro-Comintern vote by presenting a rival motion at the party congress. The left therefore agreed to co-operate with the left-centre in drawing up a motion. There was no difficulty about this since political prisoners were allowed generous visiting hours as well as newspapers and writing facilities. It is thus at least possible that Souvarine did, as he now claims,[20] write the main part of the motion to join the Third International which was presented to the Congress of Tours in the names of Cachin and Frossard.

The left and the left-centre agreed, of course, that there was no question of rejecting the Twenty-One Conditions. But they agreed also that there was equally no question of proposing them to the Congress *telles quelles*. Although they were now prepared for the party to split, the left-centre still hoped that the split would occur to the right of Longuet rather than to the left, and they wanted the right to take the blame for it. Accordingly they embarked on one final bout of negotiation with the Comintern. Daniel Renoult, a member of the left-centre, went to the USPD Congress in October at Halle, in Saxony, and there met Zinoviev who had come in person to put the case for Comintern membership. Zinoviev agreed not to insist on the expulsion of Longuet, or of the delegates who voted against accepting the Conditions at the French party congress, provided that they accepted the decision of the majority once taken. He even agreed that Longuet and his group should receive one-third of the places on the party's ruling bodies.

On this point, therefore, the Conditions were amended in the agreed motion. The call for party cells in the trade unions was also dropped. The left knew as well as the centre, if not better, that this doctrine was totally unacceptable to French revolutionary syndical-ists, who were precisely the people that a Communist Party was meant to attract. Accordingly the motion stated that though the unions and the party would 'coordinate their action, one organization would not be subject to the other'. Thirdly, as a further gesture towards the centre and the sacred cow of party unity, the motion stated that the new party would be called, not 'Communist Party', but 'Socialist Party, French Section of the Communist International'.

The USPD Congress voted by 237 votes to 156 to adhere to the Comintern, the majority then uniting with the KPD while the minority seceded in order to remain independent. It was by now obvious that the French congress would follow the same pattern. The only question in doubt was whether Longuet and his group could yet be won over; but Zinoviev did his best to ensure that Longuet would not take advantage of the concession he had made at Halle, first by a message telling the French workers that 'with a pistol at their throat, you must insist on an answer from Longuet and his followers', then by a telegram, which arrived while the congress was actually in session, denouncing both Longuet and Faure as 'agents of bourgeois influence on the proletariat'. Probably these efforts were unnecessary. Longuet and Faure were not impressed by the concessions made in the motion of the left and left-centre. Their objections to the Conditions went further. In their own motion they also rejected the Conditions dealing with clandestine organization, party discipline, periodic purges and the press. But what they objected to most of all, and what made it quite impossible for them to enter the Third International, was the very principle of rules and regulations being dictated to the French party from Moscow. Longuet tried to reply to the Twenty-One Conditions with one single condition of his own: that freedom of expression within the party should be preserved intact.[21] Evidently he no longer expected the Comintern to accept this. He knew by now that the Comintern had no intention of letting prospective members pick and choose among its Conditions, still less reply with conditions of their own. His motion for adhesion 'with reservation' was a tactical one, designed to show what those who adhered without reservations were sacrificing. Longuet took the Twenty-One Conditions seriously, and in that he was more lucid than his friends of the left-centre, who persisted in believing that the Conditions could be accepted and then ignored.

But neither Longuet's lucidity nor Frossard's calculations can have had much effect on the result. No doubt the majority for the Third International would have been a bit larger if Longuet had supported it, and a bit smaller if the motion had not been tabled in the name of the general secretary of the party. But Frossard had followed the majority, not led it, and Longuet was powerless to resist the tide. The various motions were voted on in the local federations before the congress, and the delegates came to Tours with binding mandates. In a series of speeches at the opening of the congress, they described the state of mind of their local militants. From these speeches it is clear that there was intense enthusiasm in almost all parts of France for the *idea* of the Third International, but very little interest in the details of the Conditions. The value of the Conditions, in the eyes of these militants, was that they would oblige the party to make a clean break with the recent and dishonourable past—with war socialism, with participation in government, with the whole gloomy record of compromise and failure. But most of them did not at all relish the prospect of a split, and many still hoped to preserve party unity, or at least not to lose the Longuet group: 'The Federation of the Doubs will vote for the Cachin-Frossard motion for the Third International, but if a joint motion were presented with the Longuet motion or any other, the Federation of the Doubs would vote for this motion on the one condition of an adhesion to the Third International.' 'The Socialist Federation of the Eure . . . instructs its federal secretary to make a fraternal appeal to Jean Longuet for an agreed motion at the national Congress so that the two main fractions of the Party can adhere unanimously to the Third International.' 'We are unanimous for remaining in unity.' 'Our federation has come out against any break.' 'We are not at all supporters of a split. . . .' Such is the constant theme of speakers in favour of the Cachin-Frossard motion.[22]

Another point which recurs again and again in their speeches is the strength of support for the Third International among the peasants: 'We do not speak for an industrial majority, but for an essentially rural one, and this present majority is for the immediate transformation of the workers' situation, a transformation which we see only in the Third International'. 'On one side there are the *majoritaires* who approved the Party's international policy during the war and the vote for the credits. On the other, the rural crowd. . . .' 'The Ariège, an essentially rural district, has adhered almost unanimously to the Third International.' 'In the old federations like that of the Aube, numerous peasant groups have been set up and have come with firm mandates for the Third International.' 'The supporters of the Third International are recruited especially in the rural areas.' 'The rural comrades seem to come to us with an enthusiasm that we ought to take advantage of. . . . By contrast, it is the [urban] sections of Rueil and Angoulême that give a large number of mandates to the Longuet motion.' 'It's in Vierzon and Bourges that the right-wing and centre elements live, and it's the countryside, in particular the Sancerrois and the Saint-Amandois, the peasants, the small wine-growers and the small farmers who vote for joining the Third International without restrictions.' 'I represent a rural federation. . . . The peasant comrades of the Corrèze have voted for the motion in full consciousness.' 'The federal secretary was for the Second International; the great majority in the Creuse is for the Third International. The Creuse is a specially rural department. Only Aubusson is industrial and has given the majority to the Second. That proves that it is the peasants and small farmers who are more revolutionary than the industrial workers.'[23] Two explanations are generally given for this relative lukewarmness of the urban working class: demoralization after the defeat of the May strike, and concern about the independence of the trade unions.[24] But the latter point may remind us that the most revolutionary element in the industrial working class was in any case unlikely to be enrolled in the SFIO.

The same speeches by local delegates suggest that support for the Third International was often strongest among the younger and more inexperienced militants, and that it went with a resentment of patronizing manners on the part of the party's national leaders.[25] It seems possible therefore to suggest that the impulsion of the party towards the Third International was often the work of its new members, especially of the peasants shocked into political consciousness by their experiences in the war, and to a lesser extent of the new working class; whereas the workers who had belonged to the party before the war were more wedded to the traditions of Guesde and Jaurès, more respectful of the national leadership, more circumspect in their attitude to Comintern membership and the conditions attached to it. It also seems likely, if not certain, that the political consciousness of most of the supporters of the Third International was of a fairly elementary sort, and that their grasp of the nature of Bolshevism and its implications was negligible.

In particular, they were psychologically ill prepared for a split in the party, even though from the Bolsheviks' point of view this was the object of the exercise. The exercise succeeded, and both the right and the right-centre left the party in order to preserve 'la vieille maison'—the SFIO—while the party led by Frossard and Cachin became the SFIC (it finally took the title *Parti Communiste Français* in October 1921).

We have seen that the membership of the Unified Socialist Party had been growing very rapidly since the end of the war and had reached nearly 180,000 at the moment of the split. On the basis of the voting at Tours, the Communist Party might have expected to keep at least 120,000 of these members, and it hoped to compensate for the departure of the right by a massive new recruitment of the left, among revolutionary workers who would be eager to join a section of the Communist International but had been reluctant to join a feeble social democrat party that included such tarnished figures as Renaudel and Albert Thomas. Some recruitment of this type undoubtedly did occur, though doubtless not on the scale that had been hoped. In spite of this the party found itself in October 1921 with under 110,000 members, and declined rapidly to under 80,000 by the end of July 1922. The reason for this was not that more members had followed the right than had been expected, for the new SFIO started with a membership of only 50,000. It seems clear that a large number of Socialists had voted for the Third International in the spirit of Pierre Brizon, who wrote in his pacifist newspaper *La Vague* just before the Congress of Tours: 'Let's all join the Third International, without unnecessary conditions or divisions on the left.'[26] They no doubt expected that the result would somehow be a bigger and better Socialist party, and were disillusioned when they found that instead there were now two smaller parties at daggers drawn with each other.

The Bolsheviks, however, had achieved their aim. The first stage in their operation was complete: the French Socialist Party had joined the Comintern and its right wing had been eliminated. But under the leadership of Frossard and Cachin it was by no means free from the taint of 'opportunism', and the revolutionary syndicalists remained as contemptuous of it as ever—their prejudices inflamed, if anything, by the Comintern's talk of 'cells' and 'complete subordination to the Party'.

In the next stage of the operation, the Comintern would have to destroy the influence and authority of the 'centre', which it had so skilfully exploited in the first stage.

The Defeat of the 'Centre' (1921–1923)

The Cachin-Frossard motion which was passed at Tours provided for the replacement of the old *Comité Administratif Provisoire* by a *Comité Directeur* of twenty-four members, which was to be the sovereign body of the new party. The first such Committee was elected at Tours after the departure of Longuet and the right. Its membership was agreed in advance by what had been the left and the left-centre, who thus undertook to form a kind of ruling coalition for the new party. For the time being the centre predominated, with Frossard as general secretary, Cachin as editor of *L'Humanité*, and Eugène Dondicol as treasurer. For the left, Loriot became international secretary, but more important was the election of Souvarine as representative to the ECCI in Moscow—for now, in theory at least, the leadership of the French party was subordinate to the leadership of the International. Both Loriot and Souvarine were released from prison in March 1921, when the somewhat farcical 'conspiracy trial' staged by the government ended in the unanimous acquittal of all the accused. (It had in any case achieved its object long before, by disorganizing the revolutionary groups and misleading public opinion during the strike of May 1920.)

The Bolsheviks knew well that the centre was at best only half-sincere in accepting the Twenty-One Conditions, and therefore relied on the left to take the lead in transforming the party. But the left, as it turned out, was very ill equipped to perform this task. The Committee for the Third International had never been anything more than a propaganda club. It worked by lobbying the militants of existing organizations, rather than by appealing directly to the workers, and it had avoided organizing its own supporters since its tactic was not to provoke splits in the organizations to which they already belonged. Its Socialist members especially were intellectuals and writers, men who were happier drafting a resolution or castigating their opponents in long articles than speaking in public. By their own social origins they were no better qualified to make the party a working-class party than were the leaders of the centre. They might have hoped for a reinforcement from their syndicalist colleagues. But most of the revolutionary leaders in the CGT hung back from joining the new party, either because they considered it imperfectly purged of opportunism and parliamentarianism, or because they still had scruples about membership of a political party as such, or because they felt that to proclaim their allegiance to a political party at this stage would weaken their position in the approaching battle within the CGT.

A further weakness of the left in the new party was that it was far from homogeneous. Its *raison d'être* until now had been the campaign for membership of the Third International. Once that was achieved there was little to hold it together. Its representatives on the new *Comité Directeur* included: Alexandre Blanc, one of the three Socialist deputies who had attended the Kienthal conference in 1916; Joseph Cartier, a Parisian ultra-leftist; Loriot; Victor Méric, a semi-anarchist of bourgeois origins and bohemian life-style; Charles Rappoport, a Marxist scholar of Russian-Jewish origin with very mixed feelings about Bolshevism; Boris Souvarine, also of Russian origin but at this time a quite uncritical admirer of Bolshevism as well as a merciless and often tactless pamphleteer; Albert Treint, a less subtle but equally tactless and equally passionate Bolshevik, a former schoolteacher who had emerged from the war with the rank of captain, which stuck to him as a nickname because of his authoritarian character; and Paul Vaillant-Couturier, another ex-officer but also a trained lawyer and gifted writer, a spokesman for the generation decimated and embittered by the war.

It is hardly surprising that in the course of 1921 the members of this group drifted apart. The ultra-left, in its stronghold of the Seine Federation, continued to denounce all compromises and dubbed Loriot himself an opportunist for his attempt to work with the centre. At the same time those members of the Committee for the Third International who tried to maintain a critical attitude towards Bolshevism and the policies of the Comintern—whether from a libertarian point of view, like Méric and his friend Georges Pioch (who believed that 'le Communisme est la forme organisée de l'amour'), or from a Marxist one, like Rappoport—were soon identified by Souvarine as the right of the new party, being lumped together with men like Raoul Verfeuil, a supporter of Longuet who had only stayed in the party because he held the right more to blame for the schism than the left.

70

Souvarine, Loriot, Vaillant-Couturier and Treint remained for the time being the hard core of the left, the champions of the International's policies. The Committee for the Third International itself was dissolved in October 1921 on instructions from ECCI, having ostensibly fulfilled its purpose. Supposedly the party was now inside the International, and the time for faction-fighting was over. But in reality neither ECCI in Moscow nor the left in France was satisfied with the way things were going. During the war-scare of spring 1921, when French troops occupied Düsseldorf to back up a claim for war reparations, the party had confined itself to verbal protests and had failed to back up the vigorous propaganda carried on among the troops by its youth section, the *Jeunesses Communistes* (JC). At the meeting of ECCI which preceded the Third Comintern Congress, in June, Trotsky, Lenin and Zinoviev had to defend the French party leadership against the attacks of Maurice Laporte, the JC representative, and Béla Kun, the Hungarian leader, who still wanted the Comintern to refuse admission to the French party. The Russians regarded the capture of the SFIO and the departure of Longuet as an achievement which should not be so lightly sacrificed, and they did not want to repeat the mistake they had made with the Italian party, which had walked out of the Comintern at its Congress of Leghorn in February, leaving only a small Communist rump behind. Consequently Trotsky, who had been very rude to Cachin and Frossard when they visited Moscow the previous year, now defended them in their absence against their critics. He nonetheless found plenty to criticize himself in the style and content of *L'Humanité* and in the party's inactivity on the trade union front. Immediately after the congress, in July, he began to intervene personally in 'the French question' with a series of letters to France. He wrote to Pierre Monatte, his closest friend among the syndicalist leaders, urging him that it was his duty to join the party in order to help transform it.[27] He wrote to Cachin and Frossard themselves with a whole list of suggestions for improving the party's work.[28] He wrote to Lucie Leiciague, a member of the French delegation to the Third Congress, giving in detail his criticisms of *L'Humanité* ('Stop a hundred workers in the street coming out of a factory and read them the parliamentary report from *L'Humanité*, I'm sure that ninety-nine of them will understand nothing and learn nothing; as for the hundredth, perhaps he will understand something, but he still won't learn anything.').[29]

71

It was Trotsky, too, who drafted the confidential letter sent by ECCI to the *Comité Directeur* of the French party at the end of July, demanding that Cachin and Frossard come to Moscow in person. One point in this letter was a demand that the party 'put an end to the situation in which party members, whether for financial or political motives, found newspapers and reviews which are independent of party control and frequently aimed against the Party'.[30] This was a transparent allusion to Henri Fabre and Pierre Brizon, editors respectively of *Le Journal du Peuple* and of *La Vague*. Both men were members of the party, but they ran their newspapers independently and made them organs of opposition to Comintern policy. Unwilling to resign themselves to the loss of Socialist unity, they called for a rapprochement with the Longuettistes, and openly disputed the right of ECCI to give orders to the French party. But the *Comité Directeur* took no action to discipline them, and Frossard confined himself to expressing his disagreement in some of the many articles which he himself contributed to Fabre's paper.

Souvarine, who had become an ardent disciple of Trotsky, himself took up Trotsky's arguments in a series of letters from Moscow to the *Comité Directeur* in the late summer and autumn of 1921, complaining in more and more abusive terms of the party's laxity about putting the International's directives into practice. He thus made himself the symbol of Comintern interference in French affairs, and the right wing of the party, exploiting the unpopularity which his arrogance and tactlessness had won for him in many circles, mounted a full-scale campaign against him. Frossard and Cachin, caught between the wrath of ECCI in Moscow and the wrath of Souvarine's enemies in Paris, sought refuge in inactivity and in pious statements deploring the personal animosity of both sides. They found excuses for not obeying ECCI's summons to Moscow, and they did their best to ignore the theses passed at the Third Congress which called for the reorganization of foreign Communist parties on the Bolshevik model. When in October they were visited by the Swiss Communist Jules Humbert-Droz, the first of many special Comintern emissaries, the party leaders agreed readily to all his demands—reinforced discipline, tighter control of the press, creation of a ruling Presidium, development of the party's proletarian character—but after his departure things remained much as before.

The First Congress of the French Communist Party (PCF) was held in Marseilles exactly a year after the Congress of Tours (25–30

December 1921), in circumstances of maximum confusion. A week earlier, in Moscow, ECCI had adopted a set of theses on the 'united working-class front'—a new international tactic which was in fact a more precise version of the slogan 'to the masses' adopted at the Third World Congress. It recognized, after the disastrous failure of the Communist 'March Action' in Germany, that many workers still followed the old social democrat parties, especially the 'centrist' parties of the 'International $2\frac{1}{2}$' (comprising the Austrian and Swiss Socialist Parties, the British ILP, and the rumps of the SFIO and USPD in France and Germany). In order to win their confidence, Communists must be prepared to adopt a platform of unity with social-democrat leaders for limited objectives, if only in order to demonstrate more convincingly that these reformist traitors were the real enemies of working-class unity. This amounted to an implicit admission that world revolution was no longer an immediate probability. As Trotsky had put it at the Third Congress, 'in 1919, we said to ourselves: "It is a question of months". Now we say: "It is perhaps a question of years".'[31] It was the counterpart in international labour politics of the New Economic Policy adopted in Russia in the spring of 1921, and of the pursuit of commercial and diplomatic relations with capitalist powers in Russian foreign policy.

When the Congress of Marseilles met, the 'united front' theses had not yet been published in France, but a letter to the congress had arrived from ECCI, dated the day after the adoption of the theses but in fact drafted by Trotsky three days before (15 December). This letter called for stern measures against the group round Fabre which 'is still weeping for the departure of the dissidents' (i.e. Longuet and the right-wing Socialists) 'and even preaches open collaboration with the parties of the bourgeoisie in the form of the *bloc des gauches*'[32] (the pre-war formula of alliance between Socialists and Radicals against the right). Delegates at the congress were therefore understandably bewildered to find the representatives of the International, Bordiga and Walecki, pleading with them *not* to rule out the possibility of a united front with the dissidents, on pain of finding themselves in opposition to 'almost the entire International'.

In the upshot, the congress defied the International on this point, passing a motion which specifically ruled out the possibility of any alliance with the dissidents, and also by not re-electing Souvarine (who was still in Moscow) to the *Comité Directeur*. In protest against this the four members of the left who were re-elected—Loriot, Treint,

Vaillant-Couturier and Amédée Dunois—immediately resigned. In an effort to smooth over the crisis, Frossard persuaded the congress to renew Souvarine's mandate as delegate to the International nonetheless. But the left refused to be appeased, and the International itself was far from satisfied.

The crisis got rapidly worse once the united front theses were published in France. Hard to interpret and apply in any country, the united front tactic seemed to make no sense at all in France. In France, unlike Germany and other countries, the Communist Party had—or was believed to have—more than twice as many members as the Socialist Party, while the revolutionary trade unions, now expelled from the CGT, claimed to have taken with them well over half its members. The reformist leaders hardly seemed the right people through whom to approach the masses. Besides, the Socialist split was still only a year old. Resentment and recrimination between former comrades were still being given free rein, indeed were being spurred on by the International itself. The Communist leaders did not yet feel themselves so different from the Socialists —nor were they—that they could view co-operation with them as a matter of mere tactics. The idea of a 'party of a new type'—homogeneous, disciplined, easy to manoeuvre—had as yet made little headway. To most of the party's leaders the united front tactic seemed like an invitation to undo what had been so painfully achieved at Tours, an invitation cynically issued by that very International for whose sake and at whose behest the Tours operation had been carried out.

Accordingly, those who openly regretted the Tours split and still hoped to see it reversed—notably Fabre and Brizon—eagerly supported the new tactic. Other members of the party's so-called right—for instance Méric and Verfeuil—joined with the centre in attacking it as at once opportunistic and inopportune, while the left tried weakly to think of convincing arguments for obedience to the International. On 17 January 1922 the new *Comité Directeur* unanimously rejected the united front. Five days later its position was ratified by a hastily summoned conference of federal secretaries. The party's four delegates to the 'Enlarged Executive' of the International, summoned by Zinoviev to approve the new tactic, were instructed to explain that it was inapplicable in France and to warn of its dangers for the International as a whole.

At the Enlarged Executive, which met from 21 February to 4 March, the delegation led by Cachin and Renoult tried bravely to stand up to the onslaught of Zinoviev, Radek and Trotsky. In protesting against the proposed Conference of the Three Internationals, through which the Russians hoped to apply the united front tactic at the very summit, Renoult was supported by the Italian delegation, but he was disowned by the left of his own party: Souvarine, Treint (who had accompanied the delegation as a non-voting representative of the minority) and Antoine Ker, a left-leaning centrist who had replaced Loriot as international secretary and had stayed on in Moscow after coming to report on the Congress of Marseilles. It was on this occasion that Treint enunciated his own heavy-footed interpretation of the united front, which he was never to live down: 'We move alternately towards and away from the reformists, as the hand moves towards and away from the chicken it is plucking (*la volaille à plumer*).' In the end the French, Italians and Spanish were outvoted, and Cachin read a declaration stating that they would submit out of discipline, but observing that the Executive had committed itself to applying the new tactic with the greatest possible allowances for the peculiarities of different national situations.

As a test of French 'discipline', Frossard was picked as one of the Comintern's representatives at the Berlin Conference between the Three Internationals in April. He did as he was told at the conference, but within the Comintern delegation he made no secret of his disagreement with the package deal arranged between Radek and the president of the Second International, Emile Vandervelde. This provided for a permanent Committee of Nine to organize future conferences, and for joint demonstrations during the inter-governmental economic conference at Genoa, which the Russians feared might be the prelude to a new intervention in Russia by 'all the great imperialist and reactionary states'.[33] On Frossard's return from Berlin, the *Comité Directeur* passed a resolution pointing to the dangers of the Committee of Nine, and arranged a demonstration in conjunction with the revolutionary trade unions, spurning an offer of joint action from the Socialist Party. These decisions were ratified on 22 and 23 April by a National Council of the Party, which refused to accept the ruling of the Enlarged Executive on the united front as final, and declared that only the next World Congress of the Comintern would have power to decide the issue. The Council did however re-elect the representatives of the left—Souvarine, Loriot, Dunois and Vaillant-Couturier—to the *Comité Directeur*.

The ECCI was now rapidly losing patience. At three meetings in Moscow during May the French representatives—the centrists Louis Sellier and Lucie Leiciague as well as Souvarine—were subjected to a further drubbing by Trotsky and Zinoviev both for their attitude to the united front and for their continued failure to do anything about the right-wing press. To set an example, the ECCI itself proceeded to vote the expulsion of Fabre, editor of *Le Journal du Peuple*, sweeping aside the protests of all three French delegates. On 30 May this decision was grudgingly accepted at a meeting of the French *Comité Directeur* in the presence of the Comintern's roving ambassador Humbert-Droz, who persuaded Frossard to go in person to the meeting of the Enlarged Executive in June. At the Enlarged Executive there was yet another full-dress confrontation between the Bolsheviks and the French, with Frossard trying to defend himself against Trotsky and Zinoviev while Souvarine joined in heaping abuse on his own party. A resolution was passed enjoining the French party to set up a homogeneous *Comité Directeur*, of which at least half the members should be workers and which should have the right to expel members from the party on its own authority. Above this should be a small *Bureau Politique* residing permanently in Paris. The ultra-leftist Federation of the Seine was to be brought to heel. The united front was to be applied in practice. The press was to be brought under control. The left and centre were to join forces against the right. Daniel Renoult was censured for carrying on a campaign against the United Front in his evening paper *L'Internationale*. The expulsion of Fabre was confirmed and the *Comité Directeur* instructed to explain its 'political significance' to the workers. The next congress of the party was to be accompanied by a campaign against 'all the tendencies of petit-bourgeois pacifism, anarcho-syndicalism, verbal revolutionarism, theories making the action of the proletariat dependent on the will or on the maturity of the peasant class and thereby falsifying the class character of the party, etc.' Finally the *Comité Directeur* was to circulate all these decisions to the party in the form of a manifesto.[34]

Frossard replied that his delegation remained opposed to this resolution on certain points (notably the trade unions, the united front and the personal responsibility of Renoult, who after all had only expressed the opinion of the *Comité Directeur* and the immense majority of the party). Nonetheless he again promised to submit, because 'we know that the authority of the International, which results at once from its doctrinal directions and from its revolutionary experience, can only have a beneficial effect for all parties, including the French party, whatever reserves we have at present.'[35] For the second time in two years this arch-manoeuvrer had been out-manoeuvred, and had disqualified himself as a leader of French resistance to Russian leadership. He promised to report, explain and defend the decisions of the Executive to his party. He was well aware that the party would be reluctant to swallow them, but he also realized, as he told the Federation of the Seine on his return, that 'if the French Party adopted an attitude of inertia or hostility . . . an attitude of this sort would lead us infallibly to a breach with the International.'[36] He appears to have resolved on one last effort to reconcile Bolshevik discipline with French democratic traditions—perhaps in the hope that if the French party gave an immediate example of disciplined submission, the Fourth World Congress might yet modify some of the harsher sentences of the Executive.

In fact things went the other way. The majority of the French party indulged in a final and most flagrant exhibition of indiscipline, with which Frossard at the last moment associated himself, and the Fourth World Congress was to mark his downfall.

At first, Frossard tried to apply the International's policy, working in conjunction with Humbert-Droz, who now took up residence in Paris. At the congress of the revolutionary trade unions in Saint-Etienne, at the end of June, he at least went through the motions of assembling the Communist delegates and laying down a party line. He dropped his opposition to the united front. And in August, when Souvarine at last returned from Moscow, Frossard joined forces with the left to impose more centralized statutes on the Federation of the Seine and to prepare motions for the coming party congress. But when the congress was actually held—in Paris, in October—relations between left and centre suddenly broke down, and Zinoviev's attempt to manage the congress by remote control, by dictating elaborate instructions to a small sub-committee of both factions through Humbert-Droz and another special emissary, Dmitrii Manuilsky, misfired badly. Humbert-Droz with difficulty got left and centre to accept parity of numbers on the *Comité Directeur* and on the proposed six-man *Bureau Politique*, but negotiations broke down over the editorship of *L'Humanité*. Souvarine and the left were determined to get rid of Cachin, while the centre refused to sacrifice him. As a compromise Humbert-Droz and Manuilsky proposed a joint editor-ship by Cachin and Rosmer, who had joined the party on his return from Moscow the previous year and was now a leading member of the left. This arrangement was acceptable to neither side. The centre was emboldened by the discovery that the left had less support than expected among delegates to the congress, whereas Renoult's group, which was holding out against the united front, turned out to be quite strong and to include a large working-class element. Consequently Cachin's supporters decided to fight out the issue on the floor of the congress, which quickly developed into a rout of the left. Ker, who was supposed to defend the joint motion on general policy drawn up by Frossard and Souvarine, instead found himself attacking the left and defending Cachin. On the last day Frossard himself boiled over with indignation against the left, admitted that 'faced with certain inapplicable decisions of the International' he had played for time, and announced that if the left maintained its present attitude, the centre would take over the entire leadership on its own. But, inconsistent to the last, he added: 'We will take it in order to carry out the International's policy with energy, sincerity and perseverance.'

The final night of the congress saw a scene of extraordinary confusion. It was nearly four o'clock in the morning when the *rapporteur* of the Conflicts Commission, a young member of the left, came to present his report recommending the expulsion of five right-wingers. He said of one of these that 's'autorisant de la tradition de Jaurès . . . Henri Sellier voudrait faire du Parti Communiste un grand parti démocratique.' From the back of the hall another right-winger shouted out 'Vous venez d'exclure Jaurès!', whereupon pandemonium broke out. Many slumbering delegates woke with a start and began to shake their fists, shouting 'Vive Jaurès!' Frossard, in a state of near-hysteria, barged his way to the platform and shouted: 'Je ne resterai pas une minute de plus ici; je refuse de collaborer avec des insulteurs de Jaurès!' Then, grabbing his papers and his hat, he staggered towards the exit. The left asked in vain for the exact phrase which had caused the fuss to be read again. Cachin replied solemnly: 'The report has been destroyed. A shameful text that so dishonours its authors cannot be preserved even for an instant.' Henri Sellier launched into a counterblast against his accusers and had to be dragged from the speaker's stand, while Renoult could be heard repeating in a dejected monotone: 'Vous allez nous faire un joli Parti! Vous allez nous faire un joli Parti!'

The Solution

The centre was now in no mood for compromise. While the left called for acceptance of arbitration by ECCI, which meant parity of the two factions in the leadership, Cachin pressed his motion demanding a homogeneous centre leadership to run the party until the Fourth World Congress. This was passed by the narrow majority of 1,698 to 1,516, with 844 abstentions. Manuilsky made one more attempt to force a compromise, but this too was brushed aside by Cachin who declared 'in a strangled voice': 'Au nom du centre, je déclare que nous prendrons seuls la direction du Parti.' The defiance of the International was quite blatant, and before leaving Paris Manuilsky wrote to the *Comité Directeur* warning it that in his report to the World Congress he would put the blame for the situation firmly on the centre.[37]

In the heat of the moment, Manuilsky had described the Congress of Paris as a 'French Leghorn', implying that the French party was excluding itself from the Comintern as the Italian party had done at Leghorn the year before. This might have been the result if the centre had been really united and had been pursuing a considered policy. But in fact its act of defiance was only a muddled expression of resentment, directed as much against the personality of Souvarine as against the pretensions of the International. Its members had no clear ideological standpoint, and no leader of sufficient prestige and character to hold them together. They found it easy to criticize the International's decisions in a congress-hall in Paris, but less easy when they found themselves face to face with Trotsky and Zinoviev.

Both Frossard and Cachin were by now well aware of this, and therefore did their best to avoid going in person to the Fourth World Congress, which opened in Moscow on 9 November. Summoned personally by telegram, Frossard still refused but Cachin agreed to go, taking with him Renoult and Ker. The Russians were thus able to convince or browbeat into submission the two centrist leaders— Renoult and Cachin—who had been the chief bugbears of the International and the left throughout the year, while Frossard, who until the last minute had been trying, in appearance at least, to carry out the International's instructions, now remained in Paris and became 'the centre of the resistance'.[38] Altogether twenty-four French delegates attended the World Congress, at which they knew the fate of their party would be decided. The congress set up a 'French Commission' of twenty-three members including Lenin, Trotsky and Zinoviev.

A Party of a New Type

The Bolshevik leaders were astute enough to see that if the centre were evicted *en bloc* and the left allowed to monopolize the leadership the party would be reduced to little more than a sect, whereas it was possible to break the centre as an organized force and yet make very usable Communists of some of the individual centre leaders. To achieve this, it was necessary for the International in fact to dictate the composition of the new French leadership, but to associate the French delegates with its decisions so that they would have to defend them when they got back to France. Accordingly, the representatives of each faction—the left, the centre represented by Cachin, and the Renoult group—were asked to propose names for a share of the posts. Cachin, who had been softened up in advance by Trotsky, immediately agreed, so that it was hard for the others to refuse. At the same time, the Bolsheviks succeeded in convincing Renoult that he had misunderstood the united front and had been wrong to oppose the International.* Then Trotsky hit on a new weapon of deadly efficacy against the centrist leaders: he pretended to have just learnt that a number of leading French Communists, including Ker, were freemasons. Was this true, he asked, and if so how could French workers tolerate such bourgeois aberrations on the part of a party secretary? Ker, who was present, had shamefacedly to admit that he at least was a freemason, and promised to resign from his lodge. It was decided that henceforth no freemasons or members of the *Ligue des droits de l'homme* would be allowed to hold any party post, that all Communists must resign from these organizations, and that even those who obeyed this order must also resign their party offices. In fact there were freemasons on the left as well as in the centre, so that one of the new policy's merits would be to weed out those in all factions who still kept up bourgeois associations; and it increased the pressure on Cachin, who was generally believed to be a mason though he himself said nothing about it, and who was very anxious to keep his post as editor of *L'Humanité*.

The 'French Commission' also decreed that henceforth no journalist should be allowed to write both for party papers and for the 'bourgeois' press, and that nine tenths of the party's election

* Humbert-Droz commented: 'Cachin, Ker et Renoult sont arrivés pour s'entendre copieusement engueuler. Ils ont l'échine souple et encaissent tout, ici. C'est une bande de pleutres qui n'ont pas le courage de soutenir leur position. C'était bien la peine de faire tant de saletés au congrès de Paris!' (Letter to his wife, 19 xi 22, printed in *De Lénine à Staline* [Neuchâtel, 1971], p. 116.)

candidates in future should be workers or peasants. A new list was worked out for the *Comité Directeur*, consisting of ten representatives of the centre, nine of the left, four from the Renoult group plus Renaud Jean, a peasant leader from the Lot-et-Garonne who had kept aloof from all factions. The *Bureau Politique* was to consist of three centre, three left and one from Renoult's group. Frossard was to share the general secretaryship with Treint, and for the next three months at least Frossard and Souvarine, regarded as the leaders of the two main factions, were to be joint delegates to the Executive in Moscow. Frossard's place as joint General Secretary would be taken in the meantime by Louis Sellier.

The danger was, of course, that once again the French delegates would submit in Moscow, only to ignore the resolutions once they got back to France. Humbert-Droz therefore advised Trotsky to get a personal commitment to the decisions from Cachin, and to make it clear that his editorship of *L'Humanité* depended on his carrying it out. In his memoirs, Humbert-Droz relates how this was done:

> At the end of the deliberations of the French Commission, the Russians organized a great banquet in honour of the French delegation. Vodka flowed like water. Cachin had a place of honour between Trotsky and Zinoviev. They tanked him up and, when he was *à point*, Trotsky told him how pleased the Russian comrades would be if he gave his personal undertaking to support in France the measures decided in Moscow and that in return he would be kept on as editor of *L'Humanité*. Visibly moved by the confidence in him which the leaders of the Russian Revolution showed, with tears in his eyes, Cachin promised . . . and kept his word. He remained editor of *L'Humanité* until his death [in 1958].[39]

Trotsky announced the decisions to the congress in a long speech which included a violent personal condemnation of Frossard. All the French delegates except Renaud Jean declared their full agreement with all the decisions. In spite of this, Zinoviev and Humbert-Droz remained highly pessimistic. They were saved by the inertia and indecision of Frossard, who was furious with Cachin for betraying him but unwilling to take the responsibility for defying the International alone. Cachin was not very proud of his performance in Moscow, and skulked at home until sought out. On 16 December the centrist *Comité Directeur* elected at the Congress of Paris accepted the Moscow decisions by fifteen votes to four with Frossard voting in the majority. Humbert-Droz arrived back in Paris on 27 December and immediately set about organizing the purge of the staff of *L'Humanité*. He had lunch with Frossard on New Year's Eve and found him gloomy and sceptical about the possibilities of co-operation with the left, but nonetheless preparing to leave for Moscow. Next day, however, Frossard changed his mind and resigned from the party, influenced apparently by some of his friends who had been sacked from their jobs on *L'Humanité*, and also by re-reading Trotsky's speech at the World Congress during the night. Humbert-Droz commented:

> If this attitude had been taken when the delegation came back from Moscow, there is no doubt that the delegation would have been disavowed and the majority of the *Comité Direceur* and of the Party would have broken with the International. Frossard is resigning three weeks too late to do the harm he could have done. At that time he would have taken *L'Humanité* with him.

Even so he expected to lose 50 to 60% of the party membership. In this he was not so very far wrong, for the official membership figure for 1923 is 55,598, compared to 78,828 in 1922. The real figure was probably about 45,000.[40] The effects of Frossard's departure might have been much worse had not the police come to the party's rescue. On 10 January, the day before the French occupation of the Ruhr, the offices of *L'Humanité* were raided and Treint was arrested along with other leaders who had just returned from a conference of Communist parties in Essen. On 19 January the government obtained the lifting of Cachin's parliamentary immunity and sent him too to prison. The Communist Party and the revolutionary trade unions were once again the victims of large-scale repression. In the words of Humbert-Droz, 'Frossard and the members of his new party took on the appearance of cowards and deserters in the moment of danger.'[41]

In any case, their departure ended the period when the party could seriously contest the decisions of the International. But it did not in itself ensure that the party would now be genuinely a party of the working class.

The Capture of the Revolutionary Syndicalists (1920–1924)

We must now go back and pick up the story of the trade unions where we left it, after the failure of the great railway strike in May 1920, with *majoritaires* and *minoritaires* in the CGT irreconcilably estranged from each other, and each holding the other responsible for the disaster. Up to this point the conflict between them was essentially a conflict between Frenchmen, in which the Bolshevik Revolution was used as an argument but in which the Bolsheviks themselves had not intervened. But in July 1920 a new element was introduced, when for the first time an international trade union conference was held in Moscow. This coincided with the Second World Congress of the Comintern, from the delegates at which its membership was drawn, but also with the congress at Amsterdam, at which the pre-war International Federation of Trade Unions (IFTU) was reorganized. The Moscow conference was a riposte to this, just as the founding congress of the Comintern had been a riposte to the Berne conference of the Second International. By 1920 the Second International no longer seemed a serious obstacle to the capture of the international workers' movement by the communists, but IFTU did: it included both supporters of the Second International and believers in 'Reconstruction', as well as the CGT *majoritaires* who held aloof from all brands of political socialism. After the defeat of the Kapp putsch in Germany the prestige of trade unionism was high and IFTU, with twenty million adherents in western and central Europe, was obviously going to wield considerable authority. 'The chief enemy', Zinoviev told the Comintern Congress, 'is Amsterdam, not Brussels.'[42]

We have seen (p. 58) that three *minoritaires* from the CGT were present at the Second Congress of the Comintern, as representatives of the Committee for the Third International. But only one of these, Rosmer, was present at the trade union conference, and consequently was elected vice-president of the 'International Trade Union Council', which it created. The other two, Lepetit and Vergeat, arrived in Moscow too late. This was unfortunate, since they had a mandate from the *Comité des syndicats minoritaires* set up the year before, while Rosmer did not. He had been sent to Moscow as a permanent delegate for the Committee for the Third International and, as we have seen, was at once caught up in political work in the Comintern. Trotsky tended to see him as the authentic representative of French revolutionary syndicalism, but in fact he was too much influenced by Trotsky himself for this to be correct. Until leaving for Moscow, Rosmer had been co-editor of *La Vie Ouvrière*, the review which acted as a rallying point for the minority trade unions, and was closely associated with their committee. But his eagerness to go to Moscow was itself a sign that he was moving towards Bolshevism faster than his colleagues, and once he arrived in Moscow this process was accelerated: in daily contact with the Bolshevik leaders, he quickly shed his reservations about political action and political parties; while the same reservations held by revolutionary syndicalists in France, confronted by an opportunistic Socialist Party which changed its name—but little else—to Communist, remained strong.

The object of the new International Council was to organize 'an international congress of Red trade unions' at which a new trade union international could be set up in opposition to the one at Amsterdam. But this did not mean that the Bolsheviks wanted to see two rival trade union movements—one communist, one reformist—in each country. On the contrary, Lenin had insisted at length in *'Left-wing' Communism: an Infantile Disorder* on the need for Communists to penetrate the existing trade unions and stay in them, in spite of all the efforts which 'opportunist' leaders would make to keep them out. The idea was to win over the national trade union movements from inside, and bring them one by one out of the Amsterdam International into the Red one. Accordingly, the Bureau of the Comintern Congress issued an appeal to its French supporters, signed by Lenin, Zinoviev, Rosmer and the leaders of the German and Italian parties, urging them 'not to desert the ranks of the trade unions in any circumstances'—an appeal which seems to have been directed particularly at Péricat and his friends, who having had little success the year before with their 'Parti Communiste' were now attempting to found a 'Confédération des Travailleurs du Monde', based on Marseilles.[43]

But this ultra-left was numerically as insignificant as ever. The main body of the minority was willing enough to take the Comintern's advice and fight out the next round of the battle inside the CGT. Although some members of it were less dismayed by the idea of schism than others, all agreed that if there were schism the *majoritaires* must take the responsibility for it. In August 1920, when the *Comité des syndicats minoritaires* decided to hold a series of regional congresses of the minority before the approaching Confederal Congress, it was careful to 'declare itself opposed to any kind of schism in the working-class movement'.[44]

The Confederal Congress met in Orléans in September. The minority presented a motion calling for adherence to the Moscow International and stating that the CGT would be ready 'to work with the political organization that will act in a revolutionary way, in deed and not in words, in spite of that keeping its complete autonomy'.[45] The *minoritaires* were trying to have things both ways, and were in fact divided among themselves. Their two best-known leaders, Monatte and Monmousseau, were in prison at the time, and their cause was not helped by the support of Frossard, who said that the Socialist Party had the right to expect that its members who belonged to unions would not forget they were Socialists. This partly nullified his protestations of attachment to trade union autonomy, which syndicalists were in any case reluctant to take at face value from the general secretary of the Socialist Party. When it came to a vote the *majoritaires*' motion passed by 1,505 votes to 552, a bigger majority than the year before. But the only effect was to harden the battle lines on both sides. During the congress the *minoritaires* strengthened their organization, setting up *Comités syndicalistes révolutionnaires* (CSR) with a complete hierarchy running from local or factory groups to a central committee which could issue membership cards and collect subscriptions. Monatte and his friends still saw this organization as working for the recovery of the CGT, but inevitably it looked like the embryo of a rival, schismatic confederation. In November the National Confederal Committee (CCN) began its counter-attack by giving the component bodies of the CGT—departmental unions and industrial federations—the authority to expel members who adhered to the CSR.

Then came Tours: the creation of a Communist Party which, though it did not accept the letter of the Ninth and Tenth Conditions laying down Comintern policy on the trade union question, nonetheless went a long way towards it. 'The party groups the militants in all proletarian organizations who accept its theoretical views and its practical conclusions. All of them obeying its discipline, subject to its control, propagate its ideas in the circles where they are active and influential. And when the majority, in these organizations, is won over to communism, there is between them and the party co-ordination of action and not subjection of one organization to another.' The *majoritaires* took this as a declaration of war. They set up a daily CGT newspaper, *Le Peuple*, in which to reply to the propaganda of *L'Humanité*. The first number came out on 4 January 1921. Meanwhile certain CGT federations—Agriculture, Mining, Textiles—began to expel member unions that had adhered to the CSR. In February the CCN decided that 'any group adhering to the CSR puts itself outside the CGT'.

But if the relationship between the *minoritaires* and the Communist Party was obvious to the *majoritaires*, the *minoritaires'* own attitude was ambivalent and confused. Many did join the party, but they included, paradoxically enough, some of those who were most uncompromisingly hostile to the subordination of trade unions to the party, notably Guillaume Verdier and A. Quinton; whereas Monatte and Monmousseau, the leaders of the *Vie Ouvrière* group, who were more willing to admit the need for political action, stayed outside the party. To them the party was a matter of some importance, and they felt they could not accept the party that had emerged from Tours as truly Communist; whereas Verdier and Quinton expected nothing of the party and went into it mainly in order to neutralize it. Not surprisingly, their attitude soon called forth the thunders of Trotsky.

Meanwhile, the membership of the CGT was falling catastrophically after the failure and disappointment of 1920. By the spring of 1921 it was down to 600,000, less than a quarter of the figure claimed the year before. Membership of the *Union des Syndicats de la Seine* fell from 360,000 to 120,000.[46] But the members who left seem more often to have been supporters of the confederal leadership than of the CSRs; and the latter, despite the disagreements within their ranks, intensified their efforts to win control of the Confederation. Their slogans were well calculated to appeal to the hard core of militants who stayed in the movement. Their determination impressed the hesitant and often wore out the opposition, as they called for meeting after meeting and sometimes held up the vote until well into the night. Early in 1921 they regained control of the Railwaymen's Federation, which they had lost in the immediate aftermath of the great strike, and also won the Building Federation. At the Congress of the Metalworkers' Federation, Merrheim only managed to retain the leadership by a majority of two. The *minoritaires* now controlled five of the biggest industrial federations and twenty-six of the eighty departmental unions. In June and July 1921 they won over six more departmental unions and strengthened their majority at the Railwaymen's Congress. This led to the first split in a federation, for the moderate railwaymen refused to accept defeat and seceded to set up a rival body.[47] Altogether the minority doubled its strength, capturing 700 *syndicats*, between the Congress of Orléans in September 1920 and the Congress of Lille in July 1921.[48]

But just before the Congress of Lille met, the *minoritaires* were thrown into further confusion by the founding congress of the Red International of Labour Unions, or Profintern, held in Moscow from 3 to 19 July, immediately after the Third World Congress of the Comintern. The CSRs were at this time controlled by the so-called pure syndicalists, that is, anarcho-syndicalists who rejected any role for the state or for a political party. They sent to Moscow a delegation of nine members with instructions to oppose the formula of 'organic liaison', which they interpreted as meaning subordination of the unions to the party. But the doctrinaire and arrogant attitude of these delegates made a very bad impression in Moscow, where in any case the prestige of French trade unionism was very low since the 'betrayal' of July 1919 (see above, p. 47) and the débâcle of May 1920.[49] The Bolsheviks, who were after all Social Democrats by origin, felt that they had already made a big enough concession in accepting the notion of 'liaison' rather than explicit subordination. Lozovsky, who had presided over the provisional 'International Trade Union Council' that prepared the congress and was now to become president of the Profintern itself, presented a motion calling for 'close contact and organic liaison' between Comintern and Profintern and for 'similar relations between communist parties and red trade unions'. Rosmer, who fully shared the Bolsheviks' contempt for the pure syndicalists, nonetheless considered this text unnecessarily rigid and provocative, and therefore likely to play into the hands of Jouhaux. But the only change he was able to make in it was to describe the organic liaison between individual parties and the unions as 'highly desirable', whereas that between the two internationals remained a 'necessity'. After this he agreed to sign the motion, as did two members of the French delegation: Victor Godonnèche and Joseph Tommasi. The other French delegates presented a motion calling only for 'contact' between the two Internationals and prescribing that decisions should only be binding on both if passed by a four-fifths majority in a joint meeting of the two Executive Committees. Not surprisingly, the Lozovsky motion passed by 282 votes to twenty-five.[50]

This news caused consternation among the French *minoritaires*. The *Vie Ouvrière* group, which wanted to avoid splitting the CGT, was as dismayed as the pure syndicalists at being saddled with such a text on the eve of the Confederal Congress. On 22 July *La Vie Ouvrière* published a statement signed by nineteen members of the CSRs, including prominent members of both factions: Monatte, Quinton, Verdier, Monmousseau, Julien Racamond, Pierre Sémard. They condemned the Moscow text and disavowed Tommasi and Godonnèche who had signed it on their behalf. Tommasi was forced to resign as secretary of the *Union des Syndicats de la Seine*. 'Revolutionary syndicalism,' said the CSRs' statement, 'would not be true to its traditions of trade union autonomy if it accepted this resolution. A red International founded on this conception would be unable to win over the revolutionary trade union movements.'[51]

The *minoritaires* thus arrive at the Congress of Lille in a state of confusion, most of them being in revolt against the new International of which they were supposed to be the champions. This did not prevent them from attacking the *majoritaires* with redoubled vigour. Although the unions adhering to the CSRs had been officially outlawed from the CGT in February, no serious attempt was made to stop them attending the congress, which thus brought together two irreconcilably opposed and almost evenly matched armies; and appropriately enough the first day of the congress was marked by the firing of a pistol shot in the middle of the debates. Luckily no one was hurt, and it was agreed to conceal the name of the culprit from the press and the police. The debates continued in great acrimony for five days, at the end of which the *majoritaires* succeeded in getting their report adopted, but with a much reduced majority: 1,556 to 1,348, with 46 abstentions. It seemed obvious that if the *minoritaires* were allowed to carry on their agitation as before, they would win a majority at the next congress. But the *majoritaires* had no intention of waiting for this to happen. They pushed through a motion which (1) reasserted the 'Charter of Amiens' of 1906, proclaiming the CGT's independence from all political parties, and refused 'to accommodate the necessary and total autonomy of syndicalism to the designs of any party or any government whatever'; (2) gave the leadership a mandate to carry on with its reformist 'minimum programme' as defined at previous congresses; and (3) condemned the CSRs:

> The rights of minorities remain what they must be; no one can limit the right to criticize; but minorities have a strict obligation to give way once decisions are taken; groups and factions may not on any pretext usurp the role of the departmental or national corporative organization, since this usurpation has caused confusion and made any propaganda or effort of solidarity impossible.[52]

Since the CSRs obviously had no intention of accepting this verdict, the split was now inevitable. In September, at a meeting of the CCN, Monmousseau warned that the minority would never give up the CSRs, and another *minoritaire*, Léopold Cazals, proposed the motion that 'no *syndicat* can be expelled from the confederal organization by a tendentious interpretation of trade-union discipline.' This motion was rejected in favour of a text proposed by the *majoritaires* Dumoulin and Liochon:

> The organizations which refuse to give way once decisions are taken and to co-operate in applying them, deliberately put themselves outside working-class unity. They leave the CGT no option but to admit their minorities which accept the decisions of the Confederal Congresses. Trade union organisms cannot without breach of discipline adhere to a group outside the trade unions, whether philosophical or political. In particular, they cannot adhere to the CSR.[53]

This motion passed by sixty-three votes to fifty-six, with ten abstentions. The *minoritaires* had the support of forty-four departmental unions against thirty-six, but of only twelve federations against twenty-seven. Monmousseau at once announced that in these circumstances he and his friends would take no further part in the administration of the CGT and would no longer sit on the *Commission Administrative*, its permanent governing body in Paris. A week later, on 27 September, the Central Committee of the CSRs published a manifesto calling for a Congress of the Minority. This proposal, supported by ten federations and only sixteen departmental unions,[54] reflected the policy of the pure syndicalists, who wanted to set up a 'CGT Révolutionnaire', rather than that of the *Vie Ouvrière* group or the Communists. As Monatte wrote many years later: 'a deceitful legend has grown up according to which the trade union split in France was the work of the communists. In reality it was the work of the reformists who dug a wolf-trap and of the anarchists and so-called pure syndicalists who rushed into it.'[55] According to Monatte, a group of pure syndicalists, led by Verdier and Pierre Besnard, had formed a 'little clandestine freemasonry called the Pact' while he and his colleagues were still in prison (i.e. before March 1921). The object of this group was to gain control of the CGT minority and lead it into a 'brand new revolutionary syndicalist Confederation'.[56] The same allegation appears in a Communist Party pamphlet published in 1925:

The men of the masonic 'pact' who had in their pockets a set of statutes for a revolutionary CGT did not do their utmost to resist the expulsions engineered by the leaders of the old CGT. Instead of sticking to the problems of re-integrating those expelled and slowly and methodically winning control of the confederal machine, they let themselves, in their revolutionary impatience, be pushed out of the old house of their own free will.[57]

The *majoritaires* were quick to take advantage of this situation. They condemned the proposed congress as contrary to the statutes, and when Lozovsky, in an early application of the united front policy, approached Oudegeest, one of the secretaries of IFTU, with a proposal for mediation, the CGT said it could accept this only if the minority congress were cancelled. It was not in Lozovsky's power to arrange this, and in any case it was too late. The congress was held in Paris from 22 to 24 December. Monatte, Rosmer and others still tried to avert the split, suggesting that the minority unions should withdraw from the CSRs which henceforth would have only individual members, on condition that the CGT agree to hold an extraordinary congress on 1 January. The CGT refused, but Monatte still argued that the minority should press this demand, making its pressure felt by withholding any funds from the CGT treasury until the congress was called.[58] But against him Monmousseau now joined forces with the anarchists and pure syndicalists who argued that the split had already been carried out by the *majoritaires* and was therefore the '*fait accompli* against which the minority, despite the rectitude of its conduct, is powerless'.[59]

Eventually a compromise motion presented by Monmousseau was voted unanimously. Although formally it gave the CGT a last chance, to all intents and purposes it ratified the schism: if the bureau and administrative commission of the CGT had not called an extraordinary congress by the end of January they would be declared forfeit, and the congress would be called instead by the minority bureau composed of three anarcho-syndicalists: Cadeau, Labrousse and Totti. In the meantime no membership cards or stamps would be bought from the CGT, and a provisional administrative commission would co-ordinate the work of the minority unions.

The expected answer from the CGT was not long coming: on 27 December the administrative commission pronounced that 'the agenda published creates division and in fact constitutes schism.' The CCN did not even meet to give a formal refusal to the demand for an extraordinary congress until after the minority's deadline had expired.[60]

The chief loser in the battle was Monatte, who emerged discouraged and nearly isolated. He disagreed with Rosmer about the 'organic liaison' between the two Internationals, and with most of his other friends about the split. His weekly paper, *La Vie Ouvrière*, would now become the organ of the new confederation, while his own trade union, that of the proof-correctors, belonged to the Printing Federation which would remain in the CGT. In addition, he was exhausted and in poor health. For all these reasons he decided to give up the editorship. Hesitating between Rosmer and Monmousseau, he finally picked the latter as his successor on the grounds that he 'presents more guarantees than Rosmer for the maintenance of trade union independence. . .'.[61] The choice would prove an ironic one in the light of later events, and Monatte was to regret it.

The new confederation took the name of *Confédération Générale du Travail Unitaire* (CGTU), to show that it held the *majoritaires* responsible for the split. Organized during the first six months of 1922, it was able by the time of its first congress, at the end of June, to claim a membership of 350,000 against only 250,000 for the CGT. But its leaders were quickly divided into three competing groups. The provisional governing bodies—bureau and administrative commission—were dominated by the pure syndicalists, who in fact were anarcho-syndicalists or in some cases pure anarchists. Partisans of the Profintern before it came into existence, they were now openly hostile to it and hoped to set up a Syndicalist International which would be 'neither Amsterdam nor Moscow'. Three of them—Totti, Besnard, and Louis Lecoin—did in fact attend an 'International Revolutionary Syndicalist Conference' which was held in Berlin in June 1922, and at which the Profintern and the Bolshevik government were violently and repeatedly denounced. Although the French claimed to be present only as observers and did not take part in the final votes, they did take an active part in the debates and asserted that the CGTU would not seek Profintern membership.[62]

At the opposite pole from these were the Communists, still a small group, who accepted the need for links with the Comintern and the French Communist Party, while some of the less adroit of them openly advocated the subordination of trade unions to the party. The effective leader of this faction was Tommasi, while Rosmer acted as its spokesman with the journal *Lutte des Classes*, which he founded with

Russian subsidies in May. He attacked the pure syndicalists unsparingly, but worked towards an alliance with the third group, which found itself in a decisive central position: the group of *La Vie Ouvrière*. With Monatte in semi-retirement, this group was now led by Monmousseau with the help of Pierre Sémard, who had replaced him at the head of the Railwaymen's Federation, and Julien Racamond of the bakers.

At the Congress of Saint-Etienne, which met from 25 June to 1 July 1922, Monmousseau presented a motion calling for adherence to the Profintern on condition that the autonomy of French syndicalism be respected, whereas Besnard's motion rejected membership in an International that would have any connection with a political organization, and would have authorized the leadership to send delegates to both Moscow and Berlin. Frossard fulfilled the undertaking he had just given in Moscow (see above, pp. 76–7) by assembling the Communist delegates and informing them that neither motion was satisfactory. Rosmer was instructed to write a motion for unconditional adherence to the Profintern, but it was understood that in the final vote the Communists would back Monmousseau against Besnard. In fact Rosmer did not even write his motion, so anxious was he to avoid any quarrel with Monatte and his group.[63]

The coalition of Communists and *Vie Ouvrière* defeated Besnard surprisingly easily, by 743 votes to 406. They were helped by the publication, at the beginning of the congress, of the text of the pure syndicalists' secret pact: this showed that ever since February 1921 the pure syndicalists had been applying that very tactic of *noyautage* (penetration, or burrowing from within) for which they had so often attacked the Communists. They were helped, too, by the appearance of Lozovsky in person, who had entered the country illegally to come and explain that he was not trying to subject the CGTU to his own dictatorship, nor yet bind it hand and foot to the French Communist Party. He made a good impression, especially in private talks with individual delegates, and the 'pures' further discredited themselves by their clumsy attacks on him after he had left the hall.

As a result, the 'pures' were ousted from the CGTU leadership, which was taken over by *La Vie Ouvrière* in the persons of Monmousseau, Marie Guillot, Cazals and Claudius Richetta. This leadership was instructed to send a delegation to the Second Congress of the Profintern to try and get the statutes amended in accordance with French scruples about trade union autonomy. This meant, in particular, the removal of Article II, which prescribed the 'organic liaison' between Profintern and Comintern. If the delegates obtained satisfaction on this point, they could then apply for membership.

The Profintern Congress was held in November 1922, at the same time as the Fourth World Congress of the Comintern. The French delegation was led by Monmousseau and Sémard. Their visit to Moscow was in a sense for the French trade union movement what Cachin and Frossard's in 1920 had been for the French Socialist Party. On paper they were more successful than Cachin and Frossard had been in negotiating with the Bolsheviks. But their conversion proved more whole-hearted and more lasting than Frossard's, and was arguably more important in its effects than Cachin's. Their interview with Lenin, as recorded by Monmousseau, has a place of honour among the tableaux of French Communist mythology:

No sooner had greetings been exchanged than Lenin came straight to the point:

'Tell me, Sémard, you're a member of the Communist Party? And you, Monmousseau, you aren't? How is it that you're in agreement?'

We then explained to Lenin that we were in agreement to fight a class struggle against the reformists and that, on the other hand, neither of us had confidence in the Communist Party, at the head of which were Frossard and many other noted politicoes.

Lenin pressed the question, asking me why I didn't join the Party.

'Because,' I said, 'it is led by politicoes like Frossard.'

'And if these politicoes disappeared,' Lenin went on, 'would you go into the Communist Party?'

'Good,' he concluded, 'but how can we get rid of them? We can't do anything from here. That's not our job. It can only be done in France and not from outside, but from inside the Communist Party. What must be done to get you, Monmousseau, and your comrades in the trade unions, to go into the Communist Party?'

Sémard and I then told Lenin that article II of the statutes of the Communist International [*sic*], which obliged national parties to establish an organic liaison with the trade unions, offended the feelings of the workers and involved dangers for trade union unity.

'And if we abolish this article II,' replied Lenin, 'you are sure, Monmousseau, that the revolutionary workers will come into the Communist Party?'

I assured him that they would. Article II was abolished for ever. . . . We returned to France, Sémard and I, carrying with us Lenin's concession to the traditions of the French trade union movement. . . . We gave our collective adhesion to the Communist Party. Frossard and the politicoes were kicked out; and some time later, in 1925, Sémard gave up his post as General Secretary of the Railwaymen's Federation to take over the leadership of the Party.[64]

This of course is highly simplified history. But the Profintern Congress did agree to drop Article II after Monmousseau had made a speech explaining that the CGTU wanted this not for ideological reasons but for 'technical' ones—to avoid a split in the Profintern, which would thereby lose many of its members to the anarchists. The congress unanimously passed a resolution which abolished Article II but reasserted the leading role of Communist Parties.

In a speech to the Comintern Congress, Zinoviev explained the spirit in which this concession had been made:

The French movement as a whole is extremely important for the International. To speak in arithmetical terms, one can say that the French labour movement accounts for 50 per cent of the International. Why? Because Paris and the policy of the French bourgeoisie are the home of world imperialism and the heart of world reaction. The present task lies in overcoming the prejudices of the French labour movement and in creating a party in France which brings the masses together. This is the International's most important task. In these conditions we must be ready to make the necessary concession.[65]

The concession was of course apparent rather than real. The Bolsheviks had by no means renounced their aim of dominating and controlling the trade union movement. In fact by winning over Sémard and Monmousseau they had taken a big step forward towards achieving it. As Monmousseau later admitted, it was 'from this date that the leaders of the CGTU drew close to the Communist Party'.[66]

The CGTU leaders did not in fact have to go into the Communist Party in order to get 'Frossard and the politicoes' out of it, as Lenin had suggested, for as we have seen Frossard resigned of his own accord. His departure may have helped to reassure the syndicalists that the party was now cured of opportunism, although up to now Monmousseau and his friends, unlike Monatte and Rosmer, had shown no preference for the left of the PCF as against the centre. If

94

anything they were more hostile to the left because of its proclaimed belief, which it did little to put into practice, in infiltrating and controlling the unions.[67] But in any case the CGTU leaders soon found themselves thrown together, almost literally, with the new or the remaining leaders of the PCF, as a result of the French occupation of the Ruhr.

At the Fourth World Congress great emphasis had been laid on the iniquity of the Versailles Peace Treaty, and the French party had been particularly instructed to struggle against the proposed occupation of the Ruhr.[68] Monmousseau was evidently eager to show that a revolutionary trade union organization did not need to be led by the nose but was quite capable of taking the lead itself in co-operating with the Communist Party in any worthwhile revolutionary action. Soon after his return from Moscow he took the initiative in forming a joint *Comité d'Action contre l'Impérialisme et la Guerre*, with five members from the PCF (including Cachin and Treint) and five from the CGTU (including Monmousseau himself, Marie Guillot and Cazals). On 3 January 1923 Monmousseau and Sémard both spoke at a meeting in Paris organized by this committee to protest against the threatened occupation of the Ruhr; and three days later they went, with two other CGTU delegates, to the conference of Western European Communist Parties which met in Essen to co-ordinate their strategy. Monmousseau delivered 11,000 francs supplied by the CGTU (or perhaps the Profintern?) for the strikers of Ludwigshafen, and declared that everything must be done 'to prevent and sabotage' the occupation of the Ruhr. He was supported by Cachin and Ker of the PCF. Of the eight militants arrested on 10 January and charged with plotting against the internal and external security of the state, five were from the CGTU—including Monmousseau and Cazals—and three from the PCF—including Treint, who was soon to be followed by Ker and Cachin. They remained in the Santé prison until May, when the Senate acting as High Court declared the matter outside its competence and refused to try them. But in the meantime the campaign against the Ruhr occupation went on, with party and trade unions playing more or less equal parts—and the *Jeunesses Communistes*, under the leadership of Maurice Laporte, Gabriel Péri and Jacques Doriot, being particularly prominent. The year's events reached their climax in October during the intensively planned but disastrously unsuccessful Communist uprising in Germany. At this time both the bureau of the CGTU and the National Committee of the *Jeunesses Communistes* threatened to call a general strike if Poincaré moved to crush the German revolution. Monmousseau again went to Germany himself and declared that the CGTU had concluded a 'pact of alliance' with the German revolution.

All this agitation did not come to very much, mainly because the 'German revolution' in Dresden collapsed at the approach of the Reichswehr without Poincaré having to lift a finger. But the action committee provided the framework within which collaboration between the CGTU leadership and the party's *Bureau Politique* became a habit. As early as April 1923, Humbert-Droz could plausibly suggest to Cachin that all important decisions from now on be taken in conjunction with the leadership of the CGTU.[69]

In implementing the policy of the Profintern, Monmousseau and Sémard were moving too fast for some of their syndicalist colleagues. A new minority grew up within the CGTU, led by Cazals, Marie Guillot and Benoît Broutchoux, which disputed the Communist ban on the participation of anarchists and of Frossard's 'Parti Communiste Unitaire' in the joint action committee, condemned the syndicalist commissions set up by the party as an attempt to subordinate the union movement, and criticized the CGTU leaders for conniving at these Communist aberrations. In answering these criticisms Monmousseau and the *Vie Ouvrière* associated themselves more blatantly than ever with party policy. When the party published a manifesto on 30 June demanding the right, on equal terms with the anarchists and anarcho-syndicalists, to organize a faction and spread its ideas within the unions, the *Vie Ouvrière* supported it: 'it is not up to the editorial committee of the *VO*,' it declared in a published statement, 'to judge the means by which a political or syndicalist group spreads or wants to spread its ideas in the syndicalist movement.'[70] In August Sémard went further, declaring that syndicalism was not above parties, and that the Russian Revolution had rendered the Charter of Amiens obsolete. The French revolutionary syndicalists, he said, could not hold themselves aloof from an international movement which had carried out a proletarian revolution in Russia and which constituted the revolutionary opposition in Germany, Poland, Czechoslovakia, Finland and Bulgaria.[71]

Protesting against these startling innovations in syndicalist doctrine, the Guillot-Cazals minority eventually succeeded in forcing the convocation of a congress, which met in Bourges from 12 to 17

November. But at this congress the new minority, which accepted Profintern membership but opposed subordination to the party, was discredited by the support of the old minority which opposed both, and which had been defeated the previous year. The anarchists, who went so far as to warn that if the Communists tried to monopolize the German revolution they would find the anarchists on the other side of the barricades, made it easy for Monmousseau and his friends to win sympathy as the outraged defenders of solidarity with the Russian and German revolutions. Sémard's motion to 'approve unreservedly' the CGTU's adhesion to the Profintern, paying lip-service to autonomy and the Amiens Charter but rejecting 'the thesis that syndicalism is above all and all-sufficient', was passed by the impressive score of 962 votes against 219 for the anarchist motion for withdrawal from the Profintern and only 147 for the intermediate text presented by Guillot and Joseph Lartigue, whose supporters bitterly declared: 'You have consciously voted for subordinating syndicalism to the party.' The new bureau consisted of Monmousseau, Racamond, Dudilieux, and Berrar; all were strong supporters of the new line, and all but Racamond had been in the delegation to Moscow the previous year.

The Bolsheviks had thus succeeded in the third phase of their operation: they had split the French Socialist Party and so created a Communist Party with a mass following; they had got rid of or tamed its 'opportunist' leaders; and they had now succeeded in persuading the heirs of revolutionary syndicalism to join forces with it. After the Congress of Lyons, in January 1924, the party was endowed with a *Bureau Politique* which included Rosmer (who was also co-editor of *L'Humanité*) and Tommasi, and a *Comité Directeur* which besides these included Monatte, Sémard, and other syndicalists. In July 1924 Sémard would become general secretary of the party. At first sight it was hard to say whether the party had won control over the CGTU or vice versa. What was clear was that the conjunction of the two for the first time made it possible to give the party a truly working-class leadership. As early as October 1923 a National Council of the party passed a motion submitted by Treint, barring any party official or journalist who was not already a deputy from running for office in the coming elections. This was the result of pressure from Monmousseau, who wanted concrete evidence that the party had changed.[72] From now on the party would be able to claim, with some conviction, to be *the* party of the working class.

3

'Bolshevization'

1923–1926

The slogan 'Bolshevization of the Communist Parties' was adopted by the Fifth World Congress of the Comintern in June–July 1924. But the problem it dealt with was the one already posed in 1920 by the Twenty-One Conditions: the need to transform the old western social-democratic parties, with their democratic and parliamentary traditions, into tight, highly disciplined instruments of revolution on the model of the Russian Bolshevik party.

During the struggles of 1920–3 the problem was posed mainly in personal terms: the primary object of the Bolsheviks and of their allies in France was to force out of the party those Socialist leaders who would not or could not be genuine revolutionaries, and to bring in those syndicalist leaders who were. The question of party organization fell into the background. But once the left had gained effective control of the party and the hesitations of the revolutionary syndicalists had been overcome, the remodelling of the party's structure became the next urgent task.

The most salient point about Bolshevik organization (or at least about Bolshevik organizational theory) was centralization. This was the point on which the Twenty-One Conditions had most insisted: 'the Communist Party can only fulfil its role if it is organized in the most centralized way. . . .' One man who certainly took this message to heart was Albert Treint.

FIRST MEASURES OF CENTRALIZATION (1923)

Treint, it will be remembered, had been appointed joint general secretary of the party by the Fourth World Congress at the end of 1922, but was in prison from January to May 1923 for his part in the agitation against the occupation of the Ruhr. As soon as he came out of prison he took over the effective leadership of the party, dominating his co-secretary Louis Sellier and also establishing the secretariat as the main authority in the party at the expense of the formal governing organs, *Comité Directeur* and *Bureau Politique*. Members of these bodies soon began to complain that they were not being consulted on important questions, and by June Humbert-Droz was writing to Zinoviev about Treint's 'authoritarian and brutal methods'.

In July 1923 Treint produced a plan for the reorganization of the party, which was approved by the *Comité Directeur* and published in the *Bulletin Communiste*. He diagnosed two main defects in the existing organization: there was no control apparatus to ensure that decisions taken at the centre were carried into effect by the branches, and the central office was unable to cope with the voluminous correspondence it had to keep up with the departmental federations because these were too numerous (nearly a hundred including those in the colonies). He proposed to remedy these defects by creating a network of regions (each comprising several federations) which would relieve the centre of the need to deal directly with each separate federation. In each region there would be a regional delegate from the centre, maintaining the contact between the centre and the rank-and-file members.

In practice Treint used these regional delegates as instruments to maintain a tight control over the whole life of the party. In September Humbert-Droz described them in a letter to Zinoviev as 'veritable prefects of the *Bureau Politique*, having a very great authority over the federations, directing them politically, receiving their correspondence and replying to it in the name of the party leadership without the latter knowing of it except by their reports'. He even mentioned one of them, Rieu, as complaining because the party secretariat had received a federal secretary in person and discussed with him the situation of his federation.

Treint's action in generalizing the system of regional delegates was itself an example of the growing power of the general secretary: he ignored the decision of the *Comité Directeur* to try it out first on only two or three federations.

Under this constant supervision, the federations soon became reluctant to take any decision on their own authority. An early instance is a request from the congress of the federation of the Gard, in 1923, for one of its members to be expelled by the *Comité Directeur*: a measure which under the statutes the federation was perfectly qualified to adopt on its own authority.[1]

A Party of a New Type

In the complaints voiced by readers of *L'Humanité* in the discussion in its columns preceding the congress of Lyons, in January 1924, we can recognize the criticisms habitually levelled at a bureaucratic, over-centralized party: the *Bureau Politique* had usurped the functions of the *Comité Directeur*; on pretext of maintaining discipline, all discussion at lower levels had been eliminated; the sections, barred from participating in the resolution of political questions, had become absorbed with purely administrative matters; the sections and federations had not been given enough time to read and discuss the massive documentation sent out by the central apparatus before the congress; and despite its conquest of the CGTU, the party's prestige among the proletariat remained low.[2]

FACTORY CELLS

According to Zinoviev, in his message to the congress, the blame for these ills should not be laid either on overcentralization or on Treint's personality, but on the party's structure: the party could not be effective until factory cells were created.

Factory cells were the International's latest panacea. On 21 January 1924, while the Congress of Lyons was actually in session, ECCI in Moscow published a general plan for the reorganization of the Communist Parties in the form of a 'Resolution on the organization of factory cells'. According to this, 'the basis of party organization is the party cell in the factory. All Communists who work in a particular factory must belong to that factory cell.'[3] Those not working in factories should form street cells.

The concept of the factory cell was not in itself new. Such cells had existed in the clandestine Bolshevik Party before 1917, had come out into the open during the Revolution, and had played an important part in the political education of the Russian proletariat. Nor was it new for the International to recommend this Russian example as a model for other Communist Parties. But the Twenty-One Conditions had referred to cells, not as the basic unit of party organization, but as a particular form of Communist organization formed for the purpose of working within non-Communist mass organizations such as trade unions (see above, p. 62).* This is implied also in the definition given in the 'theses on the structure of communist parties and on the

---

* The word used in the French translation is not *cellule* but *noyau*, meaning 'nucleus': from this is derived the word *noyautage*, for infiltration or 'burrowing from within'.

methods and content of their work', adopted by the Third Comintern Congress in 1921: 'Communist *cells* are nuclei for day-to-day communist work in factories and workshops, in trade unions, in proletarian co-operatives, in military detachments, etc., wherever there are at least a few members or candidates of the Communist Party.'[4] There was nothing here incompatible with the normal western system of party organization, in which the basic unit is a section covering a given territorial area, these sections are grouped into federations (corresponding in France to the *départements*), and these in turn send delegates to the party's national congress.

But the Resolution of January 1924 proposed to replace this traditional structure by a new pyramid: 'In large towns with many factory and street cells, these shall be organized into districts, and districts into areas [*rayons*].* The areas together make up the town organization.'[5] (A note dealing with France adds that 'in the big towns which are capitals of *départements*, there is no town committee. The federal conference composed of delegates from the *rayons* of the town and from those of the *département* elects a departmental committee which also fulfils the functions of a town committee.'[6])

Moreover, said the Resolution, 'in order to strengthen the influence of the factory cells, more than half the members of the district bureau and the area committee must be members of factory cells. . . .' And it summed up: 'Emphasis in the party's political organization work must be shifted to the factory cells. By taking the lead in the struggle of the working masses for their daily needs, the factory cell should guide them forward to the struggle for the proletarian dictatorship. . . .'[7]

In proposing these radical changes in the structure of western Communist Parties, the ECCI was thinking much less about France than about Germany. The fiasco of the 'German revolution' in October 1923 had been a grave embarrassment for the Comintern and particularly for its president, Zinoviev. Unwilling to take the blame for the defeat themselves, Zinoviev and the Comintern sought explanations in the inadequacies of the German Communist Party, and especially in its lack of contact with the masses. 'The experience of the German revolution,' says the preamble to the Resolution, 'has shown most clearly that, in the absence of cells based on the factories and of close connexions with the working masses, the latter cannot be drawn into the struggle and led, their minds cannot be rightly

* Literally, 'spokes' or 'radii'—i.e. connecting links between centre and circumference.

appraised, the moment most favourable to us cannot be exploited, nor victory won over the bourgeoisie.'[8]

But behind the dispute over the causes of the German defeat lay the even more intense struggle for power within the Russian Communist Party, with Trotsky on one side and the 'triumvirs'—Zinoviev, Kamenev and Stalin—on the other. In this conflict Karl Radek, the Comintern's representative in Germany during the October fiasco, had taken Trotsky's side, and moreover had threatened that the leaders of the French and German parties would support him even against the majority of the Russian Central Committee. This made it vital for Zinoviev to discredit Radek and the German leaders by putting the blame for the German disaster on them: and this led to another important change in Comintern strategy. Two days before the Resolution on factory cells, the ECCI put out a statement on the events in Germany, listing numerous mistakes made by the German party, chief among which was that it had nursed illusions about the left-wing social democrats. (The SPD–KPD coalition governments in Saxony and Thuringia had allowed themselves to be deposed by the Reichswehr without a struggle.) In co-operating with the social democrats, the German Communists had, of course, been applying the united front tactic in accordance with precise instructions from the Comintern. Zinoviev of all people could not disown the united front. But he did the next best thing, by giving it an entirely new definition: 'united front tactics are not a democratic coalition, an alliance with social-democracy. They are only a method of revolutionary agitation and mobilization.' The German social-democrat leaders had now 'completed the transition from capitalist democracy to capitalist dictatorship', and become 'nothing but a fraction of German fascism wearing a socialist mask'. Consequently the united front tactics in Germany would have to be 'modified':

> There can be no dealings with the mercenaries of the white dictatorship. . . . The KPD rejects not only any dealings with the SPD centre, but also with the 'left' leaders until they shall have shown at least enough manliness to break openly with the counter-revolutionary gang in the SPD presidium.

The slogan of the united front tactic in Germany is now: Unity from below. . . .

The party's agitation must bring home to the broadest masses that only the proletarian dictatorship can bring them salvation. This task must be linked to the goal of the political annihilation of the Social-Democratic Party; it requires the organization of united front organs and a clear objective in all partial struggles. . . .[9]

Although this statement ostensibly applied only to Germany, it was soon clear that the lessons of the German events were to be applied to the whole of the International. The 'united front from below' proved a useful weapon with which to isolate and expose the potential allies of Trotsky and Radek in the western Communist Parties. Zinoviev and his allies displayed a diabolical mixture of naivety and ingenuity. It was naive to suppose that social-democrat workers in any country could be won over by propaganda which openly vituperated their leaders and identified them with 'fascism' or 'capitalist dictatorship'. But it was ingenious to propose a tactic whose opponents could easily be stigmatized as 'right wing' or 'opportunistic', even though their opposition might in fact be rooted in a clearer understanding of the western labour movement.

THE PCF UNDER 'TROTSKYIST' LEADERSHIP

These considerations applied particularly to the PCF. Trotsky had always taken a special interest in France, and his prestige and influence there were probably greater than in any other foreign country. And by coincidence the Congress of Lyons, in January 1924, had brought about an increase in the influence of those French Communists with whom he was most closely linked. There was a general reaction against Treint's autocratic leadership of the party, and he was dropped from both the general secretaryship and the *Bureau Politique*. In the new leadership the most prominent figures were Souvarine, who had been Treint's most outspoken critic throughout the previous year, and Rosmer, who was co-editor of *L'Humanité* and had won the confidence of the Comintern's delegate in France, Humbert-Droz. These two men were very different in temperament and background, but they shared an almost unbounded admiration for Trotsky. And another rising figure in the party was Pierre Monatte, who was in charge of the trade union page in *L'Humanité* and now entered the *Comité Directeur* although he had only joined the party eight months earlier. If Humbert-Droz had had his way, Rosmer would actually have replaced Treint as general secretary and Monatte would have been given control of *L'Humanité*.[10] Not surprisingly, Zinoviev ignored this suggestion, though for the time being he gave only rather half-hearted support to Treint. In the upshot the general secretaryship was left in the hands of the characterless Louis Sellier, with two assistants: Jean Crémet, who had come up from the youth movement, and Georges Marrane, another survivor from the old Socialist centre.[11] Humbert-Droz himself was transferred to Italy shortly before the congress, and remained there throughout 1924.[12]

Treint's revenge was not to be long delayed, and the 'united front from below' was one of the weapons with which he secured it. For the first time in history a Labour government had just come to power in Britain. At the request of the British Communist Party, the *Comité Directeur* of the French party reacted by drafting an open letter to the Labour Party. This letter, drafted by Rosmer and approved by the *Comité Directeur* on 5 February 1924, took a classic united front line, old style. It congratulated the Labour Party on its electoral success and warned it, in polite but firm language, not to disappoint 'all the hopes placed in the strength of the Labour Party by five million British workers. . . . We are convinced,' it said, with disarming frankness, 'that the strictly parliamentary, peaceful methods to which you are attached, the respect which you show for the political and social structure built by the bourgeoisie for the defence of its own interests, will prevent you from carrying out even a small part of your programme.' It thus made it clear that the French Communists expected little from the Labour government, but refrained from heaping premature abuse on it and made it clear that it would be judged by the working class both in Britain and abroad on its concrete actions.[13] This was a sound approach for a propaganda document. Rosmer, who spoke fluent English (he was born in America) and kept in close touch with British affairs, knew that the Labour Party still enjoyed the confidence of the mass of the British working class and that a direct attack on it at this point would not draw British workers to communism but drive them further away.

Only two people voted against the draft in the French *Comité*

Directeur: Treint and his close associate Suzanne Girault, the secretary of the Federation of the Seine.* But these two were in closer touch with the new Comintern line than the rest. Three days earlier Lozovsky had published an article in *L'Humanité* describing the victory of the Labour Party as 'a victory of the bourgeoisie'. And on the day after the vote in the French *Comité Directeur*, ECCI in Moscow passed a resolution instructing the British Communist Party: 'Every effort must be made to help the workers to be convinced from their own experience of the utter unfitness of the Labour Party leaders, their petty-bourgeois and treacherous character, the inevitability of their bankruptcy.'[14] In the dispute which followed Rosmer was supported by Souvarine; and the two found themselves defending an apparently 'right-wing' line not only against Treint but also against Lozovsky and the Comintern itself.

Meanwhile, in mid-February, delegates from ECCI and from the German party came to Paris, apparently seeking the support of the French party for the condemnation of Brandler and the right wing of the German party (which had been made the scapegoat for the defeat of the previous October) and also for the condemnation of Trotsky which had been pronounced at the Thirteenth Conference of the Russian party in January. But on 19 February the French *Comité Directeur*, following a lead from Souvarine, implicitly refused both these requests and proclaimed its neutrality in both the Russian and German disputes.

THE 'ZINOVIEVISTS' TAKE CHARGE

This evidently convinced Zinoviev that Souvarine must be isolated and got rid of as quickly as possible, though at this stage he may still have hoped to avoid a head-on conflict with Rosmer. According to a modern account based on conversations with Souvarine, Sellier and Treint,[15] this mission was entrusted to Manuilsky. It must have been carried out with remarkable efficiency and speed, for by mid-March

---

* Ironically enough Suzanne Girault, who had been a French governess in Tsarist Russia, owed her position in the Communist movement largely to Rosmer and his wife, to whom she had attached herself in Moscow as an interpreter and guide 'à telle enseigne qu'on la prenait pour la femme de chambre de Madame' (H. Guilbeaux, *Du Kremlin au Cherche-Midi* [1933], p. 227; quoted in Christian Gras, *Alfred Rosmer et le mouvement révolutionnaire international* [Paris, 1971], p. 296). She also had connections with the Russian secret police (GPU). (Branko Lazitch, 'Two Instruments of Control by the Comintern', in *The Comintern: Historical Highlights*, ed. Milorad M. Drachkovitch and Branko Lazitch [Stanford, California, 1966], p. 48.)

at latest Treint had not only identified himself completely with Zinoviev's views but also had won back the majority of the *Comité Directeur* and with it effective control of the party. He was aided by the tactlessness of Souvarine, who had not been able to resist crowing over Treint's defeat at the Congress of Lyons. His defence of Rosmer's position on the British question turned into a gratuitous attack on Treint's conception of the united front, as illustrated by his unhappy phrase about the 'volaille à plumer' of two years before (see above, p. 75).[16] On 6 March the *Bureau Politique* requested Souvarine to stop these attacks on Treint, and when he refused it ordered him to take up the post as party representative in Moscow to which he had been elected at the congress. But Souvarine refused this too. The decisive clash came when Treint submitted to the *Bulletin Communiste*, of which Souvarine was editor, an article listing the errors of the 'majority' in its evaluation of the British Labour Party and making out that the leadership had promised support for the Labour government 'no matter what policies it followed'. Souvarine wanted to print this with a refutation by himself, but was forbidden to do so by the party secretariat. He nonetheless inserted an editorial note at the bottom of Treint's text:

> The party secretariat forbids us the slightest rectification of the inexact assertions of the author of the preceding article and the slightest commentary on his anticommunist statements about the *volaille à plumer*. Out of discipline, we naturally submit, but we consider that this conception of discussion imposed by the *Bureau Politique* is absolutely contrary to the interest of the party and of the International and we shall appeal against it at the next party assembly.[17]

By this act of flagrant disobedience, Souvarine sealed his own fate. On 18 March the *Comité Directeur*, acting on a proposal from the *Bureau Politique*, decided to remove him from the editorship of the *Bulletin Communiste*—the weekly which he had himself founded, with Russian subsidies, in the spring of 1920[18]—and 'reaffect him to his post as delegate to the presidium of the executive'. The same meeting, which was also attended by the leadership of the CGTU, passed a set of theses 'On the Tactics of the French Communist Party and on the Problems Facing the Communist International', which for the first time gave clear satisfaction to Zinoviev: they admitted the need to fight against a rightist deviation within the party, announced that the primary organizational task was the transformation of the party on the basis of factory cells, admitted that the party had not been harsh enough in its criticism of the British Labour government, condemned the German right, and proclaimed agreement with the decisions of the Thirteenth Conference of the Russian Communist Party.

This was an obvious victory for Treint, although he himself had proposed a more harshly phrased text.[19] The result showed that the soft centre of the party leadership, represented by Sellier and the youth leader François Chasseigne (Doriot was in prison at the time), had swung back under Manuilsky's influence away from Souvarine and towards Treint. Manuilsky had not succeeded in winning over Monatte, but had driven a wedge between him and his former colleagues of *La Vie Ouvrière* who were now leading the CGTU. Sémard and Monmousseau, once more jealous than Monatte in their defence of trade union autonomy, had now gone far beyond him in their enthusiasm for the Comintern. Already the previous autumn there had been signs of an alliance between Treint and Monmousseau,[20] and in February Sémard had joined Treint and Suzanne Girault in voting against Souvarine's motion on the Russian conflict. Now Monatte, Rosmer and Souvarine found themselves isolated. Monatte and Souvarine voted against the theses, while Rosmer abstained and resigned from the *Bureau Politique*.

THE GOSPEL ACCORDING TO TREINT

From now on Treint had things all his own way. Making himself the mouthpiece of Zinoviev in France, he expounded the new doctrines in characteristically brutal terms in a series of articles in the *Bulletin Communiste*. The first, entitled 'Dans la voie tracée par Lénine', appeared on 28 March. It presented the theses voted by the *Comité Directeur* and provided an analysis of the disputes in the party over the past year. The main points at issue, it transpired, were the 'Bolshevik old guard' in Russia, the existence of a right wing in the German party and the International, the British question, and 'Bolshevization'. This word, which Treint had also used in his original draft of the theses themselves, now entered the vocabulary of the Comintern for the first time.[21] Treint's slogan was: 'no de-Bolshevization of the Russian Party, but on the contrary Bolshevization of all Communist Parties'. He thus drew a clear connection between the technical problem of introducing Bolshevik principles of organization into western Communist Parties and the political struggle against Trotsky in the Russian party. Treint called on all Communists to 'continue the vigorous struggle against the weakening of Bolshevist principles and leadership within the Russian Party, and for the strengthening of the methods and discipline of all the brother parties on the rigid basis of Bolshevism'. Bolshevization was thus the slogan with which the 'Bolshevik old guard', having defeated Trotsky in the Russian party, would now establish a firm hold on the foreign parties as well. The Bolshevizers were the foreign Communists who espoused Zinoviev's new leftist line, the united front only from below: Ruth Fischer and Maslow in Germany, Treint and Suzanne Girault in France. Those who resisted this line were dubbed the 'international right'. True to this tactic, Treint's article denounced in France 'the right represented by Rosmer and Souvarine and to which we were sorry to see Monatte ally himself'. (This description of people who until now had always been regarded as on the left caused not a little perplexity in the French party. Even some of those who in later years would be the most faithful followers of the Moscow line were at first uncertain which way to turn.[22]) The alleged error of the right, in France as in Germany, was above all a misapplication (i.e. an application) of the united front. The German right had entertained illusions about social democracy, and now the French right was making the same mistake about the British Labour Party.

In another article the following week, Treint linked Bolshevization more precisely with the new organization: 'to bolshevize the party is above all, at this time, to root it in the factories'. In the same issue of the *Bulletin Communiste* (4 April) ECCI's January resolution on factory cells was published in France for the first time. But for the next two months little attempt was made to put it into practice. The leadership was preoccupied with the task of preaching the new gospel to the party faithful (and so isolating the 'right'), and also with the parliamentary elections held on 11 May, which resulted in the defeat of the reactionary *Bloc National* by the *Cartel des Gauches*, composed of Radicals and Socialists. France thus followed Britain into the 'democratic-pacifist' era which had been predicted, with unusual prescience, by the Fourth Congress of the Comintern at the end of 1922.

THE FIFTH WORLD CONGRESS

The Comintern thus assembled for its Fifth Congress, in June 1924, in a mood of self-satisfaction and optimism. The arrival of the democratic-pacifist era was hailed as 'a sign of the collapse of capitalism';[23] and although the PCF's own performance in the elections had been disappointing, it nonetheless found itself for the first time in the Comintern's good books—the more so since the KPD was now in disgrace. Zinoviev actually described it as 'the second most important party of the Communist International' after the British, and of course gave warm support to the new majority in its campaign against Souvarine and Rosmer.[24] And the whole congress followed Treint in adopting the slogan of Bolshevization, even though it was noted that the PCF had as yet made little progress with Bolshevizing itself in practice: Zinoviev complained that France still had only 120 factory cells.[25]

The practical meaning of Bolshevization was expounded in the theses on tactics adopted by the congress:

The basic features of a genuine bolshevik party are:
1. The party must be a real mass party, that is, it must be able, both when legal and illegal, to maintain the closest and strongest contacts with the working masses and express their needs and aspirations.
2. It must be capable of manoeuvre, that is, its tactics should not be sectarian or dogmatic. . . .
3. It must be revolutionary, Marxist in nature, working undeviatingly towards its goal. . . .
4. It must be a centralized party, permitting no fractions, tendencies, or groups; it must be fused in one mould.
5. It must carry out systematic and persistent propaganda and organization in bourgeois armies.[26]

Of these five prescriptions it was only the fourth which went significantly beyond what had been required of all Communist Parties by the Twenty-One Conditions; and it was also the most significant for the future. But the first also had important implications, since the theses stated that one of the 'basic conditions for the formation of mass communist parties' was 'the methodical building up of the party on a factory-cell basis'.[27]

Briefly, Bolshevization meant 'that our sections take over for themselves everything in Russian bolshevism that has international significance'.[28] A separate set of theses on propaganda activities explained that Bolshevization was also the solution to 'the present internal struggles in some communist parties', since these were 'ideological repercussions of the survivals of traditional social-democratic ideas in the communist parties':

Bolshevization in this context means the final ideological victory of Marxism-Leninism . . . over the 'Marxism' of the Second International and the syndicalist remnants.

. . . Only if the communist parties acquire theoretical understanding of revolutionary practice can they become real leaders of the masses, conscious of their aims. . . . It is therefore one of the primary tasks of the CI and its sections to make Marxism-Leninism the common property of all members. . . . For this purpose cadres must be created who are in full possession of these theoretical weapons, and who can in turn equip the broadest circles of the party membership with them. . . .[29]

Each party was therefore to set up both a central party school and elementary party courses ('evening classes, lecture series, one-day Sunday schools', etc.).[30]

The last of the theses on tactics set out the 'concrete tasks' to be undertaken by each of 'the most important sections of the CI'. In the case of the French party these included:

—'the building of a real party apparatus';
—giving 'serious attention to the creation of factory cells';
—the elimination of 'right-wing tendencies';
—improvement of international contacts, especially 'permanent and unbroken relations with the KDP';
—accelerated 'recruitment of class-conscious elements in the CGTU' ('the CGTU leaders must adopt a clear position in the struggle against anarchism and vulgar syndicalism of the old type').[31]

BOLSHEVIZATION IN PRACTICE

Back home in France, the *Comité Directeur* met on 12 August to take note of the World Congress's resolutions and start on the real reorganization of the party which, it decided, should be completed by 31 December. A circular was drawn up giving very detailed instructions for the creation of cells, and warning in particular against any confusion between cells and trade union sections: the cells were to be specifically Communist and under party control. This was the first real attempt that the party had made to compete with the syndicalist ideology inside the factories. But the new organization was not confined to factory workers. Peasants and isolated workers were also to be included in factory cells or farm cells: village cells would be allowed only in villages where there was no industry and no big farm.

At the same time the party carried out a census of its members. Each member was supposed to fill in a questionnaire giving details of his work and other activities. To judge by the complaints of the party's *Bureau d'organisation* the following year, however, this appears to have been a failure.

As for the reorganization itself, it certainly did not go on as fast as had been hoped. In January 1925 the Congress of Clichy, summoned as 'le congrès de la bolchévisation', found the work far from complete and had to postpone the deadline to 1 April.

With the creation of cells at the base of the party went that of a new organizational structure at the top. The 'regions' which Treint had introduced in 1923 (see above, p. 99) were now not merely to group together the old departmental federations but to replace them. In November 1924 the decision was taken to limit the number of regions to twenty-seven. The idea was to break the link between party organization and the administrative divisions of the bourgeois state, to adapt the former to the real economic divisions of the country, and at the same time to bring the rural departments into contact with the industrial ones.

The absurdly mechanical manner in which Treint and his colleagues carried out this reorganization can be judged from the tone of a circular which appeared in the *Bulletin Communiste* in September 1924: 'All sections in your federation are now in possession of circular 43, dealing with the reorganization of the party on the basis of factory cells. It is therefore easy for them to carry out the work which is asked of them.' The old organization was systematically destroyed, but the construction of the new one did not keep pace. The result was six months of total anarchy, during which the bewilderment of the militants was increased by a sudden profusion of Soviet-style terminology ('agitprop', 'bureau d'org', etc.). Orders arriving from Moscow were applied *en bloc* and to the letter, while the Comintern's more general advice to hold an explanation campaign before starting on anything was ignored. For nearly a year the leadership tried to bulldoze every single party member into a factory cell, completely ignoring the provision for street cells in the original ECCI resolution.

It is hardly surprising that a reorganization carried through in this manner was less than a perfect success. In February 1926, after eighteen months of intensive Bolshevization, the number of cells in the French party was given by Pyatnitsky, head of the Comintern's organization department (Orgburo), as 2,300. Since it was later admitted that total party membership at this time had been only 55,000,[32] this figure would seem fairly satisfactory. But Pyatnitsky went on to say that many of these cells had no real or organic life. A few months later Sémard (now general secretary of the party) claimed the much less credible figure of 3,188 cells, but admitted that less than half of these were in firms.

Even where the organization of factory cells was successful it was not without its dangers, as is shown by a resolution of the Central Committee (which replaced the *Comité Directeur* after the Congress of Clichy), published in June 1925. This rebuked those comrades who were treating the cell as a closed community, not recruiting new members, and ignoring or opposing the trade unions at work in the same factory: 'all these mistakes have provoked the isolation of the Communists from their fellow-workers. . . . Instead of going to the masses, we have moved away from them.'*

One important task of the cells was the publication of works newspapers. In April 1925 the *Cahiers du Bolchévisme* (the theoretical journal which had replaced the *Bulletin Communiste* in November 1924) claimed that there were now 350 of these in France, of which, however, 260 were concentrated in the Paris region. But two years later the same source gave figures for the number published in the Paris region each month during 1926: these varied from as few as nineteen in February to a maximum of eighty-eight in September. It was of course difficult to keep up regular publication of a Communist works paper in the teeth of the employers' determined hostility; and in any case very few cells had the necessary experience. It is easy to believe Piatnitsky's assertion that the works papers which did appear

---

* In 1924 party membership appears to have increased from c.45,000 to c.60,000. Mme Kriegel (*Revue Française de Science Politique*, February 1966) sees this as the result of a 'coup de fouet' given by Bolshevization. This was also the interpretation given by André Ferrat, the party's official historian in 1931, who places the increase in the *second half* of 1924. But the syndicalist opposition, on the basis of certain local data, attributed it to the election campaign in the spring (see Jederman, *La 'bolchévisation' du p.c.f. (1923–1928)* [Paris, 1971], p. 109), and a recent biographer of Rosmer relates it more generally to 'the government of the Party by the Left' *before* Bolshevization (Christian Gras, *Alfred Rosmer et le mouvement révolutionnaire international* [Paris, 1971], p. 278). In any case, membership certainly fell off again in the following years, and at the Congress of Lille (1926) this was officially blamed, at least in part, on the methods of reorganization applied by the Treint leadership. See Table on p. 113.

'Bolshevization'

were not in fact edited by the cells but by the district committees (*comités de rayon*)[33]—i.e. by the full-time party cadres.

Party Membership during and after Bolshevization
(based on A. Kriegel, 'Le P.C.F. sous la Troisième République', in *Revue Française de Science Politique*, February 1966)

Year	Most plausible estimate	Source
1923	45,000	A. Ferrat, *Histoire du P.C.F.* (1931), p. 143.
1924	60,000	Ibid.
1925	55,000	P.C.F. conférence nationale, 9–12 mars 1930: *Résolutions adoptées*, p. 19.
1926	55,000	P.C.F. 6e congrès national, 31 mars–6 avril 1929: *Rapport politique du Comité central*.
1927	52,000	*La correspondance internationale*, 30 mars 1929, p. 391.
1928	40/45,000	P.C.F. 6e congrès national: op. cit., annexe: *Etat de l'organisation du parti*.
1929	?45,000	O. Piatnitsky, *Quelques problèmes urgents, Le mouvement des chômeurs, Le travail du parti et des syndicats dans les entreprises, La fluctuation de nos effectifs* (Paris, 1931), p. 26.
1930	38,000	Ferrat, op. cit., p. 254.
1931	30,743	*La correspondance internationale*, 18 mai 1932.
1932	?25,000	A. Ferrat, in *Esprit*, mai 1939.
1933	28,825	P.C.F. (S.F.I.C.) 8e congrès national, 22–25 janvier 1936: *Quatres années de lutte pour l'unité. Le pain, la paix, la liberté*, p. 41.
1934	42,578	Ibid.

Even in this period of relative prosperity and low unemployment, it was not usually difficult for employers to repress Communist activity

113

in their factories. A few sackings were often enough to destroy the party organization in a given factory, and once sacked the militants tended to find new jobs in small firms and then lie low, rather than return to open propaganda in big ones. At the same time, lack of qualified party cadres was a serious problem. Often it had been difficult to find a competent secretary for the old party section, and the difficulty was multiplied now that each section was split into five or six cells.

All in all, the results of the first year of Bolshevization were not encouraging. The Comintern delegate Guralsky summed them up as follows in June 1925: 'The most active cells have shared out the functions among their members and have voted about ten resolutions already voted by the central committee and the regional and *rayon* committees. That is all their work amounts to. . . .'[34]

SELF-CRITICISM
Meanwhile at the Fifth Enlarged Executive (or ECCI Plenum), which was held in Moscow in March 1925, a new set of theses on Bolshevization had been adopted which gave the word a new slant:

> With the slow and delayed tempo of revolution, the slogan of Bolshevization becomes not less but more significant. . . . If the tempo of revolutionary development slows down, if the result of this is to magnify hesitations in certain strata of the proletariat and moods favourable to counter-revolutionary social-democracy are on the increase, from this we deduce *with even greater indispensability* the slogan of the Bolshevization of the parties.

Bolshevization was now coupled with another catchword, 'stabilization', and though it 'arose in the struggle against the right danger '— i.e. against those who, underestimating the revolutionary possibilities of the situation, had adopted an unduly conciliatory line towards the social-democrat leaders—it was now pronounced to be 'impossible without a simultaneous struggle against ultra-left tendencies'—i.e. against those who, underestimating the success of capitalism in 'stabilizing' the situation, adopted extremist slogans and sectarian attitudes which frightened away the masses. The new definition of Bolshevization, 'the application of the general principles of Leninism to the concrete situation of the given country', was more moderate than the one given at the Fifth Congress. It was now recalled that Lenin himself had given a warning against 'transferring Russia's experience mechanically to other countries'. The emphasis was therefore less on the exact imitation of Russian models than on the unquestioning acceptance of Comintern (i.e. Russian) leadership: 'It must be brought home to the broadest masses that in the present epoch serious economic and political battles of the working class can be won only if they are led from one centre and on an international scale.'[35]

In the ensuing months it became apparent that the 'ultra-left tendencies', like the 'right danger' which preceded them, were located above all in the German party. The new German leaders, Ruth Fischer and Maslow, were now attacked with the same virulence which they had themselves used against the right in 1923–4; and Zinoviev, whose own position was now beginning to be threatened within the Russian party, made no attempt to shield his former protégés and supporters. On 1 September 1925 an open letter from ECCI to all members of the KPD was published in both the Russian and Germany party press. It accused the two German leaders of almost every imaginable error and demanded an 'overturn' in the KPD leadership—which in fact the Comintern had already secured by obliging a KPD delegation including Ruth Fischer herself to take part in the drafting of the letter.[36]

The message for the French 'Zinovievists' was all too clear. It was inevitable that, as in 1924, the errors first diagnosed in the KPD would soon be found in other parties, and those who had led the witch-hunt in 1924 would now in their turn be made scapegoats. This was all the more likely in France in that Soviet diplomacy was currently seeking a Franco-Soviet rapprochement as a counter-balance to the rapprochement between Germany and the West achieved at the Locarno Conference of October 1925. One of the obstacles in the way of good Franco-Soviet relations was the activity of the PCF, and especially its uncompromising campaign against the French war in Morocco (see below, p. 153ff.).[37] By November some of the PCF leaders, notably Treint himself and Doriot (the former youth leader), appear to have seen the danger and to have tried to forestall the inevitable Comintern criticism. They suddenly began to propose less wildly unrealistic slogans for united front action, and in early December a hastily convened party conference,* consisting of the

---

* The conference met on the day after the arrival in Paris of Chicherin, the Soviet foreign minister, and on the day of the signature of the Locarno treaties in London (1 December 1925).

Central Committee and the regional party secretaries, sent out its own 'open letter to all party members'.[38] This advocated complete application of united front tactics 'from the base to the summit' and admitted that the slogans used against the Moroccan war had lacked 'precision' and popular appeal. It also admitted, implicitly at least, some of the damage done by the ill-considered reorganization. From now on, it said, more use should be made of 'the cadres of the older generation'. The campaign for trade union unity had been conducted with insufficient attention to 'immediate demands'. What was required was 'an internal policy and a leadership of the party which collects round itself, and assimilates, the immense majority of the party', and a 'coherent and flexible organization'.[39]

This letter marks the end of the violent phase of Bolshevization. Two months later, in advance of the Sixth Enlarged Plenum of ECCI (February 1926), an organization conference of the seven biggest Communist Parties was held in Moscow to review the whole problem. It found that in other countries progress with the creation of factory cells had been even less impressive than in France, and for the first time placed an emphasis on street cells almost equal to that on factory cells. This was confirmed by the Sixth Plenum itself, which also marked the apogee of the crusade against the ultra-left. The French party was again warned against underestimating 'the right danger', but also criticized for its 'ultra-left errors' during 1925, in connection with which both Treint and Suzanne Girault were mentioned by name. The plenum's resolution on France demanded with emphasis 'a broadening of the basis of party leadership', so as to make the leadership 'a genuine unifying centre' for all members of the party.

But neither in France nor Germany did the disgrace of the ultra-left mean that the leadership was handed back to the defeated 'right' of 1923–4. In both countries the Comintern was able to blame the 'ultra-left error' on a few intellectuals, while recuperating their working-class allies and using them for the right-wing policy it had now adopted. Thus in Germany Thälmann was detached from Maslow and Fischer, and in France Sémard and Doriot were detached from Treint and Girault. It was Sémard who, on his return to France after the Plenum, wrote an article hailing 'the unity of the working class' as the 'central idea' of the session and explaining that this implied the use of 'slogans of the most modest kind'.[40]

The results of the Plenum were confirmed by the PCF Congress of Lille, in June 1926, which admitted that there had been errors at all levels and blamed them on Treint and Suzanne Girault, both of whom were dropped from the *Bureau Politique*. It noted that the famous reorganization was still not complete after two years, and that as a result the party was suffering from weakness in its political life, from internal divisions and from a declining membership. The congress instructed the regional organizations to make a serious study of their problems, and to take more account of local circumstances. Street cells were now recognized officially, and the systematic 'rattachement' of all members to factory cells (as a result of which many so-called factory cells were composed mainly of non-factory members) was condemned. Also the *rayons*, or party districts, would henceforth correspond to the administrative divisions of the state.

Maurice Thorez, the secretary of the party's *Bureau d'organisation*, pronounced what amounted almost to an epitaph of Bolshevization:

> We have hacked about the old divisions of our party without worrying too much about the results we should reach. . . . We have set up *rayons* and regions, somewhat arbitrarily, overlapping frontiers and administrative boundaries. . . . We must get rid of all this jumble and muddle of organizations in our regions, and try to constitute, within the limits of each administrative division of the bourgeois state, a solid party organism. . . . Our policy is made in the factory, but it is also made in the locality, in the context of the *département*, and the communist party, which does not make its policy in the clouds, must absolutely take account of all these realities.

But this, he added, did not mean they would have to start the reorganization again from scratch, only that henceforth more initiative must be given to the regional committees, the *rayons* and the cells. 'The excess,' he concluded, 'is not in the centralization of leadership, but in the centralization of execution.'[41]

By 1928 the proportion of factory cells appears to have fallen below 30%. After forcing non-workers to join factory cells, the party now swung the other way and allowed many workers to join street cells. In fact both practices existed side by side, and in 1929 the proportion of party members organized effectively in their place of work was down to 22%.[42] Many workers deliberately avoided joining factory cells so as not to attract the attention of their employers. The sequence of events recorded in the Berliet factory at Lyons in 1927 was probably typical: after the Sacco-Vanzetti strike called by the party in August of that year (see below, pp. 134–5) thirty-nine out of the forty-seven party members in the factory were sacked. The other eight then abandoned any political activity in the factory, and the works paper ceased to appear.[43]

BUREAUCRATIZATION

The drive to implant factory cells was thus a fluctuating one: virtually non-existent before 1924, gathering strength during the first half of that year, intense during the second half of 1924 and most of 1925, and declining again from early 1926. But the growth of a central bureaucracy in the party was continuous and steady. In this respect the measures decreed by the International in 1924 reinforced those already carried out by Treint in 1923 (see above, pp. 98–9). The injunction of the Fifth World Congress to the PCF to 'build a real party apparatus' led to the creation of the *Bureau d'organisation*, which took charge of the day-to-day details of the 'Bolshevizing' process, and was thus enabled to interfere in every aspect of the party's life at every level. Although elected by the Central Committee, this bureau was controlled in practice by the secretariat, whose authority now became virtually unlimited. Taking advantage of the infrequency with which the *Comité Directeur* (after Clichy, the Central Committee) met, the secretariat took decisions on its own authority, presenting them afterwards to the Committee for a ratification which was little more than a formality. At lower levels, assemblies and conferences were now held only when summoned by the central leadership, without advance consultation or any genuine preparatory debate: the object of such meetings was to 'inform' the party and to dictate its political line, not to allow it to work out a line for itself. And in this respect Treint's work was completed, not undone, by the changes of 1925–6; significantly, some members of the Central Committee were not even invited to the conference of December 1925 which marked the beginning of the retreat from out-and-out Bolshevization.[44]

This type of leadership was made possible largely by the formation of a hard core of full-time, paid party officials. In March 1925 the PCF, along with the British party, was criticized by Pyatnitsky for having no such full-time paid officials to run its organization, in contrast to the better organized and better financed German and Czechoslovak parties, which were accused of leaving too much in the hands of these officials.[45] This criticism was already beginning to be out of date when it was made. The latter part of 1924 had seen both the establishment of the *Bureau d'organisation* and the creation of a central party school at Bobigny, outside Paris, whose first two-month course in organization was attended by sixty-five party members. The school was harassed by the police, and had to be closed the following year,[46] but other similar schools were set up in the Paris region and in the provinces, under the supervision of Comintern agents.[47] The deficiencies of French party finance were made good, from 1924 onwards, by massive Russian subsidies.[48] The effect of these was to create a party machine controlled very closely by the Comintern, but escaping any effective control from within the party.

Diagram of Party Organization after Bolshevization

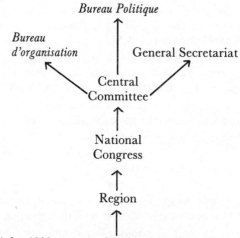

Bureau Politique

Bureau d'organisation   General Secretariat

Central Committee

National Congress

Region

Rayon (after 1926 corresponds to state administrative division)

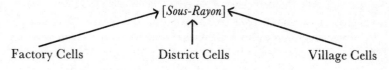

[*Sous-Rayon*]

Factory Cells   District Cells   Village Cells

PROLETARIANIZATION

Another process that was continuous throughout this period was the promotion of genuinely working-class militants to posts in the top party leadership. Doriot, a metalworker, became the leader of the

Jeunesses Communistes in 1923—a post that carried with it a place in the *Comité Directeur* of the party. Imprisoned for anti-militarist propaganda, he was put up for parliament in the 1924 elections as number two on the party list for the Paris suburbs, the area of greatest Communist strength. Triumphantly elected, he was soon afterwards released and quickly became known as the most fiery Communist orator in the new Chamber. At the Fifth World Congress he was made a candidate member of ECCI, and soon afterwards entered the *Bureau Politique* of the PCF, being given the task of organizing the party's colonial section.[49] Sémard, a railwayman, was elected a vice-president of ECCI at the Fifth World Congress, and immediately afterwards nominated by ECCI as general secretary of the PCF. In 1926, with the disgrace of Treint and Suzanne Girault, these two men became the effective leaders of the party. They were followed by others of the same stamp: for instance Henri Barbé, a mechanic, came up via the central committee of the JC and Albert Vassart, a metalworker, via the secretaryship of the CGTU Metalworkers' Federation, both to join the party Central Committee in 1926; and most important of all, Maurice Thorez, a miner, appeared as an alternate member of the *Comité Directeur* in January 1924, became a full member of the first Central Committee a year later, was put in charge of the *Bureau d'organisation*, brought into the *Bureau Politique* in July 1925 and given the title of 'organization secretary to the Central Committee'.[50]

TREATMENT OF THE OPPOSITION

We have seen that the very notion of Bolshevization originated at least partly in the struggle against Trotsky and against his actual or potential supporters outside Russia, and that these included three leading figures in the PCF: Souvarine, Rosmer and Monatte. The elimination of these men and their associates was therefore part and parcel of the Bolshevization process. Their defeat at the *Comité Directeur* of 18 March 1924 (see above, pp. 106–7) was followed by a vigorous campaign against them inside the party, for which Treint's article of 28 March (p. 107) set the tone. In early April the *Comité Directeur* obtained a vote of confidence in its new line from a conference of federation secretaries, and also organized a series of meetings of the Federation of the Seine. At these, both sides were allowed to state their case, but the account of the debates published in *L'Humanité* was highly selective—a sign of things to come. At one of these meetings the audience protested when the chairman tried to limit Monatte's speaking time, and one witness in an unpublished account concluded that the majority of those present were uncommitted, while of the minority who had formed an opinion the greater part favoured Monatte and Rosmer.[51] But Treint, undeterred, continued his campaign against the 'Right' in the *Bulletin Communiste*, and managed to provoke Monatte into resigning his post on *L'Humanité* on 22 April. The next day he was followed by Rosmer and four other sympathizers, who explained: 'we hardly feel at our ease in posts which should logically be occupied by comrades sharing the point of view of the majority of the *Comité Directeur*.'[52]

The crisis evidently caused great perplexity among the party cadres, many of whom knew the accused men as revolutionaries of long standing and unswerving conviction. Monatte in particular was regarded by many as the symbol of the revolutionary syndicalism whose allegiance the party had striven long and hard to win. But Treint and his allies had an unbeatable trump card: the support of the International and of the Russian Communist Party. The true implications of the struggles of the past four years now became apparent. For those who had fought against Longuet, against Frossard, or against the pure syndicalists it was not now possible to turn round and dispute the International's authority, still less to challenge the verdict given on a Russian problem by the Russian party. French Communists were, with very few exceptions, completely ignorant of the background to the Russian dispute. They knew only that Trotsky had been condemned, and in the last resort they had to accept the explanation for this given by the leaders of their own party, speaking in the name of the International. This consisted, of course, of a travesty of Trotsky's actual positions. For instance the secretary of one provincial federation, on a visit to Paris, was told by Treint and Crémet that Trotsky wanted to extend the New Economic Policy, open the Russian market to foreign competition, transfer Russian industry to the centres of raw materials, and give the planning commission (which was run by non-Communists) full powers.[53] The background to the dispute was obscure, and inevitably the benefit of the doubt went to the International and the party leadership. Such was the explanation given by Louis Bouët, one of the leaders of the teachers' trade union, writing with evident embarrassment to refuse Monatte space in his paper *L'Ecole Emancipée*:

We do not yet see clearly in the new party conflict. Why, in particular, was Treint removed from the leadership of the party at Lyons? How is it that today Souvarine is with Rosmer and you, when authoritarian methods formerly had no warmer partisan? . . . I could pose several other questions that would give you cause to believe that, in this new internal affair, I accord more importance to personal quarrels than to the battle of ideas; but really, for someone who lives far away from Paris and has only the *Correspondence Internationale* and the *Bulletin Communiste*—and perhaps some snatches of conversation while passing through the capital—to inform him, it is difficult to form a firm opinion.[54]

The leadership proceeded adroitly, not proposing any disciplinary sanctions at first but concentrating on the preparation of the Fifth World Congress. Strongly supported by the delegates of ECCI, one of whom was August Guralsky, a close associate of Zinoviev's,[55] they got several provincial federations to come out against the Russian opposition, and won a big majority for the *Comité Directeur*'s theses at the Congress of the Seine Federation in mid-May. Delegates were picked with great care for the National Council of the party on 1 and 2 June, with the result that Monatte found himself completely isolated and the theses went through by 2,353 votes to three, with ten abstentions.[56]

The delegations to the Fifth World Congress itself (from PCF, CGTU and *Jeunesses Communistes*) were also carefully picked and 'monolithically Bolshevik'.[57] 'The CGTU's delegation', Monmousseau was quoted as saying, 'must be made up of comrades with enough guts to smash any rightist faction in the party when they return.'[58] The Russians put strong pressure on Monatte to come, perhaps hoping to repeat on him the operation performed on Cachin in 1922, but Monatte refused, arguing that after the vote in the National Council he could bring 'only a simple personal opinion and not the opinion of certain strata in the party', and that since the delegates of ECCI had publicly compared him to Frossard his personal opinion would hardly carry any weight. He asked Zinoviev to grant him 'the freedom to remove myself from the ruling circles of the party', being convinced that he could now better serve the International 'in the ranks' as 'the most devoted of its private soldiers'.[59] Rosmer on the other hand did make the journey to Moscow (for the last time), though without a mandate from the party.[60]

Souvarine was already there, having at last resumed his post as delegate to the International (and member of ECCI) in time for the Thirteenth Congress of the Russian party in the latter part of May. Here he surpassed all his previous indiscretions by delivering a speech in defence of Trotsky (whose name, he said, was 'a synonym for revolution') and claiming to have been authorized by the French *Comité Directeur* to intervene in the debate in order to put an end to the polemics in the Russian party and in the Comintern![61]

After this, the French leaders clearly felt safe in demanding Souvarine's head. Though it had avoided seeking any mandate with regard to him before leaving Paris, the French delegation on arrival in Moscow denounced his breaches of discipline and proposed that he should be deprived of his vote in ECCI. Instead of this, a special commission of the congress was set up to consider his case. The French, after a debate amongst themselves, decided to demand his expulsion.[62] The Russians countered with a slightly more moderate proposal, stressing that the expulsion was only a temporary measure. This was adopted by the commission, and after the congress by ECCI: Souvarine was expelled from the International and from the PCF on the understanding that the latter could propose his readmission at the next world congress if in the meantime he proved his loyalty. It was also decided to send an open letter to all members of the PCF 'in order to remind them of the true meaning of party discipline'. This letter complained of the prevalence in the party of errors comparable to those of Souvarine, concluded that 'a certain individualist, petty bourgeois, anarchist spirit has dominated some leading comrades', and denounced the cult of 'personal' and 'private' opinions and unwillingness to submit to discipline.[63]

This was clearly meant as a warning to Monatte, Rosmer and their friends. But while protesting their willingness to accept decisions democratically taken, these men were not prepared to forgo their right to criticize the leaders and discuss the party line. At a conference of federation secretaries in September, Monatte defended Souvarine and pointed to inconsistencies in the accounts of the delegates who had returned from Moscow. Awkward questions were also asked about Lenin's testament, about the mandate of the French delegation to demand Souvarine's expulsion, and about the absence of any allusion to Trotsky in the reports. The leadership replied with threats, and the conference adopted a resolution proposed by Guralsky, noting the existence in the party of 'clearly anti-Communist elements of the right and the extreme left', asking them to 'submit clearly to the ideas and slogans of the International', and instructing the *Bureau Politique* to 'take all necessary measures so that these elements either submit to this spirit or resign'.[64]

After this the Rosmer-Monatte group quickly abandoned its illusions. Maurice Chambelland, a disciple of Monatte's, responded at once with a letter of resignation: 'As I have no intention of submitting, I am leaving. Herewith in consequence my resignation as a member of your so-called communist party.'[65] Monatte and Rosmer themselves, with another of their associates, Victor Delagarde, preferred to defend themselves in a letter to the *Comité Directeur*, written in such vigorous and contemptuous terms that it amounted in effect to a withering counter-attack on the leadership.[66] Six weeks later this letter had neither been communicated to the *Comité Directeur* nor published in the party press. Its authors therefore decided to send out an open 'letter to the members of the communist party', in which they both denounced the party leadership and defended Trotsky:

> The Party is in a state of permanent crisis. The latest bout of fever, which does not seem to have been cured—far from it—was provoked, a year ago, by the non-re-election of Treint to the Party secretariat. Who were the most determined artisans of this non-re-election, and therefore those responsible for the crisis? Men who had worked . . . with Treint in the *Bureau Politique* and in the Secretariat, namely Louis Sellier and Doriot, and who declared that no collective work was possible with him.
>
> Besides, they weren't the only ones to think so; Humbert-Droz, the delegate of the International, went so far as to say that so long as Treint and Souvarine were at the head of the Party, it would be impossible to have a Communist Party in France.

After this attempt to divide the new ruling coalition in the party, the three went on to give a catalogue of the mistakes made by these leaders 'in the nearly ten months for which they have had the effective leadership of the Party', and suggested that the campaign against the 'right' was really intended to distract attention from the results of this mismanagement. Noting that one of the charges against them was that they had 'obstructed the reorganization of the Party on the basis of factory cells', they countercharged that this reorganization was in fact being jeopardized by the authoritarian way in which the leadership was carrying it out.

These criticisms were largely justified, but any weight they might have carried was cancelled out by the untimely and clumsily expressed pronouncement in favour of Trotsky: after asserting that they were not 'Trotskyists' and had not even read Trotsky's latest pronouncements, the three went on to say: 'We think that it is Trotsky, at the present time, who thinks and acts truly in the spirit of Lenin, and not those who pursue him with their attacks while wrapping themselves in the mantle of Leninism.'[67]

This gave the leadership all the ammunition it needed, and made it hard for anyone in Moscow to intervene in the three's favour. They expected to be expelled at the coming party congress, but the leadership decided not to wait for this. A special party conference was hastily summoned, and voted their expulsion on 5 December, using an argument which was to be used unfailingly against all critics of the party or its leadership in the future: 'The weapons picked up by Monatte, Rosmer and Delagarde in the arsenal of Pioch and of Frossard are now being taken over by the whole bourgeoisie and directed against the Party and against the International.'[68] And Rosmer replied with a promise which would be bravely and vainly echoed by a long line of later expellees: 'As for us, expelled from the Party, far from envisaging the creation of another party, we return to the great mass of communists who are not Party members but who without doubt will join on the day when it has become a real communist party. We shall work from outside to hasten that day which the present crisis is only delaying.'[69]

Treint and his friends could afford to ignore such rhetoric. They had succeeded in putting Rosmer and Monatte beyond the pale, and had thus presented Moscow with a *fait accompli*. Zinoviev was not very pleased at being treated in this way, and ECCI appointed yet another 'French commission', which censured the French *Bureau Politique* for suppressing the original letter of the three to the *Comité Directeur*. In mid-January the CGTU's representative in Moscow wrote to inform Monatte that 'Treint has never had such a thorough head-washing as he got these last few days in Moscow': Zinoviev had told the over-zealous 'captain' to his face that 'it was very regrettable to expel workers' and that 'the regime installed in the French party cannot last'. But to revoke the expulsions now that things had reached this stage was not possible, since 'that would mean getting rid of the present party leadership. Zinoviev is not yet ready to take that step. . . .'[70] How could he be, since it would have meant sacrificing his own supporters to the avowed champions of Trotsky? All he could do was to instruct Treint to avoid any further expulsions.[71]

The result of this compromise was to permit the continued existence of a 'right' opposition within the party while ensuring that it found a platform in the journals published by those over whom party discipline had no further hold: Rosmer and Monatte's *La Révolution Prolétarienne* (founded in January 1925) and Souvarine's *Bulletin Communiste* (revived in October of the same year). The leaders of the new 'right' within the party were, predictably enough, two leaders of the old 'left': Fernand Loriot and Amédée Dunois. (Loriot had been in retirement, partly for health reasons, since 1922. Dunois, though sympathetic to Rosmer, had wavered somewhat in the heat of the 1924 crisis.)[72] They were allowed to speak at the Congress of Clichy, dissociating themselves from Trotsky and Souvarine but protesting against the recent expulsions and against the growth of centralization and dictatorship in the party. Loriot even openly attacked the resolutions of the Fifth World Congress on the united front and on the reorganization of the parties. But the 'right' was effectively discredited by Treint's reading of an intercepted letter from Souvarine to Rosmer, which included the statement that 'salvation would be found in a great crisis imperilling the revolution. Then the whole party would turn to Trotsky.'[73] Treint inevitably had the last word, and the opposition's theses were not put to a vote.

After the congress, the opposition made more effort to organize itself. On 9 February a letter signed by eighty party members was sent to ECCI, complaining of 'the suppression of all criticism and self-criticism within the party'. This was endorsed five days later by a personal letter from Loriot to Zinoviev, and in March the opposition sent a set of theses to the fifth plenum of ECCI. But these were not discussed, and no representative of the opposition was able to attend the debates and defend its point of view. (It was the first time this had happened to any PCF minority at an official Comintern gathering.) Treint and Sémard were able to denounce the 'right' unanswered, and the names of Souvarine, Rosmer and Monatte were included in a list of 'enemies of the International'. Trotsky himself was invited to disavow the support given him by *La Révolution Prolétarienne*—though he did not in fact do so until seven months later.[74]

In private, however, Treint was probably advised by the Russians not to drive the internal opposition into open alliance with *La Révolution Prolétarienne*, for in May Loriot was allowed to publish a new and lengthy set of theses in the *Cahiers du Bolchévisme*. But this was far from enough to refute his allegation that free discussion had been suppressed, while his assertion that Bolshevization in practice meant the cultivation of authoritarian methods and sectarian attitudes corresponded to the experience of an increasing number of militants. His criticisms seemed to be borne out by Communist losses in municipal elections held on 3 and 10 May. They were followed up by a further letter to ECCI, signed this time by 130 members, putting the blame for the defeat firmly on the party leaders. By October the number of signatures that could be collected for another letter in the same vein had risen to 250, allegedly including eleven Communist deputies.

At this point the leadership began to take the opposition more seriously, realizing no doubt that many of its criticisms coincided with those which the Comintern itself had now directed at the German 'ultra-left'. A meeting of the *Bureau Politique* in November passed a resolution pointing out that those who expressed disagreement should not be indiscriminately condemned as right-wingers, and admitting that fear of such condemnation had inhibited party members from speaking freely. This was followed by the open letter of 2 December (see above, p. 116) which amounted to an almost complete adoption of the opposition's platform. But this was not publicly admitted, and no offer was made to bring the internal opposition leaders into the party leadership, still less to reinstate those who had been expelled the previous year. Consequently the opposition, encouraged by rumours of Treint's impending disgrace, did not disarm. On 15 December a reply to the open letter was sent to the Central Committee by twenty-four party members. They congratulated the leadership on making 'a *volte-face* to adopt the point of view of the opposition', but attacked the undemocratic way in which the conference that sent out the open letter had been organized, and repeated the earlier complaints about 'mechanical pressure, intimidation and administrative exclusiveness'. The secretariat retaliated with a letter in *L'Humanité* on 3 January 1926, warning all party members to break off any contact with the *Bulletin Communiste* and *La Révolution Prolétarienne*. The former journal replied with a letter of defiance signed by seven party members on its editorial board, declaring that the two opposition journals were now the only platform available to 'the revolutionary spirit surviving in the party' and protesting once again against the expulsion of their founders.

The existence of this opposition helped to undermine Treint's position and provided the Comintern with useful evidence of the PCF leadership's inadequacy. But Zinoviev had no intention of allowing the 'right' to profit from Treint's downfall. At the Fourteenth Congress of the Russian Communist Party in December 1925 (the scene of his defeat by Stalin on the *kulak* question), Zinoviev criticized the French leaders but also denounced the French 'right', now lumping Loriot together with Rosmer and Souvarine. The opposition seems gradually to have realized that it had little to hope for from the International. A further broadsheet issued on 5 February 1926 by the authors of the reply to the open letter complained not only of the falsification or suppression of their statements in the party press, but also of ECCI's failure to reply to their previous letters. Meanwhile the signatories of the 'Letter of the 250' and the party members contributing to the *Bulletin Communiste* and *La Révolution Prolétarienne* were again condemned by an enlarged session of the Central Committee, held from 31 January to 2 February. This was confirmed by the Sixth Plenum of ECCI, at which the condemnation of 'ultra-left errors' in the French party was balanced by further blistering attacks on the right.[75]

After this the opposition rapidly gave up any serious struggle within the party, although there were few actual expulsions. Loriot did not renew his party card for 1926, and in June Humbert-Droz, revisiting France to attend the Congress of Lille, was told by Dunois that the right had 'dissolved'. The internal opposition had quarrelled with Souvarine and 'they are above all discouraged'. This discouragement was increased rather than otherwise by the new alliance between Zinoviev and Trotsky. Zinoviev's French supporters were not prepared to support the reinstatement of Souvarine (as Zinoviev apparently asked them to do, through Humbert-Droz's mouth); nor were the French 'Trotskyists' willing to make it up with Suzanne Girault.[76]

CONCLUSION

Although its most striking innovation—the reorganization of the party on the basis of factory cells—was only a partial success, there can be no doubt that the 'Bolshevization' was a decisive episode in the party's history. The replacement of the old territorial sections by the smaller, semi-clandestine cells (even if from 1927 onwards less than one-third of them would in fact be factory cells) gave the party a form of organization which was distinctively communist, and has distinguished it from other parties ever since. In effect, it secured the leadership against ever being openly challenged at a meeting of the party rank-and-file. The cells owed their very existence to decisions taken by the central leadership. A single cell was too small a theatre in which to stage a revolt: its members were usually unwilling to take the responsibility of contesting a decision which came from higher up; and if they did so the revolt could be quickly isolated and, if necessary, the cell itself be dissolved, the ringleaders sanctioned and the other members redistributed among other cells where they would be in a minority. Yet any attempt by party members to hold unauthorized discussions of the party line with other members outside their own cell could be branded as 'fractional' activity and promptly suppressed. The cell system ensured that democratic centralism would always be more centralist than democratic.

The changes at the top of the party went in the same direction. The bureaucratic style of leadership inaugurated by Treint was retained in its essentials by all his successors. Since his time all important decisions in the party have been taken by small groups of officials behind closed doors, and submitted afterwards for ratification by assemblies whose loyalty had been secured in advance. Power in the party has remained in the hands of its full-time paid officials. For local branches to take initiatives without the prior approval of the centre became extremely rare.

Treint also inaugurated the tradition of servile obedience to the Moscow line—though if he had not, the Comintern would no doubt have found someone else. It soon found others who would follow the line through even sharper twists and turns with even less complaint, and the tradition would survive the Comintern itself. The PCF, noted in its early years for its turbulence and refractoriness, would in due course win a reputation for exemplary discipline. It would also, after 1926, draw all its top leaders from unimpeachably working-class backgrounds. They would be men who owed all their importance and most of their education to the party and to the Soviet Union—a fact which must partly explain their unwillingness or inability to develop an independent political attitude. The contrast with the Italian party, which escaped this aspect of Bolshevization and has been led almost exclusively by middle-class intellectuals, is surely instructive.

On the positive side, there is no doubt that Bolshevization brought the party assets whose value would later become apparent. To be led by workers was itself an important psychological asset in a party that must bid mainly for working-class support. So was the formation of a hard core of party cadres whose loyalty could be depended on in all vicissitudes. Important, too, was the creation of a party machine whose structure was adapted to the penetration of non-Communist organizations, even if for the moment neither the general situation nor the line of the International were such as to give these propensities much scope; and the factory cells themselves, though singularly ineffective in the short term, provided at least a toe-hold in the factories which no other party had. Ten years later this fact would prove of crucial importance.

4

Policies and Personalities

1926–1931

'Opportunistic backslidings' (1926–1927)

The new *Bureau Politique* elected at the Congress of Lille, in June 1926, contained only two men—Cachin and Sellier—who had belonged to that of 1923. Two others, Alfred Bernard and Renaud Jean, could be described as 'belonging to the generation before Bolshevization'.[1] Five had come from the leadership of the CGTU: the general secretary Sémard, Monmousseau, Lucien Midol, Dudilieux and Racamond; and two from the *Jeunesses Communistes*: Crémet and Doriot. The remaining member, Maurice Thorez, had come up through the party's provincial organization.

The dominant figures, Sémard and Doriot, owed their rise to the fact that they had identified themselves less closely with Zinoviev and with the ultra-left line than had Treint and Suzanne Girault. But their very dominance made it inevitable that they would now be identified with the ensuing phase of Comintern policy, which would later be dubbed right-wing and 'opportunistic'. This phase is associated with the name of Bukharin, who took over the leadership of the Comintern (though not the title of president) after Zinoviev's dismissal in October 1926. Bukharin was the leader of the right wing in the Russian party, i.e. the group favouring concessions to the upper peasantry, with which Stalin had temporarily allied himself. Bukharin and Stalin together sponsored an international united front policy which can fairly be called right-wing, since it went further than anything that had been attempted during the first united front period in 1922–3—especially in China.

It would be a mistake, however, to suppose that Sémard and Doriot represented a right wing in the French party, or that they had any direct link with Bukharin such as Rosmer had had with Trotsky or Treint with Zinoviev. They simply applied the prevailing Comintern line as they understood it, and Humbert-Droz, who did have close links with Bukharin, had on occasion to take them to task for excessive 'opportunism' in his capacity as head of the Comintern's 'Latin secretariat'. For all its Bolshevization, the PCF showed an inclination to slip back into social-democratic or 'electoralist' politics whenever the united front was on the agenda. This tendency also affected the CGTU, whose leadership was now hardly distinguishable from that of the party. The official historians of the ensuing period (after 1929), when the Comintern had once again swung leftward, looked back on the actions of 1926–7 with predictable severity. According to René Garmy's *Histoire du mouvement syndical en France*, published in 1933, 'the struggle for the united front degenerated into attempts at "circumstantial agreements" with the Ligue des droits de l'homme and the Radical party, on the pretext of linking up with the petty bourgeois masses. . . .'[2]

During 1927, the Communist parliamentarians also drew the criticism of the Comintern by their 'legalistic' attitude towards repression and arrests. In June Palmiro Togliatti, who had been sent to Paris by the Comintern to reorganize the leadership in exile of the Italian party, wrote to inform Humbert-Droz of his concern about the situation in the French one:

Cachin's speech in the Chamber, when they were about to vote on his arrest, strikes me as something pathetic. The parliamentary fraction abstaining in the vote and not presenting a communist motion to make the socialists come out against the reaction is even worse. *Parliamentary cretinism!* And on top of all that comes Sémard's statement, after he was freed by mistake, that he intends to go back to prison! I think this statement is without precedent in the history of the communist movement. The same goes for the action committee's decision to go to prison at the order of the ministry of Justice. It's unheard of! The party has forgotten and is forgetting that it's a revolutionary party, that it must teach the workers to break by all methods the legality of the bourgeois republic, and that we only appeal to legality when that helps us to cover our revolutionary action and embarrass the enemy.[3]

The context of these events was the renewed government of 'national union' inaugurated in July 1926 when Poincaré was recalled to power to save the franc. The result of this swing back to the right was at once a revival of anti-Communist fervour in government circles (typified by the famous speech of Albert Sarraut, the Radical

Minister of the Interior, in April 1927, concluding with the words 'Le communisme, voilà l'ennemi!') and the return of the Socialists to opposition. This revived the possibility of an electoral united front between Socialists and Communists for the elections due in 1928. But, as in 1924, it was unlikely that the Socialists would accept a formula excluding any co-operation with the Radicals, since there was a strong element in the Radical party which opposed the 'national union' and favoured a return to alliance with the Socialists. Once again, therefore, the temptation was strong for French Communists to stretch the united front to cover electoral combinations of the old *Bloc des Gauches* type. According to Humbert-Droz, the leadership was actually encouraged to embark on such combinations (which had been explicitly condemned by the Fourth World Congress in 1922) by the Comintern agent Petrovsky, who was sent to France by Stalin early in 1927. Humbert-Droz himself opposed this, and the result was a clash between the two Comintern officials when Petrovsky returned to Moscow. The Presidium of ECCI appointed a commission to decide the issue, on which both Stalin and Bukharin sat and which held three long meetings at Stalin's secretariat. This commission also had to deal with a letter of complaints against the 'Latin secretariat' and especially against Humbert-Droz himself, sent by the PCF. Humbert-Droz attributed these complaints to 'highly tendentious reports from Treint', who after his demotion had been summoned back to Moscow (a common fate of disgraced party leaders in this period) and who, with some reason, regarded Humbert-Droz as one of the chief authors of his misfortunes.

The commission completed its work by early April, when Humbert-Droz sent the following account to Togliatti in Paris:

> It was laborious, and the battle violent. Petrovsky did a good deal to make things worse by advising the French and defending more than them the past and present errors of the party. After a first victory won in the French Commission and in the political secretariat, Thorez arrived and we had to start all over again: for three weeks we re- examined and revised the texts. . . .[4]

The result was the 'Letter of April 2nd', addressed by the Presidium to the Central Committee of the PCF to warn it against opportunistic deviations:

> The whole policy of the Party must help to get parliamentary life

out of its traditional rut, dominating next year's electoral struggle through vast class struggle movements.

The Party must envisage an electoral tactic which is not a mechanism for standing down in favour of 'left' candidates, but a method of mobilizing the masses; it must resolutely fight opportunistic attitudes towards the 'left' parties and condemn the tactic of common electoral lists with the Socialist Party by unmasking the 'socialist left'.[5]

But as it turned out the problem of common lists was rendered obsolete by the new electoral law of 21 July 1927, which reintroduced single-member constituencies with two ballots. (One of the arguments advanced for this system by the Radicals, who were its chief supporters, was that it would prevent the Communists from making big gains.) Under this system, the problem was no longer one of joint lists but of 'republican discipline'—the tradition by which, on the second ballot, all other left-wing candidates would stand down in favour of the one who had won most votes on the first. The Communists therefore had to decide not simply whether to run a joint list with the Socialists or a separate list against them (a decision which was largely academic since in most areas the Socialists could be relied on to refuse), but whether to maintain their candidates on the second ballot in constituencies where they had no chance of winning or to stand them down, in return for Socialist support in constituencies where Communists were ahead.

While it mulled over this problem, the leadership tried desperately to regain the Comintern's favour, veering uneasily from right to left. On 6 August 1927 ECCI issued a 'twelfth-hour' appeal on behalf of Sacco and Vanzetti, the two Italian anarchists threatened with execution in the United States. It called on 'all workers and all revolutionary organizations' to 'protest against the execution of the sentence; organize mass demonstrations against those responsible for this crime; organize protest strikes'.[6] Public feeling about the case did run fairly high in France and this was virtually the only issue on which, during the past year, a Communist campaign had found some measure of non-Communist support. In the Vaucluse, for example, Socialists joined Communists in a Committee for the Defence of Sacco and Vanzetti, and even Radicals agreed to share the platform at a protest meeting.[7] But the party's call for a general strike on the issue, announced two days after the ECCI appeal, was obviously disproportionate and alienated much of the support that had been won. It did however lead to violent clashes between Communists and police on 23 August. In the doubtless exaggerated version given by an official historian of the party four years later, the demonstration of that day was 'particularly vast and violent in the main working-class centres and especially in Paris where about 80,000 proletarians, sometimes dispersed, sometimes grouped in columns of thousands of demonstrators, outflanked the police for hours at a stretch'.[8] After this the leadership 'returned to legality' and held only meetings authorized by the police. The announcement in *L'Humanité* that the party 'will not tolerate' a march through Paris on 19 September by the American Legion proved an idle threat. The Minister of the Interior forbade counter-demonstrations, and the party had to be content with a sparsely-attended meeting in the suburb of Clichy while 'the accomplices of the murderers of Sacco-Vanzetti' (who had by now gone to the electric chair) marched peacefully through the heart of Paris.

These failures were the more embarrassing in that at this time there was supposed to be an imminent threat of war between the Soviet Union and a coalition of capitalist powers, and Comintern sections in the West were therefore supposed to be on a war footing. This war scare, based mainly on the situation in China and on the rupture of Anglo-Soviet diplomatic relations which had occurred in May, was in fact invented almost entirely by Stalin as a weapon against the Russian opposition. (It enabled him to coin the celebrated slogan of the 'united front from Chamberlain to Trotsky'.) But it did involve a period of tension in Franco-Soviet relations during the autumn, after a difficult round of negotiations over unrepaid French loans to Tsarist Russia. Rakovsky, the Soviet ambassador in Paris, signed a manifesto calling on workers and soldiers in capitalist countries to defend the Soviet Union in case of war, and the French government used this as an excuse to declare him *persona non grata*. (Ironically Rakovsky himself was a well-known Trotskyist, and this was actually one of the French government's reasons for desiring his recall.)[9]

CLASS AGAINST CLASS

Consequently when, in early November, the Central Committee of the PCF at last followed up the letter it had received from the Comintern in April (and further instructions sent in September) with its own 'open letter to the Party', it opened by noting that France's imperialist policy was now directed against the USSR and that war threats were accompanied by a constant decline in the workers' standard of living. It stressed the need for a recovery of the party, 'whose opportunistic mistakes are made worse by the aggravation of the class struggle', and the

> necessity of an energetic policy of resistance to repression and utilization of the 1928 elections to organize against the National Union not only a parliamentary struggle but above all a direct mass struggle by addressing not only the voters but all workers, millions of whom do not vote: women, young people, soldiers, colonial and foreign workers.
>
> During this struggle, the Party must demonstrate the nefarious and anti-working-class role of the socialist leaders, who, by their negligence, are objectively the prolongation of the National Union. The United Front must be organized class against class.

From this general principle, the open letter went on to deduce an electoral tactic: Communist candidates would not stand down for Socialists on the second ballot unless the Socialists agreed that their candidates would stand down only for Communists and not for bourgeois candidates, and unless they accepted a joint 'minimum programme'.[10]

Proposals for this, published shortly after the open letter, were fairly moderate, including such items as the maintenance of the eight-hour day and resistance to wage cuts. But the SFIO was asked to take part in joint action on a 'class against class' basis, on the understanding that this meant not just an electoral alliance but 'a class bloc including measures to ensure that it spreads beyond the electoral context into a struggle at every moment and on every ground, against the white and tricoloured reactions'.[11]

It was still not entirely clear whether the party genuinely aimed at a united front *with* the Socialist Party, or whether it proposed this only as a cover for a 'united front' *against* it. This ambiguity no doubt resulted partly from the unclarity of the Comintern line itself (Stalin had now swung over to an ultra-left line in China, but had not yet severed his alliance with Bukharin in Russia), and partly from disagreements within the French leadership.

Some members of the *Bureau Politique*, notably Sellier and the peasant leader Renaud Jean, opposed the 'class against class' tactic because they genuinely wanted to achieve a united front with the SFIO and realized that this could only be obtained by accepting 'traditional republican discipline on the second ballot'. Others such as Doriot and Bernard argued that 'we should take account of exceptional cases', and be prepared to stand down for a Socialist rather than let in a right-wing candidate, even though the Socialists had not accepted the proposed pact.[12] Doriot thus appeared for the first time as the spokesman of a right-wing opposition within the party, and therefore became the target of attacks by the young left-wingers in the *Jeunesses Communistes*, of which formerly he himself had been the most outspoken leader. It is also the first time he is known to have adopted a critical line towards a policy approved by the Comintern and by Stalin, of whom he had hitherto been an uncritical admirer. For this change of attitude there seem to be three possible explanations. One is frustrated ambition: Doriot had apparently hoped to emerge as sole leader of the PCF in 1926. Instead, he found himself playing second fiddle to Sémard and deprived of his stronghold in the *Jeunesses Communistes* by being promoted to honorary president, while at the same time the end of the Moroccan war brought a loss of importance for the colonial section of the Central Committee, of which Doriot was in charge. Then in November 1926 he was summoned to Moscow and kept away from France for eight months. The second explanation is that during those eight months he was a member of a Comintern delegation to China, and in April 1927 was virtually an eyewitness of the débâcle of Stalin's Chinese policy, when Chiang Kai-Shek massacred the Communists who, on Comintern instructions, had welcomed his troops into Shanghai.[13]

The third possible explanation is that Doriot had become a French government agent. This has been frequently asserted by Communists since his expulsion from the party in 1934. According to one version, Doriot had 'sold himself' to the police in order to escape a prison sentence with which he was threatened for mortally injuring a policeman during a riot. The implausibility of this account is convincingly demonstrated by his biographer Dieter Wolf.[14] A more general difficulty about the theory is that it does not help to explain Doriot's subsequent political career.

Against this must be set the evidence of Humbert-Droz, who went to Paris in October 1927 to take part in the discussions preceding the open letter and to impose the new 'class against class' policy on the French party. Early in November he was arrested by the French police in conditions which convinced him that he had been betrayed by a member of the French *Bureau Politique*. From prison he wrote to his wife:

It's quite obvious that the government and its political police are trying to prevent the party's recovery and to help it slide to the right and resist the directives of the Communist International. That is why, this time, I was arrested after a session of the secretariat which had come out clearly in favour of the recovery and at which Maurice [Thorez], Gaston [Monmousseau], Ferrat, Dallet, Bouthonnier, Costes had said they agreed with the C.I.'s policy and had stressed the need to fight against the party leadership in the Santé prison, in the event of resistance from that quarter. The next day Cachin and Doriot [the right] were let out of the Santé and the day after that I was arrested. Excellent preparation for the Central Committee by the government! The day after my arrest, the prosecutor asked me a series of questions proving that he knew about our discussions on Wednesday and about the C.I.'s latest letter on party tactics.

Humbert-Droz relates in his memoirs that in 1937 he was told by Vaillant-Courier that 'the member of the *Bureau Politique* who had betrayed me, in November 1927, was none other than Jacques Doriot, who had been a police spy for several years', and that though at the time he had put this statement down to party propaganda it had since been confirmed (in the 1960s) by a letter from a French intelligence agent.[15]

Humbert-Droz suggests that the French authorities' hold over Doriot might have originated in the discovery by the prefect of some administrative malpractices at the town hall of Saint-Denis. But since Doriot did not become mayor of Saint Denis till 1930, this seems hardly likely. There is, of course, also the question whether the French government would really have wished, in 1927, to facilitate the creation of a united front between Socialists and Communists rather than to encourage the PCF on a sectarian course that could only lead to its isolation.

The 'Third Period' (1928–1931)

The elections came and went, but the disagreements within the PCF smouldered on. The resentment of the new right wing was fed both by the electoral result—in which the Communist vote went up but because of its 'class against class' tactic the party lost eleven seats—and by the Comintern's accelerating swing to the left. In the spring of 1928 Stalin broke with Bukharin and began his first campaign against the *kulaks*. But in any case both Stalin and Bukharin were obliged to abandon their right-wing line in international tactics after the events of summer 1927: it was no longer possible to support the KMT (Kuomintang) in China when it had embarked on an open campaign against the Communists (as even the left KMT did in June 1927); or to maintain the Anglo-Soviet Trade Union Council when its British members failed to make any protest against the rupture of Anglo-Soviet relations and the TUC then decided to withdraw from it altogether. The united front tactics, of which the Anglo-Soviet Council had been represented as the triumph, were now implicitly abandoned and replaced by the 'class against class' slogan. The ultra-left being now eliminated almost everywhere, a new witch-hunt began in various Comintern sections against right-wing tendencies. Those who had faithfully carried out the Comintern's earlier line were now condemned as opportunists—the most flagrant injustice being the dismissal of the Chinese leader Chen Tu-hsiu, who had frequently urged the secession of his party from the KMT but had meekly allowed himself to be overruled by Moscow.

These changes were confirmed at the Ninth Plenum of ECCI in February 1928. In preparation for it the PCF held a conference (30 January–1 February) at which it accused itself of having failed to understand the nature of the capitalist offensive, or to notice the radicalization of the masses; it had kept too rigidly within the bounds of bourgeois legality, and had failed to grasp France's leading role in the preparations for war. These errors had been pointed out in the open letter, but not enough had been done to apply the new line. But just as the open letter of December 1925 had endorsed the criticisms of the 'right-wing' opposition without acknowledgement and had not rehabilitated its leaders, so now the open letter of November 1927 did not presage any mercy for the discredited ultra-left leaders. Treint and Suzanne Girault, who in 1924 had led the anti-Trotskyist crusade, were now themselves labelled 'Trotskyist fraction leaders' and expelled from the party. (Treint had already been expelled from the Central Committee, and his expulsion from ECCI had been requested, in September 1927.)

These expulsions were approved by the Ninth Plenum itself, in a resolution which also asserted that the class struggle in France was growing more acute, and the masses becoming more radical. The *Bloc des Gauches* had behaved treacherously, as had the Socialist Party and the CGT. The changed situation required changes in Communist tactics; nevertheless the party had continued to repeat the old mistakes. Old habits and traditions were obstructing the operation of the new policy; so the Plenum urged the French Central Committee to act more vigorously.[16] Sémard showed his obedience to the new line by telling the Plenum: 'We are witnessing in France a veritable fascization which is developing on an international scale with the active support of the leaders of social democracy.'

THE SIXTH WORLD CONGRESS

During 1928 the struggle between Stalin and Bukharin in the Soviet politburo grew steadily more intense. As in 1924 the swing to the left in Comintern policy was partly a manoeuvre to discredit and eliminate potential or actual supporters of the losing Russian faction in foreign Communist Parties: Stalin now used the same device against Bukharin that Zinoviev had used against Trotsky. The Sixth World Congress of the Comintern, held from 17 July to 1 September 1928, was an elaborate comedy in which Bukharin played the leading role while Stalin went off on holiday to the Caucasus. But the better informed delegates knew that Bukharin's influence was now on the wane and that some of the theses which he defended at the congress had been amended against his will during preliminary discussions in the Soviet politburo. In particular it was Stalin's idea to identify the 'third period' of post-war history, whose arrival the congress hailed, with a 'swing to the left of the masses of the working class' and 'growing acuteness of the class struggle'.[17] Starting from this premise, the congress concluded that both social democracy and fascism were merely last-ditch attempts by the bourgeoisie to forestall revolution. In the words of the Programme which the congress adopted:

> According to changing political circumstances, the bourgeoisie resort either to fascist methods or to coalitions with social-democracy, while social-democracy itself, particularly at critical moments for capitalism, not infrequently plays a fascist part. . . .
> For normal capitalism both fascism and coalition with social-democracy are extraordinary methods. They indicate the existence of a general capitalist crisis and are used by the bourgeoisie to halt the advance of the revolution.[18]

This analysis clearly ruled out any serious united front tactics, even for the defence of the labour movement against a fascist onslaught. And a further innovation of the Sixth World Congress was the doctrine that

... the Soviet Union is the true fatherland of the proletariat, the strongest pillar of its achievements, and the principal factor in its emancipation throughout the world. This obliges the international proletariat to forward the success of socialist construction in the Soviet Union and to defend the country of proletarian dictatorship by every means against the attacks of the capitalist powers. ... In the event of an attack by the imperialist States on the Soviet Union, and of a war against it, the international proletariat must answer by bold and resolute mass action and by fighting to overthrow the imperialist governments, its slogan the proletarian dictatorship and alliance with the Soviet Union.[19]

The Comintern thus became almost explicitly an instrument of Soviet foreign policy, and the western working class was told to look less to its own strength than to that of the Soviet Union for its hopes of emancipation. The premise on which the Comintern had been founded—that the survival of the Russian Revolution depended on revolution in the rest of Europe—had now been completely inverted.

Immediately after the congress the struggle between Stalin's and Bukharin's supporters in the Comintern came into the open. The so-called 'conciliator' group in the KPD, which during the congress had held meetings with the Bukharin-Rykov group in the CPSU, succeeded in swinging the KPD Central Committee against the party chairman Thälmann, who was one of Stalin's leading foreign supporters but had compromised himself over the embezzlement of party funds by his brother-in-law. This decision was summarily overruled and Thälmann reinstated by a meeting of the ECCI Presidium, held in the absence of Bukharin and most of its other members. After this Bukharin gave up direct participation in Comintern work (though he was not formally dropped until July 1929).[20] From then on Stalin dictated his orders to the Comintern through Molotov,[21] while Manuilsky took over the day-to-day political leadership. The leaders of the German right were expelled, and those who attempted to defend them—Humbert-Droz and the Italian representative Angelo Tasca—were fiercely denounced by Stalin on 19 December 1928 at a meeting of the ECCI Presidium, from which body both men were soon dropped.

The French right evidently posed a less serious threat to Stalin than the German one, and could be dealt with more discreetly. During the Sixth World Congress the French delegates, perhaps hoping to save themselves by finding a suitable scapegoat in good time, suggested that Renaud Jean, the most outspoken opponent of the 'class against class' policy, should be dropped from the *Bureau Politique* 'because he is a social-democrat or a social-revolutionary of the Russian type'. But this proposal was vetoed by Molotov 'so as not to reject him by mechanical methods, even though he is almost alone'.[22] The real reason was no doubt that Stalin did not intend to let the PCF leadership off with so restricted a purge. Instead, Manuilsky made contact with the leaders of the *Jeunesses Communistes*—Henri Barbé, Pierre Célor, Henri Lozeray, François Billoux, Raymond Guyot, André Ferrat, Gustave Galopin—and instructed them to take a leading role in the party in order to regenerate its action.

The choice was a logical one. Throughout the decade, the JC had consistently been on the extreme left of the party. The vigour of their anti-militarist campaigns had often contrasted with the weakness and hesitation of the party leadership, and they had always been ready to criticize those party leaders who showed signs of succumbing to parliamentary or legalistic temptations—including lately, their own former hero Jacques Doriot. The Comintern now wished to bring new blood into the leadership, and give the whole party a jerk to the left. Once again it looked for new leaders from two main sources: the trade union movement and the youth organization. But the emphasis was now more heavily on the latter. Henri Barbé, the general secretary of the JC since 1926, arrived in Moscow in 1928 as delegate of both Party and JC, and Manuilsky appears to have set about grooming him to take over as party leader. At any rate it was Barbé who acted as the Comintern's emissary in forming what would later be known as 'the group'. This consisted simply of the JC leaders, acting in concert, with the pretension to provide leadership for the party as a whole.

The change of leadership was formalized at the Congress of Saint-Denis in April 1929. The 'rightists' Sellier, Renaud Jean and Bernard were dropped from the *Bureau Politique*. This left Cachin, who once again had refrained from defending his 'parliamentary cretinism' when the Comintern condemned it, as the only survivor from the pre-1924 leadership. As for Doriot, he was re-elected to the *Bureau Politique* but only after he had made a speech condemning his past errors and admitting that 'against me, the Party has been a hundred per cent in the right'.[23]

The exact composition of the new *Bureau Politique* is uncertain, since the decisions of the congress were kept secret. But at least four representatives of the JC were brought into it: Barbé, Célor, Ferrat, and Lozeray. In any case its importance seems to have declined, the leadership of the party being vested in a new 'collectively responsible political secretariat' of four members. Sémard, whose post of general secretary was suppressed, thus paid for his association with the 'opportunist' mistakes of the previous period. In order to justify this a whispering campaign was organized suggesting that he was an *agent provocateur*. Being in prison at the time, Sémard was unable to defend himself against these rumours. But the accusation was not brought against him officially; he was allowed to remain a member of the *Bureau Politique* and even promised the editorship of *L'Humanité* on his release.[24]

SECTARIANISM AND ISOLATION (1929–1930)

Two of the four new party secretaries belonged to the group emanating from the JC: Barbé and Célor. Barbé was responsible for liaison with the International, and therefore returned to Moscow where he was promoted to membership of the ECCI Presidium and of the Comintern's political secretariat. Célor was in charge of 'political co-ordination'. Maurice Thorez, who had been astute enough to make himself one of the earliest and most fervent advocates of the 'class against class' tactic in 1927, was allowed to retain control of organization and propaganda. The fourth member, responsible for trade union work and representing the trade union element in the party leadership, was Benoît Frachon. He was one of the middle-rank CGTU leaders who had been brought into the party Central Committee in 1926, and at the Congress of Saint-Denis it was he who presented the main report in Sémard's absence. Predictably enough he attacked the right-wing deviations in the party, depicting them as part of a new international right, and warned that France was slipping rapidly towards fascism and anti-Soviet war. Following instructions from the Comintern, the congress decided to organize a 'National Day' of struggle against the threat of capitalist war on the USSR. At 11 a.m. on 1 August 1929—chosen by the Comintern because it was the fifteenth anniversary of the outbreak of the First World War—all workers were to stop work and go out into the streets to demonstrate their hostility to 'imperialist war'.

The next three months were employed in preparing for the 1 August demonstration, not only by the party but by the government.

The arrest of Thorez* (for whom a warrant had been out since 1927) was followed in late July by that of Frachon and virtually every other Communist leader, big or small, whom the police could lay their hands on. On 1 August itself the police were out *en masse* and the day of protest was a failure. In the Paris region only some seven or eight thousand workers took part in the strike and demonstration, while in most provincial departments the day passed quite unnoticed. The slogan 'against the threat of anti-soviet war' (a threat perceptible only to those whose view of the world was conditioned by Comintern propaganda) had evidently had little impact on the workers, while the *Bureau Politique*'s call for 'the conquest of the street by and for the working class' could fairly convincingly be interpreted by the government as a call to insurrection. Further acts of repression followed; during the autumn the police were instructed to prevent any Communist demonstration in the streets, and charges of 'conspiracy against the security of the state' were brought against the whole of the party's Central Committee (154 people).

Inevitably the 'opportunist elements' who had been condemned at the Congress of Saint-Denis saw the failure of the demonstrations and the repression as results of the sectarian policy which they had opposed. Voices were raised in both the party and the CGTU to condemn 1 August as a putsch whose only effect had been to isolate the party from the masses. During the autumn Sellier emerged as the leader of this 'right-wing opposition'. In November he and five other members of the Paris municipal council made a public statement criticizing party policy. This was by now regarded as in itself a sufficient crime to justify their expulsion; they were expelled, and in December formed their own 'Parti Ouvrier et Paysan', which took away some of the PCF's support in the Paris suburbs, the area round Saint-Etienne and the Seine-Inférieure. The PCF was left with only one representative on the Paris municipal council.

The winter of 1929–30 marked the high point of the leftist line. As Ferrat was obliged to admit in 1931: 'It is noticeable at the end of 1929

---

* Thorez was arrested on 9 June after a secret meeting of the Central Committee at Achères, west of Paris. Other leaders on the wanted list were able to leave the building before the police closed in on it, and Thorez later claimed that he had been betrayed by Célor (who in 1932 was accused of being a police spy). Célor and Barbé assert, however, that Thorez was caught because he remained in the building out of panic after the alarm had been given, and tried to hide in a cupboard whose door did not reach down to the floor, so that the police had a clear view of his shoes and trouser turn-ups. (*Est & Ouest* no. 177 [1–15 July 1957], p. 8.)

and at the beginning of 1930 that, in spite of the positive results achieved thanks to the policy of *redressement*, the state of the Communist movement in France is not satisfactory in spite of a favourable objective situation.' Party membership declined (from perhaps 45,000 in 1929 to 38,000 in 1930), and the print order of *L'Humanité* 'fell to 150,000'—though even this figure seems improbably high.[25]

In fact not all the party's difficulties were the leadership's fault, except in so far as by calling the 1 August demonstration the leadership had given the government its pretext for repression. One of the most embarrassing acts of repression, from the party's point of view, was the police raid of 16 August on the premises of the *Banque Ouvrière et Paysanne*, in which the funds of the various organizations controlled by the party were deposited. The accounts of the bank were seized, and as a result it had to go into liquidation. This posed a serious threat to *L'Humanité*, which had guaranteed the bank's original capital and which, moreover, itself enjoyed a large overdraft: on both these heads it was in danger of being called on to satisfy the bank's creditors by the public receiver. In order to stave off this threat drastic cuts were made in the paper's expenditure (by means of an administrative reorganization) and the overdraft was gradually paid off by Comintern subsidies disguised as advertising revenue from an international press combine which the Comintern controlled. This of course was on the quiet. In public, the paper launched an appeal to the working class (the first of many), which had a certain success. Those willing to contribute were organized into 'Comités de défense de l'Humanité', which survive to this day.[26] (Their main function is now to provide unpaid salesmen for the Sunday edition.)

But, says Ferrat, these committees in their infancy were 'virtually liquidated . . . by a clumsy, mechanical and sectarian policy'. At the same time local elections showed a decline in the Communist vote, and CGTU membership also fell off. All this was later blamed on 'a certain underestimation of the immediate demands of the working class' and on the abandonment of the united front tactic.

> An inadmissible attitude towards the socialist workers, considered as enemies, in the same category as their leaders, spread throughout the Party. Our methods of agitation and propaganda, and our approach to the masses, remained too often at the level of repeating general phrases, stereotyped clichés and abstract formulae inaccessible to the masses.

(One such formula was the phrase 'social fascism', imported from Germany and applied to the SFIO.) Ferrat, himself a member of the *Bureau Politique* responsible for this state of affairs, goes on to list the vices prevalent inside the Party:

> . . . a certain practice of abusive and mechanical purging and a certain resistance to recruitment. Failure to deploy a real self-criticism involving the initiative and activity of all Party members. Failure to explain clearly and in detail, so as to convince all Party members, the organizational measures taken, especially against the 'popiste' renegades [i.e. Sellier and his group]. Denial or under-estimation of the sectarian leftist deviation and tolerance of 'left' methods which, under cover of intransigence and unshakeable fidelity to the Party line, in fact favour the development of opportunist deviations. Inadequate use of methods of explanation, conviction and re-education in the training of cadres, who remain very weak.[27]

THE DAWN OF CORRECTION (1930)

These errors were not at once appreciated by the Comintern, since they were only a reflection of its own extremist line. In October 1929, at the Tenth ECCI Plenum, Molotov asserted: 'The CP of France is one of the best sections of the International. It is improving considerably; that is beyond doubt.'[28] But by June 1930 more accurate information appears to have filtered through to the leaders of the Comintern (which at this time had no permanent representative in Paris), and ECCI summoned a special delegation from the PCF to review the situation. The delegation included Barbé (who had now been replaced by Ferrat as the PCF's permanent delegate in Moscow), Thorez, Frachon, Doriot, and representatives of the Paris region, the Nord, Alsace-Lorraine and the *Jeunesses Communistes*. (Thorez had been released from prison in April after voluntarily paying the fine imposed on him by the court. This was a breach of party discipline which Thorez, with some courage, took it on himself to declare 'in conformity with the Party's interests'.[29])

At the *ad hoc* conference in Moscow, Molotov drew attention to the PCF's errors, and especially its failure to apply the united front (a first hint that the Comintern was preparing yet another change of tack). Doriot was again criticized, but this time for not taking a sufficiently active part in the party's affairs. This perhaps implied that there had been some sense in his attitude to the 'class against class' policy after all.

In July the delegation reported back to the PCF Central Committee, explaining that from now on the party must pay more attention to the workers' everyday concerns. Thorez explained that the term 'social-fascism', though correct, should not be taken as meaning that social democracy was *completely* fascist, since then it would not be social fascism but fascism *tout court*: 'The characteristic of social-fascism is that it retains a series of elements which enable it to preserve its influence over the majority of the working class.' He warned that the Socialist Party was making progress, and called on the Central Committee and *Bureau Politique* to take urgent measures to stop this, by carrying out a 'tournant' (i.e. embarking on a new tack) in united front policy:

> That doesn't mean an attenuation of the struggle against social-democracy. . . . No, on the contrary, we must move on to a more vigorous, more systematic and, above all, much more consistent offensive against the Socialist Party and its leaders, but at the same time develop our united front tactic to win over the socialist workers. It is indispensable to draw a distinction between the Socialist Party, its leadership, its cadres and the workers who are behind or who are still in the Socialist Party. You cannot lump together Boncour [one of the right-wing Socialist leaders] and a miner who votes for the socialist candidate.[30]

This was in essence a revival of Zinoviev's 'united front from below', which had been a left slogan in 1924 but now came as a corrective to the ultra-left line of the past two years. Within the party, according to Thorez, opportunism was still the 'principal danger', but once again it was also necessary to fight against 'leftism, which feeds opportunism and in practice comes to the same thing'. This policy was encapsulated in a new Comintern slogan, to be generalized the following year: the 'internal struggle on two fronts'.

Thorez also criticized the structure of the party leadership: 'The *Bureau Politique* is heavy and slow to act. . . . We need a single comrade to be politically responsible.' It had evidently been decided in Moscow that he should be that single comrade, probably because he could not be held responsible for the sectarian excesses committed while he was in prison. Accordingly the *Bureau Politique* was reduced to seven members (Barbé, Cachin, Doriot, Frachon, Monmousseau, Sémard, Thorez) and Thorez became its 'secretary'.

The other members of the 'collective secretariat' were thus downgraded, but there was as yet no suggestion that Barbé and Célor would be held specially to blame for its errors. Barbé remained for the time being a high dignitary of the party, with even a hint of a martyr's crown because he was on the run from the police. Thus at a National Conference held from 28 February to 1 March 1931, Thorez said: 'I must salute, in the name of the Conference, comrade Henri Barbé, whom the repression prevents from being with us . . .'—and who, he added, had written and presented to the Central Committee the report which he, Thorez, had just read out.[31] Célor was elected to both presidium and secretariat of the ECCI by the Eleventh Plenum in April 1931.[32]

CAMPAIGN AGAINST THE GROUP (1931–1932)

The decision to make scapegoats of Barbé and Célor must have been taken by Manuilsky soon after this Plenum, at which the previous ultra-sectarian line was criticized and the 'struggle on two fronts' generalized. Once again events in Russia and Germany helped to determine the fate of French Communist leaders: Stalin was anxious to get rid of Heinz Neumann, who had been one of the leading exponents of the leftist line both in the Comintern and in the KPD, because of his connections with the Lominadze group which had come out against Stalin's forced collectivization policy in 1930.[33] The hunt for leftists was therefore on throughout the Comintern. There were plenty of people who could suitably be denounced, but as usual the denouncing was not done by their former opponents but by those who had shared in their errors. In early June the PCF Central Committee passed a resolution denouncing the 'group spirit' which prevailed in the party, and in July Raymond Guyot 'confessed' to the *Bureau Politique* that he was one of the members of a 'Group' (composed of the former JC leaders and led by Barbé and Célor) which had been secretly manipulating the party for the last two years.

The affair was treated as a scandal, and sanctions were taken against the leading members of the 'Group': Guyot himself was 'excused', having so to speak turned King's Evidence, but Billoux (the author of an article which was now described as the Group's 'theoretical' brochure) and Lozeray were censured, while Barbé and Célor, the alleged ringleaders, were demoted from their party offices.*

* According to Lazitch, Manuilsky made a personal visit to France to organize the 'elimination of the Barbé-Célor faction'. Lazitch's account is based on information from Barbé and Célor themselves, and from Ferrat and Vassart. ('Two Instruments of Comintern Control', in *The Comintern: Historical Highlights*, ed. Milorad M. Drachkovitch and Branko Lazitch [Stanford, California, 1966], p. 52.)

THOREZ AND FRIED

The most important effect of this development was to enthrone Thorez as the official party leader (though, contrary to later mythology, he did not yet enjoy the title of general secretary). The decision was probably not taken without some hesitation by the rulers of the Comintern. According to Ferrat, who was in Moscow until the summer of 1931, the Comintern secretariat had little confidence in the members of the new leadership and 'Manuilsky especially did not have a high opinion of Thorez.'[34] Certainly at the Eleventh Plenum Thorez had been severely criticized by Manuilsky and other Russian leaders.[35] They therefore decided to send to France a team of experienced international militants who would take the party directly in hand. It was led by Eugen Fried, a member of the Czechoslovak party who had worked in the Comintern's Orgburo, and who now became personally responsible for the carrying out of all the Comintern secretariat's directives in France. He was aided by a number of specialized 'instructors', including the Romanian Anna Pauker, the Hungarian Ernö Gerö and the Pole Georges Kagan, who was put in charge of agitprop and the *Cahiers du Bolchévisme*. Each member of this team was personally responsible to the Comintern secretariat for a given section of the PCF Central Committee (organization, trade unions, colonial, etc.). Their collective brief therefore went much further than that of any of the Comintern emissaries who had succeeded each other in France during the 1920s.

According to Ferrat, who returned from Moscow to rejoin the party leadership in August 1931 (his membership of the original JC 'Group' was apparently not held against him), the team headed by Fried in fact took over the real leadership of the party during the winter of 1931–2. The official and public leadership became only its 'executive agent and legal screen'. But its existence remained a secret from all but the members of the *Bureau Politique* and a few members of the Central Committee of the top party bureaucracy. 'The PCF was thus taken completely in hand by the Stalinist machine, and politically domesticated to an extent that probably no other party ever was.'

As for Thorez, he cultivated a close personal relationship with Fried which, says Ferrat, gave him a new authority in the *Bureau Politique*: each member knew that his directives and explanations were exactly those given him the day before or that very morning by Fried, and therefore no one dared to contradict him. 'Hence when he spoke

149

in party assemblies or in public, everyone was struck by his new assurance and saw him as the party leader.'[36]

Thorez began to assert himself as early as August 1931, soon after Guyot's 'revelations' to the *Bureau Politique* and before the campaign against the 'Group' had been made public. He wrote a series of articles in *L'Humanité* which appeared to appeal to the working class over the heads of the other party leaders. He deplored the lack of free discussion in the party and the overbearing, sectarian attitude of the cadres. 'Formally,' he wrote, 'we proclaim the benefits of self-criticism, but as soon as a comrade does criticize he is covered with reproaches and it is held against him, if indeed he is not accused of trying to break up the Party. If anyone comes out with an idea, people at once start asking: *Which deviation can that be?*'[37] This was followed up with an article entitled 'The Mouths Are Opening', in which Thorez printed extracts from readers' letters to show that his campaign was finding an echo in the party rank-and-file.[38] And on 26 August he took up the theme at a meeting of the Central Committee: 'The mouths have begun to open, from now on they must not be closed.' At this meeting he passed on the Comintern's criticisms of the PCF's failure to bring off the 'tournant' decreed the previous year, but rather than take responsibility himself he hinted that the 'Group' was to blame. He thus began to assume the role in which party hagiography would later depict him, that of restorer of the democracy of which Barbé, Célor and their acolytes had conspired to deprive the party. But this claim is scarcely borne out by the record: there is little evidence of more active discussion within the party after 1931 than before. If anything the reverse. Ferrat, admittedly not an impartial witness, asserts that the atmosphere of the party became more stifling than before. Up to 1929–30 there had still been some discussion in the party on political problems, and it had been possible to identify different 'courants de pensée' or even 'tendances'. But 'from then on it was all over. You can always call on mouths to open in a party which doesn't work out its own policy, which has no right to question its policy but only to discuss ways of applying it. A leaden mantle descended on the party.'[39]

5

The Party and
the Nation

1920–1934

In the last two chapters we have been concerned principally with the internal life of the PCF and its relations with the International. The party's impact on French politics and society has been referred to only incidentally. This impact was in fact small in the period before 1934. Party members numbered only a few tens of thousands; Communist voters were one million or fewer in an electorate of over eleven million; and the party's political line was such as to ensure its isolation from the other political forces in the country. The interest of the period therefore lies mainly in the party's internal development, as it progressively acquired the characteristics which were to mark it later on, when its impact on general French history would be much greater.

In this chapter, however, I shall try to summarize briefly the impact which the PCF *did* have on the French nation before 1934. It made itself felt in four main ways: first by attacking two institutions then considered of overriding national importance—the empire and the army—and thereby drawing on itself measures of judicial and administrative repression; secondly by its control of an important fraction of the trade union movement; thirdly by its participation in elections; and fourthly by the influence it exerted among certain categories of intellectuals.

Anti-Militarism, Anti-Imperialism and Repression

In accepting the Twenty-One Conditions, the Congress of Tours had admitted 'the absolute necessity to carry on systematic and persistent propaganda and agitation among the troops', if necessary by illegal means, and had acknowledged a duty 'to support every colonial liberation movement not merely in words but in deeds, to demand the expulsion of [French] imperialists from the colonies . . . and to carry

151

on systematic agitation among [French] troops against any oppression of the colonial peoples'. In so doing the nascent Communist Party knew well that it was committing itself to head-on conflict with the forces of the bourgeois state, which regarded the army and the colonies as sacrosanct national institutions, to be preserved at all costs from subversion.

WAR SCARE OF 1921

This commitment was put to the test almost at once, during the war scare of 1921 (see above, p. 71). It was fulfilled less by the party as such than by its youth wing, which took the initiative in urging reservists of the class of 1919 not to obey the recall to the colours ordered by the government, and warning the class of 1921 not to let itself be used against workers on strike or against 'a revolutionary Germany or Russia'. The results were police raids on the offices of the JC (whose title at this time was in fact *Fédération nationale des Jeunesses socialistes communistes*), proceedings against their anti-militarist paper *Le Conscrit*, and the arrest of numerous JC militants including the leaders Laporte and Doriot. The party was of course obliged to support its youth wing against the repression, but in doing so it ill concealed its embarrassment at the boldness of the JC slogans. The regular JC newspaper *L'Avant-Garde* complained on 15 June: 'Never had the threats of war been so acute. Yet never had such a torpor benumbed the working class and also, alas, its conscious vanguard.' The party contented itself with backing up the JC in editorials in *L'Humanité*, without taking any action comparable to theirs on its own account.[1]

RUHR CAMPAIGN (1923)

The next important wave of anti-militarist agitation came with the Ruhr crisis of January 1923. As we have seen (above, pp. 82, 95–6) this came immediately after the resignation of Frossard, at the moment when the left assumed effective leadership of the party. Once again the lead in the agitation was taken by the JC, but this time the party leadership (and that of the CGTU) also committed itself fully, and shared the burden of the repression. Marcel Cachin himself, the former 'social patriot', was one of the French delegates at the Essen conference of Western European Communist Parties on 6 January, and made a speech to a largely German audience attacking the French government's policy towards Germany in violent terms. The

conference pronounced in favour of sabotaging the military undertakings of the French bourgeoisie and preparing for a general strike in
France in case of war or a lasting occupation of the Ruhr. Steps were
taken to distribute Communist propaganda among the French troops
and undermine their morale. The French delegates then toured
western Germany making inflammatory speeches.[2] Soon after their
return to France they were arrested and charged with plotting against
the internal and external security of the state. Gabriel Péri, one of the
JC leaders, was also charged with 'inciting soldiers to disobedience'.[3]
From 11 January onwards, the JC carried on an intense agitation
among the French occupying troops in the Ruhr itself, distributing
over two million tracts, leaflets and manifestos, many of them inside
the barracks. They created cells in army units and established
contacts with local KPD organizations. Leaders like Doriot moved
clandestinely in and out of the occupied area. By May 1923 there were
nearly 200 cells in French military units. French soldiers fraternized
with German workers, gave them food, and sometimes refused to fire
on them when ordered.[4]

All this contrasted sharply with the party's previous achievements,
and made a great impression on the Communists themselves. Yet
little trace of it can be found in the general history books;[5] there was
nothing like a general mutiny of the French army in the Ruhr, and
certainly no upheaval in France remotely comparable to the near-
collapse of the German state which the occupation produced. The
majority of the French troops remained loyal, if not aggressively
anti-German. Technically the occupation was a success: the French
were able to operate German coal-mines, railways and factories in
spite of German 'passive resistance'. Politically it was a failure,
largely because of Poincaré's failure to exploit it. But as it turned
against the government French public opinion was much less
influenced by the PCF than by the nascent 'Cartel des Gauches'
(Radicals and Socialists) which was to win the elections the following
year.

MOROCCAN CAMPAIGN (1925)

A further wave of anti-militarist activity came with the Moroccan war
of 1925. This was also the first large-scale anti-colonial agitation
which the party had undertaken. In its early years it had had some
difficulty in getting its own members to accept the International's
programme of total hostility to French colonialism and unconditional

support for all colonial liberation movements. A first step had been taken in 1921 with the creation of a Colonial Studies Committee at party headquarters and the passage of a resolution at the Congress of Marseilles recognizing 'the need to create as soon as possible in the colonies an opposition movement, animated by the communist spirit, against capitalism and its two special forms, imperialism and militarism'.[6] But although the party had some success in recruiting immigrants from the colonies in France, its sections in the colonies themselves were composed mainly of European settlers. Hence the prevalence of heresies such as that expressed in a resolution of the section at Sidi-bel-Abbès in Algeria, which was singled out for condemnation by Trotsky at the Fourth World Congress. According to this resolution, 'A victorious rising of the Moslem masses in Algeria which did not come after a victorious rising of the proletarian masses in the mother-country would inevitably bring Algeria back towards a regime close to feudalism, which cannot be the aim of a communist action.'[7] Eighteen months later, on the eve of the Fifth World Congress, the party was again obliged to admit that its activity 'has not responded, on the colonial front, to the directives of the Communist International';[8] and at the congress itself its inactivity was vigorously attacked by one of its own colonial members, Nguyen Ai Quoc (the future Ho Chi Minh).[9]

In this domain, as in others, Bolshevization made the party more responsive to the Comintern's directives, and in the first instance this meant a swing to the left. Events in the Rif mountains of northern Morocco, where since 1921 the Berber leader Abd-el-Krim had been carrying on a successful resistance against the Spanish army, gave the PCF the chance to demonstrate its new anti-colonial zeal. In September 1924 a telegram was despatched to Abd-el-Krim, signed by Sémard for the party and Doriot for the JC, congratulating him on his latest victory and expressing the hope that he would continue the struggle 'against all imperialists, French included, until the complete liberation of Moroccan soil'.[10] This caused a considerable scandal in France, and the bourgeois press announced solemnly that henceforth the Communists could no longer be considered Frenchmen since they were deliberately betraying French interests.[11]

In April 1925, after a series of frontier incidents, Abd-el-Krim duly invaded the French zone of Morocco, with the result that French troops became directly involved in the war. The party at once began to campaign against the war with four slogans:

Fraternization between the French soldiers and the Rif army.
Not one man and not one penny in France for the Moroccan war.
Peace in the Rif.
Total evacuation of Morocco by France.[12]

The first of these slogans was clearly treasonable, and only the third was supported by the Socialist Party. An 'action committee' was set up which therefore included only organizations more or less controlled by the PCF (JC, CGTU, *Association Républicaine des Anciens Combattants*, 'committees of proletarian unity' and the *Clarté* group of intellectuals). On 17 May some 15,000 Parisians attended a mass protest meeting against the war at Luna-Park. The party combined its anti-war campaign with that for the 1925 municipal elections, and with the traditional commemoration of the Paris Commune in the Père-Lachaise cemetery, attended by over 50,000 people on 24 May. Similar meetings and demonstrations were held in most of France's big cities during May and early June. The campaign was backed up by the party press, and by fiery speeches from Communist deputies in the Chamber, notably Cachin and Doriot. For the first time, the party made a special effort to mobilize women: a meeting of working women from the Paris region was held on 7 June and a delegation of women whose sons were in the army in Morocco or whose husbands had been killed in the Great War was sent to the prime minister's residence.

Once again the JC took the lead in organizing agitation inside the army, publishing and distributing leaflets in French and Arabic as well as their regular anti-militarist journals *Le Conscrit* and *La Caserne*. As in the Ruhr, this agitation had some success. There were demonstrations in barracks, on military trains heading for ports of embarkation for Morocco, and on ships of the Mediterranean squadron. Incidents occurred even among units in Morocco itself, where the culprits risked summary execution.

In July a second colonial war broke out in Syria, where the Druze tribesmen wiped out a French column and a rebel government was set up in Damascus. The PCF extended its campaign to include this war too, and began to win some support from left-wing Socialists who were disillusioned with the 'Cartelliste' government which the Socialist Party had supported, but which seemed to be drifting into a policy of high taxes to pay for overseas wars rather than social reform. In certain areas workers from the Socialist Party and the CGT began to join the PCF-sponsored 'committees of proletarian unity' in the factories. The first of a series of 'worker and peasant congresses' was held in Paris early in July. Its 2,470 delegates (including 130 'Socialists' and 160 'Confederates', i.e. CGT members) voted for a twenty-four-hour general strike which would link the war issue with domestic social problems. They also voted to transform the 'action committee' into a 'central action committee', of which Thorez, newly returned from his first visit to Moscow, was elected president. This committee took over the running of the anti-war campaign and organized further 'worker and peasant congresses' in the provinces to prepare for the proposed general strike.

But the three-month notice given for the strike also gave the government time to organize repression. Judicial proceedings were opened against the party, against the organizations adhering to the 'central action committee' and against *L'Humanité*. Altogether 274 militants were arrested and over 120 years of prison sentences handed out. And though a few Socialist sections and CGT departmental unions came out unequivocally against the war, the leadership and the mass of the rank-and-file in both organizations remained deeply suspicious of a Communist campaign whose obvious aim was to 'plumer la volaille'.* In particular, they were unwilling to condone the 'demagogic excitation of the soldiers', which, in the words voted by a Socialist congress on 15 August, 'makes them at once the victims of French militarism and of the foreign policy of Bolshevism'.[13]

The strike was finally held on 12 October, despite a last-minute demand from the provincial organizers that it be put off yet another week. The party claimed that 900,000 workers took part; but its success was limited to the Paris suburbs and the northern mining area, and the general impact was small. The usual battles occurred between demonstrators and police. In Suresnes, outside Paris, a Communist demonstrator was killed. In Paris itself Doriot was arrested after injuring a policeman (who later died—see above, p. 137).

The Rif war went on until May 1926, but the PCF's campaign against it dwindled rapidly after the 12 October strike. Its vigour had proved embarrassing to Moscow at a moment when the Soviet leaders were seeking to improve relations with France. The fact that it had clearly failed to interest the majority of the French working class was

---

* Treint, the author of this notorious interpretation of united front tactics (see above, p. 75), was still the dominant figure in the PCF at this time; and the campaign was addressed to 'Socialist workers', not the Socialist Party as such, in accordance with the 'united front from below' doctrine which was still in force.

blamed on the sectarian attitude of the Treint leadership which had authorized collaboration only with those who accepted the party's most extreme slogans, such as evacuation of Morocco and fraternization with enemy troops. At the PCF National Conference which drew up the open letter of 2 December, marking the end of the 'Zinovievist' ultra-left period (see above, p. 116), it was implicitly admitted that a much wider united front could have been achieved on a more moderate anti-war platform. This point of view had all along been urged by the right-wing opposition (Loriot, Dunois, etc.) but their contention that the 12 October strike had been a failure was of course firmly rejected. At the Sixth ECCI Plenum, in February–March 1926, the PCF and CGTU received a formal *satisfecit* for their 'fine and courageous campaign against the Moroccan and Syrian wars', which to all intents and purposes marked the closure of the episode.

Even while it lasted, the campaign had given little satisfaction to some of those most directly interested. At a meeting of the party's 'central colonial commission', probably in February 1926, an Algerian speaker was reported as denouncing the campaign for its essentially verbal nature: '. . . meetings which serve no purpose except to satisfy loud-mouths like Cachin and Berthon who go and hold forth at Luna Park while the capitalist bosses continue shamefully exploiting the colonials'. (André Berthon was a Communist deputy who had met Abd-el-Krim's brother in Paris in 1923; during the 1925 campaign much was made of this rather tenuous connection, and the two-year-old conversation was even published in *L'Humanité* as an interview with Abd-el-Krim himself.[14]) Two years later, at the Sixth World Congress, an Algerian delegate was to point out that local PCF organizations had made little or no attempt to involve North African workers in France in the campaign, which consequently found hardly any response among them. It was at this time that the 'Union Intercoloniale', which the party had more or less controlled, began to break up into separate national movements. Many colonials were disillusioned with the PCF's attitude to colonial problems, which seemed to have no consistent theme except the desire to recruit support among colonial immigrants for its own domestic activities. In June and July 1926 *Cahiers du Bolchévisme* carried two articles in which a West Indian leader, soon to leave the party, accused it of practising 'une politique de clientèle' while paying little or no attention to specifically colonial interests or aspirations and remaining ignorant of colonial political realities.[15]

But 'French imperialism' was not active only overseas. The 'worker and peasant congress' held at Strasbourg in September 1925 to organize the campaign against the Moroccan war in Alsace-Lorraine was also the point of departure for a longer-lasting campaign against the oppression of the Alsaciens-Lorrains themselves.

The return of Alsace-Lorraine to France was of course part of the Versailles settlement, which the PCF and the Comintern had many times denounced. But at the time when it occurred it was one of the least contested parts of that settlement. Cachin himself, in December 1918, had quoted with approval the British ambassador's comment on the delirious welcome given to Poincaré and Clemenceau in Metz: 'On a parlé d'un plébiscite: le voici!'[16] Socialists in fact had an additional reason to welcome the recovery of the lost provinces, since it brought them a valuable reinforcement in the shape of a strong and well-organized section of the pre-war SPD. But this factor also obliged them to take account of the particular problems and aspirations of the inhabitants of the recovered territory, 83% of whom spoke a dialect very close to German.

In the immediate aftermath of victory these problems and aspirations were submerged in the general enthusiasm, and in the 1919 elections the *Bloc National* won an absolute majority in the three 'recovered' *départements* (Moselle, Bas-Rhin and Haut-Rhin). But much of this enthusiasm was soon dissipated by the tactless policy of the victors, who forbade the use of German for official purposes and set about subjecting the territory to the full rigours of French bureaucracy. The opportunities for a party which could associate national and economic grievances were suggested as early as 1920, when the language question played an important part in the local success of the great railway strike. Within the local Socialist Party the pull of the Third International proved strong, especially in the Moselle which at Tours was one of the nine federations giving all their mandates to the Cachin-Frossard motion, and which brought with it to the PCF the Socialist newspaper *Volkstribüne*, published in Metz. In 1923 the CGTU was able to launch a three-week strike among the Lorraine miners in sympathy with their colleagues in the Ruhr; and in 1924 the Moselle and the Bas-Rhin were among the seventeen *départements* in which the PCF won more than 10% of the votes.

Particularist feeling grew stronger in Alsace-Lorraine after 1924, when the anticlerical 'Cartelliste' prime minister Edouard Herriot set out to abolish all legal distinctions between Alsace-Lorraine and the rest of France, notably the special educational and religious laws. A vigorous protest campaign against the government's plans was carried on by an alliance of Catholics, 'regionalists' and Alsatian separatists, and in January 1925 Herriot was forced to recognize the legal validity of the 1801 Concordat in Alsace and abandon his attempt to enforce the separation of church and state in that province. But the political problem remained in suspense and the resentment of the Alsaciens-Lorrains was largely unappeased. Since the Socialists had discredited themselves by supporting the Cartel (the Socialist deputy for Strasbourg had actually proposed an increase in the number of administrative services to be transferred to Paris), it was relatively easy for the Communists to win the support of the workers and poorer townsfolk by putting forward autonomist slogans together with economic demands. Accordingly the 'worker and peasant congress' of 1925 addressed a manifesto 'to all the workers, peasants and artisans of Alsace and Lorraine', calling for 'the right of free determination'. The people of Alsace-Lorraine, it said, should be able 'to determine their own choice by a free plebiscite'. At the same time it warned them against following the Catholic-dominated autonomist movement, whose only purpose was to protect the interests of the clerical bourgeoisie. Following Lenin, who before 1918 had attacked the French Socialists for 'compromising with the French bourgeoisie which wants to annex the whole of Alsace by force' and 'being afraid to see the formation of a separate state, even a small one',[17] the congress recalled that 'the communists of the oppressor state must defend the right to self-determination, up to and including separation—which does not mean obligation to separate'. A plebiscite, it added, would only be valid if Alsace-Lorraine were first evacuated by the French civil and military authorities; and the concluding slogan was: 'Alsace-Lorraine for the Alsaciens-Lorrains!'

The Treaty of Locarno signed the following month, under which Germany agreed to regard her new western frontiers as inviolable, did not by any means discourage the French Communists from their championship of self-determination for Alsace-Lorraine. Nor did the Comintern's disavowal of ultra-left policies during the ensuing winter: this merely made them less fussy about their allies. In 1926 the various autonomist groups, of mainly religious inspiration (Catholic and Protestant), joined together to form the *Heimatbund* whose manifesto also proclaimed the right of Alsatians to self-determination. The Communists formed an alliance with this movement, and both were victims of government repression in 1927. For the 1928 elections the Alsatian autonomists were made an exception to the 'class against class' tactic, with the result that the party was able to win a seat at Strasbourg and score above 10% in all three Alsace-Lorraine *départements*. The following year the same alliance triumphed in the municipal elections at Strasbourg and Mulhouse, and one of the local Communist leaders, Charles Hueber, became mayor of Strasbourg. But by then the ultra-left wind was blowing strongly once more. 'Profound opportunist tendencies' were suddenly diagnosed among the Alsace-Lorraine Communist leaders, who were accused of practising 'an electoralist policy of unprincipled alliance with the clerical autonomist movement, separating themselves from the French proletariat and its party'. Hueber was expelled from the party along with the deputy, Mourer, and some others.

From then on the party had no further truck with the 'bourgeois' autonomist movement (soon to be compromised by Nazi support). But for several years more it continued to denounce the *de facto* incorporation of Alsace-Lorraine into France and to call for free self-determination. Mere autonomy was discarded as an inadequate goal and replaced by the demand for independence. As late as April 1933, after Hitler had come to power in Germany, Thorez was calling (in a speech made in German in Strasbourg) for 'the absolute and unconditional independence of the people of Alsace and of Lorraine, the immediate withdrawal of all occupation troops and all French officials from Alsace-Lorraine'.

'LE COMMUNISME, VOILÀ L'ENNEMI' (1927)
Although 1926–7 was a period of relative moderation in PCF activities, this was not generally perceived by public opinion. The party's self-criticism for the extremist anti-colonial slogans of 1925 was based explicitly on tactical grounds, not on any doubt that these slogans were fundamentally right. In any case, it was confined to internal party meetings and the pages of *Cahiers du Bolchévisme*, and wrapped up in theoretical language, so that most sections of public opinion remained quite unaware of it. For the bourgeois press the

PCF had placed itself, by its attacks on the empire and the army, outside the national pale, and for most sections of public opinion its advocacy of self-determination for Alsace-Lorraine made matters even worse, since this was tantamount to demanding partition of the French homeland. Moreover, anti-Communist fears were kept alive during 1927 by the continued anti-militarist campaigns of the JC, now directed mainly against the military laws, providing for the 'organization of the nation in time of war' and for a general reform of army organization and recruitment, which came before the Chamber of Deputies during the spring and summer.

But probably more important than the Communist agitation itself was the government's attitude towards it. In 1924–5, when the right-wing press made a great song and dance about the Communist danger after the success of a Communist demonstration at the transfer of Jaurès's ashes to the Pantheon (while Treint at the height of his ultra-left zeal launched a number of untimely slogans such as 'fascism is here' and 'revolutionary tribunal for the instigators of price rises'), the *Cartel des Gauches* government had done its best to minimize the danger, and had confined itself to a few token acts of repression such as the raid on the party school at Bobigny. It also announced that it would not use 'systematic violence' against Communism, refusing to be deterred from amnestying Jacques Sadoul (who though condemned to death *in absentia* had just returned to France), and even prosecuting one of the right-wing newspapers which accused it of conniving at Communist preparations for insurrection.[18] The attitude of the Poincaré government which came to power in July 1926 was quite different. It had an interest in emphasizing the Communist danger in order to cement the 'national union' and to embarrass the Socialists who had refused to join it. In addition, the Radical Albert Sarraut, who was Poincaré's Minister of the Interior, was anxious to persuade his right-wing allies to accept a return to the pre-war electoral system of single-member constituencies, to which the right was traditionally hostile. The best way of doing this was to emphasize the Communist danger and put it about that under proportional representation the next parliament would contain seventy Communist deputies, who would 'paralyse the whole mechanism', whereas in single-member constituencies nearly all the Communist candidates would be beaten on the second ballot by an alliance of right and centre.[19] With these considerations in mind Sarraut sent out special instructions to the prefects in April 1927 for the repression of Communist activities in the army, and three days later followed these up with a public speech at Constantine (Algeria) on the theme 'le communisme, voilà l'ennemi'. To show that the minister meant what he said, Monmousseau, the general secretary of the CGTU, was arrested in the middle of the 1 May demonstrations at Dunkirk and given a four-month prison sentence for inciting soldiers to disobedience. And the following day Poincaré himself took up the anti-Communist theme in a speech to the general council of the Meuse department.

A wave of prison sentences followed, including ones of eight months on Sémard, who was arrested on 10 June but released by mistake a fortnight later, and on Thorez, who eluded the police and went into hiding. In most cases the charge was 'provocation of the military to disobedience', relating to speeches or articles dating back to the Moroccan war. The party had had the sense to entrust legal responsibility for most of its publications to militants covered by parliamentary immunity, with the result that in a number of cases the government was obliged to ask the Chamber of Deputies for permission to arrest one of its members. For the next three and a half years the question of proceedings against Communist deputies became a recurrent parliamentary problem. In spite of the acrimonious relations between the two parties, the Socialists always voted against imprisonment out of solidarity, while the Radicals were torn between their love of parliamentary privilege and their loyalty to Poincaré's 'national union'. On several occasions deputies were arrested during the parliamentary recess, only to be freed again by a vote of the Chamber when the session resumed. During the general election of April 1928 the party made much of the fact that several of its candidates were victims of repression, either in prison or on the run. Cachin and Doriot were triumphantly re-elected while in prison and Jacques Duclos, who slipped in and out of election meetings under the noses of the police, was able to hold a working-class district of Paris against no less an opponent than Léon Blum. Neither he nor Marty, who won a by-election while in prison in February 1929, were allowed to take their seats until January 1931 (when the Radicals momentarily returned to power after two years in opposition).

REPRESSION OF 1929–1930

During 1929 and 1930 there was a more or less continuous trial of strength between the party, now set once again on an ultra-left course, and the right-wing governments of Poincaré, Briand and Tardieu. Following the line of the Sixth World Congress, the party intensified both its anti-military and its anti-colonial agitation. From 1928 onwards, *L'Humanité* published regular statements on colonial problems calling in the most intransigent terms for national independence for all French colonies, and the party gave strong support to a passive resistance movement which developed in the French Congo. But at the end of 1929 it again had to be criticized by ECCI for the essentially verbal nature of its anti-colonial work, and undoubtedly during that year much more of its energy had gone into the campaign against the government's supposedly bellicose intentions towards the Soviet Union (see above, pp. 143–4), which drew down on it the most severe repression it had yet experienced. The ultra-left slogans of the Congress of Saint-Denis were immediately answered by some 4,000 preventive arrests in Paris on the eve of the traditional 1 May demonstration. At the end of May an appeal court confirmed a four-year prison sentence on André Marty (for an open letter to Marshal Foch written in 1927) and reduced him to the status of a common-law criminal. In June followed the arrest of Thorez, in July raids on *L'Humanité* and the party headquarters, the arrest of Frachon and ninety-five other party cadres at a meeting to prepare the 1 August demonstration (all were charged with conspiracy against the security of the state), and a further wave of arrests of party and trade union leaders in the days preceding the demonstration itself. The extent of the repression was such that even the Socialists became worried, and Paul Faure wrote in *Le Populaire* on 25 July of 'a redoubtable crisis of reaction in which republican liberties and the principles of democracy are in danger'. On 1 August itself both *L'Humanité* and *Internationale Communiste* (the French edition of the Comintern journal) were seized, and the police brutally dispersed such small groups of demonstrators as dared to gather. As Ferrat wrote two years later in his official history of the party:

> For the first time the Party was in fact reduced almost to illegality; not only the Party leadership but the leaderships of regions and *rayons* became illegal. *L'Humanité* was suspended; the premises of the Party, of the CGTU and of *L'Humanité* were rifled by the police, most of the militants arrested on the eve of August 1st and the whole leadership of the Party were charged with conspiracy against the internal and external security of the State. They were not to be released until May 1930.[20]

By the end of the year, according to *L'Humanité*, 1,127 Communists had been prosecuted and 597 sentenced to a total of 260 years in prison and over a million francs of fines and legal costs.[21]

In 1930 the same scenario was re-enacted but on a somewhat smaller scale, both sides no doubt feeling less conviction about its seriousness. Again the Comintern decreed an international anti-war day for 1 August, and again the government forestalled it by numerous arrests on 31 July for 'incitement to disorder'. Those arrested included the manager of *L'Humanité*, who was given a two-year prison sentence. The following year 1 August was again declared an 'international day of struggle against war', but passed without notable incident in France. But a demonstration in Saint-Denis to mark 'international youth day', on 6 September 1931, was forbidden by the strongly anti-Communist prefect of police, Jean Chiappe, and resulted in some hundred arrests.

The trial of strength had in fact been won by the government. By 1932 the party had been reduced to some 25,000 members and was no longer capable of posing a serious threat to public order. Until 1934 it continued to reserve a page in all its publications for anti-military propaganda, while colonial work, now placed under the authority of André Ferrat, received more serious attention than at any time since the Moroccan war. But the effect of this was scarcely perceptible except in the debates of the party's Seventh Congress (March 1932), when for the first and only time the colonial question appeared as a separate item on the agenda, and in the pages of *Cahiers du Bolchévisme*, where a series of lucid articles on North African affairs appeared between 1932 and 1935.[22] Communist activities continued to be severely repressed in the colonies (when they occurred) and more sporadically in France (notably by a further rash of arrests in autumn 1932), but public opinion no longer paid much attention.

The Role of the CGTU

The Congress of Bourges, in November 1923, had established in all but name the subordination of the CGTU to the Communist Party, in return for which the CGTU leaders, notably Sémard and Monmousseau, were given an important role in the party leadership (although for form's sake Monmousseau, as general secretary of the CGTU, did not actually join the party until 1925). At the time of its first congress in 1922 the CGTU claimed to have taken away over half the members of the CGT, so the party should in theory have been able to dominate the French trade union movement from 1923 on. But this hope soon proved illusory. Just as SFIO membership overtook that of the PCF in 1924,[23] so by 1926 at latest CGT membership had overtaken that of the CGTU—if in fact it had ever been below it. Claiming 350,000 members in 1922 the CGTU probably overestimated its own strength, and certainly underestimated that of its rival, which it put at 250,000. Reliable estimates of both can only be worked out from the mid-1920s, when both organizations adopted a system of voting rights in proportion to membership for the different industrial federations at confederal congresses. These estimates are as shown in the following table.[24]

	CGT	CGTU
1924	491,114	?
1926	524,960	431,240
1928	554,796	370,260
1930	577,280	322,545
1932	533,197	258,575
1934	490,984	264,085

In other words, while the CGT's membership figures followed a gentle upward slope until 1930, those of the CGTU followed a curve roughly similar to that of the PCF between 1923 and 1932, although somewhat less steep. Membership of the trade union organization seems usually to have been between eight and ten times that of the party. The rise in CGTU membership which occurred some time between 1922 and 1926 perhaps corresponds to the recovery of PCF membership in 1924—and both could be due at least partly to the convergence of the two organizations. (For other explanations of the PCF recovery, see above, p. 112n.) Certainly the decline of the CGTU from 1926 onwards must be due, at least in part, to the same general causes as that of the party. One of these was the expulsion or departure of political opponents—notably Troskyists in the party and anarchists or anarcho-syndicalists in the CGTU. The departure of the latter began in January 1924 with the secession of the Lyons builders' union and culminated in 1926 with the formation of the *Confédération Générale du Travail Syndicaliste Révolutionnaire* (CGTSR), led by Besnard. Meanwhile a new 'revolutionary syndicalist' opposition grew up within the CGTU, consisting essentially of the former 'Communist syndicalists' who had been associated with

Rosmer and until 1924 had strongly supported close ties between CGTU and PCF, but whose outlook changed rapidly after the Bolshevization of the party and its expulsion of Rosmer and Monatte. Although tarred with the Trotskyist brush in 1924, most of these men soon moved away from communism and back towards classic revolutionary syndicalism, feeling that the experience of the Comintern had justified their original hostility to all political parties as such. This was the line followed by Monatte's review *La Révolution Prolétarienne* (see above, pp. 126–8) after 1925. Its supporters remained in their respective trade unions, whether these belonged to the CGT or the CGTU, and in May 1926 they formed the *Ligue Syndicaliste*, whose programme was the emancipation of the CGT from 'governmental collaboration' and of the CGTU from 'political collaboration', and the reunification of both in a single revolutionary CGT.

The main spokesman of this group in the CGTU was Maurice Chambelland, who had been the first member of it to resign from the PCF in 1924 (see above, p. 124). He and his colleagues were not expelled from the CGTU, but the leadership was able to isolate them by much the same methods as were used against the opposition in the party. At the CGTU's fourth congress, in 1927, they could muster only sixty votes against 1,995.[25]

Yet the number of conscious political 'defections' from the CGTU should not be exaggerated. As a modern historian puts it, 'it is less a matter of *defections* than of *disaffection*':[26] disaffection due in the first instance to the defeat of the 1920 railway strike and the world economic crisis of the same year (not really felt in France until 1921, and then only in an attenuated form[27]), then to the CGT split. 'The trade union forces, already diminished by the crisis, were further weakened by their division: the period from 1921 to 1933 was thus dominated by a rivalry whose justification escaped the workers. The magnetic power of both wings was thereby reduced.'[28] That of the CGTU was evidently reduced even further by the secession of the anarchists (even though their rival organization had little success) and by the internal struggle against the syndicalists (even though their leaders remained within the movement).

Many workers who knew little of the precise criticisms levelled at the CGTU leadership by anarchists or syndicalists must nonetheless have been discouraged from supporting a movement which bound itself so closely to the Communist Party, if only because the party itself was so unsuccessful. For if in this period the reformist CGT was powerless to achieve reforms, the revolutionary CGTU seemed even further from achieving revolution. Its extremism only ensured that its militants were persecuted by employers (especially in large firms), while its willingness to organize strikes and campaigns on purely political themes at the behest of the Comintern meant that they were also victims of repression by the state.

The link with the party was formalized as early as 1924 with the creation of a permanent joint committee of eight members: four from the *Bureau Politique* and four from the CGTU's confederal bureau. Some disagreements arose within this body—notably about Treint's more absurd analyses and slogans such as the demand for a revolutionary tribunal—as a result of which it was decided to go one step further and make the four CGTU representatives (Monmousseau, Midol, Dudilieux and Racamond) ex-officio members of the *Bureau Politique*. And in 1925, at its third congress, the CGTU adopted a pattern of organization exactly parallel to that of the Bolshevized PCF, the eighty-two 'departmental unions' being replaced by twenty-eight 'regional' ones.[29] Similarly, local unions were brought into line with party '*rayons*', and factory sections with party cells.[30] This of course made it easier to set up Communist fractions at all levels.

In spite of this the PCF gave relatively little attention to trade union work during the years of active Bolshevization (1924–5), and tended to build up its own factory cells at the expense of CGTU sections. In October 1925 the *Cahiers du Bolchévisme* noted that 'Communists have a propensity to neglect trade union work and slogans embodying immediate, everyday demands'. Instead they went in for 'abstract propaganda' and underestimated 'the fact that factories and trade unions are the natural field in which to organize the united workers' front'.[31]

The united front tactic in the trade union field consisted chiefly in putting forward proposals for reunion with the CGT. The Communists had opposed the split in the CGT when it occurred (see above, p. 89), and formally at least they never reconciled themselves to it. But proposals for unity combined with abuse of the CGT leaders were naturally not taken very seriously by most CGT militants. Hence the failure of the 'committees of proletarian unity' during the Moroccan war and of the attempted 'unity congress' in September 1925, which was attended by only twenty-three delegates from unions belonging to the CGT, some of whom left before it ended.

In 1926, of course, the pendulum swung the other way and it became one of the main aims of PCF trade union policy to persuade the CGT to join the Anglo-Soviet Trade Union Council. In the hope of achieving this the party gave noisy (and compromising) support to the left wing which had now emerged in the CGT and which advocated a negotiated reunion with the CGTU (whereas Jouhaux maintained that unity could only be achieved if the CGTU members were individually to rejoin CGT unions); it also adopted moderate and even nationalistic slogans such as 'stop the collective importing of foreign labour'; and at its 1927 congress the CGTU actually dropped the formula of the dictatorship of the proletariat.[32]

The majority of the CGT remained unimpressed by these manoeuvres, and at the end of 1927 the party swung back to a sectarian line. Unity once again receded into the far distance; in spite of a relatively large number of strikes in 1928, CGTU membership continued to fall, and the subordination of trade unions to party was again emphasized. Obedient to the directives of the Comintern's Sixth World Congress, the CGTU proclaimed the 'radicalization of the masses'; and, at its fifth congress, in 1929, it officially recognized the Communist Party as 'the directing vanguard of the labour movement'.[33] Under the direction of that vanguard, CGTU troops were sent into battle on behalf of the 'true fatherland of the proletariat' and bore the brunt of Tardieu's repression. Worse, they found themselves increasingly isolated from the mass of the working class which refused to be 'radicalized'. Not surprisingly, there was a revival of opposition: the *Ligue Syndicaliste* was joined by the Federations of the Ports and Docks, the Food Industry and the Printers, and at the 1929 congress Chambelland was able to rally 209 votes, against 1,364 for the report of the leadership.[34] He formed a *Comité pour l'Indépendance du Syndicalisme*, which soon made contact with the autonomous Civil Servants' Federation and with elements in the CGT who favoured reunion (including Dumoulin and Monatte). The result was the formation, in November 1930, of a 'Committee of Twenty-Two' (seven from the left of the CGT, seven 'autonomous' and eight from Chambelland's group in the CGTU). Meanwhile a separate 'unitarian opposition' developed in the CGTU, based on the Teachers' Federation and supported by Rosmer, which opposed the existing Communist leadership but rejected the thesis of trade union independence, arguing that to revive the Amiens Charter now would mean going back to the old revolutionary syndicalism which had failed in 1914 and 1920.[35]

As the great depression began to affect France in 1930–1, the lack of a strong and united trade union movement to defend the workers was more acutely felt. The Committee of Twenty-Two's campaign for reunion had considerable success, partly owing to the prestige of Dumoulin in the CGT. In the early months of 1931 Chambelland's weekly, *Le Cri du Peuple*, achieved a circulation of 5,000,[36] while the SFIO gave space to the Committee in its daily, *Le Populaire de Paris*.[37] But the leadership of both CGT and CGTU remained resolutely hostile, and the Twenty-Two were defeated in the 1931 congresses of both organizations. Monmousseau dismissed their programme with the formula: 'C.G.T. unique, C.G.T. de trahison'. Jouhaux more subtly exploited the situation by an apparent concession—no longer insisting on individual returns to the fold but allowing mergers between unions on the local level: when these were achieved there could be federal merger congresses in each industry, and only after that a congress of reunion at confederal level. This proposal—which given the current attitude of the CGTU was in no immediate danger of being put into practice—was adopted by the CGT congress of September 1931. After this the Committee of Twenty-Two quickly disintegrated, and many of its supporters in the CGTU crossed over to the CGT.[38] Little more was heard of trade union unity until 1934.

Apart from its political campaigns, the CGTU distinguished itself during these years chiefly by its opposition to 'rationalization'—the current phrase for technical and organizational improvements in the interests of increased productivity. The Congress of Bordeaux, in 1927, declared: 'We cannot regard as progress practices which lead rapidly to the physical and moral exhaustion of the worker and whose rigour obliges the old and the weak to take underling jobs at starvation wages.' At the 1929 congress a certain Dorel, reporting on the CGTU's programme of demands, went even further: 'It should be said quite frankly that we must be against the development of modern techniques under capitalism, against the introduction of high-yield machines which work against the workers and their living-conditions. In certain cases we must even envisage collective action by the workers including refusal to work on high-yield machines. . . .' Rationalization, it was alleged, enabled employers to replace skilled workers who had developed a revolutionary consciousness with unskilled, apolitical ones from the countryside; and from 1931 onwards it was also blamed for rising unemployment.[39]

This essentially Luddite policy made sense only on the assumption that capitalism was about to collapse and that technical change could therefore wait until socialism enabled it to be introduced humanely. The same assumption lay behind the CGTU's general programme of economic demands, which was aimed especially at capitalism's chief victims, the low-paid workers and unemployed.[40] But these under-privileged groups were precisely those least inclined to carry on trade union work at a time when there were no obvious advantages it could bring, but obvious disadvantages in the shape of extra fatigue and the risk of dismissal. The CGTU thus got the worst of both worlds: among the relatively secure and well-off workers of the tertiary sector it lost ground while the CGT gained (at least until 1932), and among the more vulnerable and nomadic work-force of manufacturing industry it did not escape the general contraction of trade unionism resulting from the social and political climate.[41]

Nonetheless the CGTU continued to exist, and once its leaders had been integrated into the leadership of the party its allegiance could never be seriously in doubt. This fact was of crucial importance for the future, for no other political party had a trade union movement, however weak, directly under its influence; and as long as the CGTU existed the mass of workers—those who remained in the CGT and those who dropped out of union activity altogether—felt that their movement was disunited and incomplete. When the moment came for the labour movement to make another leap forward, the leaders and militants of the CGTU would be needed; and their allegiance, combined with the existence of the factory cells, would give the PCF an incalculable advantage.

The Communist Electorate

The PCF of 1920–34 was in no danger of winning power in an election, nor did it expect to do so. But, as good Leninists, the French Communists sought to exploit bourgeois electoral and parliamentary processes for their own propaganda; and as bad Leninists they were often accused, by the Comintern or by their own left wing, of slipping back into the excessive preoccupation with electoral success and with the winning of parliamentary seats which had characterized the pre-war SFIO. From either standpoint, their electoral performance was a yardstick by which they were bound to be judged; and since France during those years was a parliamentary democracy, it is as good a yardstick as any for an objective measurement of their importance and influence.

We have seen (above, pp. 48–9) that in the 1919 general election the SFIO won 23% of the votes cast, and that in the view of the left this total would have been much higher if the party had taken a clear revolutionary and pro-Bolshevik line. A year later, when the party split, the Communists represented two thirds of its members. The speeches at Tours showed that their support was particularly strong among the socialist peasantry, while it was taken for granted that communism would be better than social democracy at mobilizing the industrial working class. Consequently the PCF leaders tended to assume that they would inherit the SFIO's electoral patrimony and perhaps even improve on it: this was why they could see so little point in the united front tactic when it was first imposed on them in 1922. Rather than take warning from the defection of fifty-five out of the sixty-eight Socialist deputies elected in 1919, they saw this as proof that the party had chosen the truly revolutionary path,[42] and hoped to replace the opportunist black sheep with true spokesmen of communism at the next election.

Trotsky saw the fallacy in this reasoning as early as February 1922. At the Enlarged Executive of that month, he warned the French delegates that the strength of their party resulted only from the feeling of the masses that 'revolution was going to break out today or tomorrow'. If elections were held in a non-revolutionary situation, the mass of the party's potential supporters would desert it:

> What will the French worker think? He says to himself that the Communist party is perhaps a good party, that the Communists are good revolutionaries; but, today, there isn't a revolution, there are elections. . . . The elections arrive. A great mass of French workers will then probably reason in the following manner: 'In the last resort, a *Bloc des gauches* Parliament is after all preferable to a Poincaré, *Bloc national* Parliament.' And that will be the moment for the dissidents [*sc.* the SFIO] to play a political role. There aren't many of them in their political organization. True enough. But the reformists, especially in France, don't need to have a big organization. They have newspapers which few people read, it's true, because the most passive and most disillusioned mass of the proletariat doesn't read; it's disenchanted, it waits on events; it scents what's in the air without reading. . . . So, this little instrument of the bourgeoisie, this organization of the dissidents, can, in those conditions, take on a great political importance.[43]

This was a remarkably accurate prediction of what was to happen two years later. Trotsky's recipe to deal with this situation was, of course, the united front. (Indeed, the context of his remarks was the defence of the united front against the criticisms of Renoult and the Italian delegate Terracini; see above, pp. 74–5.) The PCF, he said, should forestall the *Bloc des Gauches* by forming a Workers' and Peasants' Bloc and inviting the SFIO to join it. The SFIO leaders would in fact prefer to join the bourgeois *Bloc des Gauches*, and would thereby unmask themselves as enemies of the proletariat.[44]

The PCF did in fact attempt to use this tactic, but it failed almost completely. Partly, perhaps, because they left it too late: they did not announce their plans for a *Bloc Ouvrier et Paysan* until June 1923, when the *Cartel des Gauches* was already forming in reaction against Poincaré's Ruhr policy and the violence of *Action Française*. But also because the Communist leaders were confused and divided about the precise electoral tactic which the *Bloc Ouvrier et Paysan* was supposed to imply, and never managed to make it sound as though they sincerely wanted a united front with the SFIO leaders. (The launching of the formula coincided with the virtual sabotage by the PCF of a big anti-*Action Française* demonstration organized by the *Ligue des Droits de l'Homme*.) It was not until December that the PCF in fact made a formal proposal to the SFIO and to Frossard's splinter party, stating the choice clearly: 'With the Communist Party in constituting the fighting unity of the working class against the Right and Left bourgeoisie; or with the Radical Party against the Communist Party, which refuses absolutely to practise class collaboration'.[45] As expected, the Socialists refused. But their refusal did not 'unmask' them so devastatingly as the Communists had hoped. They made it clear that they would have been glad of the Communist alliance, at least on an *ad hoc* local basis, but could not forgo the Radical alliance which was essential in order to defeat the *Bloc National*. It was the Communists, they argued, who, by their untimely exclusion of any alliance with the Radicals, were dividing the working class and risking the victory of 'capitalist reaction'.[46] This argument had its effect, even among Communist sympathizers. Those quoted in the *Bulletin Communiste* of May 1924 were probably fairly typical: 'At heart we are with you, but today let us throw out the *Bloc National*. That's the most important thing. . . . If thanks to you the reactionaries get in, we'll never forgive you.'

172

This was precisely the response that Trotsky had predicted in 1922. But though in principle the party had adopted Trotsky's tactic of 'unmasking' the Socialist leaders, it does not really seem to have believed his warnings about the revival of Socialist support, and it made little real effort to reach the SFIO rank-and-file directly in its propaganda. (By January 1924 Trotsky's warnings were also ignored by the Comintern: the message from ECCI to the PCF's Congress of Lyons asserted that the SFIO was a dead party for which few workers still voted.)[47] The election campaign itself came immediately after Treint had regained control of the party and begun his witch-hunt against the 'right' (see above, pp. 105–8), and was therefore conducted in an extremist tone, using not only the united front slogan of a 'workers' and peasants' government' (of dubious application in the circumstances), but also straightforward-ly Communist ones such as 'power to the soviets' and 'dictatorship of the proletariat'.[48] The party was also handicapped by the resolution of the Fourth World Congress that nine tenths of its election candidates should be workers or peasants, and by the Treint doctrine that no party official or journalist who was not already a deputy could stand (which had been ratified, on Zinoviev's instruc-tions, at the Congress of Lyons in January). This may have been a good propaganda point, but it meant that individual PCF candi-dates were usually inexperienced and unconvincing speakers.

The leadership concentrated most of its efforts on the Paris area, where the party did in fact score a considerable success, winning 26% of the vote and electing nineteen deputies. Its greatest success was in the inner suburbs round Saint-Denis, where the *Bloc Ouvrier et Paysan* list was headed by Vaillant-Couturier and Doriot: the latter, who already had a certain local following in Saint-Denis, conducted his campaign from a prison cell and had the good luck to appear in court two days before the poll, which enabled him to make a resounding speech from the dock about the iniquity of French policy in the Ruhr.

But the Paris area was almost alone in justifying the optimism of the party leaders. In the country as a whole the *Bloc Ouvrier et Paysan* won only 876,000 votes, barely half the score of the united Socialist Party in 1919 and amounting to just 10% of the total poll. The new Chamber contained only twenty-six Communist deputies in all, while the Socialists, thanks to their alliance with the Radicals, had 104, just overtaking the total reached by the united Socialist Party in

1914. (The *Cartel des Gauches* lists—Socialists and Radicals combined —won 3,394,000 votes, or 38.1%.)

One third of the PCF votes came from the Paris region (Seine and Seine-et-Oise). But the remainder did not come mainly from industrial areas. Of the fifteen provincial departments in which the *Bloc Ouvrier et Paysan* got the votes of more than 10% of the registered voters, only four could be described as industrial; and in one of these, the Nord, its votes in fact came from the rural districts while the working-class constituencies remained faithful to the SFIO. Its most notable successes were in the rural areas on the northern and south-western flanks of the Massif Central—particularly in the Cher and the Lot-et-Garonne, where it had over 20% of the votes. In several cases the peasant voters seem to have been strongly influenced by a sitting Communist deputy who had built up a local following before 1920, such as Renaud Jean in the Lot-et-Garonne or Alexandre Blanc in the Vaucluse. (The PCF got 14% of the vote in the Vaucluse, and would probably have done better if Blanc had not had to withdraw from the list at the last minute owing to ill health.[49]) By contrast, the party did very badly in areas where all the pre-1920 Socialist *élus* (deputies, mayors, *conseillers généraux*, etc.) had stayed with the SFIO.[50]

It is thus clear that the Communist electorate of 1924 was of two quite distinct types. On the one hand were the Parisian workers, on whom the influence of Comintern propaganda and of the party leadership was relatively direct, and who can therefore reasonably be described as Communists. On the other were scattered pockets of rural voters, especially small farmers, whose image of the party was to some extent shaped by the personality of its local leaders. It seems fair to assume that this latter group had relatively little interest in or knowledge of Communist ideology. They were the heirs of the republicans of the 1850s, the radicals of the 1880s and 1890s, the Jauressiens of 1905–14, but with an added bitterness resulting from their experiences in the war and from the galloping inflation of the post-war years. Their tradition was one of republican extremism and opposition to the rich and the powerful, and if a Communist candidate seemed the most genuine exponent of that tradition they were ready to vote for him.

The existence of this rural tradition was to prove one of the PCF's greatest long-term assets. But the PCF of the 1920s was not yet ready to exploit it. Immediately after the 1924 elections it embarked on the process of Bolshevization, which thrust electoral preoccupations into the background and for a time so disorganized the party as to make the coherent conduct of an election campaign almost impossible. It was therefore not entirely surprising that in the municipal elections of 1925, held on a two-ballot system, the party's score on the first ballot in the Paris region was 30% lower than the previous year.[51] In order to avoid losing the three municipalities it already held the party had to swallow its principles and come to at least a tacit arrangement with the *Cartel des Gauches*: it agreed to withdraw its lists on the second ballot where they were running behind those of the *Cartel*, in return for Socialist and Radical support where they were ahead. Where there was a pure SFIO list in the field, the Communists proposed to merge with it in a united front list. This tactic enabled the party to win control of six suburban town halls (two of them in alliance with the SFIO), and to hold two of the three it had controlled before. (In the third a Socialist became mayor after the victory of a joint list.)[52] But the municipalities elected in this way were not very amenable to party control, and in 1926 the local party *rayons* had to be taken to task for not supervising them strictly enough.[53]

1926–7 saw a further revival of the party's 'electoralist' tendencies. Treint's demotion was accompanied by the abandonment of his rules about election candidatures which, it was explained, were no longer necessary since 'our Party is now a solid, healthy, working-class party'.[54] Early in 1927 the PCF was presenting joint lists with the SFIO in by-elections, and in the senatorial elections of January it backed a joint list in the Seine which included dissident Communists, Socialists, Radicals and a 'Republican Socialist' (Pierre Laval).[55] It was in order to put a stop to such practices that the Comintern imposed the 'class against class' tactic (see above, pp. 133–6) for the 1928 legislative elections, which were held under the two-ballot system with single-member constituencies; in its open letter of November 1927 the PCF Central Committee announced that Communist candidates would be maintained on both ballots against all bourgeois candidates, including Radicals; on the second ballot there could be a *Bloc Ouvrier* with the Socialist Party if the latter would accept a minimum programme and would agree not to withdraw in favour of bourgeois candidates anywhere. If the Socialist Party refused this, the Communist Party reserved the right to maintain 'proletarian' candidates on the second ballot against 'all the Socialist leaders who are performing a counter-revolutionary task and call themselves defenders of democracy against communism'.

The Socialist Party at once rejected the proposed minimum programme, and denounced the Communist ultimatum as 'blackmail'. Consequently in the 1928 elections Communist candidates had to fight Radicals or Socialists in all constituencies on the second ballot,* and the party lost thirteen of its twenty-seven seats, although on the first ballot its vote had gone up to over a million (11.4%).† Worse, 40% of the Communist voters ignored the maintenance of their party's candidate and transferred their votes on the second ballot to the Socialist or Radical who had a better chance of winning. This was enough to show that the 'class against class' line had not been understood by the voters, but not enough to prevent it doing considerable damage to the moderate left and helping to ensure the victory of Poincaré and the right. (Thirty-six right-wing candidates got in with a simple majority on the second ballot because the Communists were splitting the left-wing vote.)[56] The party thereby incurred great odium among many left-wing voters.

The first ballot did not reveal any great change in the Communist electorate. The party's score was somewhat less impressive than in 1924 in the Paris region, and in the Lot-et-Garonne where some peasant discontent may have been pacified by Poincaré's stabilization of the franc. The gains were made in the coalfields of the Nord, in Alsace and in central France where there was now a solid swathe of eleven *départements* in which more than 10% of registered voters supported the PCF, stretching from Lyons right round the northern and western slopes of the Massif Central, through Limoges and down to Agen in the south-west.[57] But the second ballot confirmed that, with the exception of the area round Lyons itself, the voters of this central bloc were republican rebels rather than disciplined Communists. The most disciplined areas—those in which the party kept at least 80% of its vote on the second ballot—were the industrial ones:

* According to Humbert-Droz, this decision was almost reversed at the last moment by Stalin, who failed to grasp the workings of the two-ballot system and panicked at the news that no Communists had been elected outright on the first ballot. (*De Lénine à Staline* [Neuchatel, 1971], pp. 281–2.)

† The PCF had 1,064,000 votes, compared to 1,698,000 (18.2%) for the Socialists. The new Communist voters were presumably disillusioned *Cartel des Gauches* supporters of 1924. But the net loss in seats was only three for the SFIO, which benefited from Radical withdrawals on the second ballot. It is perhaps worth noting that the combined vote of PCF and SFIO was nearly 30%, much higher than that of the united Socialist Party in 1919.

the Paris region, especially, but also the Nord, Lyons, Rouen and the Gard, plus the Haut-Rhin, where the Communist candidates benefited from a mutual stand-down pact with the Alsatian autonomists.[58]

The real electoral débâcle for the party came in 1932. The 'class against class' tactic was applied again. At the Central Committee meeting of 26 August 1931 Thorez reminded the party that this did not rule out united front tactics but made them all the more necessary. He instructed Communist local organizations at all levels to approach those Socialist sections most likely to be receptive and offer them a mutual stand-down pact for the second ballot on the basis of a common platform of 'immediate demands'. Lest there should be any misunderstanding of the objective of this offer, he added: 'We will not revise our policy, we will put up even harder arguments against social democracy, we will use them with even greater force in order to snatch the workers away from social democracy.'[59] In spite of this, some bourgeois papers interpreted the approach, after the ultra-sectarian attitudes of the party during 1928–30, as a 'revolution' in Communist strategy. The Socialists hailed the new *tournant* as evidence of the PCF's total collapse, but saw all the less reason to make concessions to it: 'The house,' exulted *Le Populaire* on 6 September, 'is crumbling. The tenants are moving out. So they attempt to patch it up. These alarms that can be seen opposite us are a good sign. As for us we shall never ask anything of the Bolshevists. We shall mash into them (*On leur rentrera dedans*).' A week later Paul Faure wrote that it would be insulting the Socialist workers to suppose that their answer could be more than five letters long. On the whole the vote was to prove him right. The first ballot, on 1 May 1932, showed that the PCF had not merely failed to make any significant inroads on Socialist support but had lost 27% of its own electorate. The Communist vote fell to 795,000 (8.4% of votes cast) while the Socialist one went up to nearly two million (20.7%). Almost the only Communist gains were in the mining area of the Pas-de-Calais, from which Thorez himself came. In the Paris region the PCF lost votes to the *Parti d'Unité Prolétarienne* (PUP), composed of dissident Communists, and elsewhere to the SFIO. The number of *départements* in which more than 10% of registered electors voted Communist was reduced to eleven (including six northern industrial ones, but now only five southern rural ones). It was evident that many Communist voters, especially in rural areas, had been discouraged by the sectarian excesses of the party leadership, the consequent isolation of the party, and the government's repressive measures against it. So indeed were many party members, to judge by the strictures of the *Cahiers du Bolchévisme* on the lassitude and lack of conviction with which the election campaign was carried out.[60]

On the second ballot, party discipline was even less effective than in 1928: 45% of the Communist voters transferred their votes to the moderate left in spite of the maintenance of Communist candidates, and this time the phenomenon occurred in industrial as well as rural areas. (This helped to ensure the victory of the left: the SFIO gained seventeen seats, thus bringing its total to 129, while the 'Republican Socialists' gained five and the Radicals forty-eight.) Only three of the ten sitting Communist deputies (four had left the party or been expelled since 1928) were re-elected, and they were the three who were in more or less open disagreement with the class against class tactic but had concentrated on building up support in their own constituencies: Doriot and Clamamus in the Paris suburbs (both re-elected on the first ballot), and Renaud Jean in the Lot-et-Garonne. Among those beaten in Paris were Duclos, Marty, and Cachin—who had the humiliation of losing his seat to his former comrade Louis Sellier, now one of the leaders of the PUP. (Thanks to the concentration of its support in a few constituencies, the PUP was able to win eleven seats although it had less than one tenth of the PCF's votes.) Nine new Communist deputies were elected on the second ballot (making twelve in all), most of whom owed their seats to unilateral withdrawals by the Socialists. (One of these was Maurice Thorez, who took his seat for the suburb of Ivry-sur-Seine.) This was humiliating, but it did represent a glimmer of hope for the future: it showed that, however bad the relations between the two parties, Socialist candidates would not take the responsibility for ensuring the defeat of a Communist by the right, and some at least of the Socialist voters preferred to vote Communist on the second ballot rather than let the right-wing candidate in. The behaviour of the Communist voters showed that many of them felt the same way, whatever the party line. But before this fact could be exploited, the party line—and indeed the Comintern line—would have to change.

The Intellectuals

PACIFISM

For intellectuals, even more than for the working class and almost as much as for the peasantry, the First World War was a traumatic experience. Their horror at the bloodshed was heightened by their more highly developed sensitivity, their anger at its senseless-ness by their rationalist education. It was an intellectual, Romain Rolland, who made the first public protest against the war in his article 'Au-dessus de la Mêlée', published in Geneva in September 1914. At first he was almost totally alone, finding more response among the handful of syndicalist *minoritaires* than among his fellow-intellectuals, who responded almost unanimously to the call of patriotism, believing in the justice of a war for liberty which some persuaded themselves would be a new revolutionary war like that of 1792.

But in many of the intellectuals who lived the experience of trench warfare at first hand, these patriotic sentiments were soon replaced by a growing hatred of the world order which had secreted such barbarism and a growing contempt for the values of the pre-1914 liberal enlightenment. The gap quickly widened between the older men, especially the writers who sought to use their talents to sustain the country's morale and fighting spirit, and the young intellectuals in the trenches who saw what fighting meant for those who were actually doing it. The patriotic writing of their non-combatant elders filled these men with disgust, and they labelled it 'bourrage de crânes' (skull-stuffing).

In 1916 the trench generation found a spokesman in Henri Barbusse, a writer who in fact had been over forty when the war started but out of patriotism had volunteered for active service. Barbusse was already a well-known writer before the war, and his war novel *Le Feu*, published in serial form from August to November 1916, attracted attention at once. Subtitled 'Diary of a Squad', it was essentially a brutally realistic description of trench warfare and its effect on the minds and bodies of the rank-and-file. Its conclusions, necessarily in view of wartime censorship, were relatively general: military glory was an illusion; after the war another battle might have to be fought against one's own countrymen to ensure that there were no more wars like this one. 'The future is in the hands of the slaves and it is easy to see that the old world will be changed by the alliance that will one day be built amongst themselves by those whose number and whose misery are infinite.' Even so, the fact that publication was allowed is a tribute to the leniency of the pre-Clemenceau wartime governments (though also to Barbusse's prestige). Published in book form in December 1916, *Le Feu* was at once awarded a Goncourt prize, and by the end of the war 230,000 copies had been sold in spite of the paper shortage.

Among the thousands who recognized their own experiences and their own feelings in *Le Feu* were two young writers who had been students together at the Sorbonne when the war broke out: Raymond Lefebvre (born 1890) and Paul Vaillant-Couturier (born 1892). They sought out Barbusse in 1917 and with him formed the *Association Républicaine des Anciens Combattants* (ARAC), an ex-serviceman's association which aimed not only to defend the material interests of its members but also 'to give body to the impulses of anger and disgust born on the battlefields and to show their true duty to the survivors, their duty as human beings and their duty as a class'.[61] In fact these intellectuals did not start from a strictly 'class' viewpoint themselves. Like others, they evolved from a more-or-less 'Wilsonian' pacifism to militant Marxism, via enthusiasm for the Russian Revolution, stimulated in part at least by allied intervention and by the virulent anti-Bolshevism of the French bourgeoisie.

By the end of the war there was a large body of opinion among French intellectuals which expressed strong hostility to the war and general sympathy for the Russian Revolution. But events were soon to reveal the existence within this body of two quite different schools of thought: on the one hand the 'idealists', like Romain Rolland, for whom peace remained the first priority, and on the other those like Barbusse, Lefebvre and Vaillant-Couturier, whom the war had shocked into a determination to change society, if necessary even at the price of further violence. Although both groups had had initial reservations about Bolshevism, these tended to become stronger in the first group with the passage of time, while in the second group they were gradually dissipated. Rolland and his friends were temperamentally close to the Longuettistes in the SFIO, who wanted to support Bolshevism in Russia but did not consider it applicable to western Europe, whereas Lefebvre and Vaillant-Couturier became active members of the Committee for the Third International, working for the formation of a French Communist Party on the Bolshevik model.

In 1919 Barbusse formed the *Clarté* movement (named after his latest novel). This was intended to be an international organization of intellectuals, with national and local sections, 'to fight against the prejudices, the errors (too ably nurtured) and above all the ignorance which separate and isolate human beings and until now have made it possible to throw them blindly against each other'.[62] This seemed harmless enough, and the first members of *Clarté* included Léon Blum and a wide range of liberal pacifists and bourgeois journalists. Among the members of the first international Directing Committee were Georges Duhamel, Thomas Hardy, E. D. Morel, Jules Romains, Upton Sinclair, H. G. Wells and Stefan Zweig. But the activity of the movement was organized mainly by Barbusse himself with Lefebvre and Vaillant-Couturier, under whose influence he moved rapidly towards the Third International. In effect both *Clarté* and the ARAC soon became Communist 'front organizations', agitating for the formation of a French Communist Party during 1920, and rapidly falling under its control thereafter. As early as February 1921, *Clarté* published a declaration affirming the 'absolute principles of international communism', though disclaiming any official ties with the party.[63] Barbusse himself did not join the party until 1923, but by his own admission this was because he believed he could be more use to it outside.[64]

Intellectuals played a relatively important part in the early history of the PCF. Among the first party leaders, Dunois, Rappoport, Vaillant-Couturier, Loriot and Souvarine were all indubitably intellectuals, and in fact only four of the thirty-two members of the original *Comité Directeur* were classified as workers.[65] The youth leader Gabriel Péri was of both bourgeois origin and literary pretensions. Other intellectuals who played a role in the creation of the party included Sadoul, Marcel Martinet (writer and close friend of Monatte), Henri Guilbeaux (a pacifist who worked with Rolland in Switzerland, then went to Russia and joined the 'Groupe communiste français de Moscou'), Georges Pioch (poet and secretary of the PCF Seine Federation in 1921–2), and the poet and novelist Noël Garnier, a founder-member of the *Clarté* group whose dismissal from *L'Humanité* in December 1922 was one of the immediate causes of Frossard's resignation. In its first two years especially the party enjoyed the sympathy and often the active support of a substantial fraction of the Parisian intelligentsia. The young historians André Julien and Ernest Labrousse, the economist Charles Gide, the lawyer Henri Torrès, for example, were all active party propagandists and regular contributors to *L'Humanité*. The veteran feminist Séverine joined the party soon after Tours, and even Anatole France 'affirmed his solidarity'.[66]

But many of these intellectuals had never really gone beyond a generous Jauressian pacifism, and almost all of them were individualists to whom the Bolshevik idea of discipline was wholly foreign. Consequently it is not surprising that a large group of them fell away from the party at the time of Frossard's resignation, and almost all the remainder in 1924 as a result of Bolshevization. Souvarine's expulsion in July of that year was followed by a stiffening of the party's attitude to intellectuals in general—perhaps an inevitable counterpart of the drive to promote working-class leaders. At the same time the intellectuals themselves were embarrassed by the campaign against Trotsky and the dishonest methods used to discredit the opposition in France. Most of them were friends either of the expelled syndicalists Monatte and Rosmer, or of the former 'left' leaders who now went into opposition, like Dunois and Loriot. A typical example was Magdeleine Marx, an anti-war writer and founder member of *Clarté* who had become an ardent party propagandist in 1921–4 but now joined the opposition of which her husband, Maurice Paz, became one of the leaders. The *Clarté* movement itself had by now withered away, and its organ, the review *Clarté*, gradually escaped from Barbusse's control. The editors, Jean Bernier and Marcel Fourrier, espoused the Trotskyist cause and at the same time went in for *avant-garde* literary criticism which found little favour with the party leaders. In the autumn of 1924, after *L'Humanité* had published fulsome obituaries of Anatole France, *Clarté* responded with a pamphlet entitled 'L'Anti-France' in which the deceased writer was damned as a 'social-democrat, social-traitor, social-chauvinist' and much else besides. Its authors had the whole spectrum of critical opinion against them, but found themselves in alliance with the surrealists, whose pamphlet on the same subject, 'Un Cadavre', caused a considerable scandal. During the following year the two groups drew rapidly together, and at the end of 1925 *Clarté* announced that it was merging with the surrealist group to form a new journal, *La Guerre Civile*.[67]

SURREALISM

In fact the *Clarté* group and the surrealists had met on a road which they were travelling in opposite directions—the former towards surrealism, the latter towards dialectical materialism. Surrealism too may be said to have originated in the disgust and shock felt by young intellectuals exposed to the First World War, but it was not in its original form a political movement. The surrealist objection to the existing world order was not confined to political or social issues; it concerned the whole of the rationalist approach to life, and at first concentrated especially on its literary and artistic effects. Though some of them expressed admiration for Lenin in 1921, they felt no need for any specific political commitment until 1925 when, as a result of the Anatole France episode, they became involved in discussions with the *Clarté* group. At the same time, under the influence of Antonin Artaud, they were beginning to express their rejection of existing society in quasi-political slogans such as 'Open the prisons, dismiss the army'. In Number 4 of *La Révolution Surréaliste*—the first which he edited personally—André Breton wrote: 'In the present state of society in Europe, we continue to support the principle of any revolutionary action, even one that takes as its starting-point the class struggle, provided only that it leads far enough.'[68] To a certain extent the surrealists' move into politics was a reaction of self-defence against the French ruling class, which displayed unrestrained hostility to them, especially after the Anatole France pamphlet. Breton and his friend Louis Aragon had been dismissed by their employer, the art collector Jacques Doucet, and some critics had even called for legal sanctions against them. Paul Claudel, then French ambassador to fascist Italy, informed an Italian newspaper that surrealism had 'only one meaning: pederastic'.[69] All this may help to explain why the surrealists, who had taken no part in the campaign against the occupation of the Ruhr, reacted strongly against the Moroccan war of 1925 and joined with other intellectuals in signing protests.

Although this placed them alongside the PCF on a negative platform, their approach to a positive commitment was still hesitant. As late as November 1924 Aragon had written:

> The Russian Revolution? You can't stop me shrugging my shoulders. On the scale of ideas it is, at most, a vague ministerial crisis. . . . The problems posed by human existence cannot be dealt with by the miserable little revolutionary activity which has occurred to the East of us these last few years. I must add that to call it revolutionary is a veritable abuse of language.[70]

But this was going too far for Breton, who was now reading Trotsky on Lenin and finding in the latter's ideas 'the greatest power of attraction'. The result was the publication in 1925 of the pamphlet *La*

Révolution d'abord et toujours. This manifesto, stressing the social nature of true revolution, was a joint production by the surrealists and other groups of intellectuals who opposed the Moroccan war—notably *Clarté* and the review *Philosophies* (see below).

Through the *Clarté* group, the surrealists met Souvarine and the Russian oppositionist Victor Serge, both of whom influenced them in favour of Trotsky rather than Stalin. But it must be remembered that in 1925–6, with the exception of Souvarine himself and the handful of syndicalists expelled in 1924, the French 'Trotskyists' still constituted an opposition within the PCF, while Trotsky himself was still a member of the CPSU. The party, whatever its faults, was still regarded as the indispensable instrument of revolution. As one of their associates has put it, 'the solemn joining of the communist party by Aragon, Breton and a few others at the end of the 1926 occurred under the patronage of Hegel, Marx, Lenin and Trotsky'.[71]

Not surprisingly, the five leading surrealists who joined the party (Breton, Aragon, Paul Eluard, Pierre Unik and Benjamin Péret) soon found that they were the object of total incomprehension and intense suspicion. The title of their journal, *La Révolution Surréaliste*, was taken politically by the Communists and led them to suspect the surrealists of that most heinous of crimes, an attempt to constitute a political tendency within the party. Many years later, Breton was to recall with irony

> those sessions which, on a personal summons to appear, at a very early hour, either in a school playground in the rue Duhesme, or in a room in the maison des Syndicats, avenue Mathurin-Moreau, before successive 'control commissions', led me to attempt to justify surrealist activity and to give sureties for the loyalty of my intentions.

These commissions, he said, were generally composed of three foreigners who introduced themselves only by their first names and had 'a very imperfect knowledge of French'—'Apart from that, now that I think of it, it was like nothing so much as a police interrogation.' Whenever Breton appeared to have answered their questions satisfactorily, one of the investigators would bring out a copy of *La Révolution Surréaliste* and it would start all over again.

> The most amusing thing, looking back on it, is that what invariably put them beside themselves with rage was some of the illustrations, and above all the reproductions of works by Picasso. . . .

... these tiring harassments were by no means at an end when the investigation was over and I at last obtained my assignment to a cell. In face of the persistent hostility which I met with—not to mention the deliberate provocations—I had to abandon any hope of going further on this road. Those of my surrealist friends—notably Aragon and Eluard—who had taken the same initiative as me at the same time, carried out the same withdrawal on their own account.[72]

But Breton and his friends did not accept this failure as final. They continued to regard themselves as strongly committed supporters of the party. Indeed a number of important figures (Soupault, Artaud, Vitrac, Masson, Queneau, Prévert) were to be expelled from the surrealist group or leave it during 1928–30 precisely because they did not accept the priority which Breton gave at this time to social and political revolutionary commitment. In his *Second Manifesto of Surrealism* (1929) Breton reasserted his loyalty to the Comintern and made a brilliant attempt to integrate surrealism into Marxist-Hegelian philosophy. The following year *La Révolution Surréaliste* was replaced by the more reassuring title (from the Communist point of view) *Le Surréalisme au service de la Révolution*. The first number of the new journal opened with a telegram signed by Breton and Aragon, in which the surrealists assured the 'International Bureau for Revolutionary Literature', in Moscow, that 'if imperialism declared war on the Soviets' they would obey whatever orders were given them by the Comintern.

This spectacular announcement contained an implicit challenge to Henri Barbusse, who as literary editor of *L'Humanité* since 1926 had acquired a quasi-official status as the party's leading intellectual. The surrealists had never concealed their low opinion of Barbusse, whom they regarded as pompous and unoriginal. Breton had attacked him in the pamphlet *Légitime Défense*, published in 1926 shortly before he himself joined the party; and the party's hostility to the surrealists had certainly been encouraged by the small caucus of Communist intellectuals around Barbusse who saw their position threatened. That position became more vulnerable after 1928 with the arrival of the 'third period'. There was an obvious dissonance between Barbusse's pacifism, his attempt to present Jesus Christ as a revolutionary hero, his editorship of the journal *Monde* whose contributors included non-Communists (and worse, ex-Communists), and the 'class against class' sectarianism now professed by the party leadership. The surrealists, for whom the extremism of the Barbé-Célor leadership held no terrors, saw their chance to drive a wedge between the party and the second-rate intellectuals who, they believed, were preventing them from playing the revolutionary role that was naturally theirs.

At first the surrealists scored some successes: André Thirion, an active party member who had joined the surrealist group in 1928, was entrusted with the organization of the party's tenth anniversary exhibition, for which he recruited the talents of Yves Tanguy and Salvador Dali. Meanwhile Aragon and another surrealist, Georges Sadoul, set off for Russia. Both had belonged to the party in 1927, and thanks to Thirion they were able to resume their membership before leaving for the 'homeland of socialism'. There seemed a good chance that they would be able to persuade the Russians that the surrealists, and not Barbusse and his group, were the true revolutionary intellectuals in France. During their absence, Breton and Thirion drew up plans for an 'Association of Revolutionary Artists and Writers' which would be a kind of intellectuals' trade union aligned on the Profintern, ruling out any collaboration with soggy liberals who were not willing to repudiate bourgeois democracy and national defence.[73]

The result was quite the opposite to what the surrealists intended. Aragon and Sadoul were allowed to attend the second 'International Conference of Revolutionary Writers', held in Kharkov in November 1930, and were able to obtain the passage of a resolution condemning *Monde* and its editor, Barbusse. But the congress nonetheless elected Barbusse (who was not present) to its presidium, and passed a general resolution which included a condemnation of 'the errors which found their expression in *The Second Manifesto of Surrealism*'. Worse, before leaving the Soviet Union, Aragon and Sadoul were obliged not merely to appeal publicly for the execution of the 'saboteurs of the Industrial Party' (Stalin's current victims) but also to sign a long 'confession' of their own shortcomings as Communists, in which they dissociated themselves from Breton's *Second Manifesto*.

This extraordinary episode requires explanation on two levels. First, why did the Comintern prefer Barbusse to Breton? Secondly, why did Aragon and Sadoul capitulate so easily? The first point seems less surprising now than it did at the time. Barbusse was the prototype of the Communist intellectuals who would become rapidly more numerous after 1934, and especially after 1944: a prestigious, 'respectable' figure who improved the party's image in non-Communist circles and helped to mobilize other intellectuals, and the liberal bourgeoisie in general, on the Communist side in campaigns on specific issues, while glossing over any disagreements he might have with the party line. Although in *Monde* he occasionally published articles that were critical of the Communists, he himself, in public at least, was careful always to defend the party line and the Soviet Union. When Victor Serge spoke to him of oppression in Moscow, he feigned a migraine and talked of 'the tragic destinies of revolutions'.[74] It was clear that Breton's prickly character and uncompromising honesty made him quite unfit for such a role.

The sudden about-face of Aragon and Sadoul is more perplexing. Breton attributed it to the fact that Sadoul had just been given a three-month prison sentence by a French court for an insulting postcard which he had sent to the officer cadet who had passed out top from Saint-Cyr, and was therefore 'ready if necessary to make concessions to a regime in which he saw the negation of the one which had struck him'; and also to the influence of Elsa Triolet, the Russian-born woman with whom Aragon had lived since 1928–9 and whom he later married. No doubt it is true that on his own 'Aragon would never have taken upon himself to do anything which might separate him from us'.[75] But evidently one must also add the powerful psychological effect which a visit to Soviet Russia could still have on a well-disposed foreign intellectual, if he happened to be less sure of his convictions than he outwardly appeared. Aragon wrote later that direct contact with the Soviet Union and the Writers' Congress had humiliated 'the surrealist Aragon, his head full of lyrical images . . . sceptical and superior . . .', and that he returned animated by a new energy, ready to sever a thousand links.[76] Much the same mixture of humiliation and stimulation had worked on Jacques Sadoul in 1917, on Frossard in 1920, on Renoult in 1922—and on Cachin in all three of those years.

It took some time for the results to become fully apparent. On their return Aragon and Georges Sadoul, under strong pressure from Breton and Thirion, published a manifesto *Aux Intellectuels Révolution-naires* which was in effect a withdrawal of their Moscow confession; and they rejoined the surrealist group. The PCF leadership, influenced no doubt by Barbusse and his friends, took umbrage and decided to cancel the tenth anniversary exhibition. Thirion was accused of irregularity in readmitting Aragon and Sadoul to the party; and in January 1931 he decided to resign his party membership.[77] But the surrealist group as a whole, and Breton in particular, still showed great eagerness to work with the party. In July 1931 Aragon published a long poem, *Front Rouge*, which put into verse form the most extreme slogans of the current party line:

> Descendez les flics
> Camarades
> Descendez les flics
>
> . . . .
>
> Feu sur Léon Blum
> Feu sur Boncour, Frossard, Déat
> Feu sur les ours savants de la Social-démocratie

On the strength of these lines, and many more in the same vein, Aragon was charged in January 1932 with 'incitement of soldiers to disobedience' and 'provocation to murder for the purposes of anarchist propaganda'. Breton rushed into print to defend him with a pamphlet *Misère de la Poésie*, but felt obliged at the same time to protest against the party's renewed attempt to censor surrealist publications, and especially against a recent attempt to force Aragon and other surrealists who were party members to condemn a 'pornographic' piece by Salvador Dali in the latest issue of *Surréalisme au service de la Révolution*. In his pamphlet, Breton served notice that the surrealists would not accept this kind of party veto. Aragon felt that Breton had betrayed his confidence by publicizing an internal party problem, and replied with an announcement in *L'Humanité*, on 10 March 1932, that he condemned Breton's pamphlet 'in its totality' since its attacks on the party were 'incompatible with the class struggle and therefore objectively counter-revolutionary'.

That was the end of the friendship between Breton and Aragon. Aragon and his supporters—Sadoul, Unik and Maxime Alexandre —left surrealism and became Communists first and foremost. Breton had made it clear that for him surrealism came first, and the party's hostility to him increased steadily from then on.

MARXIST PHILOSOPHY

Another small group of intellectuals attracted to the party during these years was the one associated with the review *Philosophies*, which had a brief existence in 1924–5 and was afterwards replaced by *L'Esprit*. Initially these young philosophers proclaimed their adher-

ence to a new 'mysticism', but like the surrealists they began to give
their revolt a more political expression at the time of the Moroccan
war. For a time they attempted to collaborate with the surrealists
and the *Clarté* group, but were forced to withdraw when some of
their ideas (notably those of Henri Lefebvre) were found to be
incompatible with Marxism. But their interest in Marxism grew
rapidly, and it was as Marxists that they joined the party in the late
1920s. In February 1929, with the help of Charles Rappoport (still a
party member though long since banished from the leadership), they
launched *La Revue Marxiste*, one of the first serious attempts to make
Marxist studies generally known in French intellectual circles. Most
of the members of this group—for instance Lefebvre, Georges
Politzer, Paul Nizan —belonged to a new generation. Born in the
first decade of the century, they had experienced the war not as
combatants but as children or adolescents. 'During the years which
were adorned by the presence of war,' said Nizan in 1927, 'a childish
fantasy reigned. Yet I was compelled on days of victory to take my
hat off in front of flags to whose destinies I was indifferent.'[78] Pre-
selected by academic success as members of the intellectual élite,
they rejected the place offered them in a post-war world that seemed
dominated by the elderly, the self-satisfied and the second-rate.
Unsure at first of their reaction—Nizan was successively royalist,
communist and fascist, and tried fleeing to Arabia, before opting
finally for communism in 1927—they were gradually drawn to
Marxism as the only coherent intellectual system with which to
oppose the faded positivism of the academic establishment. Since
the SFIO seemed less and less mindful of its Marxist heritage and
more and more anxious to participate in the bourgeois parliamentary system, it was almost inevitable that this intellectual choice
should lead to a political commitment in the PCF, whose very failure
in parliamentary and electoral terms rendered it more attractive. By
1929 commitment was achieved. Politzer applied his knowledge of
philosophy and psycho-analysis to politics and economics, taking on
the job of demonstrating the relevance of ideological tendencies,
however specialized, to the political arena.[79] Lefebvre and Norbert
Guterman concentrated on translating and interpreting Marxist
texts—and Lefebvre became one of the chief guardians of the party's
ideological orthodoxy against heresies and deviations. Nizan stood
as a Communist candidate in the 1932 elections and became a
full-time party worker the year after, writing book reviews for

L'Humanité, lecturing at the 'Workers' University' and running the party bookshop.[80]

ANTI-FASCISM

One of the reasons for the Comintern's indulgence towards Henri Barbusse in 1930 was no doubt the role he played in campaigns against fascism and against war. Even at a time when social democracy was officially regarded by the Comintern as a more dangerous enemy than fascism itself, a distinction was drawn between social democrat political leaders, guilty of betraying and misleading the working class, and left-leaning non-party intellectuals (however moderate) whose support might be obtained for the 'defence of the Soviet Union'. Such intellectuals were usually very far from a Leninist view of the world, their strongest political emotions being love of freedom and horror of violence. They were nonetheless potential allies for communism if the latter could make itself appear the strongest bulwark against fascism or against renewed war. Barbusse, himself a product of this intelligentsia and retaining much in common with it, was an ideal mouthpiece through whom the party could approach it. Throughout the 1920s he had some success in rousing French intellectual opinion against fascist outrages in Italy and acts of white terror in the Balkans. After a tour of the Balkans in 1925 he invited a number of international figures to form an International Anti-Fascist Committee, and got a favourable response from Romain Rolland who, after a period of withdrawal into 'Gandhism', now began to draw gradually nearer to a communist point of view. In February 1927 Barbusse was able to organize a big anti-fascist meeting in Paris with the participation of Rolland and of Paul Langevin, a distinguished physicist who had expressed support for the Russian Revolution in the early twenties and was now vice-president of the Ligue des Droits de l'Homme. In March 1929 a first International Anti-Fascist Congress was held in Berlin.

The Comintern took no special interest in these activities at first, presumably because fascism did not yet constitute a serious threat to the Soviet Union and its existence was deemed more favourable to the prospects of world revolution than any revival of bourgeois democracy. Communist energies were canalized mainly into the campaign against 'imperialist'—i.e. anti-Soviet—war, which as yet evoked no great response among intellectuals because the threat of such a war did not seem very credible. But the situation changed with the Japanese invasion of Manchuria in 1931 and the rise of Nazism in Germany. Stalin was initially more worried by the former than the latter, but both made the threat of a new world war—and the possibility that the Soviet Union would be its chief victim—much more plausible. In addition, many western intellectuals were impressed by the contrast between the crisis of the capitalist world and the success of the first Soviet Five Year Plan. Some time in 1931 the Soviet leaders must have decided on a new propaganda campaign aimed at pacifist and liberal opinion in the West; but officially at least this campaign was not conducted through the Comintern, which continued to treat social democracy as equivalent to fascism if not worse—a line hardly likely to appeal to liberal intellectuals. The problem was presented, not as one of revolutionary politics, but as concerning the interests of the Soviet Union as a state. (Litvinov, the Soviet foreign minister, attended the opening of the Geneva Disarmament Conference in February 1932 and insisted on general and total disarmament. In the prevailing international climate this proposal was in no danger of being accepted, but it sounded impressive.)

The next stage in the campaign was the appeal for an 'international congress of war against war', published by Barbusse and Rolland in May 1932. The idea is said to have come from Willi Münzenberg, the great German Communist front organizer whose experience went back to Zimmerwald days. The text had been drafted by Barbusse under the title 'Appeal for the Defence of the USSR',[81] and it was clear that war against the USSR was the only major war which the authors expected or feared. The possibility of a new war between France and Germany was nowhere mentioned; and though there is a reference to the 'reorganization of German militarism', the words 'fascism' and 'national socialism' are nowhere to be found in the text. The theme of the appeal is that the Japanese attack on Manchuria is part of the preparation for a general war of the 'great imperialist powers' against the USSR, and that 'all men, all women, whatever their political affiliation, and all working-class organizations—cultural, social and syndical—all forces and all organizations, *en masse*' should join together in a congress 'to throw a clear light on the historical situation and to confront the masses with the realities which threaten them and to organize the determination of the workers *en bloc* around the USSR in danger'.[82]

191

The appeal had a considerable success, and a Committee of Initiative for the congress was formed including such figures as Einstein, Bertrand Russell, Langevin, Maxim Gorky, John Dos Passos and Mme Sun Yat Sen. Specialized committees were formed to rouse support among women and doctors, and in France a whole range of associations—not only Communist-controlled ones like the ARAC but 'bourgeois' ones such as masonic lodges and branches of the *Ligue des Droits de l'Homme*—quickly announced their support. So did the PCF itself, of course. But the leaders of the SFIO and of the Second International opposed the congress, arguing that the threat to the USSR was imaginary and that the whole thing was really a Communist infiltration manoeuvre: they threatened to expel any Socialist militants who took part in the congress or the committees it set up. This in turn enabled the PCF to combine support for the congress with vitriolic denunciations of the Socialist leaders, in accordance with the 'class against class' line.

In these circumstances the 'International Congress against Imperialist War', which met in Amsterdam in August 1932, must be regarded as a considerable success for its organizers. Out of 2,196 delegates only 830 were card-carrying Communists, while 291 were Socialists (twenty of them French) defying the ban imposed by their own International. The congress produced a manifesto calling for a united front of struggle against imperialist war and for the defence of the USSR, and set up a 'World Committee against Imperialist War', generally referred to as the 'Amsterdam Movement', with national and local branches.

This movement was not of course restricted to intellectuals, although they assumed most of the prominent roles in it. By contrast the *Association des Ecrivains et Artistes Révolutionnaires* (AEAR), founded in the spring of 1932, with Paul Vaillant-Couturier as its general secretary, was specifically aimed at writers and artists. Its title was in fact a simple inversion of the 'Association of Revolutionary Artists and Writers' proposed by Breton and Thirion at the time of the Kharkov Congress; but whereas they had envisaged a militant revolutionary organization from which mere left-leaning pacifists or liberals would be excluded, Vaillant-Couturier used it precisely as an avenue of approach to such uncommitted intellectuals, many of whom were brought through it gently closer to the party.[83] In the first instance the surrealists themselves, including even Aragon, were kept out of it.[84] Later Aragon became one of its most active members, along with Nizan, André Malraux (who was not a party member), and two of Barbusse's associates, Léon Moussinac and Jean Fréville. In October 1932 Breton and the other surrealists were admitted, and Breton himself was even made a member of the 'bureau'. In spite of his quarrel with Aragon he seemed closer than ever to Communist orthodoxy, going so far in February 1933 as to recommend the production of a 'Marxist manual of general literature'![85] At the same time the AEAR had considerable success among the more traditional intelligentsia, and when the first number of its journal *Commune* appeared in July 1933 the editorial board included André Gide as well as Barbusse, Rolland and Vaillant-Couturier.

By this time, however, Hitler had come to power in Germany and the anti-war movement had become specifically anti-fascist. This development would no doubt have occurred earlier had not Stalin consistently underestimated the fascist danger. Left to themselves, European intellectuals in 1932 would no doubt have worried more about the rise of Nazism in Germany than about the Japanese threat to the USSR—and the same probably goes for the leaders of European Communist Parties. Maurice Thorez relates in his autobiography that 'about this time' (December 1932) he visited Barbusse at his villa near Senlis, and that they 'spoke of the means of achieving the unity of the workers to fight effectively against fascism, whose spectre was poised over Germany, threatening with a new catastrophe the universe which had barely recovered from the terrible wounds of war'.[86] Yet Barbusse in the report which he delivered that same month to the Second Plenum of the Amsterdam Movement still spoke of German rearmament as if it threatened only the USSR, being part of a plot by the 'ruling imperialists' of Britain, France and Germany to unite their forces against 'a common enemy'.[87] Not until the catastrophe had already occurred in Berlin did Barbusse return to his anti-fascist preoccupations. But in June 1933 he led the delegation of the Amsterdam Movement to the 'European Anti-fascist Workers' Congress' held at the Salle Pleyel in Paris. At this congress, called formally by Italian and German trade unionists but in fact stage-managed by Willi Münzenberg, one third of the delegates were Communists. A 'European Committee for the Struggle against Fascism' was set up, which quickly merged with the Amsterdam Movement into a 'World Committee for the Struggle against War and Fascism', generally known as the *Comité Amsterdam-Pleyel*: 'Since war and fascism have their common root in the capitalist system,' explained Barbusse, 'the opponents of war and of fascism have only one enemy: capitalism.'[88] The idea of a war against fascism in which capitalist states would take part was evidently still far off; the contradiction between pacifism and anti-fascism in a country threatened by fascism was not yet perceived. But probably this very confusion helped to ensure the movement's success, especially in France. Many Frenchmen feared fascism in Germany precisely because they feared it would lead to a new war: the Amsterdam-Pleyel Movement enabled them to protest against fascism without as yet facing the issue of whether they were prepared to fight a war to stop it.

For the PCF, the movement provided a much-needed channel through which the masses could be approached over the heads of the SFIO and CGT leaders. The moment was propitious, since the SFIO itself was absorbed in an internal struggle with a right wing whose theses had strong overtones of fascism. During the autumn of 1933 local anti-fascist committees (sections of the Amsterdam-Pleyel Movement) were set up all over France, usually on Communist initiative but winning support from many Socialist sympathizers and even some SFIO members. After a World Youth Congress held in Paris in September (and again sponsored by Barbusse) forty sections of the *Jeunesses Socialistes* defied their party leadership and joined the movement. For the first time since Bolshevization there were signs that PCF support was beginning to revive.[89]

PART TWO

A National Party
1934–1947

6

The Turning-Point

Relatively little affected by the world economic crisis of 1929,
France found herself in the grip of an acute depression after the
devaluation of the pound sterling in September 1931. The indices
of economic activity, which had peaked at various times during
1929–30, declined steeply until mid-1932, then recovered slightly,
only to plummet down again from 1933 to 1935. From being a
'happy island' in the first year of the crisis (thanks to the
devaluation—or so-called 'stabilization'—of 1928), France became
part of a shrinking 'gold bloc' whose prices were less and less
competitive. After the Belgian devaluation of March 1935 she was
virtually alone, with prices 20% higher than those of the rest of the
world. The global effect was catastrophic. By 1935 industrial
production had shrunk to three-quarters of its pre-crisis level.
Official unemployment rose from under a thousand in 1929 to half
a million in February 1935 (the real figure being no doubt at least
750,000), while the 'working population' (including unemployed)
had declined by 1.3 million. In big factories especially (those
employing over a hundred people) the number of wage-earners had
declined by 24%. Money incomes declined overall by 30.5%
(28.5% for wage- and salary-earners, 48.1% in agriculture).

In fact, thanks to the fall of prices expressed in francs, most
categories of the population were not as badly off as they seemed.
The overall purchasing power of incomes fell by only 8.5%, and
that of non-agricultural wages and salaries by only 5.9% (profits
—of firms and especially of farms—being much worse hit than
wages and salaries). The wage-earning population having shrunk
(thanks to emigration, early retirement, and the ageing of the
population as a whole), there was actually more purchasing power

197

to go round among those who remained. The purchasing power of the weekly wage of the employed worker went up by 18.5%, and even that of the average worker's income, whether employed or not, increased by 12%. But averages can be misleading. Those whose money incomes were fixed by law or by long-term contract (pensioners, government bondholders, civil servants) inevitably did much better than the average, while others did correspondingly worse. For those thrown out of work or put on short hours the hardship was real, and for the working class as a whole the climate of insecurity was highly demoralizing. As for the peasants, their situation as direct victims of falling prices was truly desperate. And even those who objectively were benefiting from the crisis were not subjectively aware of it, and bitterly resented the government's attempts to reduce their money incomes. By June 1935, when Pierre Laval came into power at the head of a right-wing government committed to applying a savagely deflationary policy by decree, resentment and discontent had spread to almost every category of the population.[1]

The scale of the crisis in France was hardly comparable to that in Germany, where unemployment reached a figure of over six million in January 1932. But it was serious enough to put a very severe strain on the political system. The inability of successive governments to find an economic solution, or even to balance their budgets as taxable resources dwindled, coupled with the series of politico-financial scandals which the recession flushed out into the daylight, brought the Third Republic into a disrepute such as it had not suffered since the great scandals of the 1880s and 1890s. Now as then humiliation swelled the ranks of the extreme right. Theories were canvassed in a wide variety of circles which linked political and economic recovery with the establishment of a more authoritative, if not authoritarian, system of government; and such theories began to carry greater conviction, but also more ominous overtones, after 1933 when the arrival in power of Hitler coincided with Germany's economic revival. On the left, resentment against conservative governments was soon coupled with the fear that they would prove unable or unwilling to resist the onslaught of fascism. For all those who represented the poor and the weak, the need to unite against the rich and the strong was more and more acutely felt. Not many people on the left accepted the argument that liberal democracy had failed and that the choice was now only between fascism and communism; but many did see communism as a necessary ally against fascism, and the Soviet Union—which alone seemed strong enough to protect itself from the crisis—as a necessary ally against Nazi Germany.

COMMUNISM AND FASCISM

The same reasoning applied to the Communists themselves, but they took a long time to see it. During the 1920s they had seen fascism primarily as a useful propaganda bogey. If the bourgeoisie resorted to fascism, it meant that the revolution was near, since the classic bourgeois methods of holding down the working class were no longer adequate. In countries where bourgeois democracy appeared to survive, the game was therefore to detect the signs of fascism's approach. This served two purposes: it encouraged the belief that the revolution was near, and it discredited the existing enemies of communism by identifying them with fascism. Exaggeration of the fascist danger was a sure sign of the prevalence of an ultra-left line. Treint proclaimed in 1924 that 'fascism is already here' (under the *Cartel des Gauches*!), and after 1928 the description of social democracy as 'social fascism' became a commonplace.

By crying wolf at some particularly harmless sheep, the Comintern prepared itself very ill for the appearance of a real and highly dangerous wolf in the shape of National Socialism; and it was slow to perceive its error. Its first reaction was one of pique at the suggestion that the sheep might be all right after all. Rather than accept this unpalatable proposition, the Comintern leaders asserted that the wolf was really quite harmless and would soon go away. 'Fascism, à la Hitler, may decline,' announced Manuilsky in April 1931, 'and is probably already on the wane thanks to the influence of our party.'[2] Thälmann, the German Communist leader, went further, suggesting that the wolf had actually been invented by the sheep in an attempt to save their skins: 'By raising the spectre of Hitler's fascism, Social Democracy is attempting to sidetrack the masses from vigorous action against the dictatorship of finance capital. . . . There are some people who fail to see the Social Democratic forest for the National Socialist trees.'[3] Although there were daily street battles between Nazi storm-troopers and the Communist *Rotfrontkämpferbund*, the Communists on several occasions helped the Nazis in their task of destroying the Weimar Republic and the Social Democrat government of Prussia.*

COMMUNIST STRATEGY IN FRANCE

In France too the Communists long continued to regard Social Democracy as their main enemy. Their Seventh Congress, in March 1932, again defined it as 'an instrument of capital' and reaffirmed the 'class against class' tactic—with, as we have seen, disastrous results in the May general election. But this defeat gave new ammunition to those in the PCF who had accepted the tactic out of discipline rather than conviction and still hoped to see it abandoned. At the Twelfth ECCI Plenum, in September 1932, Doriot was able to point out that his own constituency of Saint-Denis had provided almost the only exception to the general débâcle. Thinking that he had won the argument and that the Comintern's confidence in him was now restored, he returned to Paris to organize the *Fête de L'Humanité* (an annual demonstration-cum-funfair started in 1930 as part of the public campaign to save *L'Humanité* from its financial difficulties). But Thorez, who stayed in Moscow a further twelve days, was able to turn the tables on him by persuading the Comintern to decide on a 'decentralization' of the party organization in the Paris region, thereby withdrawing it from Doriot's influence.[4] Evidently Thorez had already grasped the advantages of being in Moscow when decisions were taken, and the disadvantages of criticizing a Comintern line which had not been officially condemned. He was at pains to make it clear that the PCF's support for the Amsterdam Movement did not imply any weakening of the class-against-class line, quite the contrary: 'The effervescence visible in the Socialist Party and the CGT, in connection with the Amsterdam Congress, opens wide perspectives, provided that we carry on, thanks to the tactic of the united front from below, an effective struggle *against social democracy* [my italics]. The important thing is to ensure, in this mass action, the leadership of the Communist Party.'[5]

The Amsterdam Movement could thus be seen as a new weapon in the Comintern's struggle against Social Democracy—and that was

---

* For instance they supported the Nazi initiative to dissolve the Prussian parliament by referendum in April 1931; in summer 1932 they rejected offers of weapons from the Berlin police chief and made no attempt to oppose Von Papen's illegal dismissal of the Prussian government; and they co-operated with the Nazis in organizing the Berlin transport strike during the November 1932 general election.

certainly how it *was* seen by the leaders of the Second International. But its ostensible purpose was the prevention of a general war against the Soviet Union, and this was certainly not a matter of indifference to the Soviet leaders themselves. They had, however, other means of securing this object than agitation among western intellectuals: the means supplied by inter-governmental diplomacy. During the 1920s they had concentrated mainly on building up a system of non-aggression treaties with their immediate neighbours and on cultivating good relations with Germany. The hostility of France was normally taken for granted, and the main objective of Soviet diplomacy was to detach from France her potential allies in any anti-Soviet crusade. In 1931, however, the French government, alarmed by the rise of Nazism and by the proposal for an Austro-German customs union, began to show interest in a *détente* with Russia. Stalin and his advisers, without abandoning their *entente* with Germany, were glad to take out reinsurance in the form of better relations with France. A Franco-Soviet Non-Aggression Pact was initialled as early as August 1931, but France's desire to bring in her Polish and Romanian allies, coupled with the hostility of many right-wing elements in France itself, postponed its signature for over a year. It was eventually signed by the second Herriot government (which had come to power after the electoral victory of the *néo-Cartel des Gauches*) on 29 November 1932.[6]

A FALSE START

But this development did not redeem the '*néo-Cartel*' in the eyes of the Communists, any more than the recognition of the USSR had redeemed the original *Cartel* in 1924. The PCF was chiefly anxious to exploit the government's inability to solve the economic crisis, and especially the unpopularity which it thereby earned among the rank-and-file Socialists. (In fact there had been a partial economic recovery since the summer, but this was a world phenomenon, not attributable to any government measure; and neither public opinion nor the government itself was aware of it.[7]) As in 1924, the SFIO had refused to join Herriot's government but was giving him support in parliament. PCF propaganda therefore emphasized the 'bourgeois' and 'imperialist' nature of the government, and the responsibility of the Socialists for its unpopular economic policies: salary cuts for civil servants, tax increases, refusal to increase unemployment benefit, involvement in financial scandals, and even conversion of government bonds, described by Thorez as a 'new amputation of the small investor's already-nibbled coupon'. This was a somewhat surprising set of economic grievances to enumerate in a speech which once again summed up the party's 'whole policy' as 'these three words: *class against class*'. But the same speech (delivered in Paris's *Salle Bullier* on 2 December 1932) contained even greater surprises for those familiar with the party line over the past four years. In sharp contrast to Monmousseau's attitude the previous year, Thorez welcomed recent joint meetings of CGT and CGTU workers in the public sector and called for 'one single trade union, one single party of the proletariat'. This admittedly could be taken as simply a more vigorous application of the 'united front from below', but Thorez went further. He revealed that the PCF had invited both the Socialist Party and the PUP to send delegates to a series of public debates on 'the unity of the working class', including the meeting at which he was now speaking. He claimed to have accepted conditions on the organization of the meetings which had been requested by the other parties, and to have sent a special emissary to Paul Faure, the SFIO general secretary, asking him to be present. This was unmistakably the 'united front from above', and lest it should be interpreted as a mere propaganda exercise Thorez was careful to make it clear that, although 'nothing can justify the absence of the socialist and *pupiste* leaders from this assembly', the door remained open:

> To enlighten the proletarians we are organizing throughout the country a series of public debates, starting with this evening.
>
> We are ready to agree with the Socialist Party and the P.U.P. on the organization of these debates, on the places, the dates, the joint bureaux, and on equal speaking-time to ensure that each has full freedom of expression.
>
> We publicly renew this proposal to the Socialist Party and the P.U.P.

Interestingly enough this speech, which clearly foreshadows the rapprochement of the Communist and Socialist Parties in 1934, contains no reference to a fascist threat. It was delivered at a moment when, as a result of the November 1932 German elections, most people in France believed that Nazism was on the wane in Germany and communism on the way up. Thorez saluted the 'great victory' of 'our glorious brother party in Germany' and once more 'solemnly affirmed' that we are fighting and will fight hand in hand with the proletarians of Germany for the abrogation of the treaty of Versailles; for the complete liberation of the German people; the free self-determination of the people of Alsace-Lorraine, up to and including separation from France. . . .[8]

The Socialists were understandably cautious about accepting the PCF's sudden change of heart, but they could hardly refuse to talk. On 16 January 1933 Paul Faure and Jean-Baptiste Sévérac represented the SFIO at a summit meeting of the three parties (PC, SFIO and PUP) which agreed at least on the principle that working-class unity was desirable and necessary. But this Platonic statement was without concrete results. The whole episode is obscure, and the Socialist leaders were certainly not enthusiastic, but it seems that the talks were broken off on orders from Moscow. A year later, at the Thirteenth ECCI Plenum (December 1933), Thorez referred to 'the mistake committed in January' and 'the necessary correction applied at that time'.[9] The mistake was, no doubt, to have anticipated a change in the Comintern line which did not in fact occur until the spring of 1934. In making this mistake Thorez (or Fried?) was probably influenced not by the non-aggression pact—since the formation of a united front on the lines of the *Bullier* speech would, so far from encouraging the government in its application of the pact, have destroyed its parliamentary majority—nor yet by the fascist threat, but by the grass-root demand for working-class unity resulting from the economic situation, and by the anti-sectarian slogans which the Comintern had authorized in the campaign against the 'Barbé-Célor group'.* These slogans, if taken literally, did indeed imply a revision of the united-front-only-from-below policy. But Stalin did not mean them to be taken literally—yet.

HITLER IN POWER

On 30 January 1933 Hitler became Chancellor of Germany. Inevitably many people believed that this could have been avoided if only Communists and Social Democrats had formed a united front

---

* This campaign had gathered strength during 1932 and marked a new degree of viciousness in the party's treatment of dissidents. Célor was the first of many who, after being eliminated from the leadership on ostensibly political grounds, would then be accused of having been police agents all along. Similar accusations were made against discarded leaders in other Communist Parties about the same time, notably in Estonia, Poland and China. See Borkenau, *The Communist International*, pp. 350–6.

against him instead of fighting each other. On 19 February the Second International announced its willingness to negotiate with the Comintern for a joint struggle against fascism. On 5 March, a week after the Reichstag fire, the Comintern replied by instructing its individual sections to propose 'joint action against fascism and the offensive of capital' to the central committees of individual Socialist Parties; but only on certain conditions, one of which was the organization of joint 'action committees' in factories, labour exchanges and working-class districts. 'Committees of joint struggle' were to be set up without waiting for the result of the talks at leadership level. The message concluded by proclaiming the ECCI's conviction 'that the socialist and non-party workers, whatever the attitude of the socialist leaders to the creation of the united front, will overcome all the obstacles and, together with the communists, will achieve the united front not in words but in action'.[10]

All of this suggested a classic operation of infiltration 'from below' and was calculated to revive the Socialists' suspicions. The Second International warned its sections not to reply until a common international line had been agreed; this hesitant attitude was justified by Léon Blum in articles in *Le Populaire* on 7 and 8 March, and the PCF's proposals were left without further response. This was no doubt the reaction which the Comintern had hoped for: the united front tactic was fulfilling its classic function of 'unmasking' the Socialist leaders in front of their own rank-and-file. But the Comintern virtually unmasked itself on 1 April when ECCI published a further statement, this time calling only for a 'united front of Communist and Social-Democrat workers' (i.e. from below), and positively welcoming Hitler's arrival in power: 'The establishment of an undisguised Fascist dictatorship, by dispelling the democratic illusions of the masses and freeing them from the influence of Social Democracy, is accelerating Germany's march towards a proletarian revolution.'[11] It was soon after this that Thorez made his speech in Strasbourg calling for the 'immediate withdrawal of all occupation troops and all French officials from Alsace-Lorraine'.[12] The sincerity of Communist appeals for united action against fascism seemed more and more doubtful. On the Socialist side, the Second International was clearly in no hurry to come to terms. When its Executive Committee at last met on 18–19 May, it decided to ban any separate negotiations between Socialist and Communist Parties so long as 'an effective contact between the two Internationals has not given positive results'. Both sides were clearly intent on avoiding each other, for the Comintern made no attempt to establish contact on the international level but concentrated its propaganda on the rank-and-file of the individual Socialist Parties—with some success after the Pleyel Congress in June (see above, p. 193), at which 200 delegates (out of 3,000) were members of parties belonging to the Second International and a further 300 came from reformist trade unions. The Amsterdam-Pleyel Movement gathered strength in France during the autumn, helped by the brilliant performance of Georgi Dimitrov at the Reichstag trial and by the counter-trial of the Nazi leaders which Münzenberg organized in London and Paris: 'the acquittal of Dimitrov and Torgler came to be regarded as the acquittal of communism in general on the charges of conspiracy and violence.'[13]

THE 'DORIOT LINE' CONDEMNED

On 5 November 1933 the SFIO split. The right-wing 'Neo-Socialists' led by Renaudel, Marquet and Déat were at last expelled. They had been the element in the party which most strongly defended the policy of supporting Radical governments, and would indeed have liked the party to join such governments. The majority had refused to follow them and had insisted on bringing down the government (now headed by Edouard Daladier) rather than support its policy of salary cuts for civil servants. The event seemed to provide a new opportunity for the 'united front from above': would not the Socialist leaders, Léon Blum and Paul Faure, having purged their party of its most anti-Communist elements, now be ready for an agreement with the PCF? The case for a new approach was urged by Doriot at meetings of the *Bureau Politique* on 9 and 11 November. But Thorez was in no hurry to repeat 'the mistake committed in January', and Doriot found himself faced with the familiar charge of 'opportunism'. He then tried to appeal over the heads of the official leadership to the Comintern representative, Fried, who had presumably been the initiator of Thorez's approach a year earlier. But on 1 December ECCI in Moscow gave a ruling in favour of the *Bureau Politique*, and Doriot was conspicuously not invited to the Thirteenth ECCI Plenum convened for the end of the month.[14] Not surprisingly the Plenum rejected the 'Doriot line', and once again called on Communist Parties to fight 'against Social-Democracy and for a United Front from Below':

While carefully exposing to the masses and refuting the hypocriti-
cal and treacherous sophistries of social-democracy, the communists must win over the social-democratic workers for active
revolutionary struggle under the leadership of the communist
parties. . . .

The thirteenth Plenum of the ECCI calls upon all sections of the
Communist International persistently to fight for the realization of
a united militant front with the social-democratic workers, in spite
of and against the will of the treacherous leaders of social-
democracy.[15]

Yet in the discussions at the Thirteenth Plenum a sensitive ear
could detect echoes of disagreement among the Comintern leaders.
Manuilsky in particular did not show quite the same serenity about
Hitler's triumph that had coloured Comintern pronouncements
earlier in the year. He admitted that 'the setting up of a fascist
dictatorship in Germany has inflicted a most severe defeat on the
whole international working class'.* It was therefore 'impossible' for
Communists to 'disregard this event, to neglect to make use of the
lessons which all the other sections of the Comintern have to learn
from this murderous blow'.[16] Fascism was making gains among the
urban and rural petty-bourgeoisie, and not a single Communist Party
in the capitalist world had paid attention to winning over or
neutralizing the urban petty-bourgeoisie.[17]

For Piatnitsky, on the other hand, the main danger was still the
growth of 'social-fascism' in the working class, attributable to the
failure of Communist Parties to expose it correctly. The PCF Central
Committee had not been wrong to negotiate with the SFIO; but
instead of suggesting public discussions on how to organize the united
front they should have proposed a united front of action on a definite
platform for specific purposes (i.e. they should have put forward
proposals which the SFIO leaders were in no danger of accepting).[18]
Thorez himself said that his error had been to 'allow the idea to arise
that in certain circumstances we communists were ready to discuss

---

*According to Albert Vassart ('The Moscow Origin of the French Popular Front', in
Drachkovitch and Lazitch (eds.), *The Comintern: Historical Highlights* [Stanford,
California, 1966], pp. 234–52), Manuilsky was hoping that Thorez would take the
initiative in condemning the present Comintern strategy as ineffective. But this
evidence is of doubtful value since Vassart was not in Moscow at the time. Thorez was
scolded at the Plenum by Piatnitsky for his approach to the Socialists a year before, and
he replied with an orthodox self-criticism. He could hardly be expected to take a risk
that Manuilsky himself was not prepared to take.

organizational union with the socialist party'.[19] (This was presumably a reference to the *Bullier* speech of 2 December 1932, in which he had called for 'one single party of the proletariat'; although in the same speech he had carefully spelt out that there could be no question of sacrificing either the independence of the Communist Party or any of the 'essential principles' accepted at the Congress of Tours.) He went on to criticize those comrades who were not convinced about the error 'and reproach us for the necessary correction which we made at that time' (i.e. the breaking-off of the talks). 'They think it possible,' he added, referring obviously to Doriot, 'to make a special approach to the leaders of the Blum-Faure fraction, on the pretext of unmasking them, whereas such proposals made at this moment would help the cause of the so-called "left-wing" demagogues and would obstruct our effort for the practical realization of the united front from below.'[20]

Fortified by the knowledge that the line had not changed, Thorez returned to Paris and redoubled his campaign against social democracy; he was aided by André Marty, who had spent the last two years in Moscow as French delegate to ECCI but now temporarily took over the running of *L'Humanité*.[21] More than ever the party paper lumped together social democracy and fascism, presenting socialism as the last resort of capitalist democracy and the SFIO leaders as accomplices in the 'fascization' of the country. On 7 January an article by Thorez again insisted on the united front from below (*à la base*), against the Socialist and CGT leaders.

A session of the Central Committee, held on 23–25 January 1934, was told by Thorez:

> The Party is making little progress because it is not carrying on the offensive against social-democracy in a resolute and systematic way. . . . In no case do we seek an agreement with the leadership of the socialist party, whom with good reason we regard as enemies.

Again, Doriot disagreed:

> The way for us to increase the difficulties of the socialist party and to strengthen the revolutionary action front is to make constant proposals simultaneously at the bottom and at the top. . . . I don't believe that the tactic of the united front from below is enough. . . . We absolutely must *complete* our tactic of united front from below by timely proposals at the summit.

Doriot's argument here was no doubt disingenuous: he must have hoped that an agreement with the Socialist leaders could actually be reached. But at least he had the sense to see that the 'united front from below' could never have more than a limited success so long as there was not at least the appearance of sincerity in seeking a united front at the top. More important, he realized that the notion of social democracy as communism's main competitor and rival was out of date. Whereas Thorez scoffed at the 'fascist danger' as a mere slogan, not corresponding to the political situation in France, Doriot warned that 'already there is a struggle between fascism and us to win the masses'.

The result was a foregone conclusion: the Central Committee followed Thorez, who had the authority of the Comintern behind him. On 31 January *L'Humanité* celebrated Doriot's defeat, not naming him but stressing that the opposition had come from 'one single comrade' and had been unanimously condemned. It also distorted his position, asserting that he wanted 'to *replace* the obstinate work of the communists for the united front from below by proposals at the summit'.

THE EVENTS OF FEBRUARY

This quarrel was carried on against a background of rapidly swelling agitation by the extreme right. Cashing in on the 'Stavisky Affair'—latest and most spectacular in the series of politico-financial scandals—*Action Française* and other right-wing 'Leagues' had been holding nightly street demonstrations since 7 January. The discredited Chautemps government had resigned on 27 January, and a new Daladier government was formed in an atmosphere of great tension on 30–31 January. France was in turmoil, and the leaders of the Communist Party were almost alone in seeming unconcerned. Doriot's demand to be allowed to explain his views to the party, and his suggestion that a concerted counter-demonstration against the Leagues be proposed to the SFIO and CGT, were rejected by the Bureau Politique.[22] On 1 February the headline of *L'Humanité*'s editorial was: 'Pas d'énervement'.

Two days later the government announced the removal of Jean Chiappe from his post as prefect of the Paris police. Chiappe was detested by the whole of the left for his toughness in repressing demonstrations (especially Communist ones) and his openly right-wing opinions and sympathies. For the same reasons he was something of a cult-figure with the right: a hymn to his glory, with

music by the conductor of the police band, had even been published in
1929! His sudden promotion to the post of resident-general in
Morocco (which he refused) was transparently aimed at securing
Socialist support for the government in the Chamber. This seemed
the final provocation to the right-wing leagues and war veterans'
associations, which decided to mobilize all their forces for a massive
demonstration against the 'abject regime' on 6 February. Whether or
not their leaders had any definite plan to overthrow the republic (a
point which remains obscure), the fate of the Weimar Republic was
fresh in everyone's minds. To democrats of all persuasions it was
evident that the Third Republic in its turn was threatened by fascism.
But the Communist Party was not yet ready to rally to its defence.
L'Humanité of 6 February called on the workers to demonstrate, not
only against the 'fascist bands' but also 'against the government
which protects and develops them, and against social-democracy
which, by dividing the working class, is trying to weaken it and thus to
open the way to a rapid accentuation of the brutal class dictatorship'.
In the Chamber of Deputies, while Daladier strove to make himself
heard above the hoots and whistles of the right, the handful of
Communist deputies added to the pandemonium with chants of 'Les
Soviets!', 'En prison Chiappe!', and the *Internationale*. In the streets
Communist demonstrators found themselves fighting alongside the
men of *Action Française* against the police, who remained loyal to the
republic.[23] At one point, when it looked as if the rioters might actually
succeed in storming the Palais Bourbon and lynching the deputies,
two Communist deputies—Doriot and Renaud Jean—urged Thorez
to issue an appeal to the working class and to start immediate
discussions with the Socialists. Thorez refused.[24] Later that evening
delegates went from the SFIO Federation of the Seine (dominated by
the left wing of the party) to try and make contact with the
Communists at the head office of *L'Humanité*; but Marty refused to see
them.[25] (Twenty years later, after his expulsion from the PCF, Marty
was to be blamed for the 'sectarian' attitude of *L'Humanité* during this
crisis.)[26]

The following days were ones of great confusion both in the country
at large and in the PCF. Daladier resigned on 7 February and was
replaced two days later by a government of 'national union' under
Gaston Doumergue, a former president of the republic: this meant in
effect that the Radicals agreed to govern in coalition with the right,
while the Socialists returned to opposition. Meanwhile *L'Humanité*

continued to proclaim that there could be no 'unity of action' with those who 'abandon the class battlefield and collaborate in the defence of the capitalist regime'. But visibly the party leaders were losing control of their troops. In several provincial towns Communists joined Socialist demonstrations, while in Saint-Denis, at the very gates of Paris, Doriot held talks with local SFIO leaders in defiance of party instructions, and arranged for his 'Ninth Rayon' to take part in an SFIO protest demonstration planned for 8 February. The first sign that the PCF leadership might bend before the storm came on the morning of 8 February, when *L'Humanité* invited five Communist trade unions to 'study the possibilities' of taking part in a general strike which the CGT had called for 12 February, in protest both against the 6 February riot and against Daladier's resignation. But the same issue contained an appeal for a mass demonstration to be held the next day (9 February) to demand the arrest *both* of the 'fascist' leaders *and* of the 'killers Daladier and Frot'—the latter being the Minister of the Interior under whose orders the police had defended the Chamber of Deputies, and who was therefore held responsible for the deaths of some twenty people killed when the police fired on the rioters. The demonstration was to be accompanied by a twenty-four-hour general strike in the Paris region, organized by the local CGTU and (hopefully!) CGT unions.

Understandably confused by the Communists' behaviour, and frightened by a ban on all public gatherings, the SFIO decided to abandon its planned demonstration and support the CGT general strike on 12 February instead. Bu. the *Bureau Politique* of the PCF, meeting on 8 February, decided to ignore the ban and go ahead with its demonstration the following day. (The call for an accompanying strike was, however, abandoned—and the CGTU decided, presumably on party instructions, to join in the CGT general strike on 12 February.) The same meeting of the *Bureau Politique* apparently decided, in spite of protests by Doriot, that the party leaders should avoid the risk of arrest by sheltering outside Paris during the demonstration. Thorez, Duclos, Marty and Cachin accordingly left town and Thorez remained at Barbizon, near Fontainebleau, until 12 February.[27] This enabled Doriot to occupy the limelight in Paris during these four days, and particularly during the demonstration on 9 February when he was at the head of the Communist forces in repeated and violent battles with the police.

After that events moved quickly. On 10 February a representative of the PCF, Guy Jerram, went to the SFIO headquarters to discuss the possibility of Communist participation in a mass demonstration at Vincennes which the SFIO was now organizing, with the permission of the new government, for the afternoon of 12 February; and on 11 February *L'Humanité* at last came off the fence and urged Communists to join the demonstration. Under the pressure of events, and after much hesitation, the party had momentarily accepted the united front at the top as well as the bottom. The decision was apparently taken by Fried on his own responsibility;[28] he would hardly have had time to refer it to Moscow.

12 February 1934 was to become something of a left-wing legend. According to the CGT 75% of all workers, manual and white-collar, went on strike. Demonstrations were held all over France, and the Paris one, marching from Vincennes to the Place de la Nation, was estimated at 150,000 people, including some 20,000 Communists. The latter initially formed a separate cortège, but soon mingled with the Socialists and joined in the general cry of 'Unité d'Ac-tion! Unité d'Ac-tion!' Cachin and Duclos spoke to the crowd from the same platform as Blum and Paul Faure. To Blum's assertion that 'we are all here to defend the Republic because we know that only the Republic can enable us to move forward', they replied prudently: 'our only slogan must be the struggle against fascism!'[29] But in Saint-Denis Doriot had now abandoned all inhibitions and the demonstration there was organized in close collaboration with the local SFIO branches and the non-Communist trade unions. A 'Comité de vigilance antifasciste de Saint-Denis' was set up including the local leaders of both parties.[30]

THE CAMPAIGN AGAINST DORIOT

On the morning after the great day, the PCF leaders found themselves in an embarrassing situation. The 'united front from below' had worked, but in a quite unexpected sense: pressure from below had forced them to co-operate with the Socialist leaders, and so to contribute to the prestige of the very people whose treachery the Comintern had instructed them to expose. Anxious no doubt to forestall the wrath of Moscow, they immediately set out to unsay what had been said and to undo what had been done. An obvious scapegoat was to hand in the person of Doriot, who had had the impudence to carry the party with him in more or less open defiance of both the national and the international leadership. But he could be attacked only with circumspection because of the popularity his actions had won him in the party, and especially in his own area of Saint-Denis.

L'Humanité of 13 February praised 'red Saint-Denis' for the outstanding success of the demonstration there. But that very day the 'Comité de vigilance' was criticized. Soon afterwards a member of the *Bureau Politique* described it as 'a crime against the working class' and demanded its dissolution.[31] On 17 February the Communists prevented Jean Zyromsky, one of the left-wing Socialist leaders, from speaking at the funeral of the Communists killed on 9 February.[32] Next day in *L'Humanité* Vaillant-Couturier thanked the Socialists who had attended the funeral, but added: 'We do not forget that our comrades were killed by bullets paid for out of credits voted by the Socialist deputies.' And on 19 February he wrote: 'Defend the Republic, says Blum? As if fascism were not still the Republic, as if the Republic were not already fascism.' But the anti-fascist movement was growing willy-nilly, and inevitably Communists and Socialists competed for the control of it. On 24 February the Socialists formed a 'Centre de liaison des forces antifascistes' for the Paris region. The PCF reacted by insisting that Communist organizations could only affiliate (or stay affiliated) to local anti-fascist committees if the latter in turn affiliated to the Amsterdam-Pleyel Movement. The Socialists refused this, whereupon the Communists refused to work with the 'Centre de liaison'.[33]

Needless to say, Doriot did not meekly accept this reassertion of the 'class against class' line. He kept his 'Comité de vigilance' alive, and in internal party meetings he continued to argue for a pact of united action with the SFIO[34] and to criticize the leadership. He also tried again to win over Fried to his point of view. Fried's reaction is not known: probably he felt some sympathy for Doriot but felt unable to support him so long as the instructions from Moscow remained unchanged. And so far there was no sign of their changing. In March an article in *Communist International* laid down that the PCF's job was now to prevent the Socialists from 'diverting the anti-fascist mass movement on to the lines of "defence of the Republic"', and to continue the struggle against the 'social-fascists' and expose their manoeuvres, while extending and leading the united front movement;[35] and in April ECCI issued a May Day manifesto calling on the workers to fend off fascism by 'breaking with social democracy and uniting under the fighting banner of the Communist International for the revolutionary struggle for working-class power, for a Soviet Government'.[36]

On 1 March the *Bureau Politique* of the PCF requested Doriot to drop his attacks on party leaders and henceforth 'discuss' the party line only at *Bureau Politique* meetings. Doriot prevaricated and managed to get the issue postponed until the next meeting a week later—at which, however, he failed to turn up. Preferring to fight the battle on his own ground, he called a conference of the Ninth Rayon for 9 March and challenged Thorez to come and defend his point of view. Surprisingly enough Thorez did so: probably he and the other leaders feared that if they took disciplinary measures against Doriot at this stage they would lose almost the whole party organization in the Paris region. After a three-day debate the conference supported Doriot by 110 votes to sixty-one, and adopted a motion calling on the Comintern to settle the dispute by 120 votes to fifty-five. (This motion was proposed by one of Doriot's supporters, which suggests that Fried may have encouraged him not to despair of winning the Comintern's favour.) Doriot remained secure in his bastion, but meanwhile the leadership was working on other party branches in the Paris region to get them to condemn him. As March wore on, the campaign came progressively into the open. At first *L'Humanité* did not attack Doriot by name, but concentrated on his associates—one of whom, conveniently enough, was the already-vilified Henri Barbé (proving that 'sectarian' and 'opportunist' errors are but opposite sides of the same coin . . .). Then on 31 March Thorez accused the whole Ninth Rayon of pursuing a 'bloc policy' with the SFIO, described as 'a social democracy which neither can nor will fight against fascism'. The following two days a conference of the Communist organizations of the Paris-North region was held at Saint-Denis, and voted eighty-four to fifty-four in favour of the *Bureau Politique*. The leadership's campaign was clearly having its effect, but the existence of such a large dissident minority was still abnormal and embarrassing for a 'Bolshevized' party. The conference was not mentioned in *L'Humanité* until a week later, and even then the voting figures were not published.

Thorez thundered more violently than ever against social democracy and those who advocated dealings with it:

It's at this moment that a few opportunists 'propose' that our party renounce its policy of united front from below and practise a bloc policy with social-democracy. It's at this moment that we are invited, in effect, to abandon the positions of bolshevism and return to the social-democratic vomit. . . .

All the babblings about marriage between communists and socialists are completely foreign to the spirit of bolshevism. We do not want to unite with social-democracy. You cannot marry fire and water. . . . What we want is to make it easier for the socialist workers to turn towards communism, towards Moscow.

A big anti-fascist demonstration planned by the CGT for 8 April was deliberately sabotaged by the Communists.[37] On 9 April Doriot himself brought the conflict right into the open by resigning as mayor of Saint-Denis and promising to resign his seat in parliament as well if he were defeated in the resulting municipal election.[38] Two days later the Ninth Rayon transmitted to the *Bureau Politique*, for forwarding to Moscow, its open letter to ECCI. The letter was also printed as a pamphlet and distributed to all party members. It not only defended Doriot and attacked the 'impotence and inertia' of the party leaders during February, but also put forward a new thirteen-point programme for the party, including benefits for the peasants and the middle class, nationalizations and—most daringly—a policy of alliance with the USSR rather than unconditional support.[39]

After this the *Bureau Politique* had nothing to gain by further circumspection. On 12 April it censured Doriot and apparently forbade him to attend its meetings.[40]

THE COMINTERN INTERVENES

Formally, the issue of the quarrel now depended on the verdict of the International. In practice, and with good reason, both sides treated it as a foregone conclusion. Whatever difficulties they had encountered with the rank-and-file, the one thing Thorez and his colleagues were sure of was that they had defended the Comintern line with exemplary fidelity; and Doriot, whatever lingering hope he may have entertained after talking to Fried in early March, had evidently by now despaired of winning the Comintern's support. The content of the open letter was hardly likely to appeal to Moscow, and in any case by making it public Doriot had transgressed the most elementary rules of party discipline. His resignation as mayor—the only object of which could be to bring an internal party dispute before the mass of the electors—was an equally flagrant breach. There can be little doubt that Doriot had by now resolved on a complete break with the party, and was merely manoeuvring so as to take as many party members with him as he could. The events of February must have convinced him that he had an important political role to play in France, but that this role could not be played inside the Communist Party. Albert Vassart, who was sent by the leadership to argue its case in Doriot's own cell, relates that he told Doriot he was about to leave for Moscow (to take up the post of PCF representative) and offered to get Doriot invited there by the Comintern: 'But Doriot was skeptical. He believed that such an invitation would be of no avail and stated in a disillusioned tone that he expected nothing of such a trip. He gave the impression of a man who, considering his efforts futile, was expecting reprisals by the Comintern.'[41]

On 21 April, however, the invitation arrived, in the form of a summons from ECCI: 'We consider it necessary to cease the internal struggle in the party. Send Doriot and Thorez here. The Communist International will examine the fractional disagreement in the French Party.' This was evidently not what the PCF leadership had been expecting. Instead of condemning Doriot's indiscipline the Comintern appeared to be treating the affair as a personal rivalry between two leaders, each of whom must take a share of the blame. On 24 April *L'Humanité* tried to correct this impression, stressing that the disagreement about the united front was between Doriot and the Central Committee as a whole. On 26 April Cachin, accompanied by the whole *Bureau Politique* and the leading figures of the Central Committee, was sent instead of Thorez to a public debate with Doriot in Saint-Denis. Thorez himself was already on his way to Moscow.

But Doriot refused to go, asserting that he could not leave Saint-Denis before the municipal elections on 6 May. The Comintern displayed quite unprecedented patience: a second summons, on 30 April, was accompanied by the promise of an 'armistice' pending final arbitration of the dispute (as an earnest of which *L'Humanité*'s attacks on Doriot were at once suspended); and even after its refusal the Comintern declared that 'the question of expulsion does not arise'. The election arrived, and Doriot (whom the leadership had finally decided not to oppose) scored a brilliant personal success. But still he showed no sign of leaving for Moscow. On 10 May a final summons was sent, over the signatures of the four leading figures in the Comintern—Dimitrov, Manuilsky, Piatnitsky and Pieck. Doriot replied with a list of his coming engagements and a promise to come to Moscow, at the head of a delegation of Saint-Denis workers, when the

French situation had calmed down! A more insolent reply is hard to imagine. Even so the Comintern itself did not pronounce his expulsion, but merely announced (16 May) that he had forfeited its 'defence' and that the PCF Central Committee was therefore free to take 'all the measures of an ideological or organizational order that it considers necessary'.[42]

In this purely disciplinary pronouncement the political content of Doriot's errors was not mentioned. The reason for this, and for the surprising leniency with which he had been treated, became clear a week later when the essence of his policy received the solemn imprimatur of the Soviet Communist Party. *Pravda* of 23 May carried a long unsigned article which, after asserting that before Hitler came to power the KPD had 'more than once approached the leadership of the SPD to propose a united front of struggle', went on to say: '*A fortiori*, such an appeal to the Socialist leaders is possible in a country like France. . . . The question of addressing the leadership of the Socialist Party has never been, for the communists of France, a question of programme. Their position on this point resulted from considerations of revolutionary opportunity.' Underneath appeared another long article, signed by Maurice Thorez. According to this: '. . . the situation in France is now shaping up in such a manner that the Communist Party will once again have to make a frank proposal to the leadership of the Socialist Party and of the CGT for a joint struggle against the fascist threat.'[43] The author (or at least signatory) of this article had in fact already returned to Paris, and that same night he told a meeting at the Grange-aux-Belles, in Paris, that the official conception of a united front did not rule out negotiations with the SFIO leaders.[44]

Evidently Thorez had been instructed in Moscow to prepare a change of tactics. But probably he himself did not yet realize how sweeping the change was to be. He may well have thought that the object was—as in the original united front tactics of 1922—to 'unmask' the Socialist leaders more effectively by proposing contacts at the top as well as at the bottom. For another month the party appeared to play its old game of getting the SFIO leaders to take the blame for the failure of the united front. On 29 May *L'Humanité* announced the convocation of a national party conference for 23–25 June, the theme of which was to be 'The Organization of the United Front of Anti-Fascist Struggle'; but Thorez wrote that one of the objects of the conference would be to prove the 'unshakable unity of the Communist party in the face of the confusion and decomposition of the parties of the bourgeoisie, including the Socialist party'.

Two days later, on 31 May, the *Bureau Politique* made its first direct approach to the SFIO leaders: a proposal to discuss a joint campaign in favour of Ernst Thälmann, the German Communist leader imprisoned by the Nazis. The Socialists, though somewhat bewildered, could hardly refuse this ostensibly humanitarian suggestion.[45] After an exchange of letters, a meeting was arranged between representatives of the two parties for 11 June—at which, however, the Communists refused to promise to abandon their verbal attacks on the SFIO and its leaders. Such a 'non-aggression pact' was always the first preoccupation of Socialist leaders in this period when approaching any discussions with the Communists. They did not believe that an alliance with the PCF, small and weak as it was, could do them much positive good; but they were very sensitive to the harm done them by constant vilification in the Communist press, remembering especially how Communist propaganda had helped the Nazis to destroy social democracy in Germany. (The first reaction of the SPD, after Hitler's arrival in power, had been to propose—unsuccessfully—a 'non-aggression pact' with the KPD.) On 12 June they repeated their request by letter, to which the PCF replied two days later, calling for a decision on united action 'within forty-eight hours', protesting that 'insult and defamation are methods foreign to our party', but warning that 'we intend to retain our entire right to doctrinal criticism, to analyse the facts and events and to draw the tactical conclusions in the exclusive interest of the working masses'.[46]

Next day, 15 June, appeared a number of *Cahiers du Bolchévisme* in which the Socialists were once again attacked as 'the principal social defenders of the bourgeoisie', whose only intention was to 'fool the working class', etc. It is not clear how long beforehand the issue had actually gone to press, but inevitably its publication appeared perfectly timed to sabotage the negotiations. On 20 June the Socialist leadership met and decided to suspend them.[47] (Only the left-wing Federation of the Seine, disregarding the decision of the national leadership, went ahead and signed a local agreement with the Communist Region of Paris.)

This news was apparently received in Moscow with incredulity and fury. It looked as though Fried and Thorez, resentful at the sudden *volte-face* which had been imposed on them, were deliberately sabotaging the Comintern's new policy.* But on 24 June there arrived in Moscow the previous day's issue of *Le Populaire*, containing a Socialist proposal for a 'Pacte de Non-Aggression Socialo-Communiste', closely modelled in form on the Franco-Soviet Non-Aggression Pact of 1932 (although in substance it foreshadowed the 1935 Pact of Mutual Assistance, since it proposed that the two parties 'render each other mutual aid and assistance' in repelling fascist aggression). Vassart, the PCF representative in Moscow, discussed this with Manuilsky. They agreed that the chance must be seized, and accordingly cabled instructions to the PCF to reach agreement quickly with the SFIO, including in the telegram a draft counter-proposal which accepted the Socialist demands for non-aggression but at the same time expanded them into a positive pact of struggle against fascism.[48] This telegram arrived while the PCF's national conference was actually in session at Ivry-sur-Seine, and caused it to be prolonged for an extra day. On 26 June Thorez told the conference that the success of the united front was now 'a matter of life or death for the proletariat' and that unity of action was therefore necessary 'at any price'. If such unity were obtained, 'neither from the mouth of any of our propagandists, nor from the pen of any of our writers, in *L'Humanité* or even in the *Cahiers du Bolchévisme*, as in our entire press, will there be the slightest attack against the organizations or against the leaders of the Socialist party.' Citing the recent local agreement in Paris as evidence of the PCF's sincerity, Thorez with superb disingenuity asserted that it was Doriot who all along had treated the united front as a pure manoeuvre, who like Treint had wanted only to 'plumer la volaille'; and to prove this he quoted a passage from Doriot's speech at the January Central Committee meeting in which Doriot, arguing for an approach to the Socialist leaders and no doubt anxious to reconcile this as far as possible with the then Comintern line, had said that he would be delighted if Paul Faure again replied

---

* The Comintern leaders might have made more allowances for the technical difficulties involved. Their own French-language journal, *L'Internationale Communiste*, appeared on 20 June with an article by Togliatti, presumably written some time before, which argued to the following conclusion: 'At the present time and in the near future the most obstinate struggle against social-democracy, a struggle which must smash its influences among the masses, is a necessity for the PCF if it wants to live and to develop politically.' But according to Vassart, Manuilsky was so angry with Fried that he recalled him to Moscow and threatened to deprive him of his post. ('The Moscow Origin of the French Popular Front', in Drachkovitch and Lazitch (eds.), *The Comintern: Historical Highlights* [Stanford, California, 1966], p. 249.)

with a five-letter word—'that would be very useful to us'.[49] Next day, 27 June, Doriot was expelled from the party.

DORIOT: A POST-MORTEM

The Doriot episode remains a fascinating enigma. Did the Comintern, or a faction within it (Manuilsky? Dimitrov?), intend to combine its change of tactics with a change of leadership in the French party, replacing the 'sectarian' Thorez with the 'opportunist' Doriot? Or had they always preferred Thorez's blind obedience to Doriot's intelligent insubordination? Did Doriot have inside information which encouraged him to appeal to the Comintern in March, but discouraged him from going to Moscow in April? Or was it simply his own growing prestige and the prolonged obtuseness of the Comintern's public pronouncements that persuaded him that his future lay outside the party? Or again, was it merely an instinct that told him that if he went to Moscow he would repeat the experience of Cachin in 1922, find himself unable to defend his views when far away from his supporters and subjected to intense moral pressure by the Soviet leaders, and return deprived of his prestige and relegated to an honorific but secondary role? Was Thorez really unaware until May that the Comintern line was about to change? Or was the return to a sectarian attitude after 12 February a brilliant manoeuvre to provoke Doriot and his supporters into an open breach of discipline?

None of these questions seems likely to receive a conclusive answer. What is certain is that the episode marks a turning-point of crucial importance. Crucial in the first instance for Doriot himself. His break with the party at the precise moment when it adopted his own views made it impossible for him to play the role in which he had cast himself, as leader of a reunited working class in a crusade against fascism. Believing as he did (and as many others did at that time) that the decisive struggle would now be between communism and fascism, once expelled from the Comintern he was driven by the logic of his own ambition to espouse the fascist cause. Exactly two years later (28 June 1936) he was to found the *Parti Populaire Français*, 'the only French party which fully corresponds to the definition of "fascist" '.

The agreement between socialists and communists left Doriot space only to be flattened between the two machines. The mechanisms of rejection, so highly tuned in political bureaucracies, worked against Doriot. In the courts of unity it was Thorez who sat and not Doriot. The latter had a general staff to find places for; not until Vichy came along could these men find shoes to fit them under Pétain or Laval. Doriot, to remain the leader, invented ever more aberrant political combinations. The antifascist of the 9th February founded a fascist party, sank into collaboration and thought himself obliged to settle his personal accounts with the Comintern by going to fight the Russians in German uniform. As always, he fought bravely, and ended up a traitor in the manner of the constable Bourbon.

And if Doriot had become leader of the PCF in 1934? It is of course idle to speculate, but here again one may quote the view of André Thirion, who broke finally with communism at the same time as Doriot and became a Gaullist during the Second World War:

> I never liked Doriot's personality whereas I felt some sympathy for Thorez. Nonetheless I think that Doriot would have given the Popular Front and the action of the communists a dimension that Thorez was incapable of reaching. No doubt with Doriot the French Communist Party would have been likely to move away from Moscow, especially in 1940. But if Doriot, who fought courageously against the German army in 1940, had then been the leader of the communist party, he would have become, barring accidents, the chief figure in the Resistance, or at least the popular French politician of importance whom General de Gaulle lacked, in London, on the 18th June.[50]

Perhaps it was some such development that the Comintern vaguely foresaw, and wished to avoid.

SIGNIFICANCE OF THE 1934 'TOURNANT'

But whatever the effect on the party of Doriot's expulsion, the adoption of the slogan 'unity of action at any price' marks a watershed in its history. Not all the implications became apparent at once, but they could already be glimpsed in an article by Thorez in the *Cahiers du Bolchévisme* of 1 July 1934:

> We want to prevent the white-collar workers in the big towns, the civil servants, the middle classes—little shopkeepers, artisans— and the mass of working farmers (*paysans-travailleurs*) from being won over by fascism. . . . Then, in order to fight the penetration of the chauvinist ideology in the strata of the petty-bourgeoisie, we have said openly 'we love our country'.

Ostensibly the Pact of Unity of Action signed on 27 July 1934 between the PCF and the SFIO brought together two working-class parties, and was therefore an application of the 'united working-class front' originally prescribed in 1921, a battle front drawn up for international class war. The object of this tactic, it will be remembered, was to forestall or sabotage the forming of a 'left bloc' between social democrats and the left bourgeoisie, and so to prevent the working class from being misled into illusions about the possibilities of piecemeal reform or democratic progress. In other words, the success of the united front should have sounded the knell, in France, of the alliance between Socialists and Radicals.

Thorez's words, and indeed the whole national and international context, made it obvious that this was not the intention. Fundamentally, the Comintern leaders' analysis of the nature of social democracy had not changed. They still regarded it—and to a large extent rightly—as a party of class collaboration, voicing the aspirations at once of the less revolutionary part of the working class and of the more advanced section of the petty bourgeoisie, and expecting progress from parliamentary democracy rather than from social revolution and proletarian dictatorship. By agreeing to the united front at the top they were not suddenly endorsing social democracy as a genuinely working-class movement; rather they were admitting the need, in the present historical circumstances, for the working class to find allies, not merely in the peasantry, as Lenin had prescribed, but within the ranks of the bourgeoisie itself, and more specifically in the ranks of the petty bourgeoisie and 'middle classes'. Why? Because these strata, to which a precise political role had seldom been attributed by pre-war Marxist writers, had now assumed an unforeseen role as the main social support for fascism, which in turn had become the biggest threat to the working-class movement and had even succeeded in robbing it of some of its working-class support. In these circumstances the strategy of the Communist Parties had to become defensive instead of offensive. The theory of an imminent revolutionary crisis was abandoned; the immediate task was now to head off the rise of fascism by competing with it for middle-class support and constituting a defensive alliance which, by preserving bourgeois democracy, would also safeguard the chances of revolution at a later stage.

Obviously this involved a radical revision of the theses put forward by the Comintern during the 'Third Period' (1928–34), and especially of the notion that a fascist victory would actually bring the proletarian revolution nearer by dissipating social-democratic illusions. This revision may have resulted simply from a sober, if belated, appraisal of the objective results of Hitler's coming to power in Germany—an appraisal in which Dimitrov, who arrived in Moscow at the end of February 1934, certainly played an important part. But in all probability it was also influenced by—as it certainly had repercussions on—the development of relations between the Soviet Union and the bourgeois nation states. For just as the rise of fascism put the working class on the defensive in individual countries, so the rise of Nazi Germany put the Soviet Union on the defensive in its international relations; and just as the working class was obliged to seek allies within the bourgeoisie, so the Soviet Union was obliged to seek allies among the bourgeois states.

In strict theory, the revision involved here was less radical: the Soviet state had in fact been militarily on the defensive since the failure of the Polish campaign in 1920; and since 1922 it had practised a policy of alliance with bourgeois Germany. This had proved quite compatible with a Comintern policy of 'class against class' in Germany as elsewhere. Stalin probably hoped at first that the same dual policy could be operated towards France: from the end of 1932 onwards Litvinov was allowed to edge towards an alliance with France (involving a complete reversal of the Soviet stance on the issues 'security versus disarmament' and 'Versailles settlement versus revision'), while, as we have seen, the French Communist Party was obliged to carry on an intransigent class-against-class policy. Inevitably this involved a contradiction between the attitude of the PCF and that of the Soviet state to French bourgeois politicians who favoured the Soviet alliance—a contradiction joyfully exploited by the PCF's critics, as for instance in a cartoon which appeared in *Le Populaire* in August 1933, when Herriot was in Russia as the guest of the Soviet authorities: a French Communist (reading *L'Humanité*) exclaims, 'Ah, there's that infamous Herriot who is plotting an imperialist war against Soviet Russia!', to which a Russian Communist (reading *Izvestya*) replies, 'But, no, comrade, that's our dear little father Herriot. Here we call him "the indefatigable fighter for peace".'[51]

Such contradictions were not in themselves likely to worry Stalin. But there were other considerations. The French bourgeoisie was not as weak, or did not feel itself as weak, as the German bourgeoisie had been in 1922. By no means all its political representatives were convinced of the necessity, still less the desirability, of a Franco-Soviet alliance; and one of the aspects of it which most worried them was the encouragement it would give to revolutionary propaganda and activities in France. Successive French foreign ministers gave Soviet diplomats to understand that the Comintern's anti-national agitation in France was one of the main obstacles to an *entente* between the two countries. Stalin did not by any means give in to this pressure overnight. It was not until after the Franco-Soviet Pact of Mutual Assistance had actually been signed, in May 1935, that, in response to a direct request from Laval, he publicly expressed his approval of France's national defence policy. Until then the PCF's anti-military and anti-colonial propaganda continued unabated. But well before that, in the autumn of 1934, the party had begun to make overtures to the Radicals. Thorez's speech at Nantes on 24 October (on the eve of the Radical Party congress there) was perhaps directed more at the Radical electorate than at the party as such; but Duclos recounts in his memoirs that shortly before this he and Frachon paid a formal visit on behalf of the PCF leadership to Herriot, who was then a member of the Doumergue government.[52] This was just after the death of Barthou, the foreign minister, who had been working fast towards a Franco-Soviet alliance. It is hard to believe that the desire to reassure his prospective allies was not one of Stalin's motives for approving the change of Comintern tactics.

One may doubt, however, whether this argument would have sufficed if France had had a strong, united government composed of more or less conservative anti-fascists like Barthou and Herriot. If Stalin had had confidence in the existing French government, he would surely have been reluctant to encourage the 'popular front' whose only possible purpose was to weaken and destroy the government of 'national union' in order to replace it by a government of the united left. The French politicians favourable to an alliance with Russia were, in 1934, more numerous among right-wing nationalists than on the moderate left. The Socialist Party, and the left wing of the Radical Party led by Daladier, were predominantly pacifist and preferred to seek a *détente* with Germany, even a Nazi Germany, rather than to recreate the pre-1914 situation with an 'encircling' Franco-Russian alliance.[53] On the face of it, therefore, it seems hard to explain the decision of the PCF to seek an alliance with Blum and Daladier against the right in terms of Soviet foreign policy. But on the other hand it was essential to the success of Soviet foreign policy that France herself should not fall into the fascist camp. For this purpose it was essential to weld together the anti-fascist forces inside France, and these were essentially the forces of the left. On 6 February Daladier's government, eagerly supported by the Socialists, had firmly repressed the right-wing rioters; but the Communists, instead of supporting it, had joined in the attack. Next day Daladier resigned. There was hardly a direct connection of cause to effect here, but the lesson seemed to be that next time, if there was a next time, the left should be solidly united against the 'fascist' threat so that there could be no excuse for vacillation. By contrast, the right-wing government which succeeded Daladier could not be relied on to hold the line against fascism. Indeed it was widely regarded as 'pre-fascist'—a kind of French equivalent to Brüning or even Von Papen—and it included Tardieu, the hero of the leagues, who had done nothing to quell their violence on 6 February. Above all, it was a heterogeneous coalition based on a fragile parliamentary majority and foredoomed, by the economic crisis and the nature of its policies, to growing unpopularity. Under such a government, France was unlikely to be either a reliable or a strong ally for the Soviet Union.

In the 1920s, Russia had given Germany some help in rebuilding her military strength; but it had never been a requirement of Russian policy to make Germany politically strong—merely to keep her from forming an anti-Soviet bloc with the western Allies. The situation after 1934 was different: Russia felt a need for positive French strength as a deterrent to Germany's aggressive policies. In these circumstances a French Communist Party seeking to undermine the French state became an embarrassment to Soviet policy in a way that the German Communist Party in the 1920s had not been. Equally an unpopular, and therefore weak, French government was a danger to the Soviet Union in a way that a weak German government had not been. It became desirable that the French government should be popular, and therefore strong, and that the French Communist Party should be able to contribute to its popularity and its strength—in other words, that it should be a left-wing government with a popular programme enjoying Communist support.

From an internationalist party working to sap the vitality of the nation state, the PCF was thus asked to transform itself into a factor of national cohesion; and at the same time to make itself attractive to strata of society whose attachment to the nation was regarded as unshakeable. It therefore had to adjust itself to exalting those very

224

patriotic ideals and symbols (the tricolour, the *Marseillaise*) which it had long and ardently derided. This adjustment, at which Thorez already hinted in his article of 1 July 1934, was a much more fundamental one than the mere acceptance of a united front with the Socialist leaders, and it took about a year to complete. But the party militants, schooled by the experience of Bolshevization and the Third Period to unquestioned acceptance of chops and changes in the party line, were able to make the adjustment with astonishingly little complaint; and the adjustment once made was to bring the party a popularity and success it had scarcely dreamed of in the preceding period. It became a national party, not only in the sense of supporting the nation but also in the sense of having nationwide support and playing a major role in national politics.

The 'turning-point' of 1934 thus had two crucial and closely connected effects on the PCF: it enabled it to transcend class barriers and make itself the champion of a broad, inter-class alliance; and it enabled it to do so in the name of national unity and a shared national interest. The immediate aims of this new strategy were defensive and circumstantial, a reaction to the rise of fascism abroad and (supposedly at least) at home. But the effect on the party's outlook and character was to survive the fascist threat and model the whole of its later history. Though there were periods in its later history (notably 1939–40 and 1947–52) when it appeared to return to a narrowly class-based and anti-national position, and though of course it continued to affirm its allegiance to the Marxist-Leninist theory of class war, it remains today what it became in 1934–6: a national party.

7

The Popular Front

From 'Unité d'Action' to the Election of 1936

When Thorez called for Unity of Action 'at any price' he meant what he said. On 2 July 1934 the Comintern's proposal for a 'pact of struggle against fascism' was published in *L'Humanité* and presented to the SFIO. It accepted the main points of the Socialist draft 'non-aggression pact' (whose authors had probably not expected or even intended that it should be accepted), and added proposals for a positive campaign against fascism in France and in favour of Thälmann and other anti-fascists imprisoned in Germany. On 15 July the SFIO National Council, still suspicious of Communist motives but borne along by a groundswell of unitarian enthusiasm from the rank-and-file, agreed to joint action with the PCF, provided certain conditions were included in the pact: one of the objects of the campaign should be 'the defence of democratic freedoms'; it should be directed against the 'fascist' regime of Dollfuss (which had brutally suppressed the Austrian Socialist Party in February) as well as that of Hitler; insults against the other party should be banned outside as well as inside the joint action; joint meetings and demonstrations should not be allowed to degenerate into doctrinal or tactical disputes; the responsibility for correcting breaches of the pact by members of one party should lie exclusively with that party; and a co-ordination committee composed of representatives of both parties should deal with any disputes or conflicts that arose. All these conditions were rapidly accepted by the PCF,[1] and embodied in the 'Pacte d'Unité d'Action' signed on 27 July.*

* By this time Dollfuss had been murdered by the Nazis (25 July), but his 'fascist' regime continued, propped up by Mussolini; and the pact named Karl Seitz, the Socialist ex-mayor of Vienna, as an imprisoned anti-fascist to be campaigned for along with Thälmann.

The PCF had made all the concessions, yet it managed to present the agreement to the public as a triumph for its longstanding 'united front' policy. With perfect discipline and unanimity the party militants threw themselves into the application of the pact. By contrast the SFIO, which had in fact scored a considerable victory, did not attempt to conceal the misgivings and divisions which the agreement aroused within its ranks, and did not even draw attention to the fact that it had supported the anti-fascist vigilance committees during the spring while the PCF had condemned them. Consequently the PCF rapidly built the foundations of a new reputation as *the* party of working-class unity.[2]

CANTONAL ELECTIONS (OCTOBER 1934)
At the same time, it very quickly began to extend the policy of union against fascism beyond the frontiers of the working class. On 19 August it issued a manifesto for the local elections (*cantonales*) due in October, which not only promised a mutual stand-down pact with the Socialists but even proclaimed the party's readiness, rather than permit the election of 'an avowed or covert representative of fascism', to envisage standing down in favour of a Radical. To qualify for such support, the Radical candidate would have to 'come out categorically against the Government of National Union, against the policy of [deflationary] decree-laws, of support for fascism and of preparation for war, against the decisions of the Radical congresses which approved this policy, against the Radical ministers who have carried it out', to 'promise to denounce and combat them publicly', and to defend democratic freedoms by calling for proportional representation and the dissolution of the Chamber.[3] These were conditions which few Radicals were likely to accept; but even so the proposal marked a complete departure from the previous 'class-against-class' policy. In addition, the demands in the manifesto were essentially reformist, and several of them were obviously aimed at the middle classes. On 1 September *Cahiers du Bolchévisme* published an article by Monmousseau with the significant title 'Pour l'Alliance avec les Couches Moyennes'.

The party scored a first diplomatic success when the SFIO announced that it too would stand down only for those Radicals who explicitly condemned the Doumergue government. More encouraging still was the result of the first ballot, on 7 October, which showed a 15% increase in the Communist vote since 1932.[4] Two days later, at a meeting of the co-ordination committee, Thorez suggested to the Socialists that the pact be extended 'to draw in new forces', by means of a 'positive programme' which would interest the middle classes. On 10 October, in a public speech, he called for a 'common front of liberty and peace' which would unite the middle and the working classes. He quoted speeches of two left-wing Radicals, Daladier and Pierre Cot, to prove that parts of the 'middle classes' were already receptive to the idea of a 'common front'. On 12 October this speech was printed in *L'Humanité*,[5] under the title 'For a Broad Anti-Fascist Popular Front'.*

The word was launched, and the second ballot of the local elections on 14 October showed that the idea was already having some success: the mutual stand-down pact paid off, and Communist representation on departmental councils went up from seventeen to thirty-three (out of a total 1,512). Both Socialists and Communists had taken votes from the Radicals, and this in turn strengthened the faction within the Radical Party which objected to its participation in the government of National Union.[6] The Radical Congress was due to open in Nantes on 25 October. On 24 October Thorez appeared in that city and made a speech calling for 'a popular front of freedom, labour and peace'. At this point he did not apparently conceive of the popular front as an alliance between political parties as such, but as a network of committees elected *à la base*—'by all the workers' in each town or village.[7] The united front 'at the top' would thus be complemented by a popular front 'at the bottom', which would enable the Communists to influence the Radical Party through its electorate or, if the Radical leaders proved obdurate, to 'unmask' them and wean their electors away from them.

ATTITUDE OF THE RADICALS

If it was intended to have an immediate effect on the Radical Congress, this appeal was a failure. Herriot was once again able to impose his authority and the congress voted to allow him and his

---

* The expression 'front populaire' was apparently coined by Fried. See Dominique Desanti, *L'Internationale communiste* (Paris, 1970), p. 192, quoting Vassart; Maurice Thorez *fils* (in *Le Monde*, March 1969); and André Ferrat, 'M. Fauvet saisi par la légende' (*Preuves*, February 1965): 'J'entends encore Cachin me dire, en 1934, d'un ton à la fois admiratif et quelque peu dépité: "C'est tout de même formidable que ce soit un étranger qui ait trouvé le mot d'ordre du Front populaire!" ' The formulae most often used were 'Front populaire du travail, de la liberté et de la paix' and 'Front populaire pour la paix, le pain, la liberté'.

colleagues to remain in the government. But the Communists took some comfort from Daladier's speech, in which he stated that the working class was 'on our side' for the defence of the Republic.[8] (*L'Humanité*'s comment that he spoke like a 'future head of government destined to destroy the "enemies of the Republic"' was to prove an ironic prophecy in 1939.) Less than a fortnight later, the Radical ministers did in fact resign in protest against Doumergue's projects for constitutional reform, which Herriot considered dangerously authoritarian. This brought about a brief cabinet crisis during which the Socialists offered to join the Radicals in a 'strong republican government'. The Communists did not associate themselves with this offer: they were not yet ready for parliamentary coalitions with the bourgeoisie. In any case, Herriot had no intention of forming a left-wing coalition: he simply wanted to get rid of Doumergue. The Radicals remained in office under a new conservative prime minister, Pierre-Etienne Flandin, who agreed (8 November) to drop the 'anti-republican' aspects of Doumergue's plans.[9]

DISAGREEMENT BETWEEN COMMUNISTS AND SOCIALISTS

On 25 November a meeting of the SFIO National Council (the sovereign body of the party between congresses) found itself confronted by a letter from the PCF *Bureau Politique* proposing, for the first time under that name, a 'Popular Front programme'. This included such measures as the dissolution of the leagues, the forty-hour week, generalization of unemployment benefit, aid to poor farmers, a moratorium on commercial debts, a public works programme, and lower taxes for the poor. The Socialists protested that this list did not include 'a single measure of a socialistic nature', and proposed that it be reinforced by adding measures for the 'socialization of the main means of production and exchange'. But this the Communists absolutely refused. Already the great difference between the Socialist and Communist conceptions of the popular front had come into the open. The Socialists believed that by healing the rift in the working class which had occurred at Tours, it opened the way to the democratic introduction of socialism in France. The Communists remained as sceptical about this as ever, continuing to believe that socialism could only come about after the violent destruction of the bourgeois state. Their aim was to create as broad as possible an anti-fascist front, and they were determined not to frighten away any of the peasants or petty bourgeois by unrealistic socialist proposals. Consequently the negotiations marked time until in January they were broken off 'amicably' with no agreement in sight.[10]

HESITATIONS OF THE COMINTERN

By this time the Comintern appears to have been assailed by doubts about the usefulness of its new line. An article in *Communist International* of 1 December emphasized that the defensive alliance with social democracy against fascism remained subordinate to the 'principal aim' of the united front, which was still to 'facilitate the passage of the social-democratic masses to communism'. The PCF, in its application of the pact, had succumbed to the 'rightist danger', 'given in to the pressure of the Socialists', and 'at times interpreted incorrectly the conditions of the pact'.[11] Understandably confused by this warning, the PCF was slow to react. Probably the 1 December article represented only one side in an internal debate within the Comintern. Thorez eventually replied to it, stressing the PCF's positive achievements in the 'struggle for the united front', but admitting the need 'to expand the guiding role of the party'. He promised that the party would lead the workers in an offensive against capitalism, would 'create a vast network of local committees in the cities and the countryside', and would strive to obtain a Popular Front programme as another means of achieving the 'mobilization' and the 'extra-parliamentary action of the masses'.[12] These ideas were approved by the PCF Central Committee on 15 February. But they had little effect except to put additional strain on relations with the Socialists. At the SFIO National Council on 3 March there were many complaints about the 'unfriendly procedures' of the Communists. The Socialists felt that the pact was being exploited against them by their allies/rivals, and countered by reviving their old demand for negotiations on the restoration of organic unity between the two parties. Meanwhile Thorez stressed the extra-parliamentary nature of the united front ('obviously no parliamentary programme is called for') and declared that the Socialist offer to the Radicals in November had been an act of 'disloyalty' which the PCF ought to have publicly criticized.[13]

By the spring of 1935, it seems that Moscow had almost decided to abandon the new tactics (so far applied only in a few countries, of which France was the most important). According to Vassart, both the Comintern and the PCF leaders themselves were convinced that united action with the Socialists 'would not last and was not profitable'. Preparations were made for a break, and Vassart even wrote a pamphlet putting the blame for the failure of the pact on the SFIO.[14]

FRANCO-SOVIET PACT

But these hesitations were overtaken by events. In France, whatever the misgivings of the party leaders, the move towards reunion of the left had aroused hope and enthusiasm among the voters, while the impotence of the Flandin government faced with the continuing economic crisis made the Radicals more and more restive. A series of by-elections were won by Radicals who accepted Socialist and Communist support against members of other parties in the governing coalition.[15] In Europe, the decisive event was Hitler's announcement on 16 March reintroducing conscription and raising the strength of the German army to six times the size authorized by the Versailles Treaty. Laval, as foreign minister since the death of Barthou in October 1934, had been stalling the negotiations for a Franco-Soviet pact and seeking a rapprochement with Germany. Now the cabinet overruled him and it was decided to press ahead with the Franco-Soviet negotiations without further delay. The Franco-Soviet Pact of Mutual Assistance was signed on 2 May.[16]

MUNICIPAL ELECTIONS (MAY 1935)

Municipal elections were held in France on 5 and 12 May. The first-ballot results were confusingly complex, but showed an increase in the Communist vote. If Communists and Socialists stuck together on the second ballot they could clearly expect an important success. This they agreed to do, announcing on the 7 May that they would stand down not only for each other but also for 'candidates who are supporters of freedom, other than communists and socialists' where these were leading the field against 'candidates of reaction'.[17] The most spectacular display of left-wing unity was in the Latin Quarter of Paris where the right-wing candidate was the president of the *Union Nationale des Combattants*, Lebecq, who had been one of the leaders of the right-wing demonstrators on the Sixth of February. On the first ballot he was only twenty-seven votes short of an absolute majority, so that his election on the second ballot seemed a mere formality. Of the four left-wing candidates the Communist was in fact in the lead; but all four agreed to withdraw in favour of Professor Paul Rivet, one of the leaders of the anti-fascist movement among intellectuals, and Rivet was able to defeat Lebecq by 152 votes.[18]

Overall, the second ballot was a triumph for the PCF, which nearly doubled the number of municipalities it controlled (from 150 to 297), and more than doubled the number it controlled in towns of more than 5,000 inhabitants (from thirty-eight to ninety). This was by far the largest gain of all parties.[19] It affected some rural departments in central and south-western France, but the main centres of Communist electoral strength were still the industrial areas, especially the Paris suburbs and the Nord. Already in 1929 the PCF had fought the municipal elections in the Paris region on its record of efficient municipal administration: improvements in housing, welfare services, etc. From now on it would establish a reputation in almost all industrial areas as the party of honest, efficient city government, while at the same time finding employment for its activists and gaining useful administrative experience for its leaders. In many areas the belts of Communist administration spread 'en tache d'huile', one or two new contiguous municipalities being added at each election. After 1935 it became rare for the party to lose control of a municipality once gained.[20]

This time not only the general and official alliance with the SFIO, but also the *ad hoc*, unofficial agreements with the Radical Party had paid off handsomely. All three parties scored victories on the second ballot with the help of each other's voters, while the right, and particularly the extreme right, suffered a severe defeat. The Popular Front thus came into existence before there was any formal agreement or even negotiation between the leaders of the three main parties concerned. 'For the first time since the war,' commented a right-wing journalist bitterly, 'we have seen the overwhelming majority of the Radicals, the Socialists and the Communists closely united in the red front.'[21]

SOVIET ATTITUDE

After such success, and after the signature of the Franco-Soviet Pact, it was hardly likely that the PCF would break off its pact with the Socialists and return to a class-against-class policy. On the contrary, the time was clearly ripe for an extension of the pact to include the leadership of the Radical Party. France was now the ally of the Soviet Union, committed on paper to assisting her if she were attacked by Germany. But the Soviet leaders were well aware that Laval, who had signed the pact, had dragged his feet until the last few weeks and had restricted its force as far as possible. The main drive for its conclusion on the French side had come from Herriot. They also knew that the French economy was in a worse state than ever and that Flandin's government was weak and increasingly unpopular. From the Soviet point of view, it was high time for Herriot and his Radical colleagues to desert Flandin and Laval and form a government based on the Popular Front, which would rebuild France as an economic and military power in close alliance with the USSR.

PROBLEM OF NATIONAL DEFENCE

One of the obstacles to such a development was the attitude of the PCF and SFIO to national defence. The SFIO was still dominated by the pacifist outlook which had been that of the *minoritaires* during the Great War, while the PCF remained faithful to the Leninist tradition of revolutionary defeatism. In March 1935 both parties had strenuously opposed the government's decision to extend military service from one to two years. Léon Blum argued that France's existing army could hold back any German aggression for long enough to permit a *levée en masse* of the working class, and that the real aim of those who advocated an increase was to embark on a militaristic foreign policy that would bring the danger of war nearer. Thorez declared: 'We shall not permit the working class to be dragged into a so-called war to defend democracy against fascism.'[22] But what if it were a war to defend the Soviet Union against fascism, or a war in which the Soviet Union intervened to defend France against fascism? Once these obligations had been formally accepted by the two governments, the question became hard to avoid.

'M. STALIN UNDERSTANDS . . .'

Ironically it was Laval, one of the popular front's chief enemies and victims, who facilitated its birth by eliciting a clear answer to this question from Stalin himself. Visiting Moscow on 13–15 May, Laval told Stalin that French public opinion could not accept that he had no control over the Comintern and 'certainly would not understand if Stalin did not now give orders to the Communists in France to cease opposition to the army budget and to the two-year service law'. Stalin (according to Laval) replied simply 'I agree'; and the following sentence was inserted into the joint communiqué: 'M. Stalin understands and fully approves of the policy of national defence carried out by France in order to maintain her armed strength at the level required for her security.'[23] Laval's aim was no doubt to embarrass the PCF, and this was certainly the immediate effect of Stalin's pronouncement. But the party was by now well-trained in executing rapid about-turns: within a week it had covered France with posters announcing 'Stalin Is Right'. It explained that the Communist attitude to defence expenditure and rearmament must depend on the general policy which the armament in question was supposed to serve: if this policy reflected the interests of the imperialists, Communists would fight it; but if it was a policy of collaboration with the USSR in defence of peace and of the independence of peoples, then they would support it.[24]

In fact the Socialists appeared more concerned about Stalin's statement than the Communists did. Léon Blum wrote: 'The more I think it over, the less I understand. . . . Thus, Stalin disapproves those who refused their vote to the two-year law. . . . He approves, against us, the government which we have fought and whose representative will now return from Moscow displaying his good-conduct medal.'[25] Blum himself was to come round very gradually to the view that rearmament was justified by the fascist threat, but many members of his party never did. Meanwhile, the new attitude of the Communists, implying as it did a duty for the working class to join in the defence of France in the event of German aggression, made co-operation with the Socialists and especially the Radicals much easier. Inevitably many Radicals were sceptical at first about the PCF's sincerity. But the new patriotic tone of Communist propaganda (from which the anti-military and even anti-colonial elements were almost completely purged) soon began to have its effect in overcoming the reluctance of those Radicals who had hitherto been hostile to the Popular Front.

PARLIAMENTARY MANOEUVRES

The PCF leaders now began actively to canvass the Popular Front as a parliamentary alliance. On 24 May they suggested an agreement between Communist and Socialist deputies to fight Flandin's request for special decree powers to cope with the economic crisis, and invited other left-wing deputies to join them. This proposal was discussed at a meeting of Communist and Socialist deputies on 28 May which produced a joint letter to the parties of the left, including the Radicals and the 'Republican Socialists', inviting them to send delegates to a further meeting on the 30 May. This invitation, whose evident aim was the creation of a new centre-left parliamentary majority, was according to Léon Blum 'even more' the work of the Communists than of the Socialists. At the same time, the Communist attitude to Herriot and the other Radical ministers changed suddenly from opposition and abuse to praise and support.[26] Clearly the PCF now hoped to persuade the Radicals to abandon the 'national union' and revive the *néo-Cartel* which had governed France (with no encouragement whatever from the Communists) in 1932–4. During the debate (30 May) on Flandin's request for special powers Thorez actually declared that his party 'would be ready to bring you our support, President Herriot, if you or any other head of your party wished to lead a Radical government . . . which would really apply the policies of the Radical party'. Support did not, of course, imply Communist participation in the government; and the Communist leaders let it be known that they expected the SFIO too to support such a government from outside, as it had done in 1924–5 and 1932–4.[27]

The immediate success of the Communist initiative was limited. All the parties contacted sent delegates to the meeting on 30 May, which set up a permanent *Délégation des Gauches* as a forum in which the different left-wing parliamentary groups could at least try to co-ordinate their tactics; and Flandin's government was overthrown by the Chamber. This, however, was the result of right-wing as well as Radical defections, and Herriot stuck by the prime minister to the last. On 1 June he agreed to join yet another centre-right coalition, this time headed by the president of the Chamber, Fernand Bouisson. This in turn was overthrown as soon as it met the Chamber on 4 June. During the ensuing crisis the *Délégation des Gauches* met twice, but Radicals and Socialists were unable to agree on a programme; and to the Communists' great chagrin the same coalition was re-formed with Laval as premier as well as foreign minister. Herriot remained in office, arguing that this government was the only alternative to national bankruptcy; and on 7 June Laval came before the Chamber to request the special powers which had been refused to Flandin and Bouisson.[28] During the debate the Communist spokesman, Arthur Ramette, criticized the Radical leaders for 'yielding to the blackmail of the fascist leagues, to the pressure of the speculators', but promised the Radical deputies that 'our constant effort will tend toward the achievement of this popular government'.[29] Laval got his majority, but more than half the Radical deputies abstained. The supporters of

Herriot (who had not spoken in the debate), and of the deflation policy, were now a minority within the Radical group.[30] The time was at last ripe for the launching of the Popular Front.

Already in May the PCF had called, through the Amsterdam-Pleyel Movement, for a joint demonstration on 14 July 'under the tricolour' by all the organizations which 'defended peace and freedom', and which should then resolve 'never to separate until they have finally defeated fascism and reduced the danger of war'.[31] This invitation was accepted by the Committee of Vigilance of Anti-Fascist Intellectuals and the *Ligue des Droits de l'Homme*, and on 17 June the three organizations decided to hold a 'common celebration of a democratic July 14', in which the CGT and the Socialist and Radical parties would be asked to take part.[32] The acceptance of the Socialists, who at their Congress of Mulhouse had just called for 'a great popular movement to defend democratic freedoms against the political, economic and social effects of the capitalist crisis', was a foregone conclusion. The reaction of the Radicals was harder to predict. Herriot, as a member of the government, could hardly be expected to accept, but the left-wing 'young Radicals', led by Jean Zay, were favourable, and they were now joined by the former prime minister, Daladier. The latter attended a public meeting on 20 June, chaired by Paul Langevin, at which members of all the left-wing organizations appointed a provisional commission to prepare the 14 July demonstration and obtain the formal consent of all the parties concerned. Finally on 2 July the Executive Committee of the Radical Party agreed that the party should take part. Herriot avoided a humiliating defeat by a carefully worded speech in which he first defended his decision to join the Laval government but then welcomed the demonstration as a 'homage which will be paid to the regime', i.e. the Republic.[33]

The Communists hailed this decision with great enthusiasm, heaping praise on the Radical Party as 'the worthiest party' in France, and pleading with the Socialists not to spoil things by raising controversial issues of financial and economic policy![34]

In the end forty-eight national organizations took part in the *Rassemblement Populaire* of 14 July, including both CGTU and CGT and even the right-wing 'neo-socialists' who had left the SFIO in 1933. It was the first time that Communists and Socialists had joined in the commemoration of the storming of the Bastille—which only two years before Vaillant-Couturier had called a 'bourgeois festival ... as dead as the Palais Royal';[35] and again the Socialists showed more embarrassment than their partners: they insisted on singing the *Internationale* even while the Communists were singing the *Marseillaise*. The Communists themselves, eagerly espousing the new line but not yet free of the habits of the old, mixed the slogan 'All power to the soviets' with that of 'Daladier for premier'.[36] Daladier and Pierre Cot were there at the head of the cortège (reputedly half a million strong), alongside Blum, Paul Faure, Thorez, Barbusse and Langevin;[37] and this *Rassemblement* was not to be an affair of one day only. In an atmosphere of intense enthusiasm, all present took the oath:

> to remain united for the defence of democracy, the disarmament and dissolution of the factious Leagues, and to put our liberties beyond the reach of fascism. On this day which brings to life again the first victory of the Republic, we swear to defend the democratic liberties won by the people of France, and to give bread to the workers, work to young people, and to the world the peace of mankind.[38]

THE SEVENTH WORLD CONGRESS

Later that same month the long delayed Seventh Congress of the Comintern at last assembled in Moscow. All hesitations about the Popular Front tactic were now swept aside, and the PCF was held up as an example for all other Communist Parties to follow. Dimitrov, who was elected to the new office of general secretary of the Comintern, called both for mass anti-fascist movements uniting the working and middle classes, and for agreements among Communist, social-democratic and bourgeois parties. Togliatti urged Communists to support measures of civil and national defence necessitated by the threat of war from fascist countries, especially Germany.

The congress adopted a long resolution on 'fascism, working-class unity, and the tasks of the Comintern' which embodied these new principles, though in a somewhat cautious form of words. 'In face of fascist danger' the Communists were authorized, in election campaigns, to 'declare for a common platform and a common ticket with the anti-fascist front, depending on the growth and success of the united front movement, and on the electoral system in operation'. They were urged to 'unite, under the leadership of the proletariat, the struggle of the toiling peasants, the urban petty bourgeoisie and the

toiling masses of the oppressed nationalities', and so 'to bring about
the establishment of a wide anti-fascist people's front on the basis of
the proletarian united front'. In certain circumstances, 'when the
ruling classes are no longer in a position to cope with the powerful
sweep of the mass movement', it might 'prove possible, and necessary
in the interests of the proletariat, to create a proletarian united front
government, or an anti-fascist people's front government, which is
not yet a government of the proletarian dictatorship, but one which
undertakes to put into effect decisive measures against fascism and
reaction'.[39]

This was evidently what Thorez had in mind when he declared, in
October, that the Communists were 'ready to take their responsibilities in a Popular Front government'.[40] But equally clearly the
'essential prerequisites for the formation of a united front government' which the Comintern had laid down—including the paralysis
of the bourgeois state apparatus and the willingness of 'a considerable
proportion of the organizations of the social-democratic and other
parties participating in the united front' to fight for 'ruthless measures
against the fascists and other reactionaries'—were not fulfilled in
France; and lest there should be any misunderstanding about this
Thorez spelt it out a few weeks later: 'We do not think that a Popular
Front government as we understand it can be constituted in present
conditions.'[41] Indeed, so far from putting forward 'fundamental
revolutionary slogans . . . which lead the working masses right up to
the point of the revolutionary seizure of power', as the Comintern had
recommended in circumstances where such a government might
prove possible, the Communists were striving to make the programme of the *Rassemblement Populaire* as moderate as they could, and
even suggested inviting such reactionary (but potentially anti-fascist)
parties as Flandin's 'Democratic Alliance' to join it.[42]

The Socialists, in fact, were bewildered to find the Communists
apparently to the right of them in the National Committee of the
Rassemblement Populaire, allying with the Radicals to oppose the
inclusion of any nationalization measures in the draft programme of
economic and social reforms, and supporting the Radicals when they
refused to make the programme a binding electoral platform or the
basis of a new coalition government.[43] Inevitably as the 1936
elections approached the *Rassemblement* took on the guise of an
electoral alliance, even though it included such bodies as the *Ligue des
Droits de l'Homme* and the trade unions as well as political parties; but

the Radicals wanted to keep their governmental options open, and the Communists were still thinking in terms of a Radical government with Socialist and Communist support from outside. In January 1936, when the Radicals finally brought down Laval's government, the Communists, who happened to be assembled for their Eighth Congress at Villeurbanne (a suburb of Lyons), indignantly rejected suggestions from the Socialists that the time had now come for a 'Popular Front government'. 'To those who think that the Popular Front tactic should lead us to a vulgar policy of ministerial collaboration,' said Thorez, 'we reply very clearly: We are not a party of the bourgeoisie, we are the party of the working class. We have never promised any kind of participation in the bourgeois government. What we have said . . . is that we are ready to support in the Chamber and in the country any measures that will ensure the safety of the franc, the energetic repression of speculation, the protection of the interests of the toiling population, the defence of democratic liberties, the disarmament and dissolution of the fascist leagues and the maintenance of peace. In other words, so long as conditions do not permit the constitution of a Popular Front government such as we understand it, we are determined to support with our votes the left-wing government that will carry out a programme corresponding to the interests and wishes of the people of France.'[44] The Socialists, as a supposedly working-class party, were rebuked by the congress for their 'offers of ministerial participation';[45] and though the Communists were disappointed that the new Radical government, headed by Sarraut, still included conservatives (notably Flandin at the Ministry of Foreign Affairs), they nonetheless refrained, for the first time, from voting with the opposition when the cabinet was presented to the Chamber on 31 January.[46]

It soon became apparent, however, that the Sarraut government, which took no effective action either against the leagues after a physical assault on Léon Blum in February, or against Germany after the reoccupation of the Rhineland in March, was not 'the left-wing government' to which the PCF had promised support. In March the party leadership sent a letter to the National Committee of the *Rassemblement Populaire*, demanding that it be made clear that 'the Sarraut government is not the emanation of our movement', and that after the elections a new 'left-wing government supported by the Popular Front' would have 'entirely different' policies.[47] But they continued to see this as a government without either Socialist or

Communist participation, and harried the SFIO for its 'Néo-Millerandisme'. (Millerand was the Socialist who had joined the Waldeck-Rousseau government in 1899, and had subsequently been condemned by the Second International.) The idea that the Socialists might, after the election, be in a position not merely to join the government but to lead it does not seem to have occurred to anyone.[48]

Irritated by these attacks which seemed to come simultaneously from right and left, the Socialists understandably showed little interest in proposals which the PCF put forward for the fusion of the two parties into a single party of the working class, constructed however on strictly Bolshevik lines.[49] They joined forces with the Radicals to resist the PCF's demands that the local committees of the *Rassemblement Populaire* be allowed to admit individual members as well as delegates of the component organizations—a measure which might have enabled the Communists to pack the committees with their own activists and thereby win effective control of the *Rassemblement* 'from below'.

In this state of uneasy alliance, the Popular Front parties went into the general election of 26 April and 3 May 1936, which almost in spite of themselves was to make them masters of the country. But meantime there had been important developments on the trade union front.

Trade Union Unity and the Growth of the CGT

REUNIFICATION

The 'turning-point' of June 1934 affected not only relations between the Communist and Socialist Parties, but also those between the CGTU and the CGT.[50] On 8 June, a week after the first direct approach from the *Bureau Politique* to the SFIO leadership, the CGTU proposed joint action with the CGT. But the CGT leaders, though they had accepted Communist support in the crisis of February, were in no mood to lend the CGTU a helping hand. They were angry with the Communists for sabotaging their attempt to organize joint action against fascism in April (see above, p. 214), and considered that they had no need to make concessions to a rival organization which was visibly on its last legs. The only unity in which they saw any advantage was a return to the fold by the schismatics of 1921, if these had at last seen the error of their ways.

They therefore proposed, not unity of action, but the restoration of the organic unity of the old CGT.

The CGTU at first refused this, encouraged apparently by Moscow where the Profintern apparatus constituted a permanent lobby against concessions to the Amsterdam International and its affiliates. But this lobby could not prevail very long against the new wisdom of the Comintern. By October the CGTU had accepted the principle of reunification. A first round of talks was held on 9 October, at which the CGTU suggested reunification 'from above' by a jointly summoned confederal congress. This was rejected. But meanwhile some success was obtained by an intermediate tactic—neither 'from above' nor 'from below', but at the level of the individual *syndicat*. A series of CGTU railwaymen's *syndicats* were allowed to leave the parent body and merge with their CGT opposite numbers into an independent *syndicat* outside both confederations. This was an ingenious manoeuvre by which the Communists put pressure on the CGT—demonstrating the strong desire for unity among the rank-and-file—without really sacrificing anything themselves. The militants who left the CGTU did not thereby cease to be Communists; and in the united *syndicats* they were able to influence a larger number of non-Commmunist workers. Realizing the danger, the CGT reacted sharply, expelling the *syndicats* concerned and setting up new ones in their place. It thus succeeded in confining the success of the tactic to the railways, where the Communists still had numerous party cells. At the same time the CGT leaders took offence at an article by Piatnitsky in the *Cahiers du Bolchévisme* (1 November) which explained that Communists should continue to work as a 'fraction' within the reunited *syndicats* and to influence their activity 'by every means'. Confronted with this article at a second meeting, on 25 January 1935, the CGTU representatives refused to discuss party policy; and soon afterwards the talks were broken off, with few regrets on the CGT side.

There was then a pause during the spring of 1935, when the whole future of the united front policy seemed momentarily in doubt; but after the Franco-Soviet pact and the municipal elections the PCF's new political initiatives were again paralleled on the trade union front. On 6 June *L'Humanité* published an article by Marcel Gitton, a member of the party secretariat who had formerly held high office in the CGTU, which stated that 'there cannot be any sort of fractions within the trade unions'. Two days later the CGTU itself published a statement accepting the traditional CGT thesis of complete trade union independence from all political parties: 'Freedom of opinion and the rules of trade union democracy must not result in the constitution in the trade unions of organisms acting as fractions. Each union member being entirely free to join and work in the political and philosophical organizations of his choice, within the trade union he can speak only in his capacity as a union member.' On the face of it, this amounted to a complete abandonment of the Leninist principle which the Communists had imposed on the CGTU with such difficulty in 1922–3. The CGT leaders were rightly sceptical of their rivals' sincerity, but it was no longer possible for them to refuse talks on reunification without openly assuming responsibility for prolonging the schism. While both organizations sat in the committee which prepared the *Rassemblement Populaire* of 14 July, they also resumed direct talks with each other on 27 June. By 24 July they had agreed on a joint statement defining the independence of the trade union movement and declaring that this did not imply indifference 'to dangers which threaten public liberties or to present and future reforms'. In September the two confederal congresses were held simultaneously in Paris, and agreed on a merger procedure starting from the *syndicats*, moving up through the area unions and industrial federations, and culminating in a confederal congress of unity to be summoned by a joint National Confederal Committee (CCN) which would meet before the end of the year. Meanwhile a joint session of the two congresses was held at which Jouhaux, who privately admitted the disgust and anxiety which the new arrivals inspired in him,[51] made a lyrical speech (27 September) about the 'cosmic force' of unity and the emotion which gripped all those who could remember the good old days of the old CGT.

The CGT leaders accepted reunification secure in the knowledge that their organization was numerically stronger and that therefore they would remain in control of the reunited Confederation. Of thirty-three reunited federations, the *unitaires* (former CGTU members) were at first in control of only six: Agriculture, Building, Chemicals, Metals, Railwaymen, and Glass, representing just under 200,000 members, or about one quarter of the total reunited membership. On a geographical basis they were even worse off, being at a disadvantage because the CGT's territorial structure, not the CGTU's, was adopted: they controlled only seven departmental unions (Alpes-Maritimes, Gard, Vaucluse, Isère, Loire, Lot, Yonne) out of eighty-five. On the provisional bureau, elected by the CCN in January 1936, the *unitaires* were represented only by two out of the six assistant secretaries (Frachon and Racamond), while the general secretary (Jouhaux) and treasurer were both former 'confederates'. Among the delegates at the first united congress, in March, the 'confederates' had a majority of two thirds. They carried a motion forbidding the combination of membership of the confederal bureau with political office (including both electoral mandates and party appointments). Another motion stipulated that the administrative commission, which chose the bureau, should itself be elected not by the congress but by the Confederal Committee (CCN), composed of the secretaries of the federations and departmental unions. As a result the *unitaires* were still only able to obtain two out of eight places on the bureau, and their two representatives, Frachon and Racamond, both had to resign from the PCF Central Committee. Frachon also resigned from the *Bureau Politique*.

ADVANTAGES OF THE COMMUNISTS

In appearance, therefore, the 'confederates' had firmly secured their control of the reunited CGT. But the appearance was misleading, and the safeguards they had devised were to prove largely ineffective, for two reasons. In the first place, there was no way of compelling the PCF to make its actual behaviour conform to its public attitudes. *Bureau Politique* meetings were not public, and there is little doubt that Frachon in fact continued to attend them although his name no longer figured on the official list of members. Similarly, the ban on 'fractions' could not prevent the Communists from concerting their strategy in private or from working to extend the influence of their party. It may even have helped them, since an openly organized Communist lobby would have been a much easier target for counter-propaganda. Secondly, the 'confederates' were the victims of their own attachment to the CGT's federal structure: they were not willing to use their control of congress and of the confederal bureau to intervene in the affairs of individual federations. This meant that the Communists were free to make their own rules in the federations which they controlled; and since they did not share the 'federalist' outlook of their rivals, they insisted that the statutes of each *syndicat* within these federations be submitted to the federal bureau for approval. They were thus able to reduce the 'confederate' leaders of individual *syndicats* to impotence, while themselves retaining full autonomy as leaders of a given federation. Several leaders of CGT federations were thus able to seek and win election to parliament as Communist deputies without having to resign their trade union posts.

EXPANSION OF THE CGT

But undoubtedly the key factor in the Communists' success in 'colonizing' the CGT was the enormous increase in trade union membership which occurred immediately after reunification. The combined memberships of the two confederations in 1935 had totalled 786,000; in 1937 the membership of the reunited CGT came to 3,959,000—more than five times as much. This growth had started before the great strikes of May–June 1936. The 1935 figures were already an improvement on those of 1934, and in May 1936, before the strikes began, 'considerable' increases were already reported to have occurred since the reunification congress. Clearly trade union unity in itself was giving a great boost to working-class morale, and this, as well as the electoral victory of the Popular Front, must help to explain the spontaneous outburst of strikes.

Once the strikes started, the move into the trade unions turned into a positive stampede of new adherents. Strikes occurred even in small factories where there was not a single trade union member; and, turning to the CGT for advice and support, many of the strikers soon found it natural to take out union cards. In larger factories where trade union strength was no more than skeletal, hitherto 'unorganized' workers now flocked to join, seeing that at last industrial action was able to achieve something for them; and this new-found prestige of the trade unions was further heightened when the Popular Front government obliged employers, in law at least, to recognize the representativity of trade union 'délégués d'atelier' (or shop stewards).

Already by mid-June the CGT was claiming two and a half million members, and growth continued at almost the same intoxicating rate for months after this. The peak was probably reached at just over four million in early 1937. (Over five million were claimed at the time. It is interesting to note that the much smaller Catholic unions—CFTC —claimed a proportionally large increase, from 100,000 in 1934 to 500,000 in 1936.[52]) But this phenomenal growth was not equally distributed among the federations. It was most spectacular precisely in those which had been weakest, in both CGT and CGTU, during the period of schism—in those manufacturing industries, that is, where the CGT had done no better than the CGTU and in some cases even worse. The three federations whose growth was most spectacular were those of Chemical Industries, Glassworkers and Metalworkers, all of which had already been controlled by the Communists, but were relatively insignificant in strength, at the moment of reunion.

SUCCESS OF THE COMMUNISTS

Of the six federations which the Communists controlled at the beginning of 1936, one, the Railwaymen, with 107,000 members, was bigger than the other five put together (91,000). But by 1937 one of these five, the Metalworkers, had become the biggest in the whole confederation, with 833,000 members. The five together totalled nearly 1.5 million. The Railwaymen meanwhile had also increased their membership (though proportionately their growth was less spectacular), so that the combined total of the six was over 1.8 million. Thus even without winning the leadership of any other federations, the Communists would have controlled nearly half the vastly increased CGT membership. But in addition they had won control of three more federations, including that of Textiles which was now the third biggest. This meant that they now controlled the four biggest federations (Metalworkers, Railways, Textiles and Building), and that the total membership of the Communist-controlled federations, at nearly 2.3 million, outnumbered that of the others. In a sense, therefore, the Communists had already won a majority in the CGT before the Second World War. But the significance of this is hard to assess, either in terms of Communist support among rank-and-file trade unionists—since there is no way of knowing whether the Communist sympathizers in federations which the Communists did not yet control were more or less numerous than the non-Communist sympathizers in those which they did—or in terms of power at the confederal level, since the Confederal Congress of 1938 avoided any vote on which *unitaire* and *confédéré* delegates would have been counted separately, both Jouhaux and the Communists being anxious to maintain a united front against the 'Munichois' and against the economic policy of the Daladier government (see below, Chapter Eight). In these circumstances the 1936 leadership was maintained in office, and the *confédérés* therefore retained a numerical predominance at the top which no longer corresponded to their strength among the rank-and-file.

It is therefore not possible to say whether the Communists would have won full control of the CGT if the Second World War had not occurred when it did. No doubt the phenomenon which had helped them in the period of rapid trade union growth—their greater strength in manufacturing industry—would have worked against them once the tide started to ebb. As in 1921–34, the *confédéré* unions in the tertiary sector would probably have remained relatively stronger in a period of social calm and general decline of union membership. (Such a decline had already set in during 1938–9, especially after the failure of the strike of 30 November 1938. According to one source, CGT membership had fallen back below one million by the outbreak of war.[53])

REASONS FOR THEIR SUCCESS

Nonetheless, it is clear that in 1936–8 the Communists came very close to capturing the CGT, and established a position in the French trade union movement which no political party had ever had before; it is also clear that they achieved this largely by being entrenched in a strategic position at a moment of great social upheaval. The work of CGTU militants in the factories during 1921–34 must often have appeared ungrateful, at a time when less than 10% of workers in any manufacturing industry were willing to join trade unions at all. But when in 1936 the hitherto unorganized workers suddenly flooded into the trade unions, they inevitably accepted the guidance of the few who were already there. The fact that these were often Communists then became of crucial importance.

Yet this cannot have been the only factor. In many unions the proportion of the new members who supported the Communists did not at all correspond to the latter's relative strength *vis-à-vis* the *confédérés* before the influx. In the Metalworkers' Federation, for instance, the *unitaires* had had only a bare majority at the moment of reunion; yet at the Federal Congress of November 1936 they received 92% of the mandates. Why did these new adherents find the Communist militants so much more persuasive than their *confédéré* rivals?

Clearly the answer to such a question can only be speculative. But it seems plausible to suggest that there were two main reasons. The first is what one might call 'the mood of the moment'. The strikes of May–June 1936 were, after all, the product of a political situation — the victory of the Popular Front. The workers, who in their great majority had for five years accepted the hardships of the depression with little or no attempt to fight back, now suddenly found the necessary self-confidence to go on strike. Trade union unity was no doubt one element in this, but few would deny that the decisive factor was the belief that, as a result of the elections, political power had changed sides. The bosses could no longer count on the support of the state; the workers could. This was the achievement of the Popular Front; and the Popular Front had been the Communists' idea. In particular, it was the Communists who had pushed to link up the Popular Front with the trade union movement, by insisting that the CGT adopt the Popular Front programme, whereas the *confédérés* had wanted to stick to the 'Plan' drawn up by the CGT before reunion. In short, the Communists, at this moment of political crisis and of great political hope for the working class, were giving the trade union movement a political dimension, while the *confédérés*, loyal to the old doctrine of the Charter of Amiens, were trying to keep it out of party politics. (In fact many of them as individuals were members of the SFIO, and a few even became Socialist deputies: but the *confédérés* were very discreet about such links, and did not attempt to gain any credit from them.)

The second reason for Communist success is probably to be found in a conflict of generations among the union leaders. Many of the *confédéré* leaders now seemed to be old men harping on the battles of the past. In particular, their obsession with trade union independence related apparently to the situation of before 1914, rather than to that of 1936, now that the working class was visibly achieving something on the political front. By contrast, the Communists were usually able to present themselves as young, modern and pragmatic leaders, sensitive to the needs of the moment. Such young and up-and-coming leaders as the *confédérés* did have were not working-class militants but civil servants or primary school teachers (reflecting the growing preponderance of the white-collar unions within the CGT of 1921–34). The Communists had no lack of young working-class militants, and where these found themselves face to face with veteran *confédéré* warhorses they were quick to exploit the difference. (In federations such as that of the Railwaymen, where the Communist leaders themselves were elder statesmen like Midol and Sémard, the battle between the two sides was noticeably less fierce.)

In short, the Communists were able to appear the natural leaders for a new generation of working-class militants, whose political memory went back no further than 6 February 1934.

247

Electoral Success and Growth of Party Membership

THE ELECTIONS

But of course the revolutionary upsurge of 1936 did not only affect trade unions—it also had a profound effect on political parties.

In terms of votes, the left gained very little from the right. The important thing was the discipline of the voters on the second ballot, which enabled all the Popular Front parties to benefit from each other's votes. In fact these parties, when able to agree, had already formed the majority in the previous Chamber. The 1936 election brought them a net gain of forty seats, but the major change was not the victory of the left over the right. It was the new balance of forces within the left. The Radicals lost 400,000 votes and fifty-one seats while the Socialists gained sixteen seats (although losing 22,000 votes), and thereby became the largest party. No one could seriously contest their right, not to join, but to lead, the new government; and no more was heard from the PCF about 'Néo-Millerandisme'. But most spectacular of all was the advance of the PCF itself, from eleven seats to seventy-two. This increase of 550% resulted from a more modest, but still impressive, increase of 87% in the Communist vote. Now that it had accepted 'republican discipline' the PCF benefited from that same two-ballot, single-member constituency system which Sarraut had introduced to secure its defeat in the days of 'class against class'.

In absolute terms, the PCF vote went up from 795,000 to 1,487,000—overtaking the Radicals but falling well short of the Socialists, who polled 1,928,000. In percentage terms, the PCF received 15.3% of the votes cast, representing 12.7% of registered electors, a much higher share than it had ever had before.

The increase was general throughout France. But in many constituencies an impressive percentage increase in fact represented only a few hundred votes, since the previous score of the party had often been only in double figures. The most important gains were made in the areas where the party already had a solid base, and where it had kept some significant support even in the débâcle of 1932. These were mainly departments with a big working-class population, but also the rural ones in the south-western part of the Massif Central.

Only in 163 constituencies out of 598 did the PCF get the votes of more than 15% of the electors. The areas of real strength, where it got the votes of more than 25%, were almost all industrial ones: the Paris region (especially the suburbs); the Nord (where its votes no longer came from the countryside but from the mining districts, and to a lesser extent the manufacturing ones); the industrial districts of Marseilles, Toulon and Alès in the south-east; the suburbs of Lyons (especially Villeurbanne); Montluçon and Vierzon in central France; and Mézières in the Ardennes. By contrast there were only four rural departments where Communist candidates did really well: the Lot-et-Garonne, where Renaud Jean was triumphantly re-elected on the first ballot; the Corrèze (where again the party had popular local leaders); the Dordogne; and the Haute-Vienne—but here the SFIO did even better and all the Communist candidates had to withdraw in its favour on the second ballot. Correspondingly, the party's weakest points were all in predominantly agricultural areas: the west (Normandy, Brittany, Poitou), the western and eastern ends of the Paris basin, Champagne, Lorraine, Burgundy, Aquitaine, the western Pyrenees, the Alps, the Jura and the southern edge of the Massif Central.

In other words its success, though real, was still clearly circumscribed. It was still a new party with a predominantly urban, or industrial suburban, electorate. But the result in the Lot-et-Garonne showed that the countryside, or at least those parts of it where there were many smallholders and an anticlerical, republican tradition, could be won over to communism by long and patient propaganda.[54]

It should be added that the success was achieved at least partly by an unprecedentedly vigorous campaign. The PCF put out a greater quantity of propaganda than any French party had ever used in any election. Its posters were everywhere. The country was flooded with 7,500,000 copies of nine pamphlets, followed up a few days before the elections by a booklet enclosed in every copy of *L'Humanité*; and for the first time Communist leaders were able to address the people over the state radio.[55]

THE INFLUX OF MEMBERS

PCF membership had been declining fairly steadily from 60,000 in 1924 to possibly as low as 25,000 in 1932. The exact figure for 1933 was 28,825 (see Table on p. 113). The first signs of recovery coincided with the events of February 1934: in March 1934 nearly 10,000 more membership cards had been sent out than in May 1932. In June, at the Ivry conference, Thorez claimed that there were

10,000 new members, though later he admitted that the party had not
recruited as well as it should have during this period. The final figure
for 1934 was 42,578, the best since the repression of 1929. During 1935
this number was doubled, bringing the total to 86,902, the highest
figure for any year since 1921.

Membership continued to rise during the first four months of 1936,
reaching 106,500 by the end of April. Then, after the elections, came
the big rush. Anxious to advertise its success, the party took to
announcing its membership figures every month. The intake of new
members each month ran as follows (in round figures):

May	25,000
June	40,000
July	45,000
August	31,500
September	15,000
October	12,000
November	6,000
December	4,000

The total number of membership cards delivered to the regions in
1936 by party headquarters was 288,483. The number of 'control
stamps' sold to members for sticking on their cards at the end of the
year was 235,285. Normally one would take the latter figure as a more
reliable indication of actual membership, but in a period of such rapid
increase, which must certainly have resulted in considerable
administrative confusion, 'the number of cards sent out is likely to be
nearer the truth than the number of control stamps sold'.[56]

The growth continued during 1937, apparently reaching a peak of
328,547 in September.[57] Thereafter it levelled off, and by June 1938
decline had apparently set in: the party then embarked, for the first
time since early 1936, on a recruitment drive.[58] A more drastic decline
probably began after the strike of 30 November 1938, although by its
own account the party still had 'barely 300,000 members' on the eve
of the war.[59]

The SFIO's membership also grew very rapidly during 1936 and
1937, but it seems to have got off to a slightly slower start than that of
the PCF, which overtook it once and for all in May 1936—ironically
at the very moment when the SFIO had emerged as the largest
parliamentary party and was preparing to form France's first
Socialist-led government. The following annual totals are probably
accurate enough to be comparable:

	SFIO	PCF
1935	120,471	86,902
1936	200,852	284,194*
1937	285,461	328,647
1938	275,526	318,549

*The PCF must at this point have been the largest French party in terms of membership. But by 1939 it had probably been overtaken by the right-wing *Parti Social Français* of Colonel de La Rocque. The latter's claims of two or three million members can hardly be taken seriously; but even its rivals were willing to credit it with 750,000—i.e. more than the Socialist and Communist parties put together. See Dieter Wolf, *Doriot* (Paris, 1969), p. 254.

WHO WERE THE NEW MEMBERS?

Taken together, therefore, the two 'working-class' parties received an influx of some 400,000 new members, coinciding almost exactly with the recruitment of three million new members by the CGT (see Graph). In each case the main rush of recruits came immediately after the election in which the two parties (taken together) made a net gain of 650,000 votes and seventy-seven seats; during and after an unprecedentedly successful wave of strikes; and under a government which was the first either to be led by a Socialist or to rely on the parliamentary support of Communists. Success breeds success.

How far did these different types of recruit—new voters, new CGT members, new party members—overlap? Obviously not entirely. The CGT members included women, and men under twenty-one, who were not eligible to vote. The new party members could in theory have been recruited entirely among people who were already members of trade unions in 1934, or (a little more plausibly) among people who had already voted Socialist or Communist in 1932. The voters certainly included people who were not wage-earners and therefore not likely to join a trade union.

Nonetheless, it seems reasonable to assume some degree of correlation between a party's electoral appeal and its recruitment of new members. We have seen that the Radicals lost 400,000 votes, while the PCF gained nearly 700,000 and the SFIO score remained virtually unchanged. It would be a mistake, however, to deduce from this that the PCF necessarily won most of its votes from the Radicals or from the right. A geographical breakdown of the election result[60] shows that the SFIO, while losing heavily in constituencies where its successful candidates of 1932 had since left the party as a result of the 1933 schism, compensated for this by making extensive gains in rural areas, usually at the expense of the Radicals. This suggests that in the

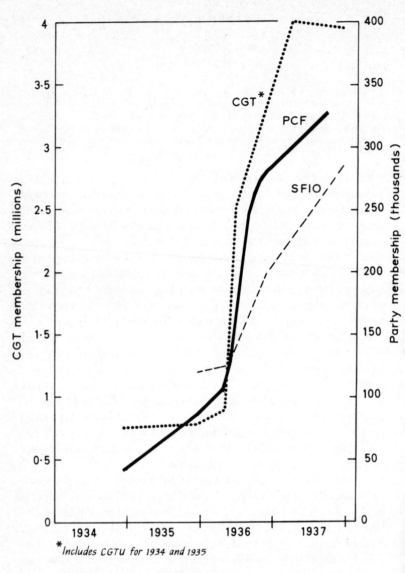

*Includes CGTU for 1934 and 1935

Comparative Rates of Growth: Trade Unions and Political Parties 1934–1937.

urban constituencies where the PCF appeared to win votes from the Radicals, it was in fact the Socialists who were gaining voters on their right but simultaneously losing them to the Communists on their left. The SFIO thus appeared a more and more successful competitor for the traditional clientele of the Radicals—smallholders, shopkeepers, artisans, school-teachers, civil servants—while relinquishing to the PCF its role as the party of the working class.

This supposition is confirmed by such direct evidence as we have about the parties' membership. Contemporaries noted that many of the new SFIO members were not workers but petty-bourgeois; and it was both to balance this development and to compete with the PCF's factory cells that the SFIO at this time tried to set up '*Amicales*' of its own in the factories. Significantly, the main success of these *Amicales* seems to have been in the tertiary sector—that is the service industries where, as we have seen, the CGT had been significantly stronger than the CGTU before 1934, and where the increase in united CGT membership was proportionately smaller during 1936–7 than in manufacturing industry. In these industries the workers usually had a certain status and security to defend, and the gesture of taking out a Socialist party card might seem as daring and revolutionary as for a metalworker or chemical worker to take out a Communist one.[61]

By contrast (and in contrast also to the Spanish Communist Party), there is no evidence to suggest that the PCF at this period recruited many members from the petty bourgeoisie. Members of this class who wanted to demonstrate their commitment to the Popular Front by joining a political party were more likely to be in contact with militants of the Socialist or Radical parties, and to find their styles of politics and types of organization more congenial, because more traditional and more respectful of the individual. Moreover, there are a number of positive reasons for thinking that the new members of the PCF were overwhelmingly working-class. In the first place, the biggest increases in membership were recorded in the most heavily industrialized areas, for instance the western suburbs of Paris, whose share of the total party membership in the Paris region rose from 14 to 30% between 1933 and 1938. A particularly impressive performance was achieved in the Renault factory at Billancourt: here there were only 120 Communists in May 1936, but 6,000 by December.*

* 1,700 was thought a good figure in 1970, in a work force almost exactly the same size (37,000 in 1936, 36,000 in 1970). See A. Kriegel, *Les Communistes français* (1970 edition), pp. 37–8, 270–2.

Secondly, there was a marked increase in the proportion of factory cells as opposed to street or district cells. In the Paris-West area, this proportion rose from 41% in May 1934 to 54% in 1937.[62] In the country as a whole the number of factory cells rose from 600 (20% of the total) in 1934 to 4,000 (40%) in late 1937.[63] Thirdly, the increase in party membership was paralleled by an increase in that of the youth wing (*Jeunesses Communistes*): from 38,000 in May 1936 to 100,000 in October.[64] Some at least of these young Communists can surely be identified with the young, inexperienced trade unionists whom we have noted as following the lead of the *unitaires* in the reunited CGT. In short we can hardly doubt that the Communist recruits, whether young or adult, comprised the revolutionary vanguard among the new members of the CGT.

HOW WERE THEY ABSORBED?

So vast and so rapid an increase in membership must certainly have put a great strain on the party's administrative apparatus. The 'newcomers' outnumbered the old members by more than two to one (ten to one if we compare the membership of 1937 with that of 1933). Clearly it was not possible to give all of them a thorough grounding in Marxism-Leninism, nor yet to organize them with the same tightness and discipline which the party had known in the years when it was reduced to a hard core. The current party line itself (see next section) made this difficult. As some dissatisfied militants later put it: 'How can you stretch out your hand to the Catholics and then object to newly recruited "communists" taking their children to catechism? How can you stretch out your hand to the jingoistic "Croix-de-feu" and then correct the chauvinistic leanings of certain new members?'[65] Inevitably, some of the party veterans were contemptuous of these fair-weather recruits who had taken no part in the anti-colonial and anti-military agitation of the previous decade and therefore never experienced the repression. They predicted—and to a large extent they were proved right—that most of the newcomers would melt away again as fast as they had come when hard times returned. Yet on the whole the surprising thing is that these internal tensions scarcely showed on the surface at all, and that the party leadership never gave the impression of being unable to control the vast unwieldy mass of which it suddenly found itself at the head. Throughout the Popular Front period there are remarkably few instances of party instructions being questioned or disputed by militants at any level. Bolshevization had done its work: the party was equipped with an inner core of some few thousand experienced militants who had learnt not to question instructions but to take pride in executing them swiftly and efficiently as soon as they were received. The mentality of the party cadres at this period is thus described by one of them in retrospect:

> I do not seek the reasons for my attitude, for my behaviour, for my unreserved approval of Thorez's attitude, either in my original education, or in my childhood, or in my nature or anything like that. I seek them simply in the fact that already at that moment, in 1936, I was conditioned by the party. Indeed, if I had not been a conditionable person I should not have been so rapidly promoted among the cadres.[66]

Borne up by their certainty that the party was right, the experienced few had little difficulty in imposing themselves on the uncertainties and hesitations of the many. It is striking that for thirty years after 1936 the party continued to be led by members of the select band that had belonged to it before 1934. Hardly any of its future leaders, even in the middle ranks, were drawn from the great mass which joined in 1936–7.

Nationalism, Leadership and a National Leader

> Jusqu'à cette date, les rapports des communistes avec la société établie étaient, par implicite accord mutuel, de purs et simples rapports d'exclusion: être communiste, c'était se voir et être vu comme l'est un paria, un intouchable, un banni. Or voici que, sans pour autant sortir de leur *in pace*, les communistes se mettent à exister: on les regarde, on les compte, on les soupèse, on les discute, on fait alliance avec ou contre eux, ils sont *reconnus*. Ce passage, de l'au-dehors à l'en-dedans, entraîne un fantastique glissement de tout leur système de valeurs. Démocratie, patrie, culture, et même, ô prodige, cette valeur entre toutes haïe: la guerre, qu'ils avaient stigmatisées comme autant de pièges infâmes tendus par l'ennemi de classe, ils vont les lui disputer.
>
> ANNIE KRIEGEL

In fact the causal relationship between the change in the party's relations with existing French society and the change in its 'system of values' was probably more complex than the above (more or less untranslatable) passage suggests. On chronological grounds alone, it seems clear that the PCF's new position in French politics resulted

255

from the changes in the party line which occurred in 1934–5, and not the other way round. On the other hand it is probably true that the successes of the Popular Front, and the apparent integration of the PCF into the existing political system which occurred in 1935–6, did in turn bring about certain changes in the attitudes of the Communists themselves, and it is perhaps even true that they did transform what had started as a mere tactical modification of the party line into a profound alteration of its 'system of values' which could never afterwards be wholly reversed.

Of course Mme Kriegel's remarks should not be taken as meaning that the PCF before 1934 had been a pacifist party, nor yet that after 1935 it became a war party in the sense of advocating a war of aggression or expansion. Both before and after 1934 it was a Leninist party and therefore a party of international class war; both before and after 1934 it condemned national war between bourgeois states as a consequence of the capitalist system. The abrupt change of May 1935 consisted simply in the recognition that, in a given set of national and international circumstances, the preservation and reinforcement of the armed forces of the French bourgeois state could be temporarily in the interests of the international working class (identified for all practical purposes with those of the only existing working-class state). In strict theory this could be presented as a very limited concession. In practice, by making the Communists for four years the most fervent advocates both of national rearmament and of a national foreign policy which implied at least the risk of war (even though presented as a means of 'defending peace'), it made it impossible for them ever again to be seen, or to see themselves, as primarily an anti-militarist party.

PATRIOTISM

More profoundly, by allowing them, indeed encouraging them, to emphasize French virtues, French traditions, French independence, the 'tournant' of 1934–5 brought to the surface a reserve of patriotic feeling in many Communists which until then they had consciously or unconsciously suppressed. However thorough their Leninist training, French Communists could hardly forget that they were French—nor indeed would a thorough Leninist training encourage them to underrate the importance of nationality. Consciously or unconsciously, they were bound to resent the identification of the various symbols of French nationality with their opponents, the bourgeoisie. Once authorized to do so, they threw themselves into the reconquest of these symbols with visible relief and enthusiasm. Jacques Duclos, at the rally of 14 July 1935, welcomed the alliance of the tricolour, the 'symbol of the struggles of the past', with the red flag, the 'symbol of the struggles and victories to come'. He recalled that the *Marseillaise* was a 'revolutionary song', and that the right-wing leader La Rocque was a descendant of the *émigrés*, those 'traitors to our country'.[67]

The following month, at the Seventh World Congress, Thorez drew attention to this utilization by his party of French revolutionary traditions (that is, the traditions of the French bourgeois revolution), and argued that it had played a part in the PCF's recent successes. 'We claim,' he declared, 'the intellectual and revolutionary heritage of the Encyclopaedists who paved the way for the great revolution of 1789 . . . of the Jacobins . . . and the Commune. We present ourselves to the masses of the people as the champions of the liberty and independence of the country.'[68] This line was endorsed and generalized by the congress, which, in its 'Resolution on the Danger of a New War', instructed Communists to 'show that the working class carries on a consistent struggle in defence of the national freedom and independence of all the people against any oppression or exploitation, because only the communist policy defends to the very end the national freedom and independence of one's country'.[69]

Whereas during the period of Bolshevization the Communists had deliberately copied Soviet terminology, now the PCF sought to demonstrate its Frenchness by using terms which fitted in with French customs and traditions. 'Do comrades think,' Thorez asked the Central Committee in October 1935, 'that the term *rayon* or the term *cellule* are really acclimatized in France? We're the only party that doesn't have *sections*. But that is the revolutionary term in France. That is the tradition. The Great Revolution had its sections. The Radical party has its sections, the *Croix de feu* have their sections. It's only the communist party that doesn't have sections. That makes it seem outside the national traditions. This gap must be filled. . . . If some comrades say we are going back to the old organization, we shall tell them it was the content that had to be changed and we have succeeded in changing it.'[70] In other words, Bolshevization had been so successful that the PCF could now be disguised as a French institution like any other without being in danger of losing the fundamental characteristics that made it unlike any other. As it turned out, the 'cell' was an institution so peculiarly Communist that no adequate 'traditional' term could be found for it. But the *rayons* were finally replaced by 'sections' at a national conference of the party in January 1937.[71]

Meanwhile, at the Eighth Congress of the PCF, in January 1936, the slogan which had been used since 1928, 'the Soviet Union is the true fatherland of the proletariat', was dropped. Instead, the congress called for a 'French Soviet Republic', and identified this with 'une France libre, forte et heureuse', which became one of the main slogans of the Communist campaign in the 1936 election. The party's election programme contained a long and lyrical passage on the virtues of the French Nation, spelt throughout with a capital 'N'; and Thorez in his electoral broadcast on 17 April proclaimed: 'It is not in Rome, or in Berlin or in any other foreign capital, and not even in Moscow, for which we communists do not disguise our profound affection, that the destiny of our country will be decided, but in Paris and Paris only.'

These nationalist themes were developed with even greater verve after the election victory. In June 1936 the party organized a special demonstration to celebrate the centenary of the death of Rouget-de-l'Isle, the author of the *Marseillaise*. In August, Duclos and Thorez called for a 'French Front' which would go beyond the Popular Front and unite right and left 'for the respect of the laws, the defence of the national economy, and the freedom and independence of France'.[72] At the same time the party started a vigorous campaign for aid to the Spanish Republic, arguing not from any ideological affinity between the two Popular Front governments but from France's national interest, which was to prevent the spread of fascism and the 'reconstitution of the Empire of Charles V'. It even began to use the slogan 'France for the French', which until then had been the undisputed propery of the extreme right.[73]

APPEALS TO NATIONALISTS, CATHOLICS AND INTELLECTUALS

The theme of national unity was a logical development of the Popular Front as the Communists understood it: a defensive alliance of classes whose long-term interests were different, but whose immediate interest was the defeat of fascism and the preservation of the French national state. The call for a 'French Front' including political opponents of the Popular Front was in fact abandoned in September 1936 after being indignantly rejected by the Socialists. But even when it was not advocating an alliance 'from above' with right-wing political parties, the PCF was in effect adopting a tactic of 'French

Front from below'—that is, seeking to win over the rank-and-file supporters of the right. At the Congress of Villeurbanne, in January 1936, Thorez quoted with approval a letter that Cachin had written to La Rocque's paper *Le Volontaire National*, assuring its readers that only the Communists could build 'a free France, a strong France, a peaceful France'; and Thorez himself, in his election broadcast of 17 April, appealed quite openly to La Rocque's supporters, young and old: 'We stretch out our hand to you, national volunteer or war veteran enrolled in the *croix de feu*, because you are a son of our people, because you suffer like us from the disorder and the corruption, because you want, like us, to prevent the country from sliding into ruin and catastrophe.'

The same broadcast contained Thorez's famous appeal to the Catholics, who traditionally made up the main voting strength of the right-wing and moderate parties: 'We stretch out our hand to you, Catholic, manual or white-collar worker, artisan or peasant, we who are anti-clericals (*laïques*), because you are our brother, and because you are oppressed by the same troubles as we are.' This campaign too was kept alive after the elections, and at the Congress of Arles, in December 1937, Thorez even spoke in defence of independent Catholic schools—hostility to which had been the main common denominator of the left ever since the turn of the century. He also strove to show that he did not underestimate the Catholic contribution to France's cultural achievement. 'Is it possible,' he asked in October 1937, 'to evoke without emotion the centuries which saw the rise towards heaven of the spires of our magnificent cathedrals, those pure jewels of popular art which protest with all their ancient stones—ancient but, for him who understands them, alive—against the legend of the gloomy Middle Ages?'[74]

The defence of French culture was a favourite theme with the PCF throughout the Popular Front period. We have seen that even before 1934 intellectuals were more or less exempt from the rigours of the class-against-class policy and that the PCF had had some success in influencing them through the Amsterdam-Pleyel Movement and the AEAR. After 1934 these efforts were intensified. The party never forgot to lavish praise on the intellectual community and its role in the life of the nation. Its election programme of 1936 listed among the elements composing the French Nation: 'the galaxy of intellectuals and representatives of learning who, faced with the decadence of our country, are turning more and more to the great ideal which is communism'.[75] An increasing number of intellectuals did indeed see communism in these terms. The *Ligue des Droits de l'Homme*, that guardian of the French humanist conscience, played an important part in preparing the *Rassemblement Populaire* of July 1935, and thereafter drew closer and closer to the PCF, which rescinded the ban on membership of it pronounced by the Fourth World Congress in 1922. By 1936 Communist influence in the *Ligue* was strong enough to prevent it making any clear protest against the great Moscow Trials. Indeed arguably the Comintern's greatest achievement in this period was to prevent the left-wing intelligentsia in the West from taking any interest in the victims of the mass purges and deportations that were occurring in the Soviet Union. This was especially true in France. Almost the only intellectuals of note to break with the party between 1934 and 1939 were André Breton—who was expelled from the AEAR after quarrelling with the Soviet writer Ilya Ehrenburg—and André Gide, who wrote a disillusioned pamphlet after a visit to the Soviet Union. For most of the others the fascist threat in western Europe seemed too serious for it to be worth risking the unity of the anti-fascist front. After 1936 especially, while social democracy became tainted by its association with Non-Intervention and Appeasement, communism gained almost unlimited credit with many French intellectuals because it appeared to be the only political force that was able and willing to stand up to fascism. Intellectuals were perhaps the only social category which fully shared the party's concern with foreign policy, at a time when many Frenchmen were amazingly oblivious of the growing German menace. Within the party, intellectuals played an important part in voicing that concern. Gabriel Péri, as chief foreign leader-writer of *L'Humanité*, wrote daily denunciations of Nazism and its accomplices; and from March 1937 onwards Paul Nizan performed a similar role in the party's new evening paper, *Ce Soir*, of which the editor was an even better-known writer, Louis Aragon. Barbusse died in 1935, and Vaillant-Couturier in 1937, but they had found worthy successors.[76]

MODERATION

National unity came first: the class struggle must wait. Such was the clear implication of the whole Popular Front line, made explicit by the 'French Front' episode of August 1936: the Communists did not urge intervention in Spain to spite the French right, but urged the conciliation of the right at home so as to make possible a bold anti-fascist policy abroad. (They knew well that Blum was deterred from helping Spain by the opposition of the Radicals and the fear that the Popular Front would either break up or find itself fighting a civil war in France. A government of national unity—headed presumably by one of the Radical leaders—need not have suffered from this kind of inhibition.)

This fundamental *parti pris* meant that the leadership which the party offered its own supporters throughout this period was essentially a leadership of restraint rather than of urging on. Its weight was thrown consistently on the side of moderation. Already during the winter of 1935–6 the Communists had sided with the Radicals against the Socialists to keep nationalization and structural reforms out of the Popular Front programme. But even more remarkable was the moderating role which they played during the great strike wave of May–June. The party did of course support the strikes when they occurred, but there is no evidence that it either expected or promoted them. (An article in *L'Humanité* on 24 May, drawing attention to the advantages which the strikers gained by occupying their factories rather than staying at home, probably did contribute to the spread of the movement; but it appeared only on page five of the newspaper and with an undramatic headline.)[77] And while the PCF supported the demands of the strikers, it did not encourage them to demand more. André Ferrat was the only Communist leader who suggested this, and his views were firmly rejected by the Central Committee on 25 May. To the left-wing Socialist Marceau Pivert, who had written that 'everything is now possible!', Marcel Gitton replied in *L'Humanité* (29 May): 'No, everything is not possible.' On 9 June Frachon, the leading Communist in the CGT, used the front page of *L'Humanité* to appeal to the strikers to accept the agreement negotiated with the government and employers at the Hôtel Matignon and resume work without further delay. Finally, on 11 June, Thorez made his famous speech to an assembly of party militants at the Jean Jaurès gymnasium:

> No, comrades, all the conditions are not yet fulfilled, are they?, for Soviet power in France. Let me mention just one of them. We have not yet got behind us, with us, determined like us to go right through with it, the whole population of the countryside.
> In certain cases we should even run the risk of antagonizing some sections of the petty bourgeoisie and of the peasants of France. What then?

> . . . *We must know how to end a strike*, as soon as our demands are satisfied. We must even know how to accept a compromise when not all our demands have been accepted, provided victory has been won on the most essential and most important demands.

It would be fatal, he insisted, to risk the dislocation of the Popular Front or the isolation of the working class.

Even the most virulent anti-Communists were obliged to admit that in this instance the party had acted as a factor of moderation, and to invent reasons why Moscow had called off its offensive at the last minute. But to less prejudiced observers it was clear that the offensive had been neither planned nor desired by Moscow. It was the French workers who insisted on seeing the Popular Front as an opportunity for radical change at home. In Moscow it was seen as a chance to strengthen the Franco-Soviet alliance. Gabriel Péri had hailed the election result in *L'Humanité* (8 May) as 'the French people's firm reply to Hitlerism', and Dimitrov in *Correspondance Internationale* (16 May) had called on the French masses to exercise 'maximum pressure on the government's foreign policy'.

Moderation except in foreign policy: this was the guiding principle of the Communists' attitude to the Léon Blum government. Before it was formed they promised it their 'loyal support'. In practice they were frequently critical of it, but it was noticeable that their criticism was usually directed at its Socialist members, while the Radicals were spared and at times even flattered. For instance, at the end of June 1936 Duclos devoted an article in *L'Humanité* to the theme 'The Radicals are right'. They were right, he wrote, to refuse any threat to private property, right to insist on limiting the reforms to what had been agreed between the Popular Front parties before the election, and right to work for 'a national union capable of standing up to the threat which hangs over us from the warlike ardour of a neighbouring country'.[78]

As the summer wore on, the Communists made gesture after gesture to reassure the Radicals and moderate opinion generally. They refused to 'sacrifice to the current fashion for attacking the Senate'[79] (when the Senate had extracted a promise from the government that no more occupations of factories would be tolerated). They expelled André Ferrat, who was attacking the current party line as one of opportunism and class collaboration;[80] and at the same national conference (10–11 July) Thorez reminded the party that the Popular Front was a contract between the working and middle classes and that therefore the reforms should benefit the latter as well as the former. The Communist Party, he added, was 'in the service of the people of France'.[81] This clearly implied that it was no longer devoted exclusively to defending the interests of the working class.

After abandoning its 'French Front' proposals in deference to the SFIO on 9 September, the PCF gave further proofs of its good will during the autumn by continuing to support the government in parliament in spite of deep disagreement both on the Spanish issue and on the devaluation of the franc. In October, fearing that the Radical Party was about to break with the Popular Front at its congress in Biarritz, the PCF abandoned the strike campaign which it had started in favour of aid to Spain. The Central Committee sent a letter to Daladier drawing attention to the moderating role which the PCF had played throughout the Popular Front and appealing to the Radical tradition of 'No enemies on the left'. As their dissatisfaction with the Blum government grew, the Communists again dropped hints that they would be glad to see a Radical-led government pursuing a bolder foreign policy. Thorez said on 29 November that the Popular Front's fate was 'not restricted to the survival of one cabinet': an alternative Popular Front cabinet could be found 'with men applying resolutely the policies wished by the masses'.[82] These hopes may have been based on reports that Daladier, now Minister of Defence, was personally unhappy about the Non-Intervention policy in Spain. But in public neither he nor his party showed any sign of agreeing with the Communists on this issue; so that when it came to the point Thorez had no alternative cabinet to propose. Accordingly the Communist deputies were instructed to abstain rather than vote against the government in the confidence vote on Spain on 5 December, after which the party leaders hastened to bury the affair as a 'passing disagreement' and to express their confidence in the government's general policies. A month later (15 January) they agreed to vote for a bill authorizing the government to prevent the departure of volunteers for Spain. And at a National Conference of the party on 22–23 January Thorez stressed the 'credit balance' of the Popular Front and the 'satisfaction of the workers'. After listing the improvements which the government, with the support of the workers, had brought about, he concluded: 'In short, one can breathe again.'

263

Not surprisingly, the Communists gave no support to Pivert during the winter when he called for a new socialist 'offensive', since this would have meant a break with the Radicals, or at very least a split in the Radical Party; but they grudgingly accepted the wage pause which Blum announced, on the Radicals' insistence, in mid-February. More remarkable was the moderation with which they reacted to the 'Clichy affair' on 16 March, when six anti-fascist demonstrators were killed by the police. Thorez criticized the government only for showing 'too much weakness towards the enemies of the people'; and carefully refrained from blaming it directly for the workers' deaths. Duclos actually tabled a motion in the Chamber to approve the government's handling of the riot.

Finally, in the crisis which brought down the government in June 1937, the Communists abandoned their initial opposition and voted in favour of Blum's demand for special financial powers. When this was refused by the Senate, Duclos and Gitton assured Blum of their party's unconditional support; and it was against their advice that he finally decided to resign.[83]

WHY DID THE PCF REFUSE TO JOIN THE GOVERNMENT IN MAY 1936?

During this crisis, the Communists for the first time offered to join the government themselves. This raises the question why they had refused to do so a year earlier when it was formed, in spite of Blum's earnest entreaties. The reason given at the time—the fear of 'offering the pretext for the panic-mongering campaigns of the people's enemies'—was not very convincing. The right was ready to panic in any case; and the left would undoubtedly have been much more reassured by the Communists' coming into the government than by their staying out. It looked to many people as if Léon Blum had been cast as Kerensky. But that interpretation can be ruled out, since nothing else in the party's behaviour during 1936 remotely recalls that of the Bolsheviks in 1917.

Much later, Thorez claimed that he had argued in favour of joining the government at the time, but had been overruled by the *Bureau Politique*—and this has now become official party history.[84] This means that it is now hardly possible for any party source to dispute the story, but it is noticeable that François Billoux, in his recent work *Quand Nous Etions Ministres*,[85] appears anxious to play it down as far as possible. He says that Thorez put forward the idea not at a *Bureau*

Politique meeting but 'in a conversation with some *Bureau Politique* members', and that finding 'no favourable echo' he decided not to bring it up at a formal meeting. It certainly seems unlikely that Thorez would have put it forward at all seriously without the support of Fried and the Comintern, and if he had had that support it is most unlikely that the *Bureau Politique* would have gone against him.

Almost certainly the real reason for the party's decision was simply that the situation in France did not correspond to the conditions laid down by the Seventh World Congress for the formation of 'an anti-fascist people's front government' (see above, pp. 237–8). The decision was first announced on 6 May, and finally confirmed on 14 May, which was actually the day of the first strike-cum-occupation in the Paris region. The mass strike wave did not get under way until the following week. In any case, as we have seen, the PCF resolutely refused to put a revolutionary interpretation on the strike wave even when it reached its peak in early June. It would therefore have been doubly surprising if, in the first half of May, it had taken a step which, according to current Comintern doctrine, was appropriate only in an immediately pre-revolutionary situation.

Although the Popular Front strategy as a whole was defensive, it is clear that until 1936 the Comintern did not conceive of a 'Popular Front government' as a defensive measure. As long as the task of the Popular Front was simply to shore up bourgeois democracy against the fascist menace, the government (even though a 'left-wing government') must necessarily be a bourgeois one, in which a working-class party had no place. (It should be remembered that the Communists went on warning the SFIO against the temptations of 'Néo-Millerandisme' until the moment when the SFIO actually became the largest party in the bourgeois parliament. They then promised support for a 'Socialist-led government'; but such a government, as Blum himself clearly recognized, was still a bourgeois government in the sense that the SFIO had not 'conquered' power on behalf of the working class but was merely 'exercising' it within the bourgeois system.) The formation of a 'Popular Front government' would have implied that the anti-fascist alliance had gone over to the offensive and was ready to proceed beyond bourgeois democracy. The Communists repeatedly denied that this was possible or desirable in the France of 1936.

But during the summer of that year the Comintern must have realized that the presence of Communists might become necessary even in a bourgeois government, as a part of the defensive strategy. The disadvantage of their not being in the government became very clear in France during the crisis over arms supplies to Spain at the end of July and beginning of August. The right-wing Radicals were then able to impose the Non-Intervention policy on a cabinet whose centre of gravity was much further to the right than that of the Popular Front as a whole. If Blum had had Communist ministers supporting him on this issue inside the cabinet, the outcome might quite possibly have been different.

Whether or not they were influenced by this episode, the Comintern leaders certainly revised their attitude to the question at about this time. For in September, when the Spanish Communists refused—with perfect orthodoxy—to join the government formed by the Socialist leader Largo Caballero, they found themselves overruled by ECCI and ordered to join.[86] The survival of the Spanish Republic was considered more important than the purity of Comintern doctrine—for no attempt was made to present the Spanish situation as pre-revolutionary. On the contrary, the Spanish Communists were to become notorious for their insistence on ignoring the revolutionary aspects of the situation and emphasizing only the 'defence of the democratic republic'. The same argument presumably applied to the French situation in June 1937: the Communists were willing to enter the government because this seemed the only way to avert the disintegration of the Popular Front. Six months later they were equally willing to join a government of national union ('from Thorez to Reynaud') when this seemed to offer a chance of arresting the slide towards appeasement abroad and reaction at home. But Blum's attempt to form such a government was frustrated by the right.[87]

CONCLUSION: THE STYLE OF COMMUNIST LEADERSHIP

The period of the Popular Front was the period of the PCF's first large-scale success—the period in which it could for the first time number its own members in hundreds of thousands, in which it could claim an important if not a dominant influence in an organized labour movement numbering millions, in which it emerged as an important electoral and parliamentary force whose leaders were treated as political figures of national standing and even asked to join governments. It was thus the period in which it was first called on to provide leadership, in one form or another, for a substantial section of the French population. The style of leadership which it provided was at once nationalistic—or at least patriotic—and socially moderate.

The reasons for this were circumstantial. The party's long-term theoretical goals remained those of class war and social revolution. Yet it could hardly escape the notice of the party leaders that their new moderate and patriotic stance was partly, if not largely, responsible for their success. Moreover, it is evident that many of them found the role of patriotic, sensible, *responsible* statesmen, which they were obliged to assume, unexpectedly congenial. This was particularly true of Maurice Thorez.

We have seen that until May 1934 Thorez had unreservedly identified himself with the class-against-class policy, and we shall see that in 1939–40 he could be equally zealous in defence of the Russo-German pact. There was never any question about where his loyalties lay or about his willingness to support whatever policy was prescribed by Moscow. It is nonetheless true that during the Popular Front Thorez found a role as a national leader which he played particularly well and which, throughout his later life, he was always able to adopt with evident conviction. No doubt he was well coached in this role by Fried, but thereafter he would need no coaching.

It would be excessive to speak of a personality cult during the 1930s. But Thorez was certainly allowed to emerge as *the* party leader in a way that none of his predecessors had done. At the congress of January 1936 the post of general secretary, which had been suppressed in 1929, was recreated for him—the same post, of course, that Stalin held in the Soviet party. The publication of his autobiography, *Fils du Peuple*, in 1937 was a further new and significant departure. Gradually the leader appeared to identify himself with his party, and vice versa, at the same time as both party and leader became known to the nation at large. Perhaps the key moment in this process was the 'outstretched hand' broadcast of 17 April 1936, of which François Mauriac wrote: 'another voice was heard, a tender, bleating voice, almost as sweet and more persuasive than that of the nightingale—the voice of the communist Thorez.'[88]

And so the French Communist Party came to identify itself with the man who said, on 6 August 1936: 'Personally I have never raised my fist. The gesture which I consider best expresses our policy is that of the hand outstretched to the people of France.'[89]

8

From Munich to Vichy

Crusade against Fascism (1936–1939)

The Popular Front brought many advantages to the Communists, but not the one which they had chiefly sought from it: the strengthening of the Franco-Soviet alliance and the containment of Nazi expansion.[1] This failure is rich in irony. What had attracted Stalin in the Popular Front strategy was no doubt the idea that he could make the western Communist Parties the instruments of his foreign policy. What happened in France was that the aims of Soviet policy were, in effect, sacrificed to the future of the French Communist Party. If the PCF had been dissolved in 1934, or if it had turned directly to a 'national front' line without first seeking to mend its fences with the Socialists and the moderate left, or even if it had simply continued its class-against-class line as before, it is quite possible that right-wing governments would have remained in office and would have pursued a nationalist foreign policy along the lines laid down by Barthou. It would have meant getting rid of Laval, but that would probably have happened anyway: Laval was hardly less unpopular on the right than on the left. Herriot in the centre and Paul Reynaud on the right were both strong advocates of the alliance with Russia against Nazi Germany, and they would undoubtedly have found much more support among their colleagues had this alliance not been identified with the Popular Front.[2]

Yet the Popular Front in power did little to implement the alliance. This was predictable. Both the Socialists and the Radicals of the Daladier school had built their careers on opposition to nationalism and militarism, on the advocacy of disarmament, international understanding and universal peace. They were slow—and in some cases totally unable—to grasp that the Nazi menace was not one that could be conjured by moderation and understanding, but one that could be contained only by the show, if not the use, of force. In the

1920s they had attacked Poincaré for pursuing a vendetta against Germany. They did not now intend to repeat Poincaré's mistake of embarking on a confrontation with Germany without British support. They therefore found themselves, through a mixture of conviction and weakness, following the British policies of Non-Intervention and Appeasement.

These policies were hard to reconcile with the anti-fascist enthusiasm which had given birth to the Popular Front, and which continued to animate many of its supporters. Together with economic difficulties, they sapped its morale and undermined its unity. In particular, they virtually destroyed the SFIO, which by 1939 had lost nearly all its popular support, while its remaining members were almost irreconcilably divided into two factions: the 'Munichois' led by Paul Faure, who still favoured preserving peace at almost any price, and the 'anti-Munichois' led by Blum, who in fact accepted the Munich agreement but nonetheless advocated rearmament and mutual assistance pacts against the dictators. The wartime division between *minoritaires* and *majoritaires* was thus revived. But, by a further irony, it was the latter who now stood closer to the Communists.

Anti-fascist resistance was the constant theme of PCF propaganda throughout these years; indeed it was the be-all and end-all of PCF policy. As the Popular Front gradually disintegrated, the Communists sought desperately to keep it alive and to impose on its leaders the foreign policy which alone could have restored its self-confidence and its sense of purpose. Part of the SFIO, and a small part of the Radical Party, was willing to follow them. But that only helped to drive the bulk of the Radicals back into alliance with the right, and to frighten the right into acceptance of Appeasement. Many of those to whom the Communists' arguments should have appealed discounted them—or were simply unaware of them—precisely because they were put forward by Communists. 'Gabriel Péri was one of the most astute analysts of foreign affairs in Paris, but only Communists read his articles.'[3] As for the mass of the population, it remained largely indifferent to foreign affairs, but grateful for peace while it lasted.

During these three years, the PCF fought the battle against fascism on two fronts: a political-diplomatic front in Paris and a military front in Spain. For Communists, the connection between the defence of the Spanish Republic and the containment of Nazi Germany was never in any doubt. As early as 6 August 1936 Thorez declared: 'The defeat of the Spanish Republic would be our own defeat. It would gravely compromise the security and the future of our country.' France should lift the arms embargo, he said, in order to 'help republican Spain against the rebels and their fascist masters, Hitler and Mussolini'.[4] The Non-Intervention policy, he said on 25 August, was 'a dangerous precedent which can only help Hitler's plans', since it would enable him to foment rebellion in any country—Czechoslovakia, Romania, Yugoslavia, Belgium, even France herself—and then demand that his agents be treated on an equal footing with the legitimate government of that country. Hitler had accepted the Non-Intervention agreement to soften the impact of his sudden introduction of two-year conscription in Germany; and yet at that very moment the French government was welcoming Dr Schacht, Hitler's Minister of Economics and president of the Reichsbank, in Paris.[5]

Already at the beginning of August a number of French Communists, who had been attending the 'Workers' Olympiad' in Barcelona at the moment when the war broke out, had helped form the 'Paris Battalion' to fight on the Republic side. Thorez himself, with Togliatti, had been put in charge of a joint Comintern-Profintern fund for Spain as early as 26 July, a week after the war began. At the end of September he took part in the discussions in Moscow which led to the creation of the International Brigades, a volunteer force for Spain recruited mainly by foreign Communist Parties. Paris became the main recruiting centre for this, and France provided the largest national contingent: probably 10,000 out of a total of about 40,000 foreigners who had fought in the Brigades by the time of their withdrawal in autumn 1938. Most of them were working-class (many coming from high unemployment areas such as Lyons). The majority were party members before volunteering, and more joined the party while in Spain. (But the most famous French volunteer, André Malraux, was not a member of the Brigades. He commanded an air squadron of his own. Nor was he a member of the party, though he was a very close sympathizer and described himself as a Communist.[6]) 3,000 French volunteers were killed in action, 'aware that in defending Madrid they were defending Paris'.[7]

The PCF also provided the uniforms for the Brigades (including an Alpine round woollen hat), as well as the commander of their base at Albacete. This was André Marty, who owed his appointment to his supposed military knowledge and to Stalin's favour (both based on his part in the Black Sea mutiny of 1919). While at Albacete he was noted chiefly for his obsessive fear of fascist spies, and impressed some observers as 'arrogant, incompetent and cruel'.[8] The portrait of him painted by Hemingway in *For Whom the Bell Tolls* as 'the butcher of Albacete', making constant use of the firing squad, is, however, contested by some of those who served under him.[9] While admitting his irascible temperament, these suggest that his violence was mainly verbal.

The French Communists who fought in Spain gained military experience which later proved useful to many of them in the French Resistance: for instance Charles Tillon, another veteran of the 1919 naval mutinies, who was to become the commander of the *Francs-Tireurs et Partisans Français*; Colonel Dumont, the former regular officer who commanded the 'Commune de Paris' battalion at the siege of Madrid in November 1936, and was to be shot by the Nazis in 1943; Pierre Georges, who volunteered for service in Spain at seventeen, and later became the 'Colonel Fabien' of the Resistance; Auguste Lecoeur, who was to run the party's clandestine liaison system in 1942–44; and Henri Rol-Tanguy, who as 'Colonel Rol' was to command the French Resistance forces during the liberation of Paris.[10]

We have already seen that during the first Blum government (June 1936 to June 1937) the PCF pressed for a more actively anti-fascist foreign policy, especially in Spain, but in the last resort refrained from voting against the government because there was no sign of any alternative government that might pursue such a policy. After Blum's fall the dilemma did not change, and nor did the party's conduct. The reshuffled Popular Front government under Chautemps was alternately coaxed and bullied to 'revive a realistic foreign policy'.* The results of both tactics were meagre. Although the government connived at a clandestine arms traffic with republican Spain, it avoided any open confrontation with Italy and Germany on this or any other issue, and tagged along behind Chamberlain's policy of seeking an understanding with the dictators. At the same time relations between France and the Soviet Union grew steadily cooler. The military value of the alliance to France seemed more doubtful than ever after the trial and execution of Marshal Tukhachevsky and other senior Red Army officers in June 1937, ostensibly for conspiring with the Germans. In December the French foreign minister, Yvon Delbos, went on a tour of East European capitals which conspicuously

---

* This goal for 'mass action' was indicated by Frachon—now officially a trade union leader without party responsibilities—in *L'Humanité*, 23 October 1937.

omitted Moscow. Soon afterwards the French Communists hard-
ened their attitude to the government's internal policy (notably the
handling of strikes and factory occupations), and in January 1938
Chautemps tried to expel them from his parliamentary majority. The
Socialist ministers then resigned. In the ensuing cabinet crisis the
Communists showed more interest in foreign policy than in the
defence of the workers. Gabriel Péri demanded Delbos's removal
from the Quai d'Orsay,[11] and blamed undue British influence for all
the French government's sins, including the attempted exclusion of
the PCF from the majority, which he presented as part of the
preparation for deals with Germany and Italy.[12] He attacked the
outgoing government for depending exclusively on London and
ignoring Moscow.[13]

But Péri's articles were ignored, as were the party's calls for a
'cabinet in the likeness of the Popular Front'—i.e. composed of
Radicals, Socialists and Communists. Blum could not get conservatives to join a national government alongside Communists; nor could
he get the Radicals to accept Communist participation in a new
Popular Front government. The result was that Chautemps came
back as head of a purely Radical government, with Delbos still foreign
minister. Once again the Communists swallowed their objections and
gave their support, since it was obvious that the only alternative was a
return to a centre-right government which they could not even
pretend to influence. For the same reason they returned to a policy of
restraint on the industrial front.

The same crisis was re-enacted when Chautemps finally resigned
in March, but in more dramatic circumstances since Hitler was in the
process of invading Austria. In spite of this international emergency
Blum was still unable to persuade the right to join a national
government, even though he was now willing to make it stretch 'from
Thorez to Louis Marin'—i.e. as far to the right as was compatible
with the defence of the Republic. He therefore formed another
government composed of Socialists and Radicals. This government
included the resolutely anti-Nazi Paul-Boncour as foreign minister. It
gave assurances to Czechoslovakia and stepped up secret arms
shipments to Spain. But no one expected it to stay in office for long,
since it was clear that most of the Radicals had now lost faith in the
Popular Front. Accordingly the Communists, visibly frustrated to
find their offers of participation spurned once more, did not waste
their energies trying to prolong its existence. They called for a

'government which governs', with a 'programme of national recovery and of struggle against war-mongers and agitators'.[10] Evidently they were still hoping for a broader government which could adopt a bold foreign policy with greater confidence and credibility. The campaign for aid to Spain was revived, and continued even after the cabinet's decision to send new arms shipments—rumours of which the Communists pretended to disbelieve.[15] Probably they hoped that the government could be provoked into a public denunciation of the Non-Intervention agreement, which in turn would provoke a breach with Britain and frustrate Chamberlain's policy of rapprochement with Germany and Italy.[16] Meanwhile a new wave of sit-down strikes broke out among the Paris metalworkers, this time clearly encouraged by the Communists.[17]

On 8 April Blum's second government, like his first, was overthrown by the Senate on its financial policy. This time the Communists did not protest, but simply proclaimed their fidelity to the Popular Front, which in reality had just received its death-blow. The Radicals considered that the moment had now come for their traditional mid-term switch from left to right. Daladier formed a centre government without the Socialists, but with Reynaud as Minister of Justice. The new Radical foreign minister, Georges Bonnet, was known to be less anti-German than Paul-Boncour. In spite of this the strikes in the automobile and aircraft industries were suddenly halted because (according to the Communist union leaders) 'the prolongation and extension of conflicts cannot avoid having their repercussions on the economy and the security of France'.[18] As the Socialist Vincent Auriol bitterly pointed out: 'the beginning, the end and the difficulties of the strikes coincided with the beginning, the end and the difficulties of the Socialist government.'[19] Daladier, after a policy statement in which he stressed the need for national defence but did not mention the Popular Front, was accorded both confidence and full financial powers by a majority including the Communists and Socialists. In May, they did not oppose his financial decree-laws, which included an 8% tax increase and new exceptions to the forty-hour working week (one of the most highly prized but economically disastrous 'conquests' of 1936).

On 31 May, however, the PCF began a vigorous parliamentary campaign against the government, probably as an attempt to halt the decline of both party and trade union membership which had now set in. Social reforms were demanded as well as aid for Spain, but the campaign was intensified on 16 June when the party leaders learned that the government had again closed the Spanish frontier. Daladier replied by cutting short the parliamentary session. During June and July the Communists tried to revive the Popular Front as a mass movement outside parliament, but with little success. A mass meeting planned for 6 July to call for aid to Spain had to be cancelled for lack of support. The collapse of the Popular Front was so evident that public enthusiasm for the idea could not be re-kindled. By the same token the PCF's inability to influence the government, whether by threats or cajolery, could no longer be concealed. The government had rejected suggestions for closer Franco-Soviet military co-operation.[20] On 21 August Daladier announced the need for a general easing of the forty-hour law, and soon afterwards he issued a decree allowing supplementary hours throughout industry. This time the Communists decided to support strike movements. During September they were clearly encouraging agitation in industry, while attacking Chamberlain and Daladier for their attempts to appease Hitler over Czechoslovakia. Foreign policy was still their overriding preoccupation. This was made unmistakably clear during the Munich crisis. No sooner had the government announced partial mobilization (24 September) than the party declared its full support and Arrachart, the Communist leader of the Building Federation, immediately instructed the Paris building workers to end their strike in order 'to take up arms against fascism'.[21] Communist union officials even announced that workers in the Paris aeronautical factories would work extra hours for the defence effort.

Inevitably after this, the party greeted the Munich agreement with intense rage and disappointment, describing it as 'scandalous', 'criminal', the 'greatest treason a republican government had ever committed against peace', and so on. These feelings were undoubtedly shared by a large number of individual Frenchmen, but few had the courage to speak out in the general atmosphere of relief that peace had been preserved. Once again the PCF appeared virtually isolated in the country, and was totally isolated in parliament. On 4 October only two other deputies joined the Communists in voting against the Munich settlement, and only five in voting against Daladier's request for special economic and financial powers. (The Socialists voted for the former but—for the first time since 1936—abstained on the latter.)

Yet Daladier and his supporters could hardly conceal from themselves that they had in fact been humiliated by Hitler. The Communist criticisms were no doubt of that peculiarly painful kind which find an echo in the subject's opinion of himself. As is common in such cases, their reaction was more violent than rational, indeed verging on the paranoiac. At the end of October Daladier, speaking at a Radical Party congress, accused the PCF of 'paralysing my action' during the Munich crisis, and warned that the Republic would henceforth prevent 'any enterprise which does not originate in the depths of the country (*qui ne surgirait pas des profondeurs de la patrie*)'. The congress voted a resolution stating that the PCF had 'broken the solidarity which united it with the other parties of the *Rassemblement Populaire*'. Accordingly the Radicals tried to expel the Communists from the national committee of the *Rassemblement*—a body which had long since lost its significance in any case. But the Communists, considering that they alone had been faithful to the ideals of the Popular Front, refused to take responsibility for its dissolution. On 2 November they reaffirmed their resolution to stay in the committee,[22] and finally it was the Radical delegate who withdrew, on 10 November. In the two months that followed, Radical newspapers actually took the lead in a campaign to get the PCF banned, which of course received hearty support from the right.

Meanwhile an ECCI manifesto called for the replacement of 'the governments of national treachery and shame in the countries menaced by fascist blows from without' by 'governments that are ready to repulse the fascist aggressors'.[23] The PCF was thus absolved from any obligation to support the Daladier government simultaneously by the Comintern leadership and by Daladier himself. It could at last afford to give free rein to the discontent of the more militant workers at the gradual dismantling of the Popular Front reforms.

By a new irony, it was Reynaud, the main advocate within the government of resistance to Hitler and a closer alliance with Russia, who now became the target of the Communists' attacks. On 1 November he was transferred to the Ministry of Finance, and on 12 November he announced a financial programme of decree-laws which included a six-day working week of up to forty-eight hours, higher taxes, the abandonment of the public works programme, and staff cuts on the state railways. The object of these measures was to put the economy on a war footing and so make it possible for France to 'repulse the fascist aggressors' (even if Reynaud would not have used that vocabulary) when the moment came. But with Daladier and Bonnet inviting Ribbentrop to Paris and preparing to sign a Franco-

275

German agreement, the workers could be forgiven for feeling that they, and not the Nazi regime, were the intended victims of the government's offensive. The working class, declared Thorez on 21 November, would be willing to make the 'maximum effort' for a programme of national recovery, but only if the 'men of Munich' were first to leave office.[24]

As it was, the working class, or at least its organized leadership, prepared for a head-on clash with the government. At the CGT congress in Nantes, held from 14 to 17 November, the Communists joined hands with Jouhaux (now as in 1914 a partisan of national resistance to aggression) to defeat the pacifist or 'Munichois' minority. But all three factions agreed to oppose the decree-laws with industrial action, 'including collective work stoppage if this proves indispensable for the defence of the social reforms'. On 21 November the first application of the decree-laws was greeted by a wave of sit-down strikes in the Paris region and the Nord. Jouhaux, who no doubt foresaw a repetition of the disaster of 1920, would have liked to avoid a general strike. But he was unable to withstand the paradoxical combination of pressures from the Communists and the anti-Communist pacifists of the *Syndicats* group. The latter were glad enough of a chance to attack Reynaud, that 'antimunichois notoire',[25] and were in any case determined not to be outflanked by the Communists in the campaign against the 'décrets-lois de misère'.

By mid-week over 100,000 workers were involved in the strike movement. Many of the strikes were spontaneous, but the Communists were now definitely egging them on rather than holding them back. On 24 November the Citroën and Renault automobile factories and the Bloch aircraft factory—bastions of the Communist-controlled Metalworkers' Federation—were occupied. But Daladier reacted with great firmness and police were used to clear the Renault factories by force. Next day the CGT's *Commission Administrative* called a one-day general strike against the decree-laws for 30 November.

Both CGT and PCF had fallen into Daladier's trap, by letting themselves be drawn into a global confrontation which could only be seen as a challenge on their part to the authority of the legally constituted government. The Communists insisted that the aims of the strike were purely economic. This may well have been true for the mass of those taking part, but was clearly not true for the Communist leaders themselves, especially as they continued calling for Daladier's resignation. Daladier of course had no intention of resigning. He was still riding the wave of popularity which the Munich agreement had won him, and he now had his opponents where he wanted them. On 28 November he 'requisitioned' all workers in public transport and public services—a measure which put strikers outside the law and threatened them with prison. The unions concerned revealed their lack of confidence by instructing their members to obey the requisition order, but the CGT nonetheless maintained its strike call elsewhere. As a result the strike, although partially successful in private industry, was deprived of its psychological impact. It completely failed to intimidate the government, but succeeded in demoralizing the CGT. Daladier may have been no match for Hitler, or even Chamberlain, but he had scored an easy victory over the French labour movement. On 9 December he received a confidence vote in the Chamber with the support of the right, while Socialists and Communists voted against him. The reversal of alliances was thus complete, and the Popular Front had suffered the same fate as the *Cartel des Gauches* of 1924 and the *néo-Cartel* of 1932.

The two levers with which the Communists had tried for two years to influence French foreign policy—their influence over the organized labour movement and their membership of the governing parliamentary majority—had thus finally shattered in their hands. But their analysis of the situation did not change. Their conviction that France's national interest and the interest of the international working class alike dictated a closer Franco-Soviet alliance and a firmer stand against Hitler remained unshaken. For eight months their voice continued to be heard crying in the wilderness, denouncing fascism, rallying Frenchmen to the defence of their national honour and national territory, reminding them of their glorious past. When Mussolini laid claim to Nice, Savoy and Corsica, no one denounced this threat to 'French soil' with greater indignation than Thorez (15 December 1938). And the same Thorez, once the organizer of agitation against France's involvement in North Africa (see above, p. 156), travelled to Algiers in February 1939 to plead the cause of a 'free union' between France and Algeria, implying the 'right to divorce but not the obligation to divorce'. On the contrary, at the present moment Algeria had a 'duty to unite even more closely with French democracy'. He warned Algerian Moslems that they would be much worse off under Hitler than under the French Republic, and Tunisians that under Mussolini they would suffer the same fate of 'ruin and death' as Libya.[26]

The collapse of Czechoslovakia in March 1939 of course gave the PCF new ammunition to use against the 'men of Munich', Daladier and Bonnet, who were subjected to further blistering attacks by Péri in *L'Humanité*. But when Chamberlain and Daladier themselves took up a tougher anti-Nazi position, the party was quick to support them. On 30 March Thorez stressed that it would support 'any efforts tending to the organization of collective security'. Throughout the spring and summer it carried on an increasingly impatient campaign for a military alliance between France, Britain and Russia, while organizing large-scale celebrations to mark the 150th anniversary of the French Revolution (including the production of Renoir's film *La Marseillaise*). The event most emphasized in these celebrations was not the storming of the Bastille but the battle of Valmy, at which the *sans-culotte* volunteers crying 'Vive la nation!' had halted the advance of the Prussian invader.[27]

The Crisis of August–September 1939

The party could hardly have been less well prepared for the news which broke at midnight on 21 August, that Ribbentrop was flying to Moscow to sign a non-aggression pact.

There can be little doubt that the PCF leadership was taken completely unawares. It was not until 25 August that any statement at all was forthcoming either from the *Bureau Politique* or from the general secretary, or from the party's usual spokesman on international affairs, Gabriel Péri, or from the editor of *L'Humanité*, Marcel Cachin. Péri is said to have been personally shattered by the Soviet decision, which appeared to make nonsense of all that he had written in the past five years. The others too must have been shaken, and were no doubt hoping for some clarification or instruction from Moscow. The only member of the secretariat or *Bureau Politique* to stick his neck out on 22 August was Gitton, who told the party's evening paper *Ce Soir* that 'the Soviet Union compelling Germany to conclude a non-aggression pact means a defeat for the fascist warmongers and a victory for peace'. This interpretation of the pact was to be the essence of the party line for the next four weeks. But for the first three days its formulation was left to party journalists —chiefly Aragon as editor of *Ce Soir* and P.-L. Darnar, an assistant editor of *L'Humanité*—without further guidance from the political leadership.

It apparently did not occur to these writers that the policy of strengthening the Franco-Soviet alliance, which they had ardently defended for five years, had simply failed; and that Stalin, drawing the natural conclusion, had abandoned it. Still less did it occur to them that the policy had been essentially a product of German hostility to Russia, and that this was the first time since 1933 that the possibility of deflecting that hostility towards the West offered an alternative means of reaching the same end, namely the protection of the Soviet Union from German aggression. What they *could* see clearly—and they could only rejoice at it—was that Stalin had frustrated the design which they attributed to the 'men of Munich', that of preserving the West by encouraging Hitler to attack Russia. It was to this that they attributed the fury of French public opinion at Stalin's 'betrayal'—a charge they could hardly take seriously when many of those who voiced it were themselves long-standing opponents of the Franco-Soviet alliance. The pact was a defeat for the 'men of Munich'. Therefore, they somewhat naively assumed, it must somehow be a victory for anti-fascism. 'Silence to the anti-Soviet wolf-pack!' wrote Aragon on 22 August: 'This is the day when all their hopes collapse. This is the day when it will have to be admitted that something has changed in the world, and that thanks to the USSR one cannot make war when one likes.' The irony was nonetheless grim for being unconsious: in the eyes of the world at large the significance of the pact was precisely that it licensed Hitler to make war when and where he wanted.

Next day *L'Humanité* appeared with a big portrait of Stalin, the 'champion of peace and of the independence of peoples'. The headline was 'Success for the Soviet policy of firmness'. Underneath, the paper proclaimed: 'The Moscow talks help the cause of peace in Europe. Without further delay, Paris and London must now sign the Franco-Anglo-Soviet pact.'

The plans of Munich [wrote Darnar] are turned upside down by the attitude of the USSR. But nothing prevents France and Britain from reaching agreement with Moscow to better ensure mutual security and the independence of peoples.

The plane for Moscow leaves every morning about eight o'clock, Monsieur Daladier.

Soviet firmness and its results give you an excellent example. *Sign the pact!* Give instructions to your military delegates to reach agreement, not to hang about. . . .

279

(Darnar could not have known that Daladier had actually done this on 21 August, and that it was the Soviet delegate, Marshal Voroshilov, who had put off resuming the military talks.[28]) Aragon in *Ce Soir* took up the same theme:

> The tripartite pact (which is not a mere non-aggression pact but a full alliance, and remains the keystone of the Peace Front) will perfectly complement a German-Soviet non-aggression pact. For the tripartite pact has never been regarded by the peoples of France, Britain and the USSR as a weapon of war, but as a weapon of peace, a weapon against aggression, against the repudiation of their signature by the specialists in aggression.

The German-Soviet Non-Aggression Pact was signed in Moscow that same night. Next morning, 24 August, *L'Humanité* again carried a piece by Darnar asserting that the pact fitted into the European system of collective security and 'in no way contradicted' earlier treaties:

> It's up to France and Britain to strengthen with their adhesion an energetic and intelligent policy which is the only one consistent with the cause of peace. All that's needed is to conclude the Franco-Anglo-Soviet alliance. All that's needed is to send instructions to the military delegations to reach agreement.

Yet even the text of the pact as published in Moscow the same day (let alone the secret protocol providing for partition of Poland) clearly ruled out such an interpretation. Russia and Germany's undertaking not to attack each other was not limited by any reservation about the case in which one of them were to attack an ally of the other; but it did explicitly include an undertaking 'in no way to support' any 'warlike action' against one of them by a third power—as it might be France and Britain fulfilling their guarantee to Poland if Germany attacked that country. Moreover, the two states undertook not to join 'any group of Powers which is directed, mediately or immediately, against the other party'. The Germans lost no time in letting it be known that they regarded this as nullifying the Franco-Soviet Pact of 1935, and on 25 August Voroshilov told the heads of the French and British military missions that Soviet-German agreement made it pointless to continue the military talks.[29]

It is true that on 24 August Daladier had not yet given up hope of an agreement with Moscow, and that some French circles still believed this possible as late as 28 August.[30] But Léon Blum had concluded even before the pact was signed that Stalin was throwing his weight 'to Hitler's side',[31] and the vast majority of French public opinion agreed with him. Few French anti-fascists had the detachment of Clement Attlee, who suggested on 24 August that Stalin's action was entirely comprehensible in view of the way he had been treated by the French and British diplomats.[32] Most of them felt intense humiliation and anger at being betrayed by the ally in whom they had urged their compatriots to have confidence. By defending the pact, the Communists forfeited the esteem of their former allies, but by no means redeemed themselves in the eyes of the 'Munichois'. They thus found themselves as isolated as they had ever been. This was at once apparent in the *Commission Administrative* of the CGT, where Jouhaux and the pacifists sank their differences on 24 August and a resolution condemning the pact was passed by eighteen votes to eight, with two abstentions.

In spite of this, *L'Humanité* stuck to its theme on 25 August, urging France and Britain not to recall their military missions from Moscow but to help work out a 'vast system of security in which the Soviet-German pact can be combined with other treaties'. The *Bureau Politique* now broke its silence at last with a public statement:

> Hitler by recognizing the power of the country of socialism is admitting his own weakness. We salute this new success of the Soviet Union because it serves the cause of peace. . . . Everyone knows that such a pact . . . will not deprive any people of its freedom, that it will not hand over a single acre of any nation's land, nor of any colony. . . . In the coming weeks the peoples will be still better convinced that the USSR has done an incomparable service to the cause of peace, to the security of the threatened peoples and of France in particular.

Thorez himself took the chair at a meeting of the Communist parliamentary group, and made a statement which was afterwards issued to the press:

> The USSR has defeated the Munich plan. But if Hitler, in spite of everything, unleashes war, then let him know that he will find in front of him the united people of France, with the communists in the front rank, to defend the security of the country, the freedom and independence of peoples. That is why our communist party approves the measures taken by the government to protect our frontiers and if necessary to bring help to the nation which might be attacked and to which we are bound by a treaty of alliance. . . .[33]

One member of the parliamentary group, Saussot, deputy for the Dordogne, suggested that the Soviet embassy be asked for information which would throw light on the pact. He was accused of acting on instructions from the foreign minister, Bonnet (who also came from the Dordogne), in order to compromise the party.[34] He and his colleague Loubradou then resigned from the party.

But if for the time being the rest of the Communist deputies were willing to be guided by Thorez, the same was not true of party militants and supporters at lower levels. The initial reaction to the pact, among the working class as elsewhere, was one of violent hostility, or at best total incomprehension. In the Pas-de-Calais, for example, the local party leaders simply failed to turn up when summoned to an emergency meeting on 24 August by the federal secretary, Auguste Lecoeur. Lecoeur himself was shouted down that night when he attempted to address a meeting in a small mining town. Several party members ostentatiously tore up their cards in front of the meeting. Lecoeur also relates that Thorez's own uncle, a local café owner, had daubed swastikas on his nephew's portrait.[35]

Like Poincaré in 1923, Daladier came to the party's rescue. On 25 August, without waiting for war to break out, without even waiting for its military delegates to return from Moscow, the government ordered the seizure of *L'Humanité* and *Ce Soir* —newspapers whose only crime was to have called for a Franco-Soviet *rapprochement* and to have suggested that this was still compatible with national defence against Germany. Communist militants handing out or sticking up copies of the *Bureau Politique*'s statement—in which the PCF had declared itself 'more than ever the implacable enemy of international fascism, and especially of Hitlerite fascism'—were arrested by the police. A kind of panic seized the French governing class, in which genuine fear that the PCF would now become an ally of Hitler inside France was no doubt mingled with resentment that its criticisms of French foreign policy should prove so largely justified. At the Foreign Affairs Commission of the Chamber of Deputies the Communist delegates, led by Péri, found their promises that the Communists would 'collaborate without the slightest reticence in national defence' swept aside by a hysterical speech from a right-wing Radical, Gaston Rioux: 'Your party is the party of the enemy, the instrument of the enemy! . . . We must not and cannot carry on the discussion here at this moment, until our communist colleagues have broken free from their slavery.'[36]

282

The party responded with fresh efforts to demonstrate its loyalty and its patriotism. Next day, 26 August, the headline of *L'Humanité*'s editorial was 'Union of the French nation against the Hitlerite aggressor'. It praised the government for taking the 'necessary measures to defend France against fascist aggression' and stressed the need for France to 'keep her promises to her threatened Polish ally'. Any threat to Poland, it added, must be considered as 'an attack on all free peoples, including ourselves'. The French Communists would be 'in the front rank of the defenders of the independence of peoples, of democracy, and of threatened republican France'. They appealed to the government to understand their position and not to weaken the country's position in the crisis by picking a quarrel with them over the significance of the Soviet-German pact. Similar statements were put out at the same time by the party's regional offices. But all to no avail. *L'Humanité* was seized as soon as it came out, and the government issued a decree suspending all Communist papers.

The only other papers to protest against this infringement of press freedom (in a country which, it must be remembered, was not yet at war) were the left-wing Radical *L'Oeuvre* and the Socialist *Le Populaire*. Not that either had any sympathy with the position of the Communists themselves. Writing in *Le Populaire* on 27 August, Blum scathingly condemned their efforts to defend the pact: 'Cease your game! You cannot believe what you are saying. Some other time we will enjoy the agility of your dialectics.' But he also advised the government to let the PCF suffer the consequences of its own obstinacy, rather than drive the workers back into its arms by using force against it. And he added a further consideration: 'Is it consonant with the interests of national defence to let the whole of France, and above all the foreigner, think that hundreds of thousands of workers belonging to communist organizations are bad Frenchmen and bad patriots?'

This shrewd advice went unheeded. By now the right was again urging the government to ban the PCF altogether. 'Shall we continue,' asked the extreme right-wing paper *Gringoire*, 'to tolerate in France the Communist Party, which gets its subsidies from Moscow, ally of Berlin?'[37] The cry was soon taken up by people more likely to impress the government: Flandin, Eugène Frot (who had been Daladier's Minister of the Interior in February 1934), a Socialist deputy, Aimé Quinson, and L.-O. Frossard, the PCF's first general secretary, who was now a dissident right-wing Socialist.[38] Meanwhile a tabloid edition of *L'Humanité* was seized in its turn, and its salesmen arrested. A regular item began to appear in the other newspapers: 'Répression des menées communistes'.[39] The 'menées' in question usually consisted simply of distributing Communist leaflets or other publications.

On 30 August the public prosecutor inaugurated a general investigation of the PCF; and on 31 August *Gringoire* called for the death penalty to be applied to four Communist leaders (Duclos, Guyot, Gitton and Sulpice Dewez), whom it accused of being Soviet spies. Such repression and such attacks probably did the party more good than harm. A more serious blow was the manifesto of the *Union des Intellectuels Français*, published on 29 August and expressing 'stupefaction at the *volte-face* which has reconciled the leaders of the USSR to the Nazi leaders at the very hour when the latter simultaneously threaten both Poland and the independence of all free peoples'. This text was signed by many of the intellectuals who had been the party's staunchest allies in the struggle against fascism throughout the Popular Front period, notably the outstanding group of fellow-travelling physicists: Frédéric and Irène Joliot-Curie, Paul Langevin, Jean Perrin, Aimé Cotton, and the president of both the *Ligue des Droits de l'Homme* and the *Rassemblement Populaire*, Victor Basch.[40]

On 1 September Hitler invaded Poland. The French government ordered general mobilization. Next day, when Daladier appeared before the Chamber, the Communist deputies joined in the applause and in the unanimous vote of military credits. On 3 September—the day on which France officially entered the war—Thorez joined his mobilization unit at Arras, and on 6 September the party announced that all the Communist deputies liable for mobilization had done likewise. The first sign of a change in its attitude came after Stalin's invasion of Poland on 17 September: meeting on the following day, the Central Committee not only acclaimed the 'liberation of the Ukraine and Byelorussia', but protested that the French government had declared war without obtaining the formal consent of parliament. (This was technically true, although the significance of the vote on 2 September had been perfectly understood by all concerned.[41]) It also demanded the recall of parliament to discuss peace proposals put forward by the Soviet government. Probably it was the announcement of these proposals that had inspired the change, for it was not until 20 September that Raymond Guyot and Arthur Dalidet arrived from Moscow with the Comintern's instructions.[42] These instructions revealed to the French Communists that their country had not after all embarked on an anti-fascist people's war, but on a classic imperialist war which it was the duty of Communists to oppose.

This change of line must have been even harder for the PCF leaders to accept than the pact itself. A new wave of defections began, which this time did not spare the top party leadership. By January 1940 the crisis had cost the party one of its two senators (Clamamus) and twenty-one of its seventy-three deputies, including Marcel Gitton who ranked third in the party hierarchy after Thorez and Duclos. Outside parliament, the most distinguished defector was the novelist Paul Nizan, who was to be killed at Dunkirk the following year. In his case, despite attempts by the party to discredit him as a traitor and police informer, there is little doubt that he resigned out of conviction. In the case of others such as Gitton and Clamamus who later co-operated with Doriot under the occupation, the fear of persecution may also have played a part.*

In any case, the party's opponents did not wait for it to digest the Comintern's instructions. Already on 18 September the confederal bureau of the CGT had declared that 'no further collaboration was possible' with those who refused to condemn the German-Soviet pact. A week later this decision was confirmed by the *Commission Administrative*. Communists who would not repudiate the pact were therefore pushed out of the CGT and had to reorganize themselves in separate and clandestine unions. Finally, on 26 September, the government officially dissolved the PCF and 'all associations, organizations or *de facto* groups connected with it, and all those which, whether affiliated to this party or not, act in accordance with slogans issued by the Third International'. It became an offence to publish any propaganda for such slogans, with maximum penalties of five years in prison and a 500,000 francs fine. All party premises and property were confiscated, and all organizations controlled by the party were dissolved, including holiday camps, artisans' associations, the ARAC (war veterans' association) and the *Amicales Laïques* (secular friendly societies).[43]

Again, Léon Blum protested, on tactical as well as moral grounds.

---

* The allegation that Gitton was a police informer is now very widely accepted; yet it seems *a priori* surprising that the police should have withdrawn an informer from the top party leadership at the precise moment when the party became illegal.

'The Communist Party's decomposition,' he argued, 'will not be precipitated but impeded.'[44] The Communist parliamentary group, itself one of the organizations dissolved, protested 'in the name of the ideal of freedom and of human dignity, inscribed on the flag of our country', and contrasted the measure with the 'clemency shown to . . . members of the *Comité France-Allemagne* and the agents of Abetz'.*
The deputies who were still in Paris at once reconstituted themselves into a 'Worker and Peasant Group', whose existence was announced in the *Journal Officiel* of 29 September. On 1 October the officers of this new group, Florimond Bonte and Arthur Ramette, addressed a letter to Herriot as president of the Chamber, asking for a parliamentary debate on the expected Soviet-German peace proposals. On the following day, deputies began to resign from the group and the party in larger numbers.† They either shared the 'nausea' at the letter's contents expressed by Blum,[45] or foresaw the reaction of the government. Avoiding action of a different type was taken by Thorez, who vanished from his military unit on 4 October. Next day the repression began in earnest with the issue of warrants for the arrest of all members of the 'Worker and Peasant Group'.

Besides deputies, the repression fell on party cadres, on town councillors, on active party militants, and on Communist trade unionists, many of whom were reported to the police by their opponents in the CGT. All of these could be charged with 'reconstitution of a dissolved association'. But many 'suspects' were held without charge in concentration camps specially set up for the purpose. In fact almost anyone known to have been a Communist in the past was in danger of arrest if he did not explicitly repudiate the party, or even if he did repudiate it after a 'suspiciously' long delay. On 19 March 1940 Sarraut, as Minister of the Interior, informed the Senate that his 'hunting-bag' to date included 3,400 arrests, 11,000 house searches, and 1,500 convictions, while 3,500 *affectés spéciaux* (i.e. people whose work would normally have exempted them from conscription) had been sent back to the army. In addition the government had suspended 300 town councils; 2,718 Communists

---

* Otto Abetz, head of the French section of the *Dienststelle Ribbentrop*, had been expelled from France for alleged fifth-column activities in the summer of 1939. He returned in June 1940 as Ribbentrop's personal representative, and was soon promoted to ambassador.
† Only three had done so before the dissolution of the party: Saussot, Loubradou and E. J. Fourrier, deputy for the fifteenth *arrondissement* of Paris.

had been dismissed from elective offices; 443 local government employees had lost their jobs; the Communist press was 'dead'; a number of trade unions had been dissolved; and 8,000 individual penalties had been applied 'whose effect is to withdraw those concerned from the *milieu* in which they were having a noxious influence'.[46]

The party's membership and influence were certainly much reduced. But Blum was probably right in thinking that without the repression the effect of the crisis would have been worse. As it was, those who broke openly with the party could easily be presented as having done so to save their skins; and, as in 1923, many who disagreed with or did not understand the party line must have felt that this was not the moment to break ranks. The timing of the government's action (before the party's switch to a pacifist line had had a chance to manifest itself), coupled with its failure to wage effective war against Hitler, made it look as if the government were more interested in attacking Communists at home (and perhaps even abroad) than in fighting the official enemy. The reactions to the news of the party's dissolution noted among his fellow conscripts by the Communist deputy Fernand Grenier may be fairly typical of the attitudes of ordinary Communist sympathizers at this time:

This war of liberty against dictatorship is taking a queer turn.

It's the social laws of the Popular Front they're gunning for; they want to use the war to take them away from us.

They didn't ask the opinion of the million and a half communist voters before doing that! *Bande de vaches!*

This was on 28 September. A week later, when the papers all carried violent attacks on the letter of the Communist deputies to Herriot (though without reproducing the text of the letter), Grenier noted the following comment from the soldier in the next bed: 'Seems to me it's not war against Hitler they want any more, but war on the communists. . . .' On 6 October, when the press reported that charges had been brought against the Communist deputies, 'several soldiers in my Company came and told me: "We don't believe in all their filth." ' And on 12 October a Communist textile worker from the Nord, on reading that the textile unions of that department have set up a new federation and given up all collaboration with the Communist leaders of the old one, remarks: 'The [employers'] Textile Consortium must be rubbing its hands!'[47]

Fighting the Phoney War (1939–1940)

The Communist press had been banned while it was still taking a strongly patriotic line. The Communist Party had been banned and its deputies arrested when they began to suggest that France should not ignore offers of a negotiated peace (a position in fact shared by some members of the government). Only when it was already outlawed did the party begin to express the new Comintern line in its full intransigence. In a clandestine appeal to the people of France, dated 16 October, it condemned the war as a war of capitalism and British imperialism 'imposed on the people of France' and asserted that it was for the German workers to fight Hitler while the French workers took on their own 'fascist imperialist warmongers inside France'. The same theme was developed by Thorez in an interview given 'somewhere in France', which appeared in the Belgian Communist paper *La Voix du Peuple* on 29 October.[48] A roneoed number of *L'Humanité*, dated 30 October, carried the headline: 'A war of right? No! A capitalists' war.' 'The communists,' it said, 'denounce the present war as a war of capitalist brigands who are massacring the peoples in a quarrel over territories and profits.' Finally a full-length exposition of the new line appeared in the *Cahiers du Bolchévisme* for the 'second half of 1939' (in fact published clandestinely in January 1940). This included an editorial (in which the party admitted and condemned its 'gross mistakes' of August and September, such as the voting of the war credits) and a number of important Comintern and Soviet documents: notably the ECCI manifesto on the twenty-second anniversary of the Russian Revolution, Dimitrov's article on the tasks of the working class in the war, the Thorez interview, an 'Open Letter to M. Léon Blum', in which André Marty had defended the Soviet invasion of eastern Poland, and Molotov's speech to the Supreme Soviet of 31 October supporting the German 'peace offensive', stressing the need for 'a strong Germany' and asserting that 'one may accept or reject the ideology of Hitlerism as well as any other ideological system'. 20,000 copies of this issue of *Cahiers du Bolchévisme* were later claimed to have been printed, and a further 30,000 of the Molotov speech on its own.[49] Other pamphlets and leaflets, produced in increasing numbers from January 1940 onwards, emphasized the same themes: attacks on 'warmongers' and 'France's imperialist war', and appeals to French workers to oppose 'their own imperialism'.

A particularly unpleasant example of PCF propaganda in this period was Thorez's article 'Léon Blum tel qu'il est', first published in German in the Comintern paper *Die Welt*. In this remarkable piece of prose Thorez released a flood of hatred and envy which no doubt he had been struggling to hold back throughout the Popular Front, and which mingled all too well with the tide of anti-semitic abuse to which Blum was subjected in the spring of 1940.[50] Here are some specimens:

> Abandoning his repulsive reptile-like convulsions and hisses, Blum now gives free rein to his ferocious instincts as a bourgeois exploiter who has trembled momentarily for his privileges ... He is barking in full cry against the working class, the Soviet Union and communism ... The jackal Blum takes the lead in the howling pack unleashed against communism and the Soviet Union ... The vile lackey of the London bankers ... The police auxiliary, the informer Blum ... The working class must nail this moral and political monster to the pillory of infamy. It cannot fail to condemn and reject with horror and disgust Blum-the-bourgeois, Blum-the-non-intervention, Blum-the-wage-freeze, Blum-the-murderer-of-Clichy, Blum-the-policeman, Blum-the-war. It is a condition of the victorious struggle for peace and socialism.[51]

There is no evidence that this work was distributed in France before the defeat of 1940 (according to Lecoeur, it was imported as an 'opuscule' from Belgium, after the defeat[52]); but other works, which later proved equally embarrassing to the party, were. This one, for instance:

> Workers, do not be the accomplices of your worst enemies who are fighting against the Soviet Union, that is against the triumph of socialism in one sixth of the globe. By all appropriate methods, using all your resources of intelligence and all your technical knowledge, prevent, delay, or make unusable what is manufactured for the war.[53]

Some acts of sabotage did occur. The most serious case was that of the Farman aircraft factory at Boulogne-Billancourt. Three aircraft engines exploded in the factory. Six workers were arrested and charged with sabotage. Three of them were executed, on 27 May 1940, after admitting to membership of the *Jeunesses Communistes*. Since the party has neither repudiated them nor defended them as victims of injustice, it seems likely that they were at least influenced by party propaganda, if not acting on specific party instructions.

But probably more damaging to the war effort than these isolated occurrences was the go-slow campaign: 'an hour of work lost is an hour won for the revolution'. There were many complaints of low yield from munitions factories. It would be wrong, no doubt, to blame this solely on the Communists, but their defeatist propaganda did help 'to prevent the working class from fully realizing the nature of the conflict'.[54] So, however, did the government's own attitude. The complete inactivity of the German front, contrasted with the support given to Finland, the talk of intervention in the Finnish war and even of a 'diversion on the Black Sea front' to back it up (made more plausible by the presence of a large French army in the Middle East under General Weygand), the repression of the Communist Party at home—all this gave many workers the impression that the war was against communism, not against Hitler. Matters were not helped by the publication of an official *Livre Jaune* of documents on the origins of the war, which revealed that on 1 July 1939—weeks before the announcement of the Soviet-German pact—the French foreign minister had told the German ambassador that in the event of war 'elections would be suspended, public meetings stopped . . . and the communists *mis à la raison*'.*

This document was quoted over and over again by the forty-four Communist deputies who in March 1949 were tried by a Paris military tribunal for 'having, in Paris, or on French territory, between September 27 and October 5 1939, . . . by taking part in the constitution and functioning of the group called "French Worker and Peasant Group", and notably in the composition and distribution of a letter dated October 1 1939, addressed to M. le président de la Chambre des députés, and urging peace under the auspices of the Soviet Union, taken part in an activity whose direct or indirect object was to propagate the slogans emanating from or belonging to the Communist IIIrd International and organisms in fact controlled by the said IIIrd International'.[55] The newspaper accounts of this trial, of the debate on the expulsion of the Communist deputies from the Chamber which preceded it in January, and of the 'repression of Communist activities' by the police, were certainly much more widely

---

* *Livre jaune français* (Paris, 1939), p. 18. In his memoirs (*Le Quai d'Orsay sous trois Républiques*, Paris, 1961) Bonnet asserts that his object was simply to refute any idea that the Germans might have about Communist revolutionary activity interfering with France's mobilization, and that what he actually said was: 'If foreign propaganda or a communist attempt sought, as has been said in your country, to obstruct our mobilization, the French government would put a stop to it at once.'

read than the leaflets circulated illegally by the party itself. Most Communist sympathizers were probably unaware of the precise party line at this point, continued to regard Hitler as the main enemy, and thought that the party had gone no further than to suggest that the Soviet Union be asked to mediate in an attempt to reach an honourable peace. The government itself could hardly use the party's more recent and more openly defeatist propaganda (to which in any case it was unwilling to give publicity) as evidence against the Communist deputies, since most of them had been imprisoned since the beginning of October.

Besides, the very virulence of the anti-Communist propaganda was enough to arouse suspicion about the real motives of its authors — foremost among whom were men who had once been prominent Communists themselves: Doriot, no longer in parliament (having been defeated by Fernand Grenier in a by-election in 1937), but still able to fulminate in his party paper *L'Emancipation nationale*; François Chasseigne, who had been Doriot's deputy as leader of the *Jeunesses Communistes* at the time of Bolshevization (see above, p. 107) and now, as a Socialist deputy, suggested that certain Communist traitors should be given 'without other form of trial . . . the pistol-shot in the back of the neck that they give in the cellars of Moscow';* and Ludovic-Oscar Frossard, who declared, in the same debate:

> It's not enough to strike down Hitler; if Stalin survives Hitler there will be no stable peace in Europe. The Communist Party is a foreign army encamped on the national soil. It's not enough to dissolve the Communist Party, or to pronounce the forfeiture of its representatives; we must continue to fight it without pity, everywhere, at every moment, at every opportunity.[56]

All three of these men were later to take part in the Pétain government or (in Doriot's case) in direct collaboration with the Germans.

1940–1941: Collaboration?

THE PCF AND THE DEFEAT

By May 1940 the official line of the PCF was not merely pacifist but virtually pro-German. The May Day manifesto of ECCI, distributed in France in early May, was full of abuse of the 'British and French warmongers and their social-democratic lickspittles', but scarcely

---

* This remark is often quoted by Communist sources, but without the last eight words!

mentioned Germany except to say that the USSR was at peace with her, and that it was 'in answer to the gross violation by England and France of the neutrality of the Scandinavian countries' that she had invaded Denmark and Norway.[57]

The PCF did not abandon this line after the German offensive against France and the Low Countries began on 10 May. On 15 May the clandestine *L'Humanité* was still attacking 'the imperialists of London and Paris': '. . . the line about "the war for right and justice" will no longer work. . . . When two gangsters are fighting each other, honest people don't rush to the help of one of them because the other has hit him below the belt.' Once again, it was for the workers on each side to fight their own bourgeoisie. What France needed, the party now declared, was a 'peace government . . . ensuring collaboration with the Soviet Union for the re-establishment of general peace'.

On 17 May the same line was repeated, but with a new ingredient: 'Vive la Commune!' The paper recalled that, sixty-nine years before, 'the communards rose against a bourgeoisie which, after dragging the country into a disastrous war, while smothering the people's liberties, went on to betray it shamefully.' It looked very much as if the party was hoping that, as in 1871, defeat would be the mother of revolution. But the article contained no echo of the Commune's patriotic slogans. The Communist leaders seemed to have forgotten that the Communards had roused the people by calling for resistance to the last man and by attacking the 'capitulards', not by calling for a 'peace government'.

On 20 May, as the German advance continued, the tone became more anti-German. The party still called for a 'peace government', but now accused the bourgeoisie of being 'ready to sacrifice the country's independence to Hitler provided that he will guarantee their privileges'. It blamed the success of Hitler's armies on the presence of the Fifth Column within the French government. Meanwhile the said government continued its intense repression of the Communists. Reynaud, after replacing Daladier as prime minister in March, had introduced the death penalty for Communist propaganda,* urged the administration, authorized night searches, and ordered the transfer of some of the internees to North Africa.[58] Now, on 21 May, the cabinet decided to 'speed up the procedure

---

* Ironically enough, this decree was not used under the Reynaud government, but was applied by the Vichy authorities and the German occupying forces. (Bonte, *Le Chemin de l'honneur* [Paris, 1970], p. 274.)

relating to the repression of crimes against state security'.[59] As the Germans neared Paris the Communist prisoners there were moved away to prisons and concentration camps in the south and west.

The Communists claim that some time at the end of May or beginning of June the party leadership approached the government through the Communist philosopher Georges Politzer, and offered to mobilize the people in defence of Paris, on five conditions:

1. Transform the character of the war and make it a national war for independence and freedom;
2. Release the Communist deputies and militants, as well as the tens of thousands of workers who are imprisoned or interned;
3. Immediately arrest the enemy agents who are swarming in Parliament, in the ministries and even in the general staff, and subject them to an exemplary chastisement;
4. These first measures would arouse the people's enthusiasm and would make possible a *levée en masse* which must be decreed without delay;
5. The people must be armed, and Paris made an impregnable citadel.[60]

Unfortunately the evidence for this claim is not very strong. The text of the alleged conditions was not published in the party's clandestine press until the end of 1943, and the full description of the circumstances in which they are supposed to have been offered first appeared in a novel(!), Aragon's *Les Communistes*, published in 1951. According to this, the terms were drawn up by Frachon in the name of the Central Committee—the latter being of course unable to meet— in response to an enquiry made by Anatole de Monzie, the Minister of Public Works, on 28 May.* But, owing to the difficulty of communication between a member of the government and the leadership of an outlawed party, the answer did not get back to de Monzie until 6 June, by which time Reynaud had dismissed him from the government because of his pro-Italian sympathies.

What is historically better established is that at the end of May the French government considered sending Pierre Cot, the former air minister, to Moscow in the hope that the USSR would agree to supply France with aircraft. This idea also seems to have originated with de Monzie. Both he and Cot were on good terms with the Soviet Embassy, and if not with the PCF as such then at least with individual

* Frachon confirmed Aragon's version of the episode in an article in *L'Humanité*, 17 August 1964.

Communists. It is at least possible that the party, or some members of it, may have encouraged them to seek help from Russia. But in the end Reynaud decided against sending Pierre Cot—probably because the Russians insisted on having an official ambassador and the government feared to arouse right-wing opposition by entrusting an official mission to a politician known for his Communist sympathies.

What is certain is that, in the absence of any encouragement from the government, the PCF did not attempt to mobilize the people against the invader. On 14 June the German troops entered Paris unopposed.

THE ATTEMPT TO RE-LEGALIZE '*L'HUMANITÉ*'

So far from resisting the invaders, the PCF leadership looked to them, as the allies of the Soviet Union, for better treatment than it had received from Daladier and Reynaud. On 19 June a PCF delegation approached the German *Propagandastaffel* and requested permission for *L'Humanité* to resume legal publication. (Similar approaches had been made in other occupied countries, and in Holland the Communist paper *Waarheid* actually did reappear legally. It is therefore hardly likely that the the French initiative was merely that of 'comrades no doubt animated by good intentions', as Duclos later asserted.[61] It must have come from the Comintern.) Next day the authorization was granted, on condition that the paper submit its articles to German censorship.

Preparations were made to resume printing,[62] but on 21 June the three party members most directly involved (including a member of the Central Committee, Maurice Tréand) were arrested by the French police. They were released two days later, on the express order of the German Military Administration,[63] but the application for permission to publish had to be renewed and this time, owing to pressure from the French authorities, it was refused. The terms of this second application, dated 25 June 1940 and signed by two members of the Central Committee (Tréand and Jean Catelas), are well worth quoting:

> We request authorization to publish *L'Humanité* in the form in which it was presented to its readers before being banned by Daladier after the signature of the German-Soviet pact.
>
> *L'Humanité* published by us would set out to be in the service of the people and to denounce those responsible for the present situation in France.

L'Humanité published by us would set out to denounce the activities of the agents of British imperialism who want to drag the French colonies into the war, and would call on the colonial peoples to struggle for their independence against the imperialist oppressors.

L'Humanité published by us would set out to pursue a policy of European pacification and to defend the conclusion of a Franco-Soviet friendship pact which would complement the German-Soviet pact and so create the conditions of a lasting peace.[64]

25 June 1940 was the very day when the Franco-German armistice came into effect. Pétain had been prime minister for little more than a week and the Third Republic still had a fortnight of life ahead of it. The same authorities who had suppressed and persecuted the Communists for refusing to support the war against Germany were now collaborating with the Germans, or rather enlisting their collaboration, in order to keep the Communists suppressed. It was thanks to them, and not through any fault of its own, that the PCF began its life under Nazi rule as a clandestine organization.

'SEMI-CLANDESTINITY'
In the long run, this rapid rapprochement between the Nazis and the French establishment was to help the Communists enormously: it virtually cancelled out the stigma of their own desertion of the anti-Nazi front in September 1939, and it discredited all the hitherto respectable political parties. But in the short term it was evidently a disappointment to the PCF leaders, who hoped that their wisdom in opposing a disastrous war would now be recognized by the French population while the German-Soviet pact would assure them the benevolent neutrality of the occupying power. Even after the rebuff over *L'Humanité* they appeared to cling to the hope that a Communist government could be installed in France with German consent. The main slogans of the late summer were: 'Vive Staline', 'Vive L'Armée Rouge', 'Thorez in power', and 'Only one Party is worthy to govern France—the Communist Party'. PCF propaganda called for 'a government of honest men with clean hands, who have struggled against the war', 'a government of the people, under communist leadership', etc., without ever suggesting that this was incompatible with the presence of the occupying forces. On the contrary, the clandestine *L'Humanité* dated 13 July carried an item on 'Franco-German fraternity' which noted with satisfaction the increasing

number of 'friendly conversations between Parisian workers and German soldiers'.

Even as late as September the leadership's central information bulletin, *La Vie du Parti*, stated that the objective was 'to come out of illegality': 'We must be without hatred towards the German soldiers. We have more possibilities of action thanks to the compromises of the occupiers.' The policy was one of 'semi-clandestinity'. Communist local councillors were encouraged to hold surgeries for their constituents, to return to their home addresses, even to make speeches in markets or cafés. To this day the party argues that this policy was right, since it was 'only by showing itself and taking risks that the Communist Party could re-establish contact with the masses and win their confidence, their respect and their support'.[65] But the result was predictable: from the beginning of July onwards there were numerous arrests. *L'Humanité* complained of this on 2 August: 'They've arrested Grandel, a member of the Seine General Council (while he was receiving his constituents), comrade Dumont, five councillors of Montreuil, two of Noisy-le-Sec, one of Bondy, two of Sèvres, seven of Corbeil, including one aged 73, etc.'

Auguste Lecoeur, who later himself took charge of the party's liaison and security work, comments acidly on this passage:

> The final 'etc. . . .' is very much *L'Humanité*'s style. . . . Yes, in application of the leadership's decisions, 'they were receiving their constituents'!
>
> How many militants were sent in this way to prisons, concentration camps and, like Grandel, to their deaths? Even the big round-ups of October 1940, in which several hundred more militants fell victim to this legalism and were arrested, did not succeed in convincing the leadership.[66]

THE 'APPEL DU DIX JUILLET'

The fullest statement of the PCF's official position in the months following the defeat is to be found in the so-called 'Appeal of the Tenth of July'. (The real date of this manifesto has been much disputed; but it is certainly not earlier than 13 July, since it includes the names of ministers whose appointment was not announced until that date, and not later than September 1940.[67]) At the end of the war this was presented by the party as the point of departure for the Resistance inside France, just as de Gaulle's 'Appel du 18 juin' was the starting-point for the Free France movement overseas. But in fact the text of the Appeal—as opposed to that of a spurious preamble which was later tacked on to it—cannot seriously be read as a call to resist the invader. On the contrary, it was carefully worded so as to avoid any attack on Hitler or on the occupying forces. It attacked the Vichy regime with great venom, not for collaborating with the occupier but for being a 'government of plutocrats and war profiteers'. It attacked the 'politicians such as Daladier, Reynaud, Mandel', not for appeasing Hitler but for 'pushing France into war to serve the interests of the plutocrats, to abolish public liberties, set up a reign of terror, crush the people and turn our weapons against the USSR, country of socialism . . .'. In certain passages the PCF seemed almost to be presenting itself to the Germans as a more deserving candidate than Vichy for their favour, reminding them that it alone had 'stood up against war, as it had stood up alone against the occupation of the Ruhr by Poincaré . . .'.

At most, the Appeal could be interpreted as a warning to the Germans that they must expect Resistance if they persisted in supporting Vichy. ('Never will a great people like ours be a people of slaves, and if, in spite of terror, this people was able in the most various ways to show its reprobation at the sight of France chained to the chariot of British imperialism, it will also be able to show the gang now in power that it is determined to be free.') But the emphasis on economic recovery ('Il faut remettre la France au travail') could hardly displease the Germans—and contrasts strongly with the encouragement of sabotage which was to become the party's stock in trade once it embarked on whole-hearted resistance in 1941. Nor could the Germans be sorry to see 'the right to independence of the colonial peoples enslaved by the imperialists' proclaimed, at a moment when France's empire was the only part of her territory that eluded their grasp and when revolts in the British empire could only help their cause.[68]

THE 'LETTRE À PÉTAIN'

But the Germans were deaf to threats and hints alike. They continued to collaborate with Pétain in suppressing communism, as in other matters. By December the PCF, in its anxiety to obtain a public platform, was even willing to approach the Marshal himself. François Billoux, who had made the principal speech from the dock at the trial of the forty-four Communist deputies in March, now wrote to Pétain from prison offering to give evidence at the trial of the republican leaders which was to be held in Riom. Billoux argued that, since Pétain now proposed to condemn those responsible for the war, he ought logically to release the Communist deputies who alone had opposed it, and who had been put in prison solely for that reason. Their evidence would be valuable at the Riom trial 'since nothing has been published about the *in camera* proceedings at our trial, in which we denounced the real warmongers'.[69] In other words, Billoux was offering to appear as a prosecution witness and repeat the denunciation of Reynaud, Daladier and Blum which he had delivered at his own trial in March, but which would have taken on a quite different significance now that those leaders had fallen from power and were themselves on trial, essentially for having tried to resist Nazism. And this was not an individual initiative of Billoux's, for near-identical letters were sent by other imprisoned deputies, including some in a different prison.[70]

NEUTRALISM

Fortunately for the PCF, Pétain ignored its offers, and this was probably the nearest that the party came to active collaboration. From the autumn of 1940 onwards the official propaganda put out by the clandestine leadership* became increasingly critical of the Germans. The protest of the German Communist Party against the Franco-German armistice, describing it as a 'monstrous act of violence against the French people', was distributed in France; and the PCF put out its own protests against the German annexation of Alsace-Lorraine in November (though demanding independence for Alsace-Lorraine, rather than its *rattachement* to France). During the winter the party also distributed a pamphlet by Georges Politzer which attacked the Nazi racialist theories of Rosenberg; and in December a commemorative pamphlet for the PCF's twentieth anniversary contained the first clear attack on the 'masters in Berlin' and on 'so-called collaboration'. 'The Communists,' it said, 'are fighting imperialism in a brown shirt as they fought imperialism in tail-coat and top hat.'[71]

The rediscovery of German imperialism certainly brought no slackening in the Communists' hostility to British imperialism, or to General de Gaulle, whom they regarded as its lackey. 'Neither British

---

* Throughout the occupation the party was led by Duclos and Frachon. Although the official histories have Thorez leading the Resistance during its early stages, it is virtually certain that in fact he had reached the USSR by the summer of 1940.

dominion nor German protectorate, France for the French. . . .'[72] 'De Gaulle pursues his career in England where he is the ally of the English reactionary government, the lords and the bankers.'[73] 'De Gaulle wants the victory of English imperialism because it is in his interests.'[74] 'The movement of the de Gaulles and de Larminats, thoroughly reactionary and anti-democratic, is . . . aiming at nothing less than to deprive our country of any freedom in the event of an English victory.'[75] Such was the line of the clandestine *L'Humanité* during the spring of 1941.

The PCF's neutralism was probably influenced both by its own leaders' disillusionment with the Germans' local attitude and, more decisively, by Stalin's view that the two imperialist camps must be left to wear each other out. The party's aims at this period were most fully expressed in a programme entitled 'For the Salvation of the People of France'. The text of this is said to have been sent from Russia by Thorez. Two hundred thousand copies were printed. In it the PCF for the first time called explicitly for the 'liberation of the national territory and of the prisoners of war'; but this was to be achieved by peaceful means—by pressure from the French people and from other countries, especially the Soviet Union—and was to be followed by the establishment of 'fraternal relations between the French people and the German people'. A Communist 'People's Government' could achieve this since it would recall the Communist campaigns against the Treaty of Versailles, the occupation of the Ruhr, etc. A Supreme Court would be set up to judge 'those responsible for the war', namely the former presidents of the Republic, the Senate and the Chamber of Deputies, all the prime ministers, defence ministers and foreign ministers from 1933 to 1939, all deputies and senators who supported 'the war policy of Daladier-Reynaud', anyone who had campaigned for war against the USSR, Generals Gamelin and Weygand, all who had been members of the higher councils of War, the Navy and the Air since 1933, and all politicians and journalists 'who since the armistice have betrayed France's interests, destroyed public liberties and shamefully sacrificed the interest of the Nation to the interests of the trusts and capitalist oligarchies'. In general, the programme was much more informative about what the 'People's Government' would do once it got into power than about the means to be used for getting it there. The party appeared to think that the Germans could be intimidated by peaceful demonstrations of popular resentment. Certainly the programme contained no call to throw out the invader by force.[76]

A further step was taken with the Appeal 'of May 15', 1941, which for the first time referred to the Germans as 'the invader'; it called for a 'National Front of Struggle for the Independence of France', and urged national unity so that France 'can live free and independent, delivered from the yoke of national oppression which is crushing her'. The National Front 'must be constituted with, as its fundamental force, the working class of France headed by the Communist Party'. It was evidently not intended to include the Gaullist Resistance, for the Appeal still insisted on neutrality between the rival imperialisms. Its object was not to bring France back into the war on Britain's side, but to prevent her from slipping into it on Germany's; and again it gave no explicit indication of how liberation was to be achieved.[77]

It appears that this Appeal was never in fact distributed.[78] Presumably it was overtaken by events. But on 25 May a special number of *L'Humanité* was issued, with the headline: 'Down with imperialist war! Long live the National Front of Struggle for the Independence of France!' This too kept to the neutralist line, but with an increased emphasis on the danger of being dragged into the war on Hitler's side:

> Our country, muzzled and bled white, has for a year been paying 400 million a day and the barbaric methods of Nazism have the force of law among us. Odious racialism, unworthy of civilized man, is forcing the France of the rights of man to take a big step backward. Liberties are destroyed, and the best sons of the people are in prisons and concentration camps. . . . So that France can be France and not become a Nazi colony . . . the Unity of the Nation must be achieved.

Yet neutralism was maintained up to the very eve of Hitler's attack on Russia. On 20 June 1941 the clandestine *L'Humanité* was still warning its readers to 'rest assured that it is not in the victory of one imperialism over another that our common salvation is to be found'.

1940–1941: Resistance

SPONTANEOUS RESISTANCE

So much for the official line of the clandestine leadership during the fall of France and the first year of German occupation. It cannot honestly be called a Resistance line, even if in the last month or two it showed some signs of shifting in that direction. But that does not mean that during this period there was no Communist Resistance activity. To start with, many Communists were probably unaware of the official line, and when they learnt what it was many chose to disregard it.

Certainly many Communists fought bravely against the Germans during the battle of France, and often were decorated for it. Aragon, for instance, received the *Croix de Guerre* twice and the *Médaille Militaire* once.[79] Fernand Grenier's diary contains no hint of pleasure at the defeat of French imperialism, only horror at the misconduct of the war by the French government and generals.[80] His attitude seems to have been very much the same as that of Jean Chaintron, who says: 'I considered it a war that had to be fought—but which was fought very badly.'[81]

Nor were all Communists willing to accept the *faits accomplis* of the defeat and armistice. In Brittany, on 22 June 1940, Auguste Havez, a member of the PCF Central Committee, issued a pamphlet which includes some attacks on French capitalism but ended: 'No respite until we have kicked Hitler's jackboots out of our country.' Havez organized the stockpiling of weapons, reconnoitred the location of powder magazines, and generally prepared for an armed struggle. To instructions which eventually reached him from the leadership, telling him to organize an open campaign on the theme 'Maurice Thorez in power', while avoiding criticism of the Germans, he claims to have replied: 'I hope Maurice will forgive me, but if he were to take power in these conditions it could only be as *gauleiter*! . . .'[82]

In Bordeaux, where the French government and parliament took refuge in the final phase of the defeat, Charles Tillon relates that on 15 June 'a communist delegation' (whose members he names) tried to reach the president of the Chamber, Edouard Herriot, to ask him to lead the opposition to capitulation and to make an appeal to the nation. 'On the point of being arrested, the delegates managed to escape from the police.' It is not clear from whom, if anyone, these delegates had a mandate. But when the German troops arrived in Bordeaux, 'pamphlets condemning treason and appealing to national sentiment against the occupying troops, for the union of the workers to resist Hitlerism brought by German bayonets, were stuck into the day's papers with the approval of several newsagents, and distributed by hand in the suburbs.'[83] At the end of July Tillon, who had been co-opted on to the *Bureau Politique* and put in charge of the whole south-western region, issued a circular to party cadres entitled 'Union of the people to liberate France'. This denounced the

301

armistice, called for unity 'to throw out both the capitalists . . . and the invaders to whom they have delivered the independence of the country', and promised a 'national liberation struggle'.[84] (This takes on all the greater significance in that Tillon was called to Paris in October to join Frachon and Duclos in the clandestine central leadership.[85])

Many more such examples could be quoted of Communists in the provinces at first ignorant of, later deliberately ignoring or at least very freely interpreting, the line taken by the national and international leadership.* As the historian René Gallissot remarks: '. . . there is no lack of communist resistance pamphlets and actions in the summer of 1940; their number is greater than for any other organization, if indeed there were any other organizations in existence at the time.'[86]

ORGANIZED RESISTANCE

As the winter of 1940–1 wore on, Resistance began to take a more organized form. The first Resistance movements were of course formed outside the PCF, but several of them had crypto-Communists among their leaders. For instance Marcel Degliame-Fouché, who was to become one of the leaders of 'Combat' (one of the three big Resistance movements in the southern zone), 'tried to conceal as long as possible his membership of the Communist Party although he never lost contact with it'.[87] Another example is François de Lescure, the leader of the famous students' demonstration in Paris on 11 November 1940. He was president of the *Association corporative des étudiants en Lettres* and delegate in the occupied zone of the Pétainist leadership of the national student union (UNEF). But he was also, unknown to his colleagues, one of the leaders of the *Étudiants communistes*, and claims to have had a regular liaison with the leadership of the *Jeunesses Communistes* and of the party itself.[88]

Whatever its attitude to resistance activity as such, whatever its illusions about German tolerance, the leadership was still Leninist enough to appreciate the need for some clandestine apparatus. In fact such an apparatus had been set up even before 1939 as a

---

* For examples in the southern zone, see H. R. Kedward, *Resistance in Vichy France* (Oxford, 1978), pp. 56–63. Freedom of interpretation was greater here because of the party's unhesitating hostility to the Vichy regime—'qui pour tout dire occupait notre place' (Lecoeur)—which contrasted to its at first ambiguous attitude to the German occupation in the north.

precautionary measure under Gitton, and after his defection it had been reconstructed by Maurice Tréand.[89] After the armistice a semi-autonomous clandestine organization was set up in the so-called 'free zone', with its headquarters at Lyons. It was divided into ten sectors, each with its own printing-presses, liaison agents, etc., and regular contacts were maintained with the national leadership in the Paris region (Frachon and Duclos) through a system of women couriers, since in these early days of the war women travellers attracted less attention from the German and French authorities when crossing the demarcation line. But this southern organization suffered a setback when twenty-five of its leaders were arrested in March 1941.[90]

In the occupied zone too the party was obliged to defend itself, since the German authorities persisted in repressing it. A 'Special Organization' (OS) was set up, to provide armed bodyguards for Communist speakers who addressed crowds at markets or queues outside shops. 'They stood ready according to a prepared plan to protect the speaker's retreat. Sometimes they even showed themselves ostentatiously so that the police did not insist but prudently "moved on".'[91] From this essentially defensive function, the OS units quickly moved on, in early 1941, to acts of sabotage.[92] But it seems likely that these resulted from local initiative rather than central party directives. Certainly the national leadership did not attempt to claim credit for them in its clandestine propaganda.

The nearest that this propaganda came to advocating armed resistance before 22 June 1941 was in Gabriel Péri's pamphlet *Non, le nazisme n'est pas le socialisme*, published in April, which asserted that 'the Communists are struggling to free the soil of the homeland from Nazi occupation'. In this pamphlet, without contradicting the official line of the moment, Péri was evidently trying to stress as much as possible its anti-Nazi aspects while ignoring as far as possible the condemnation of de Gaulle and of British imperialism. This was recognizably the same Péri who from 1935 to 1939 had tirelessly advocated an alliance of Britain, France and Russia against Nazi Germany. Parts of the pamphlet could be read as an implicit criticism, not perhaps of the Stalin-Hitler pact itself but of the way that the French party leadership had reacted to it. Instead of denouncing the French bourgeois politicians who had tried to stand up to Hitler, Péri concentrated his fire on the Nazis themselves, exposing their consistently aggressive policies and showing that they bore the overwhelming responsibility for the war. Even more daringly, he attacked them for 'exalting the principle of the leader', contrasting the Nazi *Führer* with the 'Communist leader' who 'enjoys no privilege, or more exactly his only privilege is to be entrusted with the most difficult and perilous tasks. Communist leaders do not arrogate to themselves the right to decide the people's fate but proclaim that it is for the people alone to decide their own fate. The Communist Party doesn't tell the people of France to have faith in the genius or power of a few men. It calls on them to fashion their own destiny.' It is hard to believe that when Péri wrote these lines he did not intend some of his readers to ask themselves how far flesh-and-blood Communist leaders had lived up to this ideal in the past two years.

On 18 May 1941 Péri was arrested, in circumstances which have never been fully cleared up. Many former Communist resistants believe that he was a victim of the leadership's orders to 'drive out at gunpoint' those who didn't understand the German-Soviet pact and the 'undisciplined people who criticized the orders of the clandestine ruling group'. According to the unofficial history of the party published by a group of these ex-resistants, Péri was denounced to the police by Tréand's assistant.[93] What is certain is that he was convicted of infringing the decree of 1939 banning the Communist Party, and handed over by the Vichy authorities to the Gestapo. After torturing him in vain, the Germans promised to spare his life if he would break publicly with the party—which suggests that they too may have thought that he believed himself to have been betrayed by it. But he refused, and was executed as a hostage at the Mont Valérien on 15 December. The party at once placed him in the front rank of its anti-fascist martyrs, and rightly so. In his case if anyone's there was continuity between the anti-fascism of 1939 and that of 1941.

THE MINERS' STRIKE

At the end of May and beginning of June 1941 a successful strike paralysed the coalfields of the Nord and the Pas-de-Calais, in the 'forbidden zone' of northern France which had been placed under the direct rule of the German *Feldkommandantur* in Brussels, and in which any sign of trade union activity was ruthlessly suppressed. This was by far the most successful defiance of German authority in France during the first year of the occupation, it was unquestionably inspired by patriotic as well as economic motives (the one reinforcing the other), and it was organized mainly by Communists working through illegal trade union action committees. Consequently it has assumed great importance in Communist histories of the Resistance, where it is adduced as conclusive proof that, so far from staying out of the Resistance before Hitler's attack on Russia, the PCF was already leading. Once again, however, there seems to have been a significant difference between the attitude of Communists on the spot and that of the central party leadership, and between the party's official attitude at the time and its later interpretation. So at least it is claimed by Auguste Lecoeur, who as head of the party's Pas-de-Calais federation played a leading role in the strike. During the winter of 1940–1, Lecoeur says, he and his colleagues were already putting forward anti-German slogans which were 'noticeably different from the programme proposed by the official party press', and the same was true during and after the strike itself. He quotes an article by the youth leader Julien Hapiot in the local edition of *L'Avant-Garde*, asserting that the strike had shown the Germans what French workers thought of 'Kollaboration', and contrasts it with the 'purely economic slogans put forward by *L'Humanité*' which, he says, 'would never have succeeded in spreading the strike movement to the entire coalfield'.[94]

CONCLUSION

It is quite clear that individual Communists, and even local party organizations, did not wait for Hitler's attack on Russia before embarking on active resistance, including in some cases armed resistance, against the Germans. But it is equally clear that the party leadership, faithful to Stalin's line of the moment, sought a *modus vivendi* with the Germans for as long as it could. It is fair to suppose that the leaders in France realized the futility and danger of this policy sooner than did Stalin and the Comintern leadership in Moscow, as they saw the economic effects of France's incorporation into the German war effort and the effect which these in turn had on French public opinion, especially in the working class. By June 1941 it must have been fully clear to Duclos and Frachon that the only possible Communist platform in occupied France was a platform of whole-hearted resistance to the Germans, and that only the survival of the German-Soviet pact was preventing them from adopting this platform in a clear and unambiguous way. Whether or not they foresaw the rupture of the pact, they must have felt that such a rupture was needed before the party in France could play its full role. The point was delicately put in a report drafted for the Comintern by one of its contact men in France, Joseph Epstein, in early June 1941:

> There are many people who haven't understood the policy of the USSR and regard the German-Soviet pact as an act of treason. With time and thanks to the Party's work their number is diminishing—but it is still quite large, especially as German propaganda seizes every opportunity to make out that the USSR is the ally of the Third Reich. If one day the USSR were to go to war against Germany, she would have on her side the immense majority of the French people.[95]

Whether this report reached Moscow is not known. In any case Stalin, who ignored the explicit warnings of Sorge, was hardly likely to respond to such hints as these. But on 22 June Hitler struck. There can be little doubt that the great majority of French Communists heard the news with almost unmixed relief. Two years of awkward explanations and nagging self-doubt were now at an end. The party was once again free to adopt the nationalist persona which it had discovered with such felicity during the period of the Popular Front, and which it had never wholly abandoned. Even in the darkest days of 1940 it had claimed to be the champion of France's honour and independence. But it can hardly have been convinced by its own argument that France's honour and independence would best be restored by deserting her British ally and fraternizing with her German conqueror. Now this argument was cast aside. Honour and independence could be sought straightforwardly, by helping the courageous Soviet people and their British allies to smash the evil of Nazism once and for all, in France and throughout the world. *A chacun son Boche!*

9

Resistance and Liberation

1941–1945

The PCF's Contribution

The Communist Party's role in the Resistance did not merely repair the damage done by the German-Soviet pact. It carried the party far beyond the peak of strength it had reached during the Popular Front—in membership, in electoral support, and in general political influence. In the view of the leading historian of the Fourth Republic, there were in France at the end of the war 'only two real forces: the Communist Party and General de Gaulle'.[1] Both of these had succeeded in identifying themselves, in different ways, with the Resistance. De Gaulle, from outside, had succeeded in imposing his leadership. But inside France, as it seemed to many Frenchmen, the Communists had played the leading role.

The Communists themselves of course did their best to foster this impression, and many of their claims were exaggerated. The most obvious example was their claim to be 'le parti des 75,000 fusillés'—to have had 75,000 of their members shot by the Germans. In fact the total number of Frenchmen, let alone Communists, shot under the occupation was certainly much lower than this.* That Communists were numerous among the Nazis' victims should not be doubted, but it should also be noted that the Communists were particularly adept and zealous at turning their 'martyrs' to political account. Their clandestine press was always full of photographs, biographies and

* The official total of Frenchmen shot under the occupation is 29,620. This does not include those who were deported and died in concentration camps, those who were tortured to death, or those killed in action during Resistance operations. It is therefore possible that 75,000 Communists lost their lives as a result of the occupation (see Georgette Elgey, *La République des Illusions* [Paris, 1965], p. 36). Thorez on occasion used the more elastic formula 'the 75,000 Communists who died for France and for freedom'—which could of course also include those killed while fighting in the regular army in 1944–5. (Thorez to de Gaulle, 15 November 1945; quoted in Fauvet, *Histoire du Parti Communiste Français*, vol. II, p. 170.)

(sometimes apocryphal) 'last messages to their comrades' of the latest victims. The cult thus started was carried on after the Liberation with the publication of a series of veritable martyrologies. Among the most assiduously commemorated one should mention the twenty-seven Communist hostages executed as a reprisal measure at Chateaubriant on 22 October 1941 (including the deputy Charles Michels and the seventeen-year-old Guy Môquet, son of another Communist deputy); Gabriel Péri (already mentioned) and his fellow-editor of *L'Humanité* Lucien Sampaix; Pierre Sémard, the party's general secretary from 1924 to 1929 and both before and after that a dedicated leader of the railwaymen's union; and the leading intellectuals Georges Politzer and Jacques Decour. All of these were executed in the first year after the German invasion of Russia. But they were far from isolated examples, and as the war went on the ferocity of German repression increased. (On the other hand, Communists did get better at avoiding capture.)

Communist Resistance was, however, anything but passive. In the first weeks after the German attack on Russia the party began organizing an 'army without uniforms'—the *Francs-Tireurs et Partisans* (FTP)—around the nucleus of the mainly defensive OS, mentioned in the previous chapter. Technically, the FTP were the military wing of the *Front National*; but both, although including non-Communists at all levels, were in practice Communist-controlled (Tillon, the chairman of the FTP's National Military Committee and effectively their commander-in-chief, was also a member of the party's central leadership). Sabotage actions proliferated, and after a German officer was shot dead at a Paris Metro station on 23 August 1941 by 'le Colonel Fabien' (Pierre Georges), it became Communist policy to make direct attacks on members of the German armed forces serving in France. This provoked increasingly savage reprisals against the French population, including numerous massacres of hostages. Militarily it was of doubtful value—though it may have helped to tie down larger German forces away from the main theatres of war—and it was sharply criticized by de Gaulle and his supporters as being tactically premature and therefore counter-productive. But politically it paid off, making it easier for the Resistance in general—and the Communist Resistance in particular—to recruit new fighters. The idea of direct and immediate action against the occupiers, whatever the price, was more attractive to people of fighting temperament than the cautious attitude of the Gaullists; and the reprisals themselves, by stimulating hatred of the Germans, brought many people closer to the PCF's point of view. The party correctly calculated in advance that this would be so. A week before Fabien's action *La Vie Ouvrière* had announced: 'The blood which stains our paving-stones is the seed of future harvests.' Two months later, by which time more than twenty hostages had already been executed, the same journal declared that 'the glorious death of our heroes has called forth others in thousands.'[2]

The ranks of the FTP swelled rapidly, especially after the Germans began to conscript French workers for labour in Germany during the winter of 1942–3. Many young workers preferred to take to the *maquis*, responding to the party's call, which Aragon versified thus:

> Ne t'en va chez l'ennemi
> Ne t'en va, c'est felonie
> Ne t'en va pas, prends un fusil!

A Soviet source gives a total strength of 200,000 for the FTP throughout France at the end of 1943.[3] De Gaulle justly observes that 'the number of soldiers of the interior depended directly on the weapons they were given.' The FTP, he says, were 'almost one third of the *maquis*', whose total strength he reckons at over 200,000 'right at the beginning of the battle of France' (i.e. in June 1944).[4] By September, however, when 'we were able to establish with sufficient precision the real situation of the paramilitary elements', he gives an 'approximate total' of 400,000 for the *Forces Françaises de l'Intérieur* (FFI),[5] while Eisenhower's headquarters reckoned their contribution to the campaign as the equivalent of fifteen divisions.[6] The FFI were formed at the beginning of 1944 by the fusion of the FTP with the Secret Army (AS) in the southern zone and the *Organisation de Résistance de l'Armée* (ORA), recruited mainly among regular army officers. It is reasonable to suppose that the FTP provided between a third and a half of the total numbers (both Communist and non-Communist Resistance forces suffered heavy casualties during the Liberation, but the FTP seem to have been the main beneficiaries of the rapid last-minute recruitment which occurred).[7] During the Liberation they played a major role in the fighting both in Brittany and in Paris. In many parts of the south-west (where there were no Allied troops) the FTP found themselves in almost total control. This was probably true at Toulouse and Montpellier, and at Limoges, where the Communist guerrilla leader Georges Guingouin had controlled the surrounding countryside for months before the Liberation, styling himself 'Préfêt du Maquis', fixing prices and posting up regulations in the villages.[8]

De Gaulle himself, in his war memoirs, pays tribute to the Communist Resistance. He refers to the party as 'committed to the Resistance, in which it did not stint its losses',[9] and explained his own attitude to the Communists in August 1943 thus: 'The part which they were playing in the resistance, as well as my intention to see that their forces were incorporated into those of the nation at least for the duration of the war, led me to the decision to put two of them in the government.'[10]

Further evidence of the Communist role in the Resistance is provided by the abundance of clandestine Communist publications which have been preserved. It has been calculated that during the five years of its clandestinity (from 1939 to 1944) the party printed a total of fifty million copies of *L'Humanité* (316 'regular' numbers and twenty-four special numbers or supplements), nearly twelve million copies of 128 leaflets, and one and a half million copies of forty-three pamphlets and reviews. These are only the publications issued by the party in its own name. They do not include those of the various front organizations which it controlled—trade unions, the *Union des Femmes Françaises*, the *Jeunesses Patriotiques*, war veterans' organizations, and of course the FTP and *Front National*.[11] No other Resistance movement could claim a comparable volume of literary output, and still less any other political party. In fact the SFIO was the only other party which maintained any existence at all under the occupation, and it did not attempt to organize a Resistance movement of its own.

Reasons for its Pre-Eminence

Why was the PCF so uniquely effective as an organizer of Resistance? A number of reasons can be given.

First of all, it had a tradition of clandestine and illegal organization. Although during the Popular Front period it had become more or less 'respectable' and had behaved more or less like a conventional political party, its hard core of cadres was composed of people with experience of hiding from, and fighting, the police; of people who had joined the party in the conviction that its political ends would not be achieved without a violent struggle, and who had had that conviction reinforced by their Leninist training. Many of them, moreover, had since had actual military experience during the Civil War in Spain. Mentally at least, they were equipped for Resistance in a way that none of the other parliamentary parties of the Third Republic was. (The same factor no doubt explains the high proportion of army officers and former *Cagoulards*—extreme right-wing conspirators—in the ranks of the Gaullist Resistance.)

Secondly, the PCF had already been outlawed for nine months before the occupation began. From the point of view of Vichy, and soon also of the German authorities, membership of it was in itself proof of subversive activities. Both frequently attributed Resistance actions to the Communists without any evidence, and Communists were always the first targets of any reprisals. Since prisons and internment camps were already full of Communists, they were readily available as hostages. The French police had fewer scruples about hunting them down than they did about non-Communist resistants, and Vichy was less likely to protest at their execution. (The twenty-seven hostages executed at Chateaubriant, for instance, were actually chosen from a list of 'the most dangerous Communist internees' in the camp, provided by the Vichy Minister of the Interior, Pierre Pucheu.[12]) Both Nazis and Pétainists had a predisposition to identify opposition to themselves with Bolshevism, and also a propensity to believe that by describing the Resistance as 'Communist' they were effectively discrediting it. The actual result was, of course, that Communist prestige within the Resistance increased, as did the anti-Nazi ardour of the Communists themselves.

Thirdly, the PCF benefited from the intensity of the struggle, in much the same way as the Spanish Communist Party had done during the Civil War. When a national movement is fighting under very great pressure, the influence within it of a highly disciplined body enjoying great tactical flexibility, whose members are trained to apply the party line with total devotion rather than to argue about policy, is liable to increase. The PCF was such a body. Once Stalin had called for support for the Soviet war effort from within the German-occupied countries, the Communists embarked on resistance with complete single-mindedness and ruthlessness. They repeatedly expressed their determination to subordinate all other aims to the immediate one of inflicting as numerous and as severe blows as possible on the occupying forces, in order to hasten the restoration of national independence. By contrast the Gaullists and other non-Communist Resistants were both tactically more cautious and strategically more openly preoccupied with France's political future *after* the Liberation. The PCF and its front organizations were more obviously 'doing something' about the occupation, and this undoubtedly helped their recruitment.

Fourthly, after Stalingrad the prestige of the Red Army was reflected on to the Communists in France. Just as de Gaulle had drawn his initial prestige from his association with Britain, when that country alone was still fighting to stem the Nazi tide, so now the Communists benefited from their association with the military power that was actually rolling back the Nazi tide in Europe. In 1944 admiration for the Red Army was partially eclipsed by gratitude to the British and American forces which were actually liberating France, but it persisted nonetheless; and for some Frenchmen it was easier to identify with the heroism of the Russian people, which had itself experienced invasion, than with the successes of the well-oiled American military machine.

Finally, and perhaps most important of all, the PCF benefited from the political vacuum left by the collapse of the Third Republic. In all the European countries occupied by the Germans, the Communist Parties played a significant role in the Resistance and gained some influence as a result. But the only western European countries where they emerged from the Resistance as a major political force were France and Italy, where the war had brought not only military but political disaster for the previous regime. In Scandinavia, Holland and Belgium the Resistance fought in the name of governments in exile, and the Liberation resulted, more or less, in the restoration of the political status quo. But in France even non-Communist Resistants agreed that the Liberation must not mean a restoration of the Third Republic but a new political order. The PCF was the only political party which (thanks perhaps to its exclusion from parliamentary politics in 1939) was not implicated in the suicide of the Third Republic in June–July 1940. It was therefore the only party which could carry on activity *as a party* under the occupation without exciting general contempt.

Many Resistants had ideas about what the new France should be like, and worked on blueprints for all kinds of reform. But only the Communist Party and Charles de Gaulle seem to have realized that France's fate after the war would be determined above all by the *rapport des forces*—the relative strengths of different forces—established while the war was still in progress. That, no doubt, was the real reason why the Communist Party and de Gaulle emerged in 1944 as the only political forces that counted.

Political Rivalry within the Resistance

Superficially at least, the dispute between Communist and Gaullist Resistants during 1941–4 was over tactics. The Communists favoured preparing for 'national insurrection' by immediate direct action against the occupying forces. The Gaullists also spoke of 'national insurrection', but were anxious that this should not be attempted until the arrival of Allied forces assured it of success. In the meantime, the Resistance should hold its fire and preserve its manpower. The Liberation would be essentially the work of the Allied forces, with the Free French playing as large as possible a part. The role of the Resistance was to help the Allies by intelligence and sabotage operations, by organizing escape routes for Allied pilots and prisoners of war, and by localized guerrilla warfare (the *maquis*); but also—and in de Gaulle's eyes this was more important—its role was to demonstrate politically that France had never abandoned the struggle against Hitler, that Pétain and the armistice did not reflect the will of the French people, and that de Gaulle and not Pétain represented the 'legitimacy' of the French nation, so that France should participate as of right in the Allied war councils and in the planning of the postwar world order. It was of cardinal importance to de Gaulle that the Resistance should recognize himself as its leader, and that it should forestall the creation of an Allied Military Government (AMGOT) by providing officials who would seize power in his name and assert his authority as soon as the Allied troops arrived.

Inevitably, each side attributed ulterior motives to the other. The Communists saw the Gaullists as bourgeois whose chief aim was to prevent the Resistance from taking on the character of a 'people's struggle' (*lutte populaire*) for fear that it would damage their class interests. This suspicion was strengthened by the fact that Allied arms drops, arranged in co-ordination with the Gaullist *Bureau Central de Renseignements et d'Action* (BCRA) in London, were reserved almost exclusively for non-Communist Resistance groups and largely denied to the FTP.* Weapons were thus given to those who were holding

* I have been told by M. Geoffroy de Courcel, who was on de Gaulle's staff in London, that they had evidence that the Communists in France were receiving some deliveries of Soviet arms. But he admitted that he did not know by what route these deliveries could have reached France.

back, but denied to those who wanted to use them at once against the Germans. On their side, the Gaullists did not see the problem in class terms but suspected that the Communist Party hoped to turn an insurrection to its own advantage and seize power for itself before normal democratic institutions could be set up.

In time, however, each side was obliged to recognize the other as an essential ingredient of the Resistance. In December 1942 a meeting was arranged between 'Rémy', one of de Gaulle's secret agents in France, and a representative of the PCF, Fernand Grenier. According to Grenier, Rémy acknowledged that in northern France, as opposed to the former 'free zone', the Communist Party and the Communist-inspired *Front National* were the only effective elements of Resistance. Grenier in turn acknowledged the FTP's need of support, both material and moral, from London, and Rémy replied that this would be much more easily arranged if the PCF would send a representative there.[13] This was accepted by the party leadership and Grenier himself returned to London with Rémy the following month, as the delegate of both the party and the FTP, to de Gaulle's 'French National Committee', whose authority was thus implicitly recognized. That at least was how de Gaulle took it, for he wrote to the Central Committee:

> The arrival of Fernand Grenier, the adhesion of the Communist Party to the National Committee, which he had brought me in your name, and the setting at my disposal, as commander-in-chief of the free forces, of the valiant formations of *francs-tireurs* which you have set up and animated, are so many demonstrations of French unity and a new proof of your determination to contribute to the liberation of our country.

The party made no objection to this. Nor did it hesitate from then on to claim de Gaulle's authority for its own actions. (De Gaulle himself had made a concession of sorts by declaring that 'the detachments of *francs-tireurs* constitute the vanguard of Fighting France'—which could be taken, though it can hardly have been intended, as a *carte blanche* endorsement of the FTP's direct action tactics.)[14]

Unlike the other Resistance movements, however, the PCF and the *Front National* gave no explicit endorsement to de Gaulle in his struggle with his American-sponsored rival, General Giraud. Grenier publicly expressed his confidence in both generals, and privately informed de Gaulle of the party's view that they should join forces as soon as possible in a joint provisional government based in Algiers.

(This was also being urged on de Gaulle by the British, but he delayed accepting until he was confident that politically he would have the upper hand.) Like a number of right-wing Resistance leaders, Giraud accepted the 'non-political' nature of the *Front National*, and through him the Corsican Communists were able to obtain Allied weapons which their metropolitan colleagues were not able to obtain through de Gaulle—with the result that the *Front National* virtually seized power in Corsica at the moment of the Italian armistice in September 1943. But it did so in the name of the 'National Liberation Committee' in Algiers of which de Gaulle was by then in full political control (Giraud was nominally co-chairman but his responsibilities had been limited to purely military matters). The liberation of the island was completed with the aid of Free French troops, with whom arrived a Gaullist prefect and a Gaullist military governor, nominated by the Algiers Committee. Their authority was never seriously questioned, and de Gaulle himself, when he arrived on 8 October, was greeted with unanimous applause.[15] But the Communists succeeded in setting up municipalities under their control throughout the island.[16]

Did the Communists expect to seize power in France at the Liberation? Many Gaullists believed so, including apparently de Gaulle himself.[17] At the local level, and especially in the south, some FTP leaders did behave as if this was their intention. (In Bordeaux the local non-Communist FFI commander, Colonel Druilhe, discovered and took seriously a document addressed to the FTP of the Dordogne, which read: 'Order to wait until Limoges and Toulouse are taken before proclaiming the Soviet Republic of the South of France'[18]—but this is hardly conclusive evidence, since the document's origin is unknown and it could well have been a German or Pétainist forgery.) Throughout the south-west the FTP converged on the big towns at the moment of Liberation, often with no obvious military reason. In Montpellier, for instance, 'it seems that the FTP were above all concerned about what would happen in the town itself', rather than with the pursuit of the retreating *Wehrmacht*. On the day after the German evacuation of the city (23 August 1944) they were able to secure the election by acclamation, at a mass meeting in front of the *préfecture*, of a five-man municipal authority, the 'Délégation Générale', three of whose members were Communists.[19] Ten days later Gilbert de Chambrun, the pro-Communist local FFI commander, issued a proclamation urging the FFI to join some new battalions which were being formed to be 'sent in pursuit of the enemy with the regular army'. But he warned that some would be needed, 'and especially our valiant *Milices Patriotiques*', to 'stay in the region to ensure the maintenance of public security and to protect our Revolution at its beginnings'.[20]

These *Milices Patriotiques* were a kind of home guard of the Resistance, set up on Communist initiative during the spring and summer of 1944. They were supposed to be 'the organization of those patriots who, for reasons of age, family situation or professional situation of public importance (in industry or agriculture) have to remain within the law and attached to a given place . . .'. They were not well enough armed or organized in time to play a major military role in the liberation, but were well suited to play a political role immediately after it. In the Clermont-Ferrand region, for instance, the tasks assigned to them included '*épuration* [i.e. 'purging' of collaborators], police duties, traffic control, telephone control and postal control'.[21] In central and southern France especially, their numbers swelled rapidly after the Liberation, and they became a kind of 'parallel police', carrying out house searches, requisitioning property, arresting and even executing people, either on their own authority or in the name of the local Liberation Committees (often themselves Communist-dominated) by which they were theoretically controlled.[22] Not surprisingly, de Gaulle's Provisional Government took exception to this. 'Once justice is functioning, there remains no pretext for the maintenance of armed forces which are not regular.' The various Resistance movements were instructed to dissolve their paramilitary groups.[23] But the PCF and the *Front National* refused.

> The *Milice Patriotique* [declared Jacques Duclos on 27 October] must remain the vigilant guardian of republican order, while at the same time giving active military instruction to the popular masses.
>
> In each locality it must include thousands and thousands of soldier-citizens devoted to the public good.
>
> The Patriotic Guard, placed under the authority of the local Liberation Committee and the municipality, provided with permanent officers and endowed with a stock of weapons and ammunition, must in each locality form the safeguard of republican institutions.

Next day the government officially dissolved the *Milices Patriotiques*

316

by decree. The party ignored this, instructing the *Miliciens* to remain organized and not to give up their weapons. In many areas secret arms depots were set up.[24]

None of this, however, really amounts to evidence of a definite plan to seize power at the national level. If such a plan ever existed, it was probably abandoned during the winter of 1943–4. In the late summer of 1943 when Michel Debré, acting on de Gaulle's behalf, secretly contacted the various Resistance movements in order to draw up a list of prefects and 'Commissioners of the Republic' who would be ready to seize power in each area, the PCF and *Front National* refused to suggest any names. Meanwhile in Algiers the party was making difficulties about accepting de Gaulle's offer of a place in his embryo government, the *Comité Français de Libération Nationale*. But in March 1944 when de Gaulle officially and publicly renewed his invitation the party responded much more positively. On 4 April Grenier and Billoux became the first Communists in French history to accept office in a government (the former was given the air ministry, the latter a 'Commissariat of State' without portfolio). In France at about the same time the party belatedly start lobbying for prefectures, and complained of discrimination when only two Communist prefects were chosen (Chaintron for the Haute-Vienne and Monjauvis for the Loire), and no Communist 'Commissioners of the Republic'. (De Gaulle did, however, appoint three who were broadly sympathetic to the Communists: Yves Farge at Lyons, Raymond Aubrac at Marseilles, and Jean Cassou at Toulouse. Cassou never took office, being badly wounded just as the liberation of Toulouse was beginning.)

It was clear by this time that the PCF intended to work through the embryonic Gaullist state rather than against it. Further proof of this can be seen in the extravagant praise of de Gaulle himself which appeared in the Communist press at the moment of the Liberation. It was almost as if the party wanted to show itself 'more Gaullist than the Gaullists'. During the Liberation of Paris, Communists took an active part in producing 'Vive de Gaulle' streamers and hanging them from trees and lamp-posts.[25]

The change of line, if such it was, may have been the result of the Teheran Conference in November 1943, at which the war sectors of the different Allies were for the first time clearly delimited. Implicitly, this gave a free hand politically to each Ally in its own sector: to Stalin in eastern Europe and to Churchill and Roosevelt in western Europe.

It was in Stalin's interest to respect this arrangement, since eastern Europe was the area which most immediately concerned him. In any case, he had been pressing for the opening of a Second Front in western Europe for some time in order to divert German forces from the Eastern Front. Now that the Second Front was to be opened at last, he obviously did not want to diminish its impact by causing political trouble behind the Anglo-American lines. The emphasis of Soviet propaganda throughout 1944 was on Allied unity and the overriding importance of the war effort.

In other words, the PCF leaders must have realized, and may well have been explicitly told, that they could not expect any help from Stalin if they came into conflict with the British and Americans. They could only have seized power with at least tacit Anglo-American approval. Such approval might perhaps have been forthcoming if the Resistance had thrown up a Communist-led provisional government which was a clear expression of national unity. But in a civil war between Communists and Gaullists, the Allies would certainly have taken the Gaullist side. Events in France would have followed the Greek rather than the Yugoslav pattern.

Consequently, once the Communists had realized that de Gaulle had real support in the country, and that he would not give in to them without a fight, they were obliged to accept his leadership. Naturally they still sought to install themselves in as strong positions as possible, but they did so under de Gaulle and not, overtly at least, against him. And once this decision had been taken, once the PCF had entered the government and obtained prefectures, etc., it was obvious that the authority of the government and of the prefects would, in the last resort, have to be accepted.

De Gaulle and his immediate subordinates must have sensed this, for in the days after the liberation they brilliantly exploited their moral authority, sometimes asserting it successfully over much superior physical force. In Toulouse, for instance, the local FTP commander, 'Colonel Georges', agreed to obey orders from de Gaulle's 'Commissioner of the Republic', Pierre Bertaux, in spite of the fact that the latter had no forces at his disposal at all and that the whole region was overrun by the FTP.[26] Even in Montpellier, the city which appeared closest to Communist revolution at the moment of the Liberation, the Gaullist General de Lattre de Tassigny was greeted with wild enthusiasm when he arrived on 2 September. He took the opportunity to 'explain to the FTP leaders that he was intimate with the Soviet ambassador to the provisional government, Bogomolov, and that the latter had asked him to tell the Montpelliér-ains that they should stay calm'.[27] Whether or not this was true, it shows that de Lattre knew the real weakness of the PCF's position.

The Communists thus allowed the crucial moment of power vacuum to pass. By 1 December the state institutions were working normally again, and the chance to use the Resistance forces in a struggle for power had been lost. The *Conseil National de la Résistance*, theoretically the supreme co-ordinating body of the Resistance inside occupied France, in which the Communists had won a strong though not quite dominant position, was successfully neutralized as early as 28 August by de Gaulle, who simply announced that it had 'no longer any *raison d'être* as an organ of action', and would be integrated into the Consultative Assembly which was arriving from Algiers. The COMAC (Military Action Committee), two of whose three members were Communists, attempted to maintain its independence a little longer. Not surprisingly, Montpellier was the last bastion of Resistance power. There the COMAC's nominee, Gilbert de Chambrun, maintained himself until 1 December as regional military commander in defiance of the government. Then, realizing that the game was up—or receiving new instructions directly or indirectly from the party (of which he was not a member)—he handed over his command to the government's appointee, Colonel Zeller, asking to be given a regiment and sent to the front. His request was granted.[28]

Resistants versus Politicians

Once it recognized its inability to monopolize the Resistance and exclude de Gaulle from the leadership, the PCF found it was in its interest to reassert the primacy of politics and political parties over the Resistance and the various *ad hoc* groups which it had thrown up. As we have already noted, one reason for the PCF's pre-eminence within the Resistance was precisely that it was the only political party which had escaped involvement in the collapse of the Third Republic. It could best exploit this advantage if there was a quick return to politics, and specifically to parliamentary politics—the terrain least favourable to de Gaulle.

The PCF thus set itself firmly against any tendency in the Resistance to blame the party system for France's defeat or to suggest that the role of parties be henceforth limited or even dispensed with. It even reproached the SFIO (whose competition it no longer feared) for not withdrawing its members from the various non-Communist Resistance movements and forming a separate party militia of its own. In its contribution to the discussion within the Resistance about the shape of the new Republic to be set up after the Liberation, the PCF—in contrast to most other Resistance groups—insisted that the power of parliament, rather than that of the executive, should be strengthened.

Ironically enough, de Gaulle himself helped the PCF to achieve its aims in this respect, yet neither of them in the long run benefited. In London and Algiers de Gaulle deliberately revived the prestige of the political parties as a counterweight to that of the internal Resistance, whose political pretensions he mistrusted. He nominated representatives of the parties to the Consultative Assembly, and included some of them in his successive committees and governments. After the Liberation he gave some encouragement to the founders of a new party of Christian Democratic inspiration, the *Mouvement Républicain Populaire* (MRP), but refused to take any part in party politics himself. The result was that in November 1945 he found himself accepting office from a Constituent Assembly of which he was not a member, and which was dominated by political parties that he could not control. Within two months he had discovered that this deprived him of the authority he wanted, and he resigned.

The result was undoubtedly a victory from the Communists' point of view, but it perhaps came too quickly and easily for their purposes. Probably they had hoped that de Gaulle would either be gradually reduced to a figurehead role or would use up his authority in a long-drawn-out struggle with the parties, in which the PCF would emerge as the leader of a coalition in defence of parliamentary democracy and constitutional liberty. As it was, power was left in the hands of an assembly in which they were the strongest single party but not on their own a majority, and in 1947 the other parties were able to freeze them out.

This might perhaps have been avoided if the PCF had exploited the opportunity offered by the Resistance to restore the unity of the French labour movement. The SFIO proposed this during the occupation, and again at its first post-Liberation national congress in November 1944. Most Socialists emerged from the Resistance thoroughly ashamed of their party's role in the collapse of the Third Republic and full of respect for the role played by both the Soviet Union and the French Communists in the struggle against Hitler.

They were convinced that the Liberation offered a golden opportunity for the French working class to reunite in support of a real socialist programme. If the PCF leaders had been willing to join in a new party with a genuinely democratic internal structure, unity could almost certainly have been achieved, and in the circumstances the Communists would undoubtedly have dominated the new party by sheer force of numbers, as they did the reunified CGT (see next chapter).

Instead, the PCF Leadership replied to the Socialist proposals in a dogmatic, unconvincing way, as though it lacked confidence in its own militants and required guarantees in advance of its continued supremacy. The terms which it proposed were similar to those on which Communist and Socialist parties were to be united in eastern Europe. But of course the French Socialists, with the Red Army four hundred miles away and the British and Americans all round them, could not be subjected to that kind of pressure.

For instance, the Communist delegates on the joint committee which was set up insisted on the inclusion in the proposed charter of a paragraph promising unconditional support for Soviet positions and recognizing the absolute superiority of the Soviet Communist Party. The Socialists were hardly likely to accept this. Nor could they be encouraged by the PCF's procedure in publishing its own draft Charter of Unity in *L'Humanité* (12 June 1945) before submitting it to the Socialist delegates (or indeed to the rank-and-file of the PCF itself).[29]

Visibly, the party was anxious to use the Resistance to extend its own power, rather than to produce a new kind of power. It acquiesced in de Gaulle's abolition of the *Conseil National de la Résistance*, and made surprisingly little attempt to press for the application of the very radical programme of social and political reform which that body had adopted under the occupation, and to which Socialists, Radicals, Christian Democrats and Gaullists had all subscribed. Instead of trying to maintain unity with these various non-Communist Resistance forces, the PCF tended to belittle the role played in the Resistance by non-Communist organizations, and thus contributed to the fragmentation of the Resistance into rival political parties. The Communist leaders even discouraged their followers from extra-parliamentary agitation intended to strengthen the hand of the Communists inside the government, arguing that the party would be isolated 'if it upset the middle classes'[30]—a familiar enough argument to those who could remember the Popular Front.

One reason for this general damping-down of the Resistance, and for the PCF's enthusiastic co-operation in the return to parliamentary politics, was undoubtedly the need of the political leaders to reassert their authority within the PCF itself. The party had been so transformed by the Resistance that many of its members were too young to remember the faces or even the names of the pre-war leaders.[31] These young men and women might have learnt to respect military discipline of a sort as a necessity during the Resistance, but many of them had not yet learnt the kind of political discipline which a Bolshevized Communist Party expects from its militants. Even Communists of long experience had sometimes been affected by their responsibilities as Resistance leaders, having developed a dangerous habit of taking decisions on their own initiative—a habit all the more dangerous when combined with an inevitable feeling of superiority over other leaders who had taken no direct part in the armed struggle. Seldom directly expressed, this feeling was nonetheless sensed and resented. Indeed it was bound to be suspected even where it did not exist.*

But the pre-war leadership, in the persons of Duclos and Frachon, had managed to remain broadly in control of the party throughout the occupation, and from the moment of the Liberation it began cutting the Resistance leaders down to size. Overruling Tillon, who considered that the call to insurrection issued on 10 August by the national military committee of the FTP was quite sufficient, the party issued on 19 August 1944 an appeal to the population of the Paris region signed by the Communist *élus*—deputies, municipal councillors, etc., all of whom of course had been elected before 1939.†

On 25 August Duclos and Frachon were fetched by Lecoeur from their hiding-place in the Paris suburbs and installed in the old party headquarters at 44 rue Le Peletier, which had been recaptured from the Germans and the *Milice* a few days earlier.[32] From then on they

---

* One of the accusations against Tillon at the time of his expulsion from the leadership in 1952 was that 'when he remarked to comrade Jeannette Vermeersch in spring 1951 that *he* had been in France during the war, he was taking up the arguments of the enemy and reflecting indirectly on comrade Maurice Thorez'. (Tillon, *Un 'Procès de Moscou' à Paris* [Paris, 1971], p. 111.)

† See Tillon, *Un 'Procès de Moscou' à Paris*, p. 111; also *Histoire du Parti Communiste Français*, Tome II (Paris, Editions Unir, n.d.), pp. 205–8; and Lecoeur, *Le Partisan*, p. 205. Lecoeur says that Tillon deliberately broke contact with the party leadership 'pour marquer son désaccord', whereas Tillon claims that it was Duclos who tried to 'delay the national insurrection' by breaking contact with the FTP on 10 August.

could exercise their authority directly and were no longer dependent on Lecoeur's clandestine liaison system.

Their task was made easier on 28 August when de Gaulle ordered the incorporation into the regular army, for the duration of the war, of all Resistance soldiers who wished to carry on fighting.* The party instructed the FTP to comply with this order, and most of them did so. Only those commanders whom the political leadership considered 'friendly' were asked to stay behind and given positions of responsibility within the party.[33]

There remained the problem of the supreme FTP commander, Charles Tillon, between whom and Duclos there was already friction at the moment of the Liberation. Here too de Gaulle's interests were identical with those of the party leadership, and between them they found the perfect solution: on 9 September Tillon entered the government, succeeding Grenier as air minister. For both sides there was an element of risk: the party was in effect guaranteeing Tillon a place in the leadership at least for as long as the provisional government lasted, while de Gaulle was giving a Communist control over military personnel, with power to decide promotions.[34] But evidently both thought the risk worth taking in order to neutralize Tillon as an independent force and to associate the FTP directly with the party's decision to participate in de Gaulle's government and recognize its legitimacy.

Tillon was no doubt flattered enough to see his Resistance services rewarded with such high office in the state. Later, however, he was to complain of 'the insufficient representation of the Resistance in the new government, to which only two Communist ministers were admitted, as at Algiers'.[35] In fact it was the Communist Party rather than the Resistance as such that was under-represented, for the new government included seven non-Communist Resistants.[36] The two Communists, Tillon and Billoux, were not able to have much influence on policy outside their own departments of Air and Health. They were unable, for instance, to dissuade de Gaulle from decreeing the dissolution of the *Milices Patriotiques*.

---

* The PCF did, however, criticize de Gaulle for dissolving the FFI command structure. It wanted the FFI to be incorporated into the regular army in complete units, not as individuals. It could then have been the nucleus of a new, popular French army led by patriotic officers—i.e. one more likely to accept orders from a future government under Communist control. See J. R. Rieber, *Stalin and the French Communist Party 1941–1947* (New York and London, 1962), pp. 69–71, 174–7.

Meanwhile the party's political leadership was free to continue its work of absorbing and diluting the Communist Resistance. A pamphlet giving profiles of Communist leaders as 'Men in whom you can have confidence' contained an adroit mixture of Resistance heroes and reliable leaders who had taken little or no part in the Resistance. Gradually, as the bureaucratic pre-war leadership reasserted its authority, it was able to start demoting Resistance leaders, who were often found to be 'too sectarian', 'perverted by military action', or lacking the necessary flexibility for their new political tasks. Later still many active Resistance leaders would be eliminated from the party leadership altogether. They provided a high proportion of the victims of the 'grandes affaires' which were to punctuate the party's history in the 1950s—Tillon (1952), Lecoeur (1954), Hervé (1956), Casanova and Kriegel-Valrimont (1961)— while many lesser figures such as Guingouin, Chaintron and Prenant were to share the same disgrace although with less publicity. To fill these gaps in the ranks of its heroes, the party endowed some dead Communists with spurious Resistance records, while some who were still alive found their past becoming more glorious as time went by.[37]

De Gaulle's lofty and mistrustful attitude to the internal Resistance undoubtedly created among non-Communist Resistants a good deal of resentment, which the Communists might have been expected to exploit. One reason why they did not do so was that they themselves, like the Gaullists, acknowledged the authority of a leadership outside France: that of Thorez in Moscow and of the 'delegation of the Central Committee in North Africa', whose political secretary was André Marty. This delegation was composed mainly of Communist deputies who had been imprisoned by the Daladier government in 1939–40 and later transferred to Algeria by the Vichy regime. After the Allied occupation of North Africa they had been released and were joined by Marty, coming from Russia, and by Grenier, who followed de Gaulle from London.

Few of these people except Grenier could claim any connection with the Resistance. Thorez and Marty had been outside France probably since the beginning of the occupation (party myths to the contrary notwithstanding), while the deputies had been in prison and therefore had had little opportunity for Resistance activity. They obtained their release from Giraud, and they depended first on him and later on de Gaulle, both for rehabilitation as patriotic Frenchmen and for freedom to carry on political activity. Thorez himself asked de Gaulle's permission to come to Algiers in February 1944, and was refused. Even after the Liberation, he had to wait to be amnestied before he could return to France, since he was still wanted for deserting from the army in 1939. When de Gaulle agreed to amnesty him, on 31 October 1944, it was, in his own words, 'quite deliberately. Taking account of the former circumstances, of the more recent events, and of the present necessities, I considered that the return of Maurice Thorez at the head of the Communist Party might at that moment bring greater benefits than disadvantages. That proved to be the case. . . .'[38] De Gaulle correctly guessed that Thorez's main preoccupation on returning to France would be to get the party firmly under control, and that this would facilitate his own efforts to restore order in France and impose the authority of the state.

Thorez arrived in France on 27 November. He was soon admitted to the Consultative Assembly and began to 'take the Party in hand'. To do this he copied the methods prevalent in the USSR, including the personality cult. Huge portraits of him suddenly appeared everywhere, and the legend that he had been in France during the first years of the occupation was assiduously promoted. (But Cachin gave the game away to the alert reader, in a pamphlet which said: 'He is restored to us at last after five years' separation. . . .')[39] As a sample of the prevalent style, here is a sentence from Georges Cogniot's report in *L'Humanité* of the first meeting at which Thorez spoke after his return: 'And courageous fighters competed for the honour of embracing the great patriot, the great Frenchman beyond all others, courageous and farseeing.'[40]

De Gaulle meanwhile went on a visit to the USSR, and signed a Franco-Soviet treaty of alliance, under which both sides undertook not to sign a separate peace, to take joint action to prevent any future German threat, to assist each other in any future war with Germany, and not to join any alliances or coalitions against each other. De Gaulle's aim in making this alliance was of course to strengthen France's international position, particularly *vis-à-vis* the British and Americans. His domestic policy was always subordinated to his foreign policy and not the other way round. But obviously the alliance had a useful side-effect as an extra guarantee of French Communist loyalty, at any rate for the duration of the war. Stalin himself hinted as much, when he told de Gaulle: 'I know Thorez and in my opinion he's a good Frenchman. In your place I should not put him in prison. . . .

At least, not just yet!' De Gaulle's reply was characteristically Delphic: 'The French government treats Frenchmen according to the services it expects from them'.[41]

Thorez did not disappoint him:

> As for Thorez, while doing his best for the interests of communism, on several occasions he served the public interest as well. No sooner had he returned to France than he helped to put an end to the last remnants of the *milices patriotiques*, which some of his supporters had insisted on maintaining in a new clandestinity. As far as the harsh and sombre rigidity of his party would allow him, he opposed the attempted encroachments of the liberation committees and the acts of violence which some over-excited gangs were trying to perpetrate. To those numerous workers, especially miners, who listened to his harangues, he constantly prescribed that they should work as hard as possible and at all costs produce. Simply political tactics? That was not for me to unravel. For me it sufficed that France was served.[42]

Thorez gave an unequivocal endorsement to the legitimacy of the Gaullist state in a speech to the Central Committee at Ivry on 21 January 1945:

> Is it not necessary to track down the saboteurs, traitors, spies and enemy agents and bring them before the courts? It goes without saying that this task belongs solely to the qualified representatives of public power. The people has the right and the duty to make its voice heard, but it is for the legal authority to carry out house searches, arrests, judgements and the execution of judgements.
>
> A few words, in this connection, about the organization of *Milices Patriotiques*, which have become Republican Civic Guards. These armed groups had their *raison d'être* before and during the insurrection against Hitler's occupation and its Vichy accomplices. But the situation is different now. Public safety must be ensured by the regular police forces set up for this purpose. The Civic Guards and, in general, all irregular armed groups, must not be maintained any longer. . . . The local and departmental Liberation Committees must not usurp the functions of the municipal and departmental administration.[43]

So ended the affair of the *Milices Patriotiques*, which, as Tillon says, 'has been used for all sorts of romances well devised to confuse matters and serve the personality cult. Were the Gaullists then so weak in power that they feared the pop-guns of the militia? Those weapons counted for little on the liberated soil, once the mass of the best-armed FFI had been incorporated into the National Army.'[44] The importance of Thorez's gesture was in fact psychological rather than military. Once again, as in June 1936, he had taken upon himself to douse the revolutionary excitement of his followers with a cold appeal to the realities of power politics. Again the French working class had made a great stride forward; but the bourgeois state was still there, and once again it had to be strengthened rather than weakened because it was the ally of the world's only proletarian state in the struggle against fascism. Small wonder that this message came as a bitter disappointment to thousands of Communists who had really believed that the Resistance was the prelude to socialist revolution, and who years later were still convinced, without knowing exactly how or why, that 'at the Liberation we missed the bus'.[45]

10

The Bid for Power

1944–1947

The Strategy: a French People's Democracy

Yet the situation in 1945 was very different from that of 1936. Then the strategy of the Soviet Union and of the Comintern had been essentially defensive. But now the Red Army was advancing into the heart of Europe. The forces of fascism were being routed. The pendulum of world politics was swinging rapidly to the left. In almost every country of continental Europe the Communists, thanks to their own Resistance efforts and to the new power and prestige of the Soviet Union (the relative importance of these factors varying from country to country), were more powerful than they had ever been before. In the countries occupied by the Red Army new political structures were being set up—the 'people's democracies'—in which the Communists were clearly going to play a dominant role.

The creation of such 'democracies' was clearly a departure from the classic Leninist formula for the seizure of power. It corresponded fairly closely to the resolution of the Comintern's Seventh Congress in 1935, foreseeing 'an anti-fascist people's front government, which is not yet a government of the proletarian dictatorship, but one which undertakes to put into effect decisive measures against fascism and reaction' (see above, pp. 237–8). But whereas that resolution had still seen such a government as a prelude to the 'revolutionary seizure of power', it now proved possible, thanks to Communist control of the existing state machinery, to by-pass that stage altogether. A new pragmatism had crept into the international Communist movement, symbolized by the formal abolition of the Comintern itself (a conciliatory gesture from Stalin to his wartime allies) in 1943. As Thorez told the PCF Central Committee in January 1945, 'the

A shortened version of this chapter appeared in M. McCauley (ed.), *Communist Power in Europe 1944–1949* (London, 1977).

Marxist theory of dialectical materialism is not a dogma, but a guide for action. Its theses and conclusions necessarily change as time goes on: they are necessarily replaced by new conclusions and theses which conform to new historical conditions.'[1]

Would these new historical conditions permit the establishment of people's democracies in western as well as eastern Europe? The great, and as it turned out the insuperable, obstacle was the presence of American and British troops. This led the Russians later to regret the opening of the second front in western Europe, which at the time they had so insistently urged and so enthusiastically welcomed. By 1948 they were even suggesting that the second front had been demanded by '*émigré*' circles (including the pretender to the role of French dictator, de Gaulle) ... not so much to crush the Germans as to struggle against the popular masses and the internal Resistance movement'.[2] And if these internal French forces had not been strong enough to set up a people's democracy on their own, the Red Army could always have come to their aid. As Stalin himself claimed at the time of his breach with Tito:

> Even though the French and Italian Communist Parties have so far achieved less success than the Communist Party of Yugoslavia, this is not because of any special qualities of the CPY, but mainly because ... the Soviet Army came to the aid of the Yugoslav people, crushed the German invader, liberated Belgrade, and in this way created the conditions necessary for the CPY to achieve power. Unfortunately, the Soviet Army did not and could not render such assistance to the French and Italian Communist parties.[3]

Once the British and Americans had landed in France, it is probable that Stalin did not rate the French Communists' chance of achieving power very high. On the other hand there is no reason to suppose that he ruled it completely out. No one could assume in 1944–5 that American troops were in western Europe to stay. Roosevelt himself had told Stalin at the Teheran Conference that land armies for the maintenance of peace in the post-war world would have to be furnished by Britain and the USSR, and had expressed doubts whether Congress would favour American participation in a purely European defence system.[4] As soon as the war ended the United States began rapidly demobilizing its forces. It seemed likely enough that it would soon withdraw most of its troops from the European Continent.[5] If this had happened, and if Stalin had achieved his postwar aim of a united Germany heavily dependent on the Soviet Union, no bookmaker would have given odds against a people's democracy in France.

Certainly the possibility was taken very seriously by non-Communists, both inside and outside France. 'How many senior civil servants, even at the very top, are backing communism to win!' exclaimed de Gaulle's Socialist minister of industrial production, Robert Lacoste.[6] After de Gaulle's resignation, in January 1946, there was a real possibility of a Socialist-Communist coalition government being formed (the two parties between them had a majority in the Constituent Assembly). The acting chief of the French general staff, General Billotte, felt obliged to write to one of the leaders of the *Mouvement Républicain Populaire*, Maurice Schumann, who was a personal friend of his, urging him not to allow this to happen:

> This solution, which will quickly lead to the SFIO being completely eclipsed by the CP and allowing it political control, has been examined with objectivity by the Anglo-American commanders. They consider it as a very serious threat to the rear of their occupation troops and as likely to hasten a possible conflict with the USSR. They envisage various measures such as: strategic abandonment of continental Europe . . . , preventive seizure of bases in Eurasia—French ones of course, measures of economic coercion, etc. . . . The Anglo-American diplomats will perhaps be less blunt, but not much.[7]

Billotte also put pressure on the Socialist leaders:

> I drew them as precise as possible a picture of what a Thorez government would be like. I told them that if Thorez became prime minister he would never leave office, even if defeated in parliament.
> . . . I knew what a Thorez government would mean. The Sultan of Morocco had warned me that he would immediately proclaim independence and put himself under American protection. The troops of our Allies were ready for an equally swift takeover of the French occupation zone in Germany. . . .[8]

A year later, on 27 February 1947, President Truman was told by his adviser Dean Acheson that 'in France, with four Communists in the Cabinet, one of them Minister of Defence, with Communists controlling the largest trade union and infiltrating government offices, factories, and the armed services, with nearly a third of the electorate voting Communist, and with economic conditions worsening, the Russians could pull the plug any time they chose.'[9] Such was the general opinion in Washington at that time.[10]

In these circumstances it would have been surprising if the French Communists themselves had settled for a purely defensive strategy, or had confined their attention to foreign policy as in the period of the Popular Front. Certainly they did not ignore foreign policy, and of course in their discussions of it they laid emphasis on the need to strengthen the Franco-Soviet alliance, to avoid the creation of a Western Bloc, and so on. But they also laid great emphasis on the specific interests of France, and on some issues (notably that of the Ruhr, and those affecting the future of the French empire) they even spoke up for those interests against the current themes of Soviet policy. And greater emphasis still was laid on the reconstruction of the French economy and on the 'renewal of democracy'. In June 1945 Thorez addressed the Tenth Party Congress thus:

> In this gigantic battle, democracy has shown itself superior to fascism in every sphere: military, economic, political and moral. The more a country remained faithful to democratic principles and institutions, the more capable it was of victoriously resisting the fascist aggressor. Soviet democracy, which is certainly the most complete democracy, played the decisive role in the war against fascism. By contrast, the further a country had strayed from democratic practices, the weaker it proved when confronted by the fascist aggressor. Such, alas!, was the case of France.[11]

It is clear that in Communist eyes the degree of 'democracy' in a country corresponds closely to the power of the Communist Party there, and vice versa. In the same speech Thorez was urging de Gaulle's government to 'recognize without delay the government of democratic Poland'; and he went on to argue that France, with her provisional government, was 'beginning to cut an odd figure in a world moving towards more democracy'.[12]

In November 1946 Thorez, by then the leader of the largest party in the French parliament and a candidate for the post of prime minister, thus defined his attitude to parliamentary government in France:

> It is clear that the Communist Party, in its action as part of the Government and within the framework of the parliamentary system it has helped to re-establish, will hold strictly to the democratic programme which has won for it the confidence of the masses of the people. The progress of democracy throughout the world, in spite of rare exceptions which serve only to confirm

the rule, permits the choice of other paths to socialism than the one taken by the Russian Communists. In any case, the path is necessarily different for each country. We have always thought and said that the French people, who are rich in great traditions, would find for themselves their way to greater democracy, progress, and social justice. . . .

The union of working class and republican forces is the sure foundation of democracy. The French workers' party which we wish to create by the fusion of Communists and Socialists would be a guide towards this democracy, *nouvelle et populaire*.[13]

It is noticeable that Thorez did not feel it necessary to stress any differences between the French 'path to socialism' and those of the various eastern European countries under Soviet tutelage. In fact, though he did not explicitly say that France should follow their example, he was using the same slogans and proposing much the same recipe (including the fusion of Communists and Socialists) as the Communist Parties in those countries.*

What the Communists hoped to achieve in France was clearly very similar to what they actually did achieve during this period in Czechoslovakia, where they were able to establish themselves in power by using the democratic institutions set up at the end of the war, without direct help from the Red Army. Czechoslovakia—like France, and unlike other eastern European states—was an industrialized country in which liberal democracy before the war had allowed the growth of a strong trade union movement and a strong indigenous Communist Party, which after the war emerged as the largest party in a freely elected parliament. Gottwald became prime minister through the application of normal 'bourgeois' democratic procedure, as Thorez hoped to do. Perhaps neither Gottwald nor Thorez foresaw in 1946 exactly what would happen in Prague in 1948. But each certainly believed that the establishment of a Communist-led government was a decisive and irreversible step on his country's 'path to socialism'. Thorez certainly saw nothing unconstitutional in Gottwald's behaviour in February 1948, and would have behaved in the same way had he found himself in analogous circumstances in France.

* The 'i' was dotted by Raymond Guyot in an article in January 1947: 'In such countries as Yugoslavia and Bulgaria basic reforms have been pushed forward much farther than in France in so far as the sovereignty of the people and the real control by the popular masses of the government of the country is concerned.' (*Cahiers du Communisme*, no. 1, p. 17.)

In short, when Thorez ordered the dissolution of the *Milices Patriotiques* and urged respect for the 'legal authority' of de Gaulle's administration, and when Fajon, at the Tenth Party Congress, declared that 'the chatter about setting up socialism in France at the present time is either meaningless or the work of *provocateurs* whose task is to divide the democratic forces, for the indispensable conditions for setting it up have not been created',[14] the retreat they were ordering was tactical and not strategic. They knew that an attempt to seize power by insurrection at this stage would simply isolate the party, and bring into play overwhelming American and British forces on the side of its opponents. But they were not, as in 1936, trying to persuade the French working class to mark time in order to ensure the survival of the Soviet Union. They now had a positive strategy for installing the dictatorship of the proletariat in France. They believed their party had been so strengthened, and the bourgeoisie so weakened, by the events of the past five years, that the working class could win power not through insurrection but by the use of bourgeois parliamentary institutions.

The Power Base: 'Le Premier Parti de France'

Why did the French Communist leaders believe this? Because their party had indeed emerged from the occupation as, by almost any objective test, the strongest political force in France. It was at last winning effective control of the reunited trade union movement. It had far more members than any other party. In the first post-war election it won more votes and seats than any other party. And from then on it had at least five ministers in each government.

TRADE UNIONS

The CGT,[15] which had split for the second time after the German-Soviet pact in 1939, was clandestinely reunited on 17 April 1943 by an agreement signed at Le Perreux, in the Paris suburbs. Under this, *unitaires* (Communists) and *confédérés* were to have the same relative strengths in the local, regional and national leaderships of the CGT and of each of its component federations as they had had immediately before the war. This meant that on the confederal bureau there were three *unitaires* to six *confédérés*. But the latter were weakened by the absence of their leader, Jouhaux, who had been deported to Germany. When the bureau resumed public activity in August 1944, its *unitaire* members were Frachon, Racamond and Henri Raynaud. Officially they were outnumbered by five *confédérés*, but one of these was Louis Saillant, who was also the CGT's representative on the *Conseil National de la Résistance*, and who tended increasingly often to vote with the Communists, so that in practice there was often parity between the two sides.

At the federal level, the *unitaires* still controlled all the federations which they had controlled before the war—which would already have given them a majority at the 1938 Confederal Congress, if they had chosen to break with Jouhaux at that time (see above, p. 245). But, as elections were held in the various federations during the months following the Liberation, they also extended their control to those of the Food Industry, the Hatters, the Barbers, Clothing, Posts and Telecommunications, the Miners, Entertainment, Transport, and Commercial Travellers. By the end of 1945 the only big federations still in non-Communist hands were the Clerical Workers, the Civil Servants (including Teachers), the Printers, Seamen, Dockers, and Local Government Employees.

The Communists were helped once again by many of the same factors as in 1936: the dynamism and hard work of their own militants, the apparent irrelevance of the issue of trade union independence from political parties (on which the *confédéré* leaders took their stand), the disciplined attitude of the *confédérés* (who accepted a series of defeats by majority votes at various levels until late 1947 without threatening a showdown or a split), and the very rapid growth of CGT membership. This had peaked at just over four million in early 1937, had declined rapidly in 1938–9 and was perhaps already below one million even before the complete disorganization caused by the war, the renewed split, the occupation, and the banning of all trade unions by Vichy. Yet in 1945 the CGT delivered 5,600,000 membership cards, and in 1946 6,369,000. As in 1936 this massive influx was clearly set in motion by *political* events—the occupation and Liberation—and once again many of the new trade union members were clearly attracted by Communist leaders who offered a clear *political* programme.

In addition to these factors, the Communists were now aided, in the CGT as elsewhere, by the association of their party with the Resistance, which of course they skilfully exploited in their trade union propaganda, and no doubt also by the soaring prestige of the USSR. Conversely the *confédérés* were to some extent discredited by the fact that some of their former leaders—drawn mainly from the pre-war pacifist-syndicalist minority—had co-operated with the Vichy regime (one of them, René Belin, actually served as Pétain's Minister of Labour from 1940 to 1942). This too was vigorously exploited by Communist propaganda, which for a time took on the character of a witch-hunt. A number of CGT officials—both *confédérés* and former *unitaires* who had broken with the party in 1939—were physically eliminated during the first chaotic weeks of the Liberation, almost certainly by Communist Resistance groups. Not all of them were genuine collaborators: some indeed had spent the occupation in internment camps or had themselves been in contact with the non-Communist Resistance. Other *confédéré* leaders, such as Edmond Fronty of the Posts and Telecommunications Federation, were merely put under arrest—usually on the basis of orders or information given by their Communist opponents—during the crucial few weeks when their unions were being reorganized after the Liberation and the *unitaires* were gaining control. Yet others were simply denounced as collaborators and purged from their trade union posts. In several cases the charge was that they had joined local trade unions or 'social committees' authorized under Vichy's *Charte du Travail*. French workers had been specifically encouraged to join these organizations, in order to be better placed for disruption and sabotage, by broadcasts from the CGT's representative in London, Albert Guigui. But in the violent and vindictive atmosphere of the Liberation it was easy for the Communists to whip up rank-and-file feeling against alleged collaborators, and dangerous if not actually impossible for those falsely accused to answer back.[16]

Another reason for *confédéré* reticence in the face of Communist attacks was no doubt that many *confédérés* themselves felt a certain inferiority complex about the Communist role in the Resistance, which in turn occasioned some guilt feelings about their own past anti-Communism and about the failure of the CGT as a body to stand up against either Hitler or Vichy. In a sense 1939–40 had been the opposite of 1914: the French labour movement had sinned through pacifism rather than through chauvinism. But in another sense it was the same thing over again: war had swept away all the rhetoric and illusions about the movement's unity and strength and had shown the leaders to be muddled, frightened, impotent and divided. The success of the Resistance—and of the Soviet war effort—told against them much as the success of the Bolshevik Revolution had told against the

Socialist and syndicalist leaders of 1918. The self-confidence of the Communists contrasted with the self-doubt of the old syndicalists, whose immediate concern was to restore the unity of the movement and not to isolate themselves from the mass of the working class. In some cases, such as Saillant, this led to a gradual conversion to the Communist point of view. For others it meant a tactical reluctance to oppose the Communists during the crucial months when they were establishing their hold over the CGT. Even Jouhaux, whose consistent anti-fascist record and sufferings in a German concentration camp gave him considerable personal prestige, was not immune from this kind of complex. A revealing pen-portrait of him at this time has been given by a fellow-prisoner, André François-Poncet:

> In the main he fought against the revolutionary demagogy of the Communists. There remains something of this in him. But at the present time he is afraid of looking like a moderate, a 'soft'. He defends himself vehemently against what he calls backsliding; he is anxious to acquire new conviction in his dislike of the privileged and rich, to persuade himself that he is not a bourgeois nor in danger of becoming one, to conserve intact his class consciousness.[17]

Signs of growing Communist power within the CGT could already be seen at the first meeting of the newly elected *Comité Confédéral National* (CCN) in March 1945. In a striking breach of the CGT's tradition of non-involvement in electoral politics, the CCN agreed to allow those local and departmental unions which wished to do so (i.e. those which the Communists controlled) to take part in the drawing up of joint Resistance lists for the coming municipal elections. It also gave the *unitaires* virtual parity on the bureau, with Saillant and Frachon as joint acting general secretaries in Jouhaux's absence. Jouhaux resumed his post when he returned from Germany in May but, for the reasons given above, he avoided taking any open stand against Communist penetration. Indeed, by agreeing to intervene officially in the political debates which preceded the election of the Constituent Assembly, he indirectly helped the Communists to politicize the CGT and transform it into a vast lobby in support of their political demands. Thus in June the CGT adopted a resolution supporting the demands of the political parties for a sovereign Constituent Assembly (as opposed to the alternatives of holding elections under the 1875 Constitution, or of holding a prior referendum on the issue, which de Gaulle had suggested). In August the CGT took the initiative in co-ordinating the protests of the left-wing parties and the *Ligue des Droits de l'Homme* against the electoral system chosen by de Gaulle, on the grounds that it ensured proportional representation only on the level of each department but not for the nation as a whole. Jouhaux himself presided at the inter-party meeting on the subject, and asked de Gaulle to receive a delegation headed by himself. It was left to de Gaulle to remind the disciple of Pelloutier that the CGT's legal function was 'the study and defence of economic interests', and that it had no business to interfere in political or electoral matters.[18]

The first open defeat for the *confédérés* came in September. With the help of two other Communists who would soon be cabinet ministers—Marcel Paul and Ambroise Croizat—Frachon persuaded the CCN to give direct advice to CGT members on how they should vote in the coming referendum: 'Yes' to the first question (should the new Assembly be a Constituent one?) and 'No' to the second (should its powers and duration be limited as de Gaulle proposed?). This of course was the result which the PCF was campaigning for, whereas the Socialists, after a good deal of heart-searching, agreed to support de Gaulle's call for a 'Yes' to both questions. Jouhaux would have preferred to avoid giving a direct endorsement to either side, but he was defeated. The same meeting of the CCN voted a new composition of the bureau, making Frachon a full general secretary on an equal footing with Jouhaux. These two votes showed that there was now a clear Communist majority in the CCN. (The motion to create a second general secretary was passed by eighty-nine votes to forty-two.) But the Communists, anxious to avoid a split, still allowed the *confédérés* a nominal majority of six to five on the bureau. This was quickly changed, however, by the death of one *confédéré* representative, Georges Buisson, and the election of another, Albert Gazier, as a Socialist deputy to the Constituent Assembly. Neither was immediately replaced, so that the Communists acquired a working majority. A third *confédéré* representative, Saillant—who in any case was by now a fairly reliable fellow-traveller—took a less active part in the bureau's work after his election as secretary-general of the newly-founded World Federation of Trade Unions (WFTU) at its congress in October.

At the CGT's first post-war confederal congress, in April 1946, the Communists obtained a reform of the statutes by an overwhelming vote of 21,238 to 4,862. (This probably exaggerated their real strength among the rank-and-file, since many delegates were elected on a very low poll.) The reform provided for a much stricter system of proportional representation within the CGT, thereby increasing the weight of the big federations and virtually ensuring the permanence of Communist control. In spite of this, Jouhaux and his supporters still agreed to participate in the leadership, believing that it was better to apply a 'policy of presence' than to leave the Communists in sole command. The Communists for their part were glad enough to reassure public opinion by allowing generous representation to their opponents. Jouhaux was allowed to keep his title of general secretary, and was thus equal to Frachon in dignity though no longer in power. In the bureau too there was nominal equality between the two sides, with the supposedly neutral Pierre Le Brun holding the balance. But in any crucial vote both he and Saillant could be relied on to support Frachon, so that in practice there was a Communist majority. And if anything went wrong the bureau could be overruled by the *Commission Administrative*, on which the *unitaires* now had a majority of twenty to fifteen.

PUBLIC OPINION AND THE ELECTORATE

Many of the factors which ensured the Communist triumph in the CGT also affected other sections of the population besides trade unionists. Although the 1945 election showed that neither the new *Mouvement Républicain Populaire* (MRP) nor the revived SFIO was all that far behind the PCF in terms of quantitative electoral support, the leaders of both parties knew well that qualitatively they were not in the same class. The Socialist and Christian Democrat militants suffered from the same sort of inferiority complex towards the PCF as did the *confédérés* in the CGT. They were intimidated by the dynamism and organization of the Communists and by the violence, both verbal and on occasion physical, which they were ready to use. 'At every demonstration, every professional or political meeting, the Communists, who were used to military discipline, were all there. The same was not always true of our militants. . . .'[19] Like the *confédérés* too (indeed they were often the same people) many Socialist militants felt ashamed of their party's past record and determined in future to preserve the 'unity of the working class', or at least not to help the PCF win over the working class by allowing themselves to be labelled as part of an anti-Communist bourgeois coalition. Still less did they wish to be labelled as collaborators, a risk which almost anyone ran who was too outspokenly critical of the PCF or the USSR. About the latter, indeed, wild illusions were prevalent even in unimpeachably non-Communist circles. It was Maurice Schumann, one of the MRP leaders, who wrote in early 1945: 'The Soviet armies have already liberated, totally or partially, several of the countries between Germany and the USSR. Yet in none of these countries has the predominant, indeed exclusive, Russian influence taken the form of Leninist or even Stalinist communism.'* No doubt Schumann hoped to demonstrate that one could be pro-Soviet without being Communist in France, but inevitably the general effect of such statements was to reassure people about Communist good intentions in France as elsewhere.

The Communists benefited from the general feeling that the old order had been rotten and must be swept away, that a fresh start was needed, that the Liberation should also be something of a revolution. They benefited too from the upheaval in the press. Most of the old newspapers were suppressed for having continued publication under German censorship. The vacuum was instantly filled by a plethora of ex-Resistance publications vying desperately with each other for readership, among which the Communist press got off to a good start. By October 1945 *L'Humanité* had a circulation of 456,000 and its sister paper *Ce Soir* 419,000, compared to 382,000 and 101,000 respectively for the surviving moderate dailies, *Le Figaro* and *L'Aurore*. And in the provinces the Communist press had a similarly dominant position.[20] In addition the *Mouvement Unifié de la Résistance* (MUR), an umbrella organization of Resistance groups including the *Front National*, had its own daily, *Libération*, edited by the pro-Communist Emmanuel d'Astier de la Vigerie. Even the most influential non-Communist dailies in Paris, *Combat* and *Le Monde*, were somewhat self-consciously 'progressive'. Indeed it was symptomatic of the atmosphere that *Le Monde* had been set up with government encouragement as an entirely new paper in place of the most influential pre-war paper *Le Temps*, which had been somewhat artificially convicted of collaboration in order to prevent it reappearing, the real reason being that the provisional government considered it too conservative and too much identified with big business to be the voice of the new France.[21]

---

* Quoted in Georgette Elgey, *La République des Illusions* (Paris, 1965), p. 17. This sort of complaisance towards 'our Soviet allies' was of course not confined to countries which had been under German occupation. Witness for instance the difficulty which George Orwell experienced in getting *Animal Farm* published in Britain in 1945.

The PCF attempted, through its members and sympathizers in the various non-Communist Resistance groups, to bring about a federation between these and the *Front National* in 1945. This failed, and the non-Communist Resistance split between a minority who joined the fellow-travelling MUR (so-called deliberately to encourage confusion with the non-Communist *Mouvement Uni de la Résistance* that had existed under the occupation) and a majority who formed the *Union Démocratique et Socialiste de la Résistance* (UDSR), which in due course became a small centre-left parliamentary party. But many lesser organizations were set up to canalize the patriotic, anti-fascist and 'progressive' enthusiasms of the time: the Peasants' Defence and Action Committees, the National Writers' Committee, the Union of French Women (women were given the vote for the first time in 1945), the Union of Republican Youth, and so on. In most of these Communists played a leading role, but they were not yet written off by non-Communists as mere front organizations, and many distinguished non-Communists served on their committees. They took their place alongside old faithfuls such as the *Association Républicaine des Anciens Combattants*, which had served the party so well between the wars.

Nothing succeeds like success. The more the PCF appeared to dominate French public life, the more important it became for all sorts of people to be on good terms with it. A civil servant was bound to calculate that if he refused a Communist request for any kind of administrative favour he might not be doing his career any good. Generals, admirals, provincial governors thought it politic to call at the PCF headquarters when passing through Paris.[22] Businessmen with dubious records under the occupation found it prudent to purchase advertising space in *L'Humanité*.* Even politicians as distinguished as Edouard Herriot, who had made the mistake of lunching with Pierre Laval on the eve of the Liberation and consequently found that his popularity in Lyons (now 'the capital of the Resistance') was somewhat tarnished, were not above a little gentle flirtation with the PCF as the price of rehabilitation. Herriot became a member of the MUR and even president (at the age of seventy-three!) of the Union of Republican Youth. Under his influence the Radicals joined the Communists in opposing de

---

* This is the origin of the widespread but erroneous belief in France that the Paris department store *La Samaritaine* belongs to the PCF.

Gaulle's constitutional plans, while Communist propaganda began to rehabilitate the discredited Radicals as a party of the 'left'. The object of this was to put pressure on the Socialists to be more co-operative, and to burden the fast-rising Catholic MRP with a 'right-wing' public image.

Control of the CGT itself brought further advantages with it, for it enabled the Communists to win control of the *comités d'entreprise* (works committees) introduced into French industry by the provisional government in February 1945. These committees were composed of representatives of the employees, in practice usually nominated by the trade unions. As well as having the right to be informed about the firm's affairs and to be consulted on decisions affecting productivity, they were responsible for the management of funds devoted to the material and social well-being of the personnel—holiday camps, relief for workers' families in distress, etc. Here was yet another opportunity for Communists to make themselves popular with the workers, and also a good reason for workers to be on good terms with the Communists.

For all these reasons, no one was surprised when the PCF emerged from the general election of 21 October 1945 as the strongest party in France. De Gaulle indeed was inclined to congratulate himself on having limited it to 26% of the votes cast, even though this was a striking advance on its previous percentage of 15.3 in 1936, which at the time had already seemed a spectacular success. The party, de Gaulle later wrote,

> did not win the support of the great mass of the nation. And yet the events from which France was barely emerging had offered it an exceptional chance to triumph. The disaster of 1940, the failure of the nation by many of her leading elements, the resistance to which it had greatly contributed, the long misery of the people during the occupation, the political, economic, social and moral upheavals which the country had suffered, the victory of Soviet Russia, the abuses committed against us by the Western democracies, were so many conditions favourable to its success.

He attributed this successful containment of the Communist electoral tide partly to his choice of a proportional electoral system (he was convinced that an election in single-menber constituencies on the British model would have given the PCF an overall majority on its own, while the pre-war two-ballot system would have forced the SFIO into an electoral alliance with the PCF and ensured the victory of the resulting coalition), partly to his own prestige and the fact that the Communists attacked him during the campaign.[23]

What was remarkable about the Communist vote in 1945, especially when compared to 1936, was how evenly spread it was throughout France. In only two departments (compared to twenty-four in 1936) did it fall below 5% of registered voters, and in only another nine below 10%, while only in the Paris suburbs did it rise above 35%.[24] Though the Paris region and the industrial north were still among the areas of greatest Communist strength in absolute terms, the party's relative advance was much less spectacular there than in rural areas where the *maquis* had played an important role under the occupation, such as the Haute-Saône, the Pyrénées-Orientales, Savoy, the Nièvre, the Côtes-du-Nord, the Alpes-Maritimes and the Creuse. The PCF for the first time gained a following in many Breton and western departments, predominantly Catholic and traditionally voting for the right, from which it had been virtually excluded before the war. Here the church and the big landowners were often discredited by the débâcle of Vichy or terrorized by the *maquis*. Tenant farmers and small freeholders were emancipated from their influence, and in general sympathetic to the Resistance.[25] Many no doubt were attracted by the intensive propaganda which the PCF directed at the peasants, notably through its specialized paper *La Terre*, praising them extravagantly for their role in the Resistance and urging various forms of public assistance to the small farmer.[26] Thus while it won over some peasants in Catholic areas from the right, the PCF also won many votes in anticlerical departments from the Radicals, traditional defenders of the small farmer against church and aristocracy. It had rediscovered the role which it had begun to assume in the 1920s, as heir to the French rural tradition of Jacobin republican extremism, and was now able to play it on a much larger scale, while at the same time confirming its superiority to the SFIO as a party of the working class. This success was confirmed by further gains in rural areas in the two elections of 1946, which took the party to its peak electoral strength: 28.6% of the votes cast on 10 November 1946.

GOVERNMENT

The PCF's emergence as France's strongest party in electoral and parliamentary terms greatly strengthened its claim to a share of power in the government—a claim which de Gaulle had already recognized on the basis of its contribution to the Resistance. From April 1944 to November 1945 de Gaulle's provisional government included only two Communist ministers—first Billoux and Grenier, then from September 1944 onwards Billoux and Tillon. By contrast from November 1945 to May 1947 there were never less than five Communist ministers, except during Léon Blum's brief one-party caretaker government at the end of 1946. Apart from Maurice Thorez, who was one of the four senior ministers (*ministres d'État*) representing the different political currents in de Gaulle's government, and one of the two deputy prime ministers in those of Gouin (January to June 1946), Bidault (June to November 1946) and Ramadier (January to May 1947), the key men were Marcel Paul (Minister of Industrial Production), François Billoux (Minister of the National Economy, then of Reconstruction), Charles Tillon (Minister of Munitions) and Ambroise Croizat (Minister of Labour and Social Security). For a year these four between them, working in close co-operation with the CGT (from whose leadership Paul and Croizat moved almost directly into their ministerial offices), were in virtually undisputed control of French industry, at a crucial period when much of it was being physically reconstructed and when its whole legal, economic and social framework was being re-cast.

Not surprisingly, the Communists exploited this situation to extend the influence of their party. The way had been shown by Tillon as air minister in the provisional government. He had carried out a thorough purge of the air force and the aircraft industry, often replacing non-Communist officials with party members, and advertising management vacancies only in pro-Communist papers.[27] He had also set up a number of new aircraft companies at the head of which he appointed engineers and managers belonging to the Communist-controlled *Union des Ingénieurs, Techniciens et Cadres*; and within his ministry he had set up a so-called 'Centre for the Administration of Isolated Civilian Personnel' which in fact was simply a means of keeping several hundred party members on the government payroll. After November 1945 an even more blatant method of doing this was chosen by Marcel Paul at the Ministry of Industrial Production: he appointed a personal *cabinet* of 117 people, all party members, and created nineteen divisions in his department where there had been only three. More seriously, with the help of his under-secretary of state, Auguste Lecoeur, he was able to give the party control of the nationalized coalmines by seeing that their board included Communists in three different categories—as representatives of the trade unions, of the state, and of the consumers.[28]

Not content with its domination of industry, the PCF repeatedly demanded one of the three 'big' ministries—Interior, Foreign Affairs or Defence. In November 1945 de Gaulle refused this, arguing that in view of their connection with one of the two great world powers the Communists should not be given any of 'the three levers which control foreign policy, namely the diplomacy which expresses it, the army which supports it and the police which covers it . . .'.[29] This was typically Gaullian reasoning: no one else would have justified refusal to give the Communists control over the police by referring to foreign policy. But de Gaulle's successors were perhaps even more determined to keep the police and the army out of Communist hands, for internal reasons, than they were to preserve the independence of France's foreign policy. De Gaulle's ban was maintained, and though in January 1947 as a sop to Communist *amour-propre* François Billoux was given the title of Minister of National Defence, actual power over the armed forces was transferred to three separate departments headed by non-Communists. And although Thorez became deputy prime minister after de Gaulle's resignation, the promise made to him by the head of the new government, Félix Gouin, that he would be consulted on all decisions, was not kept. The prime minister and foreign minister were careful to weed out the more sensitive diplomatic papers before any file was passed to Thorez.[30]

Obviously the Communists would have liked more influence in foreign policy and would have liked control over the army or the police, if only to ensure that these forces did not become an exclusively anti-Communist preserve which might refuse to obey a future Communist-led government. But there is no evidence of any systematic attempt at infiltration in preparation for a *coup d'état*. In fact the largest concentration of Communists within the security apparatus, which was to be found in certain companies of the riot police (CRS), resulted not from any Communist initiative but from the decision of de Gaulle's anti-Communist Minister of the Interior, Adrien Tixier, to 'neutralize' some of the FTP after the Liberation by enlisting them as officers in the CRS where he could keep an eye on them.[31] The Communists expected to come to power constitutionally, not by a *coup de force*. The very fact that they attached as much importance to the foreign ministry as to those of Defence and the Interior suggests that their main motive for wanting one of these three posts was to increase their influence within the government and their prestige in the country at large. They wanted to be accepted as France's largest political party, with a right to any position in the government including the leadership. Thus the most potent reason for insisting on one of the three 'big' posts was precisely that other people were trying to keep them out.

MEMBERSHIP

Finally, the PCF was undoubtedly the largest party in France in the most literal sense of having the most members. Success in this respect was more a result than a cause of success in other respects. The biggest increase in membership came not at the moment of liberation, but during 1945 and 1946 (see Table).

PCF Membership Statistics 1937–1948

Sources: Annie Kriegel, *Les Communistes français* (Paris, 1970), p. 13; Michelle Perrot, Annie Kriegel, *Le Socialisme français et le Pouvoir* (Paris, 1966), p. 197.

Year	Cards Sold	Cards Sent Out (by Party HQ to local federations)
1937 (September)	328,547[1]	
1938 (September)	320,000[2]	
1939 (August?)	<300,000[1]	
1945 (January)	387,098[1]	
1945 (June)	544,989[3]	906,727[4]
1945 (December)	775,352[3]	
1946	804,229[3]	1,034,000[3]
1947 (January)		809,030[3]
1947 (June)		895,130[5]
1947 (December)		907,785[6]
1948		798,459[6]

[1] Figures taken from Léon Mauvais's report to the Central Committee on 22 January 1945. (The pre-war figures after deduction of Algeria: see Kriegel, *Les Communistes français*, 1970 edition, p. 261.)
[2] Gitton, *Cahiers du Bolchévisme*, February 1939, p. 156.
[3] *Deux années d'activité pour la renaissance économique et politique de la République française*, Rapport du C. C. pour le XIe congrès du PCF (Strasbourg, June 1947).
[4] M. Thorez, 'Rapport au Xe Congrès' (Paris, 1945), reprinted in *Oeuvres Choisies*, vol. II, p. 356.
[5] Cards sent out by 20 June 1947, according to Thorez at the Strasbourg congress.
[6] M. Thorez, 'Rapport au XIIe congrès' (Gennevilliers, April 1950).

The figure of 387,000 for January 1945 is not all that much higher than those for 1937 and 1938. But by June 1945 it has gone up to nearly 550,000 and by the end of 1946 to just over 800,000. (This was probably the peak, since thereafter the leadership stopped publishing the number of cards actually sold.)

The other striking thing about the increase, as with the Communist vote, is that it was much more marked in rural than in industrial areas. In June 1945 party membership in the Paris region was no higher than it had been in 1937, and in the city of Paris itself it was actually down. But in Brittany it had multiplied by ten and in central France by four—both these, of course, being regions where Communist *maquis* had played an important role under the occupation. Less than one fifth of party members now lived in the Paris region, compared to more than a third at the time of the Popular Front.[32] At the same time the PCF ceased to be an overwhelmingly working-class party and became much more heterogeneous in its social composition.

The Tactics

The essence of the PCF's strategy was to obtain control of the government and state apparatus through a Communist-led parliamentary majority. Tactically, the party sought to achieve this by creating a favourable climate of opinion, an appropriate institutional framework, and a pliable governing coalition.

STATESMANSHIP

Obviously it tried to maximize its own electoral support. But in a proportional electoral system it was unlikely ever to win a majority of seats in parliament on its own. It therefore needed also to win the goodwill of the supporters of other parties, and especially of the Socialist Party, so as to make it more difficult for their leaders to resist Communist pressure. Since in electoral terms it had no serious challenge to face on its left, it was free to concentrate on winning over moderate public opinion by taking a moderate and strongly patriotic line on all current political issues. As long as the war was going on, all the emphasis of PCF propaganda was placed on the war effort. Thorez set the tone in his speech to the Central Committee in January 1945: 'As for us we say frankly that only one thing worries us, because only one thing worries the people: winning the war as soon as

346

possible; so that joy can soon return to all the homes, with peace and freedom, with the return of the absent and milk for our little ones, bread for our old people and a glass of wine for all.'[33] On Communist instigation the CGT in September 1944 adopted an appeal for increased production and called for a general wage increase of at least 50%. The government decreed an increase averaging only 40%, but this was immediately accepted, and from then on both party and trade unions concentrated on appeals for greater productivity, often of a Stakhanovite nature. Strikes were discouraged, and when they occurred the strikers were often denounced as provocateurs, 'agents of the trusts' and so forth.

Nor did this change when the war ended. The goal of victory was simply replaced by that of a healthy peace-time economy. In a famous speech at Waziers, in July 1945, Thorez castigated miners who dared to go on unofficial strike, and warned that 'shirkers will never make good communists or good revolutionaries'.[34] It was also during this period that Monmousseau, of all people, made the memorable observation: 'strikes are a weapon of the trusts'.[35] The reasoning behind this paradoxical judgement was spelt out as follows by the Communist leader of the Civil Servants' union:

> The main thing to notice in the activity of leftists in the labour movement is that their policy is too closely identified with the interests of the worst agents of reaction for there not to be, behind it all, the intrigues and manoeuvres of the men of the trusts who inspire, direct and pay. You only need to ask who benefits from the provocations and attempts to divide the working class to understand the reactionary origin and nature of leftist activity.
>
> It would be a mistake to consider the action of the tiny leftist groups (*petits groupuscules gauchistes*) in the labour movement as negligible or unimportant. Their strength results not from their size but from their links with the enemies of the people. It results from their stubborn determination to provoke, to divide and to confuse. It results from their lies and their slanders. It finds support among the backward and reactionary masses and in the anarchistic conceptions of certain petty-bourgeois strata. In these circumstances it would be a serious mistake to display an outdated liberalism in dealing with such elements.[36]

The tone is strikingly similar to that of the party's and the CGT's reaction to a later wave of wildcat strikes and leftist agitation in the factories, during and after 1968.

The party did not confine itself to rhetorical denunciation. On occasion it worked actively to defeat strikes—for instance the printing strike of January 1946, during which *L'Humanité* tried to carry on publication and one of its distribution vans was actually stopped by pickets. On 1 February 1946 the paper even appeared with blank spaces, where its criticisms of the strike had been censored by its own printers. (The censored criticisms included a reprint of a broadcast in which Ambroise Croizat, the Communist Minister of Labour, pointed out that throughout the occupation the printers had produced the collaborationist newspapers without going on strike. Thorez had used the same argument in cabinet, in an outburst which astonished his colleagues and helped persuade them to reject the printers' wage demand.) The Communists then resorted to distributing anti-strike leaflets, but this too was forcibly prevented by the angry workers.[37]

Another strike carried out successfully in spite of Communist opposition was the postal strike of July–August 1946, which was run by an unofficial strike committee in defiance of the Communist leaders of the postmen's union. This time the SFIO exploited the Communists' discomfiture by supporting the strikers. The effects could be seen in the social security elections a few weeks later, when support for the union leadership had clearly declined since the previous congress. In fact the leadership got less than 40% of the votes among the higher-paid postal workers (*fonctionnaires et agents des PTT*), being outvoted by the pro-strike *Liste d'indépendance et démocratie syndicale*. Interestingly it retained its control of the union thanks to the support of the less well-off workers (*facteurs et agents des lignes*) who were apparently more willing to accept the PCF's moderate line.[38]

There can be little doubt that this line alienated some of the workers who had previously been among the party's active supporters. Lecoeur tells us that in the Nord-Pas-de-Calais coalfield many militants stopped attending party cell meetings in 1945—'militants who were conscientious and hard-working and had shown it at other times'—and did not reappear until after the Communist ministers had left the government, during the great strikes of 1947.[39] But on the whole the party was fairly successful in deflecting working-class anger on to aspects of the economic situation for which it contrived to blame the other parties in the government. In any case it knew that so long as the Socialists were sharing responsibility for government policy it would have no serious rival for working-class support, at any rate in electoral terms. As Thorez was to explain many years later: 'we had with us almost the whole of the working class, but you can't make a revolution with the working class alone. We had to win over the middle classes and the farmers. . . .'[40]

The PCF's moderation and concern for national interest extended also to colonial affairs. It condemned the nationalist riots in Algeria in May 1945 as 'a fascist conspiracy'.[41] It asserted that France 'is and ought to remain a great African power'.[42] It argued that the colonial peoples would be better off in a free union with a democratic France than left to the mercy of the 'powerful desires' of Anglo-Saxon capitalism.[43] And though during the second half of 1946 their government colleagues were increasingly irritated by the Communists' vociferous support for Ho Chi Minh, this support was given in the belief and hope that Ho's aims could best be realized within a loosely-structured French union headed by a 'democratic' (i.e. partly socialist) France. In the spring of 1946 Thorez astonished the head of the Cochin Chinese delegation to Paris by telling him 'that the Communist Party under no circumstances wished to be considered as the eventual liquidator of the French position in Indo-China and that he ardently wished to see the French flag fly over all corners of the French Union'.[44]

Within the government, Thorez frequently played a conciliatory role, sometimes ostentatiously cooling the reforming zeal of his Communist colleagues, sometimes opposing 'demagogic' proposals for nationalizations or other structural reforms put forward by the Socialists (or before April 1945 by Pierre Mendès France), sometimes bitterly denouncing strikers and urging the government to stand firm against them. All his colleagues were impressed by his 'statesmanlike' qualities.[45]

THE CONSTITUTION

Believing that it would be able to dominate a directly elected National Assembly, the PCF worked to achieve a constitution in which such an assembly would have supreme power, without checks or balances.[46] It opposed all suggestions for a second chamber, an independent executive, or any body with a right to query the constitutionality of the assembly's decisions. It hoped to obtain the constitution it wanted from a constituent assembly which would itself be directly elected and enjoy unfettered sovereign powers, whereas de Gaulle wanted an assembly with limited powers whose work would be subject to ratification by popular vote. The battle on this issue was fought out during the summer of 1945 within the government and in the Consultative Assembly, with the Socialists acting as a somewhat indecisive referee. The result was something of a draw. The Communists were forced to accept a referendum, held simultaneously with the election of the assembly, which gave the people the chance to limit its powers and duration; but de Gaulle had to accept that the proposed limits would still allow the assembly to overthrow the government and to propose legislation on its own initiative.[47] By this concession he managed to obtain a lukewarm official support from the SFIO for a 'Yes' vote in the referendum.[48] The Communists were left almost alone in campaigning for a 'No', and were defeated by a two-to-one majority (21 October 1945).

The significance of this defeat was at first eclipsed by the fact that Communists and Socialists together had an overall majority in the new assembly. The Communists succeeded in persuading the Socialists to work in close alliance with them on the drafting of the constitution, and thus were able to push through a constitution almost entirely to their taste, with a single, omnipotent National Assembly and a purely ceremonial president of the Republic. But in their anxiety to lock the Socialists into a tight exclusive alliance with themselves, they made the mistake of refusing even token concessions to the third government party, the MRP. The MRP was thus driven to oppose the draft constitution in the referendum on it which had to be held under the terms of the law adopted in the previous referendum. This split in the government was more or less deliberately engineered by the PCF, which wanted the adoption of the new constitution to be a clear victory for Socialists and Communists against the MRP.* But in the event some 600,000 Socialist voters refused to follow their party into this alliance,[49] and the proposed constitution was rejected (5 May 1946).

In political terms this defeat probably marked the decisive failure of the Communist strategy, for the SFIO was never to recover from it, and never again did the two Marxist parties together have an overall majority in the French parliament. In constitutional terms, however, the defeat was not decisive. In the new draft produced by the second Constituent Assembly the MRP was able to introduce a second chamber and to give some powers to the president of the Republic.

* Georgette Elgey (*La République des Illusions*, p. 199) quotes Thorez as telling Gouin: 'Why worry about the People's Republicans? You know we can manage without them!'

But in essence the constitution remained as the PCF wanted it, with all important powers concentrated in the directly elected National Assembly. Although the Communists initially attacked the new draft as being 'Gaullist', they immediately rallied to its defence when de Gaulle himself denounced it,[50] and it was with their support that it was adopted both by the assembly (29 September) and by the people (13 October). The battleground of parliamentary democracy, on which the PCF was to be routed in 1947, was the ground which it had itself chosen.

'THOREZ AU POUVOIR!'

As soon as the October 1945 election had made it the largest parliamentary party, and even before the resignation of de Gaulle, the PCF asserted its right to the leadership of the government and suggested that Thorez should become prime minister. This however was a purely tactical move, for the Communists knew that the Socialists, whom they had vigorously attacked during the referendum and election campaign, were not yet ready to accept a subordinate role in a Communist-led government. The Communists' immediate aim was to get rid of de Gaulle and to split the Socialists from the MRP.[51]

To this end, they next suggested a Socialist prime minister, in the person of Félix Gouin, who had just been elected president of the Constituent Assembly. But this did not seduce the Socialists, who insisted that the government must have the support of all three big parties in the new assembly—Communists, Socialists and MRP. The MRP for its part would have no prime minister but de Gaulle, and the Communists were obliged to accept this in order not to exclude themselves from the government altogether (13 November 1945). Nor, as we have seen (above, p. 344), did they succeed in obtaining from de Gaulle any of the three 'big' ministries. But, by staging a crisis on this issue, they did succeed (19 November) in manoeuvring the assembly into giving de Gaulle an 'imperative mandate' to form 'a government composed essentially of the three parties . . . with the portfolios shared equitably among them'. De Gaulle accepted this only reluctantly, since it was clear that from now on the policy of the government would depend more on the parties than on himself. Within two months he had decided that he could not govern in such circumstances, and he resigned (20 January 1946).[52]

351

Once again, the Communists put forward Thorez as a candidate for the premiership. The MRP predictably refused, whereupon the Communists again proposed a two-party Communist-Socialist coalition. The Socialists again insisted on the inclusion of the MRP, but without de Gaulle there was serious doubt whether the MRP would agree to join. Some of its leaders were tempted to follow de Gaulle into opposition, calculating that this would either hasten his return to power or at least strengthen their own position in the next elections. This was perhaps the nearest that the PCF ever came to achieving its aim, and it was precisely the fear that a Socialist-Communist coalition would lead to a people's democracy —reinforced by General Billotte's letter to Maurice Schumann (see above, p. 330)—which finally persuaded the MRP to stay in the government under a Socialist prime minister. The Communists too accepted this, but they rejected the candidate first proposed by the SFIO, the strongly anti-Communist Vincent Auriol, and obtained instead the easygoing Félix Gouin, who, unlike de Gaulle, allowed each party to choose its own ministers for the portfolios assigned to it. In return for this, and in order to avoid prolonging a ministerial crisis which might have given de Gaulle a chance to return, the PCF this time made no attempt to secure one of the three 'big' departments.[53]

It continued, however, to regard the three-party coalition as temporary, and did everything possible to divide the SFIO from the MRP. This was clearly the motive for its intransigence on the constitutional issue, which finally forced the MRP to oppose the Socialist-Communist draft constitution both on the floor of the Assembly and in the ensuing referendum campaign. During this campaign (April–May 1946) the Communists did not conceal their expectation that the victory of the left on the constitutional issue would be followed by a political victory. Jacques Duclos warned that those who voted against the constitution would 'appear as the enemies of the country, as the people of disorder',[54] and the cry 'Thorez au pouvoir!' was regularly heard at Communist meetings.[55] This was a serious tactical error, which undoubtedly helped to ensure the constitution's defeat. This in turn threw the Socialists into a mood of strongly anti-Communist recrimination, and although it was they and not the Communists who paid the penalty at the elections (2 June), that was little consolation to the PCF. Not only had its alliance with the SFIO broken up, but even if reconstituted it would no longer have an overall majority in the

Assembly. Moreover the MRP had now overtaken the PCF as the largest party.

The Communists were thus thrown on to the defensive, and tried to maintain the Gouin government in office. But Gouin, who wished to avoid taking responsibility for an unmanageable situation,[56] insisted on handing over to the MRP. The Communists looked on helplessly while Bidault was elected premier (19 June), and then agreed to serve under him (22 June) after only a token demand for one of the three 'big' ministries.[57] On constitutional issues they now found themselves outvoted by an MRP-Socialist alliance, and after some hesitation they fell into line behind this in order to defend the parliamentary republic against the more radical onslaught mounted from outside the Assembly by de Gaulle. Not until the constitution was safely ratified by the people (13 October) were they free to resume their drive for power.

Even then their election campaign (the third in just over a year) was a relatively defensive one, emphasizing the fight against rising prices and the need for working-class unity to prevent the MRP from carrying out its slogan of a 'Bidault-without-Thorez' government.[58] This moderation, combined with the declining prestige of the other two government parties, paid off handsomely. In the elections held on 10 November the PCF increased its share of the vote to 28%, becoming once again 'le premier parti de France'.

Greatly encouraged, it renewed its call for a Thorez government, this time apparently in earnest. It was at this point that Thorez outlined his plans for the fusion of the Communist and Socialist Parties and the creation of a 'démocratie nouvelle et populaire' to the correspondent of *The Times* (see above, p. 332). At diplomatic receptions Thorez could be seen button-holing fellow-deputies, reminding them of his responsible record in government, and urging them to vote for him as prime minister. Apparently he had genuine hopes that, as the candidate of the Communist and Socialist Parties, he would somehow or other attract the further thirty-seven votes needed to give him the requisite overall majority. He expected them to come from 'republicans'—presumably not in the well-disciplined MRP but in the looser ranks of the Radicals and the UDSR, who had sixty-six deputies between them. In fact, however, the SFIO would almost certainly not have agreed to vote for him had it not been confident that there was no chance of him being elected. As it was it did so only after heated discussion, and several conscientious

353

objectors were exempted from the party whip, so that in the event Thorez fell short of a majority by fifty-one votes (4 December 1946).[59]

The Communists had thus to renounce any hope of winning the leadership of the new Assembly, at least for the time being. But at first it seemed that they had at least the negative power to prevent the formation of a government they did not like. Bidault was defeated even more easily than Thorez. There was as yet no coherent majority without the Communists. Seeing this, they tried once again to obtain one of the 'big' ministries, but the MRP refused to serve under any prime minister who would grant this request. After a prolonged crisis, during which Léon Blum served as caretaker prime minister at the head of a one-party Socialist government, the Communists accepted a face-saving compromise: Billoux was given the title of defence minister but virtually without powers (23 January 1947).[60]

It was obvious that the PCF now wanted simply to stay in the government in order to keep its options open but, as the international situation deteriorated, it was able to exert less and less influence on government policy. Moreover the new government, headed by the right-wing Socialist Paul Ramadier, was no longer a three-party coalition but included Radicals and conservatives as well. The pendulum was swinging back to the right. The PCF's effort to split the Socialists from the other parties and to create a governing majority under its own leadership had completely failed.

Defeat

DEFEAT IN PARLIAMENT

In retrospect, this failure is less surprising than the fact that the strategy was ever expected to succeed. Once de Gaulle had had the sense to choose a proportional electoral system in 1945, the chances of the PCF obtaining a parliamentary majority on its own were negligible. To obtain the majority it wanted, it had therefore to obtain the co-operation of other parties, voluntary or otherwise, and in the last resort it had no means of doing this. Its powers of physical intimidation were strictly limited after the first chaotic weeks of the Liberation, once the bulk of the FTP had been incorporated into the regular army and the *Milices Patriotiques* had been disbanded.

On the other hand its powers of moral intimidation should not be underestimated. It required considerable moral courage to stand up to the Communist Party in 1944–6, and it is to the great credit of the leaders of the other parties that they did not lose their nerve. This is especially true of the Socialist leaders, on whom the moral pressure was often intense. Attacks on them from the Communists themselves were constantly echoed from inside their own party. The generation of Socialist militants which emerged from the Resistance contained a large number of convinced Marxists who were obsessed with the idea of the unity of the working class. They were infuriated to see their party being discredited yet again in the eyes of the working class by Communist propaganda which presented it as a party of bourgeois compromisers, and constantly urged their leaders not to allow the Communists this luxury.

Ironically enough the spokesman of this new generation was Guy Mollet, who in September 1946 captured the post of general secretary of the party. The parliamentary leaders often had to make tactical concessions to his point of view, but in the main they resisted both his pressure and that of the Communists, at considerable cost to their popularity inside and outside the SFIO. With only two important exceptions—the campaign for the first draft constitution in the spring of 1946 and the platonic vote for Thorez as prime minister in December—they refused to form an exclusive alliance with the Communists and insisted on maintaining co-operation with the MRP.

This attitude was easily attacked as opportunistic, since in the short run it gave the SFIO a key role as the linchpin of successive governments, thereby keeping its leaders constantly in high office, making three of them prime ministers (Gouin, Blum, Ramadier) and one the first president of the Fourth Republic (Auriol). But most of them were lucid enough to read the message of their steadily deteriorating election results and to know that in the long run Mollet was right. By deciding to resist the Communist strategy in co-operation with the bourgeois parties, they condemned the SFIO to serve as the guardian of the capitalist order until that order was strong enough to do without it, by which time many of its supporters had been alienated for good. But they made this sacrifice to a large extent consciously, because they knew that the alternative was to co-operate in the creation of a people's democracy, in which the Communist Party would sooner or later swallow them up.

It is a curious fact that the SFIO, unlike some of its counterparts in eastern Europe, unlike several of the non-Communist French Resistance movements, unlike even the *confédéré* faction in the CGT,

355

was not to any significant extent infiltrated during the Resistance by crypto-Communists. Whether this was due to its own vigilance or to the contempt in which the Communists themselves held it, is not clear. If the latter, this must be reckoned one of the PCF's major blunders. But underestimation of its Socialist rival has been a more or less permanent characteristic of the PCF, from the early 1920s right through to 1981.

In the final scene of the parliamentary drama, the PCF was outwitted by a Socialist prime minister and a Socialist president of the Republic—Paul Ramadier and Vincent Auriol—but almost saved by the obtuseness of the general secretary of the Socialist Party. A series of events in the spring of 1947 convinced the Communists that their position in the Ramadier government was untenable. It was engaged in a war against the local Communists in Indochina. It brutally suppressed a nationalist uprising in Madagascar. The announcement of the Truman doctrine in March made it clear that there was to be a world confrontation between the United States and the Soviet Union, and after the deadlock at the Moscow conference in April France came down unequivocally on the western side. Finally the government's policy of wage restraint was causing the Communists to lose ground to Trotskyists in various industrial disputes, the most important being in the Renault factory at Billancourt.

After a series of votes in which the Communist ministers supported the government while the rest of the party abstained or voted against, on 4 May, in a confidence vote on the government's economic policy, the Communist ministers broke solidarity and voted against the government to which they belonged. 'The Communist Party,' declared Jacques Duclos, 'has the right to think that if a Communist-led government had not been prevented events might have developed differently. . . .' Clearly Thorez expected that Ramadier would have to resign, and that the rules of the parliamentary game would then oblige the president of the Republic to send for him, Thorez, as leader of the party responsible for the crisis, and ask him to try and form a government.

Guy Mollet too thought that Ramadier should resign, and the SFIO's *Comité Directeur* passed a motion to that effect. But Ramadier and Auriol had planned it otherwise, and the Socialist parliamentary group managed to persuade the *Comité Directeur* to change its mind. Ramadier then proceeded with his plan. Since the Communist ministers refused to resign, he informed them that 'by virtue of the

356

powers which the Constitution confers on me, I withdraw the delegation of powers which I had accorded to our Communist comrades, and I shall replace them.' Next day the *Journal Officiel* announced that their functions 'are considered as having ended, following the vote which they cast in the National Assembly on 4 May 1947'.

On 6 May, after twelve hours' discussion, the National Council of the SFIO rejected Mollet's demand for the government's resignation. 'The Socialist party', commented François Mauriac, 'is a party worthy of Corneille: trapped between duty and self-interest, it invariably chooses duty.'[61]

The government carried on, and the PCF was forced to recognize that a parliamentary majority existed to which it did not belong. Even if Ramadier had resigned, that would still probably have been true. There would probably have been a long ministerial crisis, but Thorez would have been no more able to obtain a majority than he had been in November, and in the end a government without the Communists would have been formed. Even Guy Mollet admitted that the coalition with the Communists had become untenable: he simply wanted the parliamentary game to be played according to the rules. But that would not have altered the fact that the Communist parliamentary strategy was bankrupt.

DEFEAT ON THE BARRICADES

The PCF itself was strangely slow to admit this. On 8 May Duclos described its absence from the government as 'momentary', and added: 'People who talk of a general strike in France are imbeciles.'[62] There was no general strike, but the party switched from discouraging to encouraging particular strikes, clearly hoping to demonstrate that the country was ungovernable without its help. 'No government can be strong today if it does not have the confidence and support of the working class,' warned Fajon.[63] 'Because the people approve of us for having defended their interests and those of the Republic, we will return to the government,' declared Thorez, promising both to grant the workers' demands and to restore order.[64] At the party's Eleventh Congress, which opened in Strasbourg on 25 June, the image of a government party was carefully sustained. While Thorez was greeted with the familiar rhythmic shout of 'Thorez au pouvoir!', Cachin enquired rhetorically 'par quelle aberration on a pu se priver d'un tel homme d'État' (how they could think of doing without such a statesman).[65] Duclos asserted, 'In truth, the people of France demands that our country return to a democratic government, in conformity with the wishes of universal suffrage. There and not elsewhere lies the key to national salvation.'

Thorez and his colleagues seem genuinely to have believed that their eviction from the government was an 'aberration' by the French Socialist leaders, and not to have seen that it was no longer possible for France to keep a foot in each of the Soviet and American camps. Even after the Soviet Union and its satellites had rejected the offer of Marshall Aid, Thorez did not realize that they would object to France accepting it. 'How could any Frenchman not accept with satisfaction the aid of our American friends?' he asked on 24 July. 'How could we refuse the help which is offered us for the reconstruction of our country?'[66]

It was not until the founding meeting of the Cominform at Szklarska Poreba, Poland, in September, that the PCF realized how badly out of step with the Soviet leadership it had got. The French delegates, Duclos and Fajon, heard Zhdanov explain that the world was now divided between the imperialist camp headed by the United States and the democratic camp headed by the Soviet Union, that the Truman Doctrine and the Marshall Plan were simply the concrete expression of American expansionism, and that the role of the Communist Parties in the West was to lead the resistance against American domination and to 'unmask resolutely all the auxiliaries of American imperialism', especially right-wing Socialists such as Blum and Ramadier. From these generalities the Yugoslav delegates, Kardelj and Djilas, went on to deduce that the PCF in particular had so far failed miserably in its task, allowing itself to be duped first by de Gaulle, then by Blum and Ramadier, and even now still presenting itself as a government party. Duclos was obliged to pronounce an abject self-criticism on behalf of his party, confessing to 'opportunism, legalitarianism, parliamentary illusions', and promised that from now on it would mobilize the people against American imperialism.[67]

The message was duly relayed to Thorez, who confessed his faults in public on 29 October: 'We did not emphasize with the necessary force that we were only expelled from the government on the express orders of the American reaction. As a result of this initial mistake we did not at first pitilessly unmask the behaviour of the Socialist leaders and of the various government parties, as being a real ignominy, a shameful betrayal of national interests.'[68] From now on, any possibility of compromise with the Socialists or the other government parties was clearly ruled out.

For the next two months, France was the scene of a series of frighteningly violent strikes and riots. All the class hatred which the PCF had so strenuously bottled up during the period of *tripartisme* was suddenly released. An atmosphere close to civil war was created, and at times the government's ability to maintain order seemed in serious doubt. But once again the non-Communist politicians did not lose their nerve, in spite of a ministerial crisis at the height of a near-general strike. A new government took office on 24 November under Robert Schuman, with the Socialist Jules Moch as Minister of the Interior. He threw himself into the battle against the Communist strikers with amazing vigour and ferocity. Though often far from sure of the loyalty of his police he managed to break the strike, earning in the process the undying hatred of a large section of the French working class, as well as the sobriquet 'Moch-la-matraque'.

Yet on the Communist side there was no sign of any attempt at a general insurrection or *coup d'état*: nothing more spectacular than an all-night sit-in by Communist deputies in the Palais Bourbon. The Communists knew well that France was in the heart of the 'American camp', and that they had no military forces at their disposal. Their instructions were simply to make trouble, and this they did with great bravado, expecting worse punishment than they in fact got. They were probably even more frightened of the government than it was of them. The Minister of Labour, Daniel Mayer, was amazed when in the middle of a discussion in his office at the height of the strike, one of the CGT leaders suddenly lay down on the carpet and announced: 'I know you're going to have us arrested. Well, you can have me arrested in your own office. I shan't leave here till your police come and get me.' When Mayer assured him that no one was going to arrest him there or anywhere else, he was astonished and incredulous.[69]

The government was equally astonished when the CGT suddenly called off the general strike on 9 December, at a moment when from the government point of view the situation still seemed extremely serious. It was clear, however, that the strike had been getting increasingly unpopular with workers, both because of its blatantly political nature and because of the widespread violence and intimidation which accompanied it. One effect was a new split in the CGT, with the anti-Communist minority seceding under Jouhaux's leadership (though against his personal inclination) to form *Force Ouvrière*, with financial help from the American trade unions and also from various employers' organizations in France.[70]

More generally, the strike confirmed the political isolation of the PCF, whose unpopularity kept pace with that of the Soviet Union under the impact of the events of the next two years: the *coup* in Prague, the attacks on Tito, the political trials in Bulgaria, the Berlin blockade. Not until the 1970s would the French Communist Party again become a credible contender for governmental office.

EPILOGUE

The Years of Frustration

1947–1981

Return to the 'Ghetto'

1946 marked a peak in the PCF's fortunes from almost every point of view. Over 800,000 membership cards were sold in that year, according to the Central Committee's report to the Eleventh Congress, held the following June. We may be fairly sure that the membership declined thereafter, for subsequent congresses were not supplied with comparable figures. Not until 1974 did Georges Marchais, as general secretary, give an estimate of the number of cards actually issued to and paid for by individuals (i.e. the number of actual party members). It was then about 450,000, and this figure was presented as a major recruiting achievement.[1] In between, the only figure given was that for the number of cards requested by local federations, and this has never again passed the million mark as it did in 1946. It declined steadily to a low point of 389,000 in 1955, then held remarkably stable between 400,000 and 430,000 until 1968 when it rose to just over 450,000.[2] Here again it held steady until 1972 when it began to rise more rapidly, reaching half a million in 1974. The relationship between this figure and actual membership was clearly not a constant one, but it has been calculated that the latter reached a low point of less than 200,000 (if correct, the lowest since 1935) in 1961 and then began to climb again.[3]

The 28.6% of votes cast won by the PCF in the general election of November 1946 has likewise never been equalled since. During the lifetime of the Fourth Republic the party held the support of a quarter of the French electorate, but the return of de Gaulle to power in 1958 made serious inroads. In the election of that year the Communist vote

Much of the material in this chapter has been published as 'Un Socialisme aux Couleurs de la France' in P. Filo Della Torre, E. Mortimer, and J. Story (eds.), *Eurocommunism: Myth or Reality* (Milan, 1978; London, 1979).

361

fell to 18.9%. In 1962 it recovered to 21.7%, and oscillated around that figure until 1981 when it dropped to fifteen.

1946 was also the year in which the PCF came closest to being in power in France. Its influence within the government diminished rapidly in the first months of 1947, and after its ejection from the government in May it quickly found itself thrust into a marginal position in French politics. During the Cold War there was never the slightest doubt where its loyalties lay—and, given France's geo-political situation, it was on the wrong side. Association with the Soviet Union soon became as much a liability in France as it had been an asset in 1945. Not that there was ever a full-scale McCarthyist witch-hunt in France (though there certainly were large-scale dismissals of strikers, especially in the northern coalfield after the long and traumatic strike of autumn 1948). The party's popular support, the prestige of the intellectuals who were or had been associated with it, and indeed the genuine liberalism of many of its opponents, were all too strong for that. But after 1947 there were few careers in which it helped to be a Communist (except, of course, the party itself and the CGT) and many in which it was a definite hindrance.

Even among that substantial section of the French intelligentsia which opposed both the Cold War and American influence in Europe, the PCF's credibility was greatly diminished by its subservient copying of every detail of Stalinist propaganda. The *coup* in Prague, the attacks on Tito, the political trials in Bulgaria, Hungary, Czechoslovakia, the Berlin blockade: all were faithfully defended by a well-disciplined band of French Communist scribblers under the guidance of a specially delegated member of the *Bureau Politique*, Laurent Casanova. 'Le génial Staline' himself was the subject of endless eulogies, while Maurice Thorez, as 'le meilleur des Staliniens français', was treated to a personality cult of his own. The existence of forced labour camps in the Soviet Union was first denied, then minimized, while those who sought to publicize it were subjected to hysterical vituperation. Scarcely less violent was the denunciation of those who dared to question the authenticity of Lysenko's biological discoveries, or to criticize the 'socialist realist' art which alone had the seal of Zhdanov's approval.[4]

And, as in the 1920s, the purges of Communist leaders in Russia and eastern Europe were replicated in France, the victims in both cases being often former leaders of wartime Resistance or veterans of the Spanish Civil War, or both. The most spectacular case was the sudden disgrace of Marty and Tillon, who in 1952 were accused of 'fractional' activity and subjected to a kind of internal Moscow trial in the *Bureau Politique*. Both were known to have had reservations about Thorez's option for an exclusively parliamentary road to socialism in 1944, and to be disgruntled at the prominence assumed by Jeanette Vermeersch-Thorez during her husband's prolonged illness and convalescence in the USSR. This must have made them a convenient choice when the leadership felt the need to prove to Stalin that it was duly vigilant in seeking out traitors even in its own bosom. Happily, since the PCF was not in power it could not go to the lengths of imprisoning or executing its traitors, but once their characters had been suitably blackened in the party press they became non-persons, and their past achievements were carefully erased from all party documents.

The Long Road Back: Unity of the Left

The PCF was thus relegated, or relegated itself, to the margin of French political life—almost as it had been before 1934, or in 1939–40. In 1954, for instance, Pierre Mendès France not only refused the offer of Communist support for his government but undertook in advance not to count the Communist votes in his favour when calculating whether or not he had a majority in the National Assembly. This was undoubtedly frustrating and humiliating for a leader like Thorez, who so recently had gloried in the title of deputy prime minister and believed himself close to establishing in France a 'démocratie nouvelle et populaire'. But he had at least the negative satisfaction of seeing that his party was now so strong that its non-participation decisively altered the balance of French politics. France could no longer be governed by a *Cartel des Gauches* excluding the PCF. The non-Communist left could now govern only in alliance with so-called centre parties which in fact were on the right.

Thus Mendès France, though widely regarded as the leader of a 'new left', did not attempt to form a left-wing government in 1954. His government was a centre coalition based on a heterogeneous parliamentary majority brought together by the need to end the Vietnam war and by hostility to the proposed European Defence Community. Once those two issues were disposed of it soon broke up. Similarly the Mollet government of 1956, ostensibly a centre-left coalition under Socialist leadership and at first enjoying Communist support, soon drifted to the right and eventually fell, being replaced by centre-right coalitions led by right-wing Radicals, in part at least because without the Communists it had only a relative majority. Many on the non-Communist left deplored Mollet's hard-line policy in Algeria, and believed, rightly or wrongly, that such a policy would not have been adopted by a genuine left-wing government based on a united working class. This feeling was strengthened in 1958 by the collapse of the Fourth Republic, which many believed a united left would have been able to avert.

It was thus natural that the PCF should see in a revival of the traditional left-right polarization of French politics its best hope of escaping from the 'ghetto' to which the Cold War had condemned it. The first condition for its success was provided by the drift to the right, and then decline, of the MRP, which as a 'social catholic' party appeared in the immediate post-war period to have broken the classic left-right mould. The MRP was the victim partly of the identification of some of its leaders with a hard-line colonial policy, and partly of the resurfacing of old quarrels of issues of church and state—particularly the question of state subsidies to church schools—which might have been thought obsolete.

Significantly, this issue was exploited somewhat cynically by both Communists and Gaullists in order to split the centre coalition (*Troisième Force*) from which they were both excluded. In the short term the manoeuvre failed, but in the long term it paid off. The victory of Mendès France in 1954 (initially supported by both Gaullists and Communists, united in their hatred of the European Defence Community) was essentially the defeat of the MRP—the first Fourth Republic government to exclude it. Thereafter the *Troisième Force* was really dead, lacking the strong centre party needed to hold it together, and the Fourth Republic gradually disintegrated under the strain of the Algerian war.

De Gaulle's return to power in 1958 brought the PCF its first major—and for the most part permanent—loss of electoral support since 1932. But it also brought both political and institutional conditions favourable to the revival of a united left. De Gaulle reintroduced the *scrutin d'arrondissement*—the two-ballot, single-member-constituency electoral system. His object in so doing was to weaken the political parties (whose power had been strengthened by the use of proportional representation with party lists since 1945) and to favour the election of independent deputies who would take a lead from the executive rather than from party machines. This tactic succeeded beyond his expectations. What happened in fact was that a new Gaullist party came into existence which became the dominant element in a new majority of the moderate right. The Radicals were reduced to a rump. The MRP gradually disintegrated, and the Socialists, finding themselves powerless to influence the new government, went into opposition. There was thus now a predominantly right-wing government facing a predominantly left-wing opposition.

Then, in 1962, anxious to strengthen the executive still further, de Gaulle proposed to have the president of the Republic elected directly by the people. All the traditional parties (between them still forming a majority in parliament) opposed this, but de Gaulle bypassed parliament and had his constitutional amendment approved by the electorate in a referendum. This was followed by a general election fought largely on the same issue (being provoked by a parliamentary vote of censure on the government for calling the referendum). The Socialists, who had been damaged by the new electoral system in 1958, announced that this time on the second ballot they would withdraw in favour of the best-placed opposition candidate in each constituency, even where this meant supporting a Communist.

This was the breakthrough the PCF had been waiting for. It quickly announced that it would return the compliment, and in fact even withdrew some of its candidates who were narrowly ahead on the first ballot in favour of other opposition candidates who had a better chance of rallying moderate voters. The old tradition of 'republican discipline' was thus revived, and though de Gaulle's supporters won the election both Socialists and Communists were able to win back many of the seats they had lost in 1958.

Direct election of the president of the Republic (also on a two-ballot system) proved a further stimulus in the same direction. The Socialists did not immediately resign themselves to an alliance with the PCF, of whose intentions many of them remained deeply suspicious. They first attempted to construct a centre-left alternative to Gaullism around a Socialist presidential candidate, Gaston Defferre. But this attempt broke down in 1965 without being put to the test of an actual election, because a political consensus between the SFIO and the centre parties involved (mainly the rump of the MRP) could not be found. The Socialists realized that the centre of gravity of this reconstituted *Troisième Force* would still be too far to the right, and would prevent them from competing effectively with the PCF as a party of the left and of the working class.

The implication of this discovery was paradoxical: that the Socialists could compete effectively with the Communists only by accepting an alliance with them. The man who grasped this paradox earliest and with greatest clarity, and acted on it most consistently, was François Mitterrand—a man who, by a further paradox, came not from within the Socialist Party but from the ill-structured middle ground of Fourth Republic politics. In the wake of Defferre's failure, Mitterrand put himself forward (after discreetly sounding out both SFIO and PCF) as candidate of the left. While ruling out any negotiations on his programme, he made it clear that he would be happy to accept Communist support. On 23 September 1965 the PCF Central Committee decided officially to support him.

Communist and non-Communist left thus embarked on a partnership which was to last through twelve years of storms and upheavals, but without resolving its fundamental contradictions and ambiguities. It is clear that the two partners went into it with different aims and expectations, for whatever the PCF wanted it was surely not to help Mitterrand build a new and stronger Socialist Party that could effectively challenge the PCF's predominance on the left and its leadership of the working class. The PCF leaders no doubt understood that this was Mitterrand's intention, for he made no secret of it. But they probably calculated that his chances of succeeding were not good. The SFIO in 1965 was a party tired and discredited by its record of participation in *Troisième Force* governments, riven by internal quarrels and jealousies, deserted in disgust by many of its more talented leaders or potential leaders. Guy Mollet, its general secretary since 1946, was particularly associated in the public mind with the compromises of the Fourth Republic and the Algerian war. Yet his manipulative skills enabled him to remain in control of the party; indeed Defferre's failure had strengthened his hold. If he supported Mitterrand it was at least in part because a presidential candidate outside the party was unlikely to pose any serious threat to his own position inside it. He could be relied on to resist any attempt by Mitterrand to rejuvenate the SFIO or to absorb it in a broader-based party. It was therefore reasonable to expect that within a united left the PCF would remain easily the strongest force, that the other parties would serve essentially as channels for attracting voters to an alliance in which the PCF would set the tone, and that when such an alliance eventually came to power France would be able to resume the march towards a 'démocratie nouvelle et populaire' so untowardly interrupted in 1946–7. Then the PCF's allies had been prepared to ditch it on the instigation of the United States. Next time things would be different: the PCF itself and the French people would be on their guard against American imperialism, which de Gaulle himself was now taking steps to resist. The PCF's allies, this time elected on a clear left-wing programme, would not be able to renege without completely discrediting themselves in the eyes of the voters.

The Common Programme

Such, broadly, was the strategy that the PCF pursued from 1965 to 1977, with a consistency sometimes obscured by its abrupt variations in tactics. Periods when no sacrifice was too great to be made for the overriding cause of left-wing unity alternated with periods when the party's militants had to be reassured and its allies firmly reminded about its true priorities. One constant theme was that efforts to reach understanding with the other parties of the left must be combined with ever greater efforts to strengthen the party itself. Another was the need for the left to present itself to the country not merely united by sentiment or by tactical self-interest but by a programme of precise commitments which could not be gone back on. Two years before the 1965 presidential election, the PCF was already urging the need for a 'common programme of the left', and declaring that only on the basis of such a programme could it support a non-Communist presidential candidate.[5] In fact its leaders were realistic enough to know that the non-Communist left would not accept such an idea overnight, and that the goal would have to be approached by stages. The first stage was the agreement to support Mitterrand on the basis of a set of essentially reformist 'options' unilaterally announced by him (they included France's continued membership of both NATO and the EEC) and of his willingness to accept and publicly acknowledge Communist support. This looked very like giving something for nothing, and caused a good deal of grumbling among the party faithful. A section of the Communist Students' Union had even to be dissolved and its leaders (who turned out to be crypto-Trotskyists) expelled.

But the gamble taken by the party leaders paid off. Mitterrand did unexpectedly well in the election, winning 32% of the votes on the first ballot and 45% in a run-off against de Gaulle alone. The morale of the left rose to its highest point since 1956. Unity seemed indeed to be the recipe for success. The non-Communist left took the bait and embarked, albeit hesitantly, on a process of rapprochement with the PCF. The next stage, in December 1966, was a negotiated agreement for the general election of March 1967. The PCF and Mitterrand's *Fédération de la Gauche Démocrate et Socialiste* (an umbrella body comprising the SFIO, the Radicals and his own *Convention des Institutions Républicaines*, with a sprinkling of independent left-wing clubs) would each have their own candidates on the first ballot but on the second there would be only one candidate of the left (normally the one who had done best on the first ballot) in each constituency. This electoral pact was coupled with a political 'constat de convergence' which fell well short of a common programme but still committed the non-Communists to such measures as the nationalization of the merchant banks and the arms industry.

Again, the bargain proved profitable to both sides. The voters transferred their votes on the second ballot with unexpected discipline in both directions, and Communist and non-Communist left gained thirty-one seats each. De Gaulle's supporters all but lost their overall majority. Thus encouraged, the non-Communists agreed to move on to a third stage: a 'common platform', published in February 1968. Once again, this fell short of a common programme, for it listed not only points of agreement but also points of disagreement—notably on foreign policy and on the extent of a future left-wing government's nationalization programme. But the agreement was clearly intended as a step towards a left-wing government which would include Communists and would be committed to a radical transformation of French society.

At this point the process received a severe set-back in the shape of the 'events' of May–June 1968. A student insurrection, led by leftist groups violently hostile to the PCF's gradualist strategy, sparked off a general strike which the PCF had clearly not expected and which it was able only with considerable difficulty to keep under control. As its leaders had always feared, this kind of extra-parliamentary agitation proved detrimental to the left's electoral fortunes. De Gaulle also foresaw this, called a snap election and inflicted a humiliating defeat on both Communist and non-Communist left. This in turn provoked

368

a furious bout of recrimination within the non-Communist left, which was soon aggravated by reactions to the Soviet invasion of Czechoslovakia. The personality of Mitterrand and the strategy with which he was identified were widely condemned, and the *Fédération de la Gauche* broke up.

It was soon proved, however, that disunity could be even more disastrous than unity. In April 1969 de Gaulle resigned after being defeated in an ill-judged referendum. This was the opportunity the opposition had been waiting for ever since 1962. But the left could not have been less well prepared to exploit it. The SFIO had half-heartedly agreed to join Mitterrand's *Convention* and the various clubs in a 'new' socialist party, but the Radicals wanted no more to do with it and neither wanted to hear of a joint candidate with the PCF. In the event the Radicals decided to support the centre candidate, Alain Poher (a former MRP man), while the Socialists put up Defferre as a specifically social-democratic candidate. The PCF was left with no choice but to put up its own candidate, and chose Duclos (by now aged seventy-two), while Mitterrand refused to endorse anyone. To make matters worse there were two far-left candidates: Michel Rocard of the 'Unified Socialist Party' (PSU) and the Trotskyist Alain Krivine. The result was perfectly calculated to make Mitterrand's and the PCF's point for them. The dispersal of the left's votes left the right unchallenged masters of the field. The Gaullist and centre-right candidates, Pompidou and Poher, came in first and second, and were thus left to contest the run-off ballot between them—with Pompidou an easy winner. Among the left candidates, Duclos did much the best, with 21%, winning back for the PCF some of the votes lost in 1968. Defferre, the official Socialist candidate, won only 5.1% of the votes cast.

The effects took a good deal of time and manoeuvring to work themselves out. But two years later Mitterrand was enthroned as leader of the new Socialist Party (PS), which one year later still (27 June 1972) at last signed with the PCF a 'Common Programme of Government'. This was countersigned a few days afterwards by a movement representing most of the Radical members of parliament (the official apparatus of the Radical Party having meanwhile opted for a centrist alignment).

The PCF with good reason hailed this as a major victory: it had after all been campaigning for it for nearly ten years. It rushed out the Common Programme in paperback form, and launched a major campaign to sell it to the voters. Opinion polls soon showed, however, that it was the Socialists who would reap the main benefit electorally. Against all expectation, Mitterrand was succeeding in his effort to 're-balance' the left. There was even speculation that, for the first time since the war, the Socialist Party might win more votes than the PCF. This proved to be premature. In the general election of March 1973 the PCF won 21.34% of the votes, the PS and its 'Left Radical' allies 20.65%. But this latter figure was a marked improvement on the percentage won by the *Fédération de la Gauche* in 1967, whereas the PCF had recovered only part of the votes lost in 1968. 'For the first time, unity is to our partners' advantage and not ours, or more to theirs than ours,' commented the PCF's new general secretary, Georges Marchais, reviewing the results at a meeting of the Central Committee.[6]

The PCF's reaction was not to abandon the strategy but to shift the emphasis, stressing its own specific virtues, criticizing various signs of Socialist backsliding, but not questioning the basic value or importance of the left-wing alliance. Its big campaign in the latter part of 1973 was for the sale of Marchais's book *Le Défi Démocratique* (The Democratic Challenge), which set out in simple language the party's vision of 'un socialisme aux couleurs de la France'.

When the sudden death of Georges Pompidou plunged France into a new presidential election in the spring of 1974, the PCF came out without hesitation in support of Mitterrand as candidate of the united left, and did everything possible to help him in his campaign, notably by stressing the modesty of its own ambitions: shortly before the second ballot Marchais made it clear that if Mitterrand became president the PCF would not expect more than a third of the cabinet posts, would not seek the prime ministership, and would not even insist on being given one of the three 'big' ministries as it had tried to do in 1945–7.[7]

Only after Mitterrand's hair-breadth defeat by Giscard d'Estaing, it seems, did the PCF leaders become seriously worried, in the autumn of 1974, by the PS's still-rising score in opinion polls and by-elections, and by its success in attracting new currents of socialist opinion, notably from the PSU and from the formerly Catholic trade union movement (CFDT), which was now the CGT's largest rival/partner and which laid great emphasis on the idea of workers' self-management. (The PCF and CGT until 1978 rejected the slogan of *autogestion*, preferring a more classic model of 'democratic management' which allowed for a more tightly planned and centralized economy.) For a year after October 1974 the PCF subjected the PS to constant, even carping criticism and there were bitter quarrels between the two—particularly on the subject of Portugal in the summer of 1975. Then in 1976 and early 1977 the emphasis was again on unity, culminating in the impressive victory of the alliance in the municipal elections of March 1977. Whereupon in summer 1977 the PCF's resentment at being treated as a junior partner by the PS burst out in a new quarrel over the updating of the 1972 common programme for the general election due in March 1978.

Socialism, Pluralism and Freedom

The PCF's option for a 'parliamentary road to socialism', so abundantly emphasized in 1944–7, was put on ice rather than explicitly disavowed during the ensuing period. At the founding meeting of the Cominform in September 1947 it was only the Yugoslavs who criticized the French and Italian parties for failing to transform the struggle against Nazism into revolution. The criticism which mattered, that of Zhdanov, concerned only their failure to recognize the role of American imperialism and to denounce its local allies, especially after their ejection from government in the spring of that year.[8] There is no indication that at any point in or after 1947 the PCF believed that circumstances in France would allow a revolutionary seizure of power. The violent strikes and demonstrations that it organized were intended simply to weaken the 'imperialist camp' in its struggle against the 'democratic' camp. In fact it is difficult to find any evidence in these years for any PCF strategy for achieving power or installing socialism in France by any means at all—probably because this was not an objective in which Stalin was interested.

Not until 1956 did a clear line again emerge from Moscow on the strategy to be adopted by Communist Parties in highly developed capitalist countries, and then it was the Khrushchev line, according to which the corollary of the non-inevitability of wars and the possibility of peaceful co-existence between the blocs was the corresponding possibility of a peaceful road to socialism, brought about by an alliance between Communist and other 'patriotic forces', in particular the social democrats. Whatever their resentment at Khrushchev's denunciation of Stalinism, the PCF leaders had no cause to quarrel with the aspect of his policies, which was largely a reversion to the Stalin line of 1941–7, the line which had carried the PCF to the peak of its power and prestige. It was a line that fitted perfectly with the 'union of the left' strategy which, as we have seen, the PCF was impelled to adopt by national circumstances. And when the union of the left became a reality in the mid-1960s, the PCF was able without inhibitions to reassure its new partners about its belief in democracy and the parliamentary system, and to argue, by referring to Thorez's 1946 interview with *The Times* and other pronouncements of that epoch, that it was no recent convert to such ideas.

The trouble was, of course, that non-Communist politicians were by now well aware that Communists were liable to use words like 'democracy' in a rather special sense. What Thorez had looked forward to in 1946 was, after all, a 'démocratie nouvelle et populaire': a people's democracy. That phrase had acquired a distinctly pejorative connotation in the West as a result of subsequent events in eastern Europe, and therefore the PCF avoided reviving it in a French context. But an attentive reader of the French Communist press could see that, in the PCF's eyes, not only were the Soviet Union and its satellites 'democratic' as well as 'socialist' countries, but also the satellites remained interesting and valid alternatives to the Soviet model. In 1966, for instance, the party explicitly quoted Czechoslovakia as an example of the parliamentary road to social-ism on which it wished France to embark: 'What happened in Czechoslovakia [in 1948] is . . . a confirmation of the possibilities of making Parliament the instrument of the people's wishes. . . . The Parliament elected in 1946 confirmed its confidence in the govern-ment formed by the Communists, thus consecrating the victory of the socialist revolution by constitutional means.'[9] This was presum-ably meant to reassure party veterans that there were good Com-munist precedents for what the party was proposing, rather than to warn any French social democrat who might be so unwise as to cast himself in the role of Masaryk. But in any case leaders like Mitterrand, who had first-hand experience of Communist tactics during the postwar period, needed no such warning. From the moment the union of the left got under way in 1965 the PCF found itself under constant pressure from its allies to make its commitment to democracy more precise, and each step towards effective unity was achieved at the price of new concessions to the 'bourgeois' interpretation of the word.

A key issue for the non-Communist left was acceptance of a multi-party as opposed to a one-party system. On this a first step was made in 1964 when the PCF's Seventeenth Congress rejected the notion that a one-party state was necessary for the construction of socialism.[10] Then in 1966 René Piquet, a candidate member of the *Bureau Politique*, affirmed the PCF's 'respect' for other parties and promised 'to each its place in the common struggle but also after the struggle'.[11] This pledge was given more precise form in the manifesto adopted by the Central Committee at Champigny in December 1968:

> During the passage to socialism and for the construction of the latter, the existing democratic parties and formations which will declare for socialism and for the respect of the laws of the new social regime will be able to take a full part in the country's political life and will enjoy all the rights and freedoms guaranteed by the Constitution.[12]

But inevitably the questions asked were, what about those parties that refused to 'declare for socialism', and what would happen once the 'construction of socialism' was complete? Only the first received a partial response in the 'programme pour un gouvernement démocratique d'union populaire', adopted by the Central Committee on October 1971. This included a substantial chapter on the preservation and extension of civil liberties.

> Parties and political groups [it said] will be able to form and to carry on their activities freely provided that they respect the law. Their plurality contributes to the expression of opinion. They will be assured of access to the state information media.
>
> The political rights of the opposition will be guaranteed in law, both by the liberties defined above and by the existence of proportional representation.
>
> The regular organization of elections under universal suffrage is one of the essential methods allowing the people to express its judgement on the activity of the parties. The parties will respect the people's verdict.
>
> There will be no confusion between the parties and the state apparatus.[13]

This also gave at least a partial answer to another question constantly thrown at the PCF by its opponents, the question known as that of *alternance*, or alternation in power: once they attained power, would the Communists ever allow themselves to be defeated in an election, or would they hold on to power irrespective of the popular will? For years the PCF wrestled unhappily with this question, to the embarrassment of its allies, for clearly it did present a genuine theoretical difficulty. The PCF claimed to be offering not merely a change of government, but a change of society. The 'advanced democracy' it proposed to introduce was 'a step towards socialism'. In other words it should see at least the beginnings of a transition from the capitalist to the socialist mode of production. Such a profound change in the social structure could hardly be without effect on the political superstructure: indeed the very advent of a left-wing government would be proof that the contradictions of capitalism in France could no longer be resolved within the bourgeois political system. To suggest that after reaching a new stage on the road to socialism the majority of the people might voluntarily give back power to anti-socialist parties seemed at worst quite unscientific and at best to cast doubt on the Communist Party's claim to be the unique instrument through which the working class could achieve power.

The PCF was therefore very reluctant to go beyond the general formulation of respect for universal suffrage quoted above. But in the negotiations on the common programme in 1972 the Socialists insisted on a specific pledge to relinquish power if defeated in an election, since to omit it would inevitably be taken as admitting an intention to hold on to power by undemocratic means if necessary. The PCF eventually agreed, but insisted on inserting a curiously worded rider. The relevant passage in the Common Programme reads as follows:

> If the country refused its confidence to the majority parties, the latter would surrender power and resume the struggle in opposition. But the chief task of the democratic government, whose existence implies the support of a popular majority, will be the satisfaction of the toiling masses; and the government will therefore be strong in the ever more active confidence that the masses will place in it.[14]

The PCF thus affirmed in principle its willingness to accept defeat, while hastening to reassure its supporters that it did not expect the pledge would ever have to be honoured. Perhaps of greater practical significance was its simultaneous acceptance, in the Common Programme, that France would remain a member of the Atlantic Alliance and a full participant in the European Community.

But the Common Programme was a programme for only one five-year parliament. The PCF presented it, like its own 1971 programme, as a blueprint for 'advanced democracy' rather than for socialism itself, which would come later. Would the multi-party system survive in a socialist France? Yes, replied Marchais in his book *Le Défi Démocratique* (1973), but then immediately deprived this assurance of any value by citing as examples of multi-party socialist societies the people's democracies of eastern Europe and the German Democratic Republic, where, he said, the government was a coalition of five parties and the Speaker of the *Volkskammer* was a Christian Democrat!

The PCF was remarkably slow to realize that this kind of explanation was worse than useless, since the French public was not interested in the purely formal pluralism of eastern Europe, but wanted to see freedom preserved through a genuine pluralism in which parties, trade unions and other corporate bodies were free to oppose each other publicly and compete for popular support. It was not enough to say that socialist democracy in France would be different from the Soviet model. If the word 'democracy' was to carry any conviction on French Communists' lips, they had to show that they were aware of the *un*democratic character of society both in the Soviet Union and in its eastern European satellites.

The Breach with Moscow

At an earlier period of its history, of course, this was the one concession the PCF would have found it quite impossible to make: its very *raison d'être* had been the defence and glorification of *la patrie du socialisme*. But since the death of Stalin the bonds which held the western Communist Parties to the CPSU had slackened. Stalin himself, of course, had to all intents and purposes written them off as instruments of world revolution since the 1920s. But his successors seem to have considered them of little use even as instruments of Soviet foreign policy. The denunciation of Stalin in 1956 was carried out without regard for the embarrassment it was bound to cause to western Communist leaders who for years had not only heaped the most extravagant praise on Stalin but had themselves been carefully built up as miniature Stalins in their own countries. Krushchev and his associates perhaps thought that this would pass off as so many earlier twists and turns of Soviet policy had done, and that the western parties would have no choice but to fall into line. They either did not realize, or did not care, that this time they were demolishing

375

the very myth of Soviet perfection and infallibility on which all the previous acts of blind obedience and self-sacrifice were based.

The Italian Communist leader, Togliatti, at once grasped the implications and proclaimed his new doctrine of 'polycentrism', according to which Moscow was no longer the single, unchallenge-able centre of the world Communist movement, but merely one centre among many. But Thorez and the other leaders of the PCF, products of a more thoroughgoing 'Bolshevization' in the 1920s, lacked the intellectual independence and subtlety to make this leap. They tried to carry on as if nothing had changed. For a long time, indeed, they pretended to know nothing about de-Stalinization, referring to the 'so-called Khrushchev report' long after the full text of the secret speech had been published in *Le Monde* and other western newspapers. Then they fell into line, denouncing Stalin's crimes but not making any apology for their own party's earlier efforts to condone or conceal them, still less changing anything in its system of organization and leadership other than to phase out the personality cult. Thorez indeed rushed to the defence of Moscow's continued right to provide leadership for the whole world Communist movement, and conducted a public polemic on the issue with Togliatti.

But although officially grateful for Thorez's support, Khrushchev behaved as if he agreed with Togliatti—in large part, no doubt, because he had no choice. The dissolution of the Comintern in 1943 had been a purely formal affair because Stalin by then enjoyed an unquestioned personal authority over the whole movement. Virtually every party leader had been selected by him. Many had been accessories to, if not accomplices in, his crimes. Most important of all, he was in 1943 still the leader of the world's only socialist state, on which every foreign Communist Party depended psychologically, and most materially. Khrushchev in 1956 enjoyed none of these advantages. By crushing the Hungarian uprising in the autumn of that year he was able to reassert Soviet supremacy over the new socialist states of eastern Europe, and to win unanimous approval for this action from the foreign Communist Parties (as Stalin had done for his excommunication of Tito in 1948). But on his eastern flank he was now confronted with a Communist China which, though still receiving Soviet aid on an important scale, definitely considered itself independent. Mao had accepted the seniority of Stalin in the club of world Communist leaders, but he considered Khrushchev definitely his junior, and certainly did not accept that he had the authority to remove Stalin from his pedestal. And even in western Europe the larger Communist Parties such as the PCI and PCF were gradually freeing themselves from financial dependence on the Soviet Union, as the business enterprises they had set up after the war to exploit East-West trade began to prosper in their own right, benefiting from the skill of their managers and the rapid expansion of their domestic markets, and thus became less dependent on Soviet and eastern European concessions given for political reasons.[15]

Thus Khrushchev could no longer take for granted the support of the more important foreign parties. He had to treat them, if not as equals, at least as vassals whose continued loyalty had to be earned, and which had occasionally to be played off against each other. He implicitly recognized the accuracy of Togliatti's analysis by allowing the Cominform to wither and by readmitting Tito to the club of recognized Communist leaders essentially on his own terms. This could only mean that from now on the club would be much more loosely organized and would permit much greater diversity. It has recently been revealed, moreover, that on one ostensibly internal Russian issue (the rehabilitation of Bukharin and other 'old Bolshevik' leaders) Khrushchev backed down in spite of having a majority in the Soviet politburo, because the minority was able to invoke the support of foreign Communist leaders, and most notably of Thorez himself. (On this issue Togliatti was alone in supporting Khrushchev.)[16] Finally, and most important, when the showdown came with the Chinese, Khrushchev was unable either to bring them to heel or to have them formally condemned by a world conference of Communist Parties, since Togliatti and Tito, though both far from sharing the Chinese position, were now resolutely opposed to any kind of international discipline. Once again Thorez came down firmly on the Soviet side, but even for this Khrushchev had to pay a price, by supporting Thorez against Togliatti and against those in the PCF leadership (Marcel Servin and Laurent Casanova) who favoured a more 'Italian' line.[17] And in 1964 Thorez died, to be replaced by the cautious but more open-minded Waldeck Rochet.

Thus by the mid-1960s it was no longer possible to assume that contradictions between Soviet great-power interests and the PCF's domestic ambition would be automatically resolved in favour of the former, as had happened in 1928–32, 1939–41 and 1947–52. In fact conflicts between the two which in themselves were much less serious than those earlier ones were now to lead to unprecedented public expressions of divergence.

The sudden overthrow of Khrushchev himself in 1964 was one source of embarrassment and irritation to the PCF leaders, after all the trouble they had gone to to align themselves with his positions even at the price of implicitly repudiating their own past. It was also a source of anxiety, since his policy of peaceful co-existence was an essential prerequisite for the PCF's escape from political isolation in France. Accordingly the PCF sent a high-level delegation to Moscow to demand an explanation. Apparently it returned with reassurances: only Khrushchev's individualist methods of decision-taking would be changed. The co-existence policy would be maintained.[18]

Indeed, there is no reason to think that the Brezhnev–Kosygin leadership was unhappy with Krushchev's general line of encouraging co-operation between Communists and other socialist or 'patriotic' opposition forces in western countries. But in the mid-1960s France was coming to constitute a special case in Soviet foreign policy, because of de Gaulle's various gestures of independence from American tutelage and desire to steer a course of his own between the blocs. The Soviet leaders clearly put a high value on these signs of a breach in the front of western hostility, and were unenthusiastic about the PCF's willingness to make common cause with a French opposition that was predominantly Atlanticist. Waldeck Rochet's remark in 1962 that withdrawal from the Atlantic Pact or the Common Market should not be a precondition for co-operation between French Communists and Socialists may well have been received with indifference in Moscow, since at that time there was no serious likelihood of France withdrawing from either. By 1965, when de Gaulle was applying his 'empty chair' policy in Brussels and preparing to withdraw from NATO, the position was rather different, and the Soviet Union could hardly be expected to join the PCF in endorsing a presidential candidate running against de Gaulle on a platform including a pro-EEC and pro-NATO plank. In fact it did the opposite, and gave a discreet endorsement to de Gaulle himself, in the form of a Tass report explaining that some opponents of the French regime would probably vote for de Gaulle because of 'certain positive and realistic measures that the Gaullist government is taking in the foreign policy field'. *L'Humanité* ignored this report, and the PCF let it be known that it had protested to Moscow.[19]

Two months later the PCF was able to get its own back by publishing in *L'Humanité* an article by Louis Aragon, now the doyen of French Communist intellectuals, which protested strongly against the sentences passed on two Soviet dissidents, the writers Sinyavsky and Daniel. Both sides had thus indicated that there were limits to their solidarity well before the Soviet invasion of Czechoslovakia in 1968—but this undoubtedly was a traumatic blow for the PCF, as for other western European Communist Parties. Indeed, perhaps more so than for others, precisely because the PCF had been more thoroughly Stalinized (at any rate than the Italian party). Both its leaders and its militants had till then retained a strong instinctive loyalty to the 'patrie du socialisme'.

In April 1968 the PCF Central Committee came out rather gingerly in favour of the 'Prague spring': a demonstration that democracy and communism were not incompatible was not, after all, to be spurned as an electoral argument in France, especially when the French right-wing press had just been drawing an anti-Communist moral from the twentieth anniversary of the 1948 'coup de Prague'. Then, seeing disaster approach, the PCF in July despatched its general secretary, first to Moscow, then to Prague, in a desperate but vain attempt to find a compromise. Like his Italian colleague Luigi Longo, Rochet apparently warned the Soviet leaders that he would have to condemn any military intervention. And sure enough, on the day of the invasion the PCF's *Bureau Politique* expressed its 'surprise and reprobation'. Next day the Central Committee announced its 'disapproval'. Many commentators saw this as a significantly weaker expression. What was certainly true was that the party took no pleasure in condemning the Soviet action. For many leaders and militants to do so meant going against the mental habits of a lifetime. For Thorez's widow Jeannette Vermeersch it was too much: she resigned from both *Bureau Politique* and Central Committee. Rochet himself, who like Dubček had sought to combine a more liberal version of communism with fundamental loyalty to the Soviet Union, described his party as 'bitter' and 'torn'—implying not that it was about to split but rather that each French Communist must find himself torn by conflicting loyalties.

Undoubtedly the condemnation was as sincere as it was electorally indispensable. But having made the gesture the party's immediate instinct was to try and limit its scope, and to find a way out of a psychologically unbearable situation. It at once welcomed the 'agreement' imposed on the hapless Czechoslovak leaders in Moscow. The party's leading philosopher, Roger Garaudy, a member of the *Bureau Politique*, was censured by his colleagues for attacking the Soviet leaders in an interview with the Czechoslovak news agency: he was accused of an 'inadmissible interference in the internal affairs of brother parties'. In November a further PCF delegation travelled to Moscow and held long discussions with the Soviet leaders. They agreed to differ, but at the same time reaffirmed their 'fraternal sincerity and friendship'.[20] The PCF was thus the first of the Communist Parties which had condemned the invasion to resume formal contacts with Moscow; and it went on to accept the successive stages of 'normalization' imposed on the Czechs, never questioning the legitimacy of Gustav Husak and his colleagues as genuine leaders of a genuine Communist Party. At the Moscow world conference of June 1969 the PCF, while reaffirming the principle of the independence of each party, was one of the very few western European parties (along with those of Ireland, Luxembourg and Portugal) to give total support to the CPSU in its condemnation of China,[21] and to avoid making any reference to Czechoslovakia.

While in Moscow to attend that conference, Waldeck Rochet fell victim to a stroke which left him in a permanent coma. It was soon apparent that he would be able to play no further part in the party's affairs. The role of party leader was taken over by Georges Marchais, who was named assistant general secretary in February 1970 and full general secretary in December 1972. Marchais since 1961 had held the key post of organization secretary but was not well known outside the party. He was neither a member of parliament nor a noted public speaker, and had not been publicly involved in the party's attempts to forge new links with other opposition forces or to endow itself with a more liberal image. As his rise to the leadership coincided with the period of 'normalized' relations with the CPSU, he was at first identified as 'Moscow's man', and bitterly attacked by those like Garaudy and Tillon (still a party member, though reduced to the rank-and-file in 1952) who had hoped to see the party develop a more radical opposition to Stalinism both at home and abroad. (He was also attacked for not having a Resistance record, and had repeatedly to rebut the accusation that he had volunteered to work in a German aircraft factory in 1942.) Both Garaudy and Tillon were expelled from the party in 1970, and it seemed at first that a period of re-Stalinization had set in.

By the end of 1970, however, Marchais had consolidated his position within the party and was able to show that it would be at least as independent of Moscow under his leadership as under his predecessor. In December of that year Etienne Fajon, by now a veteran member of the secretariat (as well as editor-in-chief of *L'Humanité*) with the reputation of being an unreconstructed Stalinist, was chosen to express the PCF's criticism of the 'mistakes and insufficiencies in the working of socialist democracy' which led to the strikes and riots in Poland (culminating in the fall of Gomulka). Marchais himself confirmed the criticism in a speech to the Central Committee; and the same month the PCF publicly protested at the death sentences passed in Leningrad on two Soviet Jews who had attempted to hijack a plane, and joined in the (successful) international chorus of appeals for clemency. Marchais expressed his dislike of 'barracks communism'; and the following month the PCF made a further public protest when the 'normalized' Central Committee of the Czechoslovak party retrospectively justified the Soviet invasion.

A 'Marchais line' was thus established which remained fairly consistent until the autumn of 1975: a line which combined freedom to criticize specific actions by the Soviet Union and its satellite regimes with acceptance of East European society as genuinely socialist (and therefore in the last resort preferable to existing capitalist society in the West), and *de facto* acceptance of Soviet leadership in the international Communist movement. It could be defined as a centrist position between the uncritical pro-Sovietism of, say, the Portuguese and the 'autonomism' of the Yugoslavs, Romanians, Italians and Spaniards. Thus up to and including October 1975 the PCF supported Soviet efforts to convene a conference of European Communist Parties which would reaffirm the essential unity of the international Communist movement; and during the summer of 1975 it expressed its solidarity with the Portuguese party, then under attack from both French and Portuguese Socialists, and criticized also by Italian and Spanish Communists, for disregarding election results and trying to gain power through the armed forces. But the PCF was careful to add that solidarity did not mean 'alignment' and could not be 'unconditional'. Clearly the tactics applied in Portugal were very different from those which the PCF proposed for France. But, as it sought respect for its own right to work out its own tactics in France, so it defended the right of the PCP to do the same in Portugal. And when Konstantin Zarodov, writing in *Pravda*, sought to use the Portuguese context as basis for a general criticism of the strategy of relying on electoral alliances and 'arithmetical' majorities, Marchais bluntly recalled that 'our policy is decided in Paris, not in Moscow.'

A number of factors must have combined to convince the PCF's leaders of the need for a more radical change of policy in the autumn of 1975. Marchais himself, who had suffered a slight heart attack earlier in the year, regained his health and resumed full control of the party. Combined with carping criticisms of the Socialist Party, the relatively tough line which the PCF had taken during the previous twelve months had served only to strengthen the Socialist Party's support as revealed in by-elections and opinion polls. Support for the Portuguese party had clearly damaged the PCF's liberal image, while the Italian party, after its triumph in the local and regional elections of June 1975, became an ally hardly to be spurned. Finally, the Soviet leaders had annoyed the PCF not only by publishing Zarodov's article but also by welcoming President Giscard d'Estaing in Moscow in October and publishing an incomplete version of the PCF's statement on the visit (which stressed that *détente* did not imply acceptance of the social and political status quo in France).[22]

Whatever the relative importance of these various factors, the fact is that in November 1975 the PCF suddenly aligned itself with its Italian brother. The two parties published a joint statement which stressed a general 'concordance of solutions' for situations having a 'common character' in highly developed capitalist countries. In the discussions on the proposed conference of European Communist Parties the PCF now changed sides and joined the 'autonomists' in rejecting a draft document considered to go too far in the direction of a unified world Communist strategy. Then, in Janary 1976, Marchais came out with statements on the 'French road to socialism', indicating that the PCF would now drop the term 'dictatorship of the proletariat', which no longer accurately expressed its policy, and, after re-stating the PCF's attachment to democracy, pluralism of political parties and freedom of speech, went on to say: 'We consider that the principles which we enunciate concerning socialist democracy are of universal value. It is clear that we have a disagreement with the Communist Party of the Soviet Union about this problem.'[23] This statement was clearly crucial, and may be said to mark the PCF's true ideological breach with Moscow. Up to then the 'French road to socialism' had been different from the Soviet one, but leading essentially to the same goal. Now it was proclaimed to embody principles of universal application, which the Soviet Union was condemned for failing to observe. Criticism of specific Soviet abuses became correspondingly less inhibited and more aggressive: at the end of 1975, for instance, the PCF publicly called on the Soviet Union for an explanation of scenes said to have been filmed in a Soviet labour camp which were shown in a documentary on French television; and in January 1976 PCF leaders appeared at a press conference alongside Leonid Plyushch, the Soviet mathematician who had been interned in a psychiatric hospital, and associated themselves with his struggle for democracy in the Soviet Union.

The PCF showed a certain insolence, too, in scheduling its congress for the same month as that of the CPSU (February 1976), at which Marchais was conspicuous by his absence. The Twenty-Second Congress was the occasion for the PCF to set out in detail its conception of political democracy and its strategy for achieving socialism in France. The dictatorship of the proletariat was jettisoned, and replaced by the 'union du peuple de France'—a union of all 'non-monopolist' social classes. As summarized by the Communist historian Jean Elleinstein, 'the "union du peuple de France" can be realized around the working class which is its driving force and on the basis of the union of the left, but what is important is to see clearly that the new political power thus constituted will not be only that of the working class but that of all the social forces which will have worked to transform society and bring the new political power to birth.'[24]

The PCF thus adopted an essentially Gramscian vision of working-class hegemony (though without the word) in a class alignment apparently indistinguishable from the 'new historic bloc' which Garaudy had been condemned for proposing in 1970. As in Italy, so in France, the circumstances of advanced industrial capitalism were seen to make both possible and necessary a combination of socialism with political democracy and 'public freedoms', which so far from being obstacles were presented as instruments of social and economic transformation; whereas the bad name given to socialism by Soviet practices was frankly acknowledged as an obstacle to be overcome. 'We cannot allow', said Marchais in his report to the congress, 'the Communist ideal, whose object is the happiness of mankind, and on behalf of which we call upon the working people to struggle, to be besmirched by acts which are unjust and unjustified.'[25] And these points were bluntly repeated in his speech at the Berlin Conference of European Communist Parties, when it finally met in June of the same year. He even questioned the utility of such gatherings, and said he did not expect to take part in any more.

But the Twenty-Second Congress also set clear limits to the changes it was making. Internationally, the Soviet Union remained a socialist state under which 'great historical progress' had been accomplished, and with which the PCF was still involved in 'the common struggle against imperialism and for our great common goals'. Nationally, the hoped-for union of the French people still depended on 'the irreplaceable role of the party of the working class'. So describing itself, the PCF implicitly relegated the Socialist Party to the role of representing some of those secondary social forces over which the working class was to exercise its 'guiding role' (*rôle dirigeant*). In retrospect this could be seen as serving notice that the PCF would not agree to play second fiddle in a left-wing alliance where the Socialist Party had become dominant.[26]

The Crisis of 1977–8

It had been generally expected that the negotiations to update the 1972 Common Programme for the March 1978 elections would be difficult, but also that the prospect of victory would create a mood in which such difficulties could be overcome. Perhaps the Socialist leaders assumed a little too readily, from past experience, that the Communist leaders would share their anxiety to reassure middle-of-the-road voters, and would therefore agree in the end that any changes in the 1972 text should be in the direction of moderation and realism.

At first, indeed, it seemed that the PCF might be trying to outflank the PS by moving further and faster into 'realism', when in May 1977 it suddenly announced its conversion to the continued development of France's nuclear strike force—a decision which the PS had been manoeuvring towards for some years in spite of strong internal resistance. Later in the summer the PCF embarrassed the PS by its robust defence of France's civil nuclear energy programme, which had run into strong opposition from the 'ecologist' lobby, the newest and most vigorous form taken by youthful protest in France. The

384

'ecologists' were generally closer in outlook to the PS than to other conventional parties, and their candidates were thus a potential threat to the PS on the first ballot. Mitterrand therefore tried to hedge on the nuclear issue, suggesting that it might be dealt with by a referendum after the election. But the PCF was not inclined to let him off so lightly, and the referendum suggestion was greeted with outraged scorn by Marchais as well as by the parties in power.

It was not until September, however, that the full scope of the Communist campaign became clear. The main issue on which the negotiations finally broke down was the extent of the nationalization programme. The Communists insisted that the 1972 programme implied the complete nationalization not only of the groups named but of all companies in which they had a holding of more than 50%. This claim was resisted by the Socialists and by the small, often-forgotten third party to the alliance, the *Mouvement des Radicaux de Gauche* (MRG). The Socialists pointed out that the state would gain indirect control of the subsidiaries anyway, and that to slate them for full nationalization would mean taking over more than a thousand firms—a figure which could easily be used by the right to intimidate the floating voter.

It rapidly became apparent that the PCF leaders did not want to reach agreement, or at least did not expect to do so on what they considered acceptable terms. The final session of negotiations was broken off without serious discussion of Socialist counter-proposals, which did include some significant concessions, and almost simultaneously an edition of *L'Humanité* was on the streets including a cartoon which showed President Giscard d'Estaing thanking Mitterrand and the MRG leader, Robert Fabre, for their alleged betrayal of the union of the left. This was to be the constant theme of PCF propaganda from now on: the PS had 'veered to the right' and was secretly preparing to do a deal with Giscard for a new centre-left government which would exclude the PCF and would maintain the economic and social status quo. The Socialists replied by protesting their fidelity to the programme of 1972, even without updating if necessary, and their determination to go into government only as part of the union of the left, rejecting any reversion to the strategy of the *Troisième Force*.

The Communist accusations lacked credibility, and had manifestly issued from some secret decision of the *Bureau Politique*. (Some suggested that Marchais, hitherto strongly identified with the policy

385

of left-wing unity, must have been outvoted and now be applying a policy with which he did not really agree.) The rank-and-file of the party had had nothing to do with the origins of the campaign, and were clearly bewildered by it. The leadership had to embark on a series of intensive explanations to make it clear that the breach was the fault of the Socialists, and these appear to have been only very partially successful.

Some observers were inclined to see the change as resulting from a victory for pro-Soviet forces within the party, and intended to serve Soviet interests by avoiding a left-wing victory in France and so preserving the European status quo. But certainly what happened was not a straightforward realignment of the PCF on Soviet positions. What may be true is that the success of the PS, the growing condescension with which its leaders treated the PCF, and the reformist gloss which some of its economic specialists were putting on the Common Programme with a view to reassuring the domestic and international business communities, had convinced some wavering members of the *Bureau Politique* that the scepticism consistently expressed in private by leaders and diplomats of the Soviet bloc about the PCF's strategy was better justified than they had thought.[27] That strategy, after all, had been predicated on the ability of the PCF to hegemonize the left and to remain the uncontested 'party of the working class'. A left-wing government in which the PCF would be reduced to the role of junior partner ('force d'appoint') was of little interest. The risks involved were too great: the economic circumstances (world depression) and the constitutional circumstances (a parliamentary election, leaving the right in control of the all-important presidency of the Republic) were both unfavourable to the left in 1978. A predominantly Socialist government would be likely either to collapse quickly or to pursue an essentially reformist policy, rapidly resorting to classic deflationary measures to stabilize the economy (the examples of Britain and Portugal were cited). As in 1936–8 and again in 1947, the PCF would be asked to support, and would have to 'sell' to its own supporters, a series of unpopular policies with which it was fundamentally out of sympathy, and in the end might well be rewarded once again by the 'betrayal' of its former allies, relegating it once again to the margin of effective politics.

Rather than repeat those experiences, the PCF leaders decided to give priority to the reassertion of their own party's image as *the* party of the working class, the poor and the underprivileged, in contrast to the reformism, technocracy and opportunism of the PS. Thus one of the main points in their election platform was the immediate raising of the minimum wage from 1,700 to 2,400 francs per month—a plank which the PS soon felt politically obliged to endorse, against the advice of its own economists.

The campaign did not succeed in preventing the Socialist Party from overtaking the PCF for the first time in a national election since 1936, or in preventing an actual decline in the PCF's share of the vote. But neither phenomenon reached the landslide proportions which opinion polls had at one time predicted. The PCF total, 20.6%, was not as bad as that of 1968 (20.0%), let alone that of 1958 (18.9%). And the PS, instead of the 27% or 30% predicted by the polls, obtained only 22.6% (24.7% if the MRG votes are included).

The PCF's campaign *did* succeed (if that was indeed its aim) in preventing the left as a whole from winning the election. The left failed to secure the decisive advantage it needed on the first ballot. Arithmetically the total of left-wing votes appeared fractionally higher than that of the right, but the unity, discipline and enthusiasm needed to convert this into a majority of seats on the second ballot were lacking. A last-minute agreement between the left-wing parties enabled them to withdraw their candidate in each other's favour in the traditional manner, but carried little conviction with the voters after the months of open conflict between them. Inevitably each side's supporters tended to suspect their own leaders of giving away points that had up to now been stressed as essential. In reality the significant concession was made by the PCF in accepting an electoral pact without prior agreement on the programme; but the PCF had of course to claim that it was the Socialists who had at last yielded to Communist pressure in accepting an agreement, and this interpretation was enthusiastically supported by the right-wing parties and press. In this atmosphere it was hardly surprising that the transfers of votes between the two parties were far from perfect, and that Giscard d'Estaing's coalition, which in the hour of peril had patched up its own serious divisions, was returned with a comfortable majority.

This result came as a bitter disappointment to the Socialists, many of whom had almost taken for granted that they were about to come to power. The majority of them, not unnaturally, held the PCF responsible for their unexpected failure. They were in any case perplexed and embittered by the violence and suddenness of the PCF's campaign against them, after they had invested so much time and energy in building an alliance with it and overcoming the prejudices that this aroused in their own party and elsewhere. The effect, inevitably, was to revive those prejudices, and to extend them to a new generation of French Socialists who had no personal memories of the post-war period or the Cold War. In the aftermath of the March 1978 elections Mitterrand's strategy of the united left lay apparently in ruins. Many Socialists and 'Left Radicals', who before the election had sincerely put all thoughts of an alternative strategy—centre-left or *Troisième Force*—behind them, were now forced to reconsider. There was thus a clear danger that Marchais's accusations that his 'allies' were preparing a deal with Giscard would in time become self-fulfilling.

Yet the unity of the left had also been—and officially at least still was—the strategy of the PCF and of Marchais himself. Great sacrifices had been made by PCF and CGT militants in the hope of a left-wing victory in 1978, and great hopes had been invested in it by almost the entire working class. Even if the party leaders had secretly concluded that such a victory would not in fact be in their interests, they had certainly not communicated that view to the rank-and-file. The result was therefore a great and bitter disappointment for the members and supporters of the PCF, as well as those of the PS, and the first preoccupation of the party leaders immediately after the election was to ensure that the PCF was not blamed by its own supporters, and that they themselves were not blamed by the rank-and-file members, for what had happened. They did not dare to encourage a genuine debate in the party about their own strategy and tactics, as this would have undermined their authority. Instead they made it a party axiom that the blame lay with the Socialists. They were thus obliged to continue and even to step up the campaign against the PS which they had begun the previous summer.

What had perhaps originally been intended as a tactical manoeuvre, to intimidate the Socialists and reassert the central role of the PCF within the united left, thus developed into an apparent change of strategy. The PCF leaders behaved as if their first priority was to drive the PS into alliance with Giscard and thereby justify retrospectively their own attacks on it. They did this especially by emphasizing the European connections of the PS, notably those with the West German SPD, and presenting themselves as authentic defenders of French national interests which both Giscard and the PS were prepared to sacrifice to a German-dominated European

Community. This led them to adopt positions very close to those of the Gaullists led by Jacques Chirac (for instance in opposing Spanish membership of the Community), in an alignment reminiscent of the campaign against the European Defence Community in 1953–4. It also drove them further apart from the other main 'Eurocommunist' parties (those of Spain and Italy), both of which favoured closer European integration. But it did not imply a whole-hearted return to the Soviet fold: in July 1978, for instance, French Communist leaders took part in a mass demonstration in Paris in protest against the trials of the Soviet dissidents Shcharansky and Ginzburg.

These tactics did not avert, but helped to contain, a crisis within the party. The imposition of what amounted to a U-turn in the party line was no longer quite as simple a matter for the leadership as it had been in the past, because of the great efforts made over the preceding decade to project a liberal and democratic image of the party—an image which was taken seriously above all by many of the party's own members. (In 1976 it was calculated that two thirds of the members had joined since 1968 and at least one third since 1972.)[28] The leadership could not afford to act in a way completely inconsistent with this image without running the risk of alienating a large part of the party membership, as well as destroying what was left of its credibility outside the party. At the outset of the crisis, therefore, Marchais was obliged to declare that 'whatever happens, no one will be expelled'. Emboldened by this assurance, large numbers of party members, including some junior or middle-rank cadres, did express their dissatisfaction with the way the party had been led. Denied space to do so in the party press, they resorted to *Le Monde* and other external media. As in the past, the leadership accused them of allowing themselves to be exploited by the party's enemies (among which the PS was now given pride of place!), but this accusation was now less frightening than in the past, coming from people who had pledged their respect for plural democracy and had undertaken to tolerate dissent.

Perhaps the most damaging criticism came from Jean Elleinstein, the deputy director of the party's Marxist Research and Study Centre (CERM). He, with some encouragement from the party leadership, had made himself a kind of symbol of the PCF's new 'Eurocommunist' outlook. He had written a very critical analysis of Stalinism, been attacked in the Soviet press and defended by *L'Humanité*. He had vigorously defended the ideas of the Twenty-Second Congress against those (notably the world-famous Communist philosopher and Marx-ologist Louis Althusser) who attacked the dropping of the dictator-ship of the proletariat as 'unscientific'. He was generally accepted by the French intellectual establishment as a man of honest, indepen-dent and open mind. The fact that he was apparently at ease within the PCF hierarchy was therefore an important argument in its favour; and during the run-up to the election Marchais had thought it worth while to get a public endorsement from him of the party's position *vis-à-vis* the PS, while himself vigorously rejecting sugges-tions that the break with the PS meant going back on the decisions of the Twenty-Second Congress. 'We don't suffer from too much Twenty-Second Congress,' Marchais declared, 'but from not enough.' This remark rebounded against him after the election when Elleinstein took it up, accusing the leadership precisely of failing to live up to the democratic principles it had proclaimed, and pointing out that a series of crucial decisions had been decreed in an arbitrary manner from the top, without any attempt to consult, involve or even adequately inform the rank-and-file.[29]

Yet Elleinstein and the other critics did not at first question, at least in public, the main premise of the leadership's argument —namely, that the main responsibility for the break lay with the PS. Their criticisms were directed essentially at the way the leadership had reacted to the PS's 'swing to the right'—something it should after all have been prepared for, in view of the world Communist movement's long experience with, and well-known opinions about, social democracy. But though many of the criticisms were very cogent, this manner of posing the argument may have worked psychologically in the leadership's favour, by reinforcing the im-pression that the party was the victim of a great betrayal, and that in the last resort its misfortunes were the result of external events rather than internal failings. The leadership was also helped by the fact that the attack was joined by people whose position on fundamentals was very different from that of Elleinstein—notably Althusser himself and Thorez's widow Jeannette Vermeersch. This enabled the leadership to adopt the classic argument that it was fighting off twin deviations—left-wing sectarianism and right-wing opportunism—which as usual converged to produce a single result, namely the weakening of the party for the benefit of the bourgeoisie; the leadership's own position, by contrast, being centrist, reasonable and 'correct'.

Epilogue

1979 and After

The traditional image of a party controlled and manipulated from the top was confirmed by the preparations for the Twenty-Third Congress, held in May 1979. Discussion was organized in the party on the basis of a draft resolution and draft revision of the party statutes drawn up by the leadership and published three months before the congress. The *Bureau Politique* gave strict instructions that only members who were in agreement with the general approach of these documents should be sent as delegates to the preparatory conferences at section and federation level, and to the congress itself. There was to be no question of proportional representation for minorities.[30] Meetings from cell level upwards were organized with great care by party officials to ensure that opponents were as far as possible isolated and intimidated. Their efforts succeeded handsomely, for Charles Fiterman (one of Marchais's closest colleagues) was able to tell the congress that only eighty-two out of 28,000 cells had voted against the draft resolution 'or radically altered its general approach'. In the federal conferences, out of 20,446 delegates, sixty-three had voted against the resolution and 151 had abstained.[31] Only one overt critic of the leadership—the mayor of Sèvres, Roger Fajnzylberg—was mandated by his federation to attend the congress, and he tactfully decided not to attend.[32] As a result the congress was marked by the same ponderous unanimity as in the past. Moreover its preparation coincided with an intensification of the campaign against the PS and a definite rapprochement with the CPSU. The catch-phrase in the resolution, seized on by the leadership's critics, was the 'overall credit balance' (*bilan globalement positif*) of the socialist countries; and the new statutes, though they allowed for a 'discussion platform' in the party press on an 'important political situation or event' in between congresses, stipulated that in such a case it was for the Central Committee to take the initiative.

Nonetheless, Marchais in his opening report to the congress was careful to emphasize that 'Eurocommunism' was not dead, and declared that 'far from being outdated . . . the democratic road to a socialism in French colours, as defined by our Twenty-Second Congress, remains more than ever the only possible road . . .'[33] In a sense the congress was a success for the critics, since even though they were not officially represented in it a great part of its time was devoted to refuting their arguments.

Marchais even admitted to journalists that 'some of the criticisms addressed to us are well founded.' He added that the party regarded the intellectual 'front' as one of crucial importance, and that intellectuals were not to be regarded as second-class citizens within the party: they were there on exactly the same footing as workers. A high proportion of those promoted in the party hierarchy were indeed intellectuals, including Pierre Juquin, who had become something of a symbol of the PCF's independence from Moscow through his public handshake with Plyushch in 1976. (A photograph of this was to have been used as the cover of a leaflet on the PCF's defence of civil and political liberties in the 1978 election campaign, but the pro-Soviet faction within the leadership succeeded in getting it withdrawn: thousands of copies of the leaflet had to be shredded.) Moreover, to general surprise, Roland Leroy—who was regarded as the leading hardliner—was dropped from the party secretariat.

All this took place within the context of a struggle to win back the leadership of the left from the PS. The Common Programme was now presented as having been almost a mistake, since it had provided the PS with an apparent certificate of revolutionary purity which it did not deserve and thus had helped it to lead the workers astray. The corrective, as in the 1920s, was to apply the united front from below (*à la base*), summoning rank-and-file Socialists to joint action on specific issues (such as unemployment in the steel industry) while vigorously 'unmasking' their leaders as reformists and allies of Giscard. The immediate purpose of this was to defend the Communist vote against further Socialist inroads in the European election of June 1979, but there was much speculation about its implications for the next presidential election, due in 1981. The PCF announced that this time it would have its own candidate. What was not clear was whether it would refuse to support the Socialist candidate on the second ballot. On this as on other matters, it seemed that Marchais was keeping his options open.

In the two years which followed the Twenty-Third Congress the PCF leaders concentrated on reaffirming their party's identity and distinguishing it as sharply as possible from the PS. On the international level this involved a retreat from 'Eurocommunism' and a degree of re-identification with the Soviet Union. Though the PCF did not retract its earlier criticisms of Soviet 'democracy' or of Soviet policies in Eastern Europe these criticisms were definitely muted, while the party gave full support, in strong contrast to other 'Eurocommunist' parties, to the Soviet intervention in Afghanistan in December 1979, arguing that there was no parallel with Czechoslovakia in 1968: then the Russians had intervened unnecessarily and illegitimately to interfere with the autonomous choices of the Czechoslovak Communist Party, whereas in Afghanistan the 'progressive' regime was genuinely threatened by American-backed counter-revolution.

On the domestic level the PCF sought to polarize and radicalize industrial conflicts, with a view to discrediting the PS's moderation and economic 'realism' in the eyes of the workers and creating a climate of tension in which the PS would find it more difficult to win middle-class votes. In September 1980 Marchais went so far as to declare that Mitterrand, if elected president, 'would carry out the same policy' as Giscard d'Estaing.

The following month a national conference of the party nominated Marchais himself as the Communist candidate in the presidential election. Although Charles Fiterman, in his introductory report, did not rule out the possibility of 'political agreements . . . , in particular with the Socialist Party', other leaders stressed that the Communist candidate's campaign would be the application of a new strategy, based on criticism of, and refusal to renew, the earlier experiments with left-wing unity: the Popular Front, the Liberation, and the Common Programme. It was necessary, Fiterman explained a few months later, to fight against 'the illusion of change' represented by the PS.[34]

The overriding priority was, quite clearly, to destroy the new-found strength and popularity of the PS, by destroying the unity of the left on which Mitterrand's strategy was based. This operation at first seemed likely to succeed. The PS was badly demoralized by the defeat of 1978, and Mitterrand's strategy was widely questioned within it. Only with difficulty did he overcome the challenge of a reformist wing led by Michel Rocard, who advocated drawing the logical conclusion from the breach with the Communists and moving back towards the centre. (This must have been what the PCF leaders were hoping for, since it would have been bound either to cause a split in the PS or to leave vacant ground to its left for the PCF to reoccupy.) If Mitterrand was eventually endorsed unopposed as the PS candidate for the 1981 presidential election, that was partly because there was a general assumption that the left could not win in 1981 in any case.

In the event, however, the PCF's campaign had the exact opposite of the effect presumably intended. By allowing the PS to take sole credit for efforts to maintain the unity of the left it drove many traditional Communist voters into the PS's arms, and by emphasizing the difference between Communists and Socialists it strengthened the credibility of the latter, in the eyes of the floating centre, as an independent force able and willing to safeguard French democracy. The world recession, coupled with Giscard's increasingly monarchical manner and the bitter divisions within the ruling majority, did the rest.

On 26 April 1981 Georges Marchais, as the PCF's candidate in the first ballot of the presidential election, obtained only 15.42% of the votes—the lowest proportion achieved by the party in any national election since 1936. Mitterrand won 25.9%. In these circumstances the PCF leaders found it impossible to deny him their support on the second ballot. Mitterrand had, after all, been the candidate of the united left both in 1965 and in 1974. Many Communist voters, regardless of party instructions, would have switched their votes to him in 1981 rather than miss an opportunity to defeat the right. The PCF leadership dared not overtly take the blame for his defeat. They therefore came out belatedly in support of him, without obtaining any undertakings in exchange, and on 10 May he was elected President of the Republic with 52% of the votes.

In the entirely new political situation thus created, the PCF leaders had to execute yet another of the abrupt U-turns for which, fortunately, their training had long prepared them. Marchais's campaign had been built round the theme that the left cannot win in France without a strong Communist Party. The results had proved the opposite: the PCF was weakened, and the left had won. The Communist leaders now had to try and take credit for Mitterrand's victory, and proclaim their eagerness to co-operate with him, in order to salvage what was left of their electoral support and to profit from the massive swing of opinion in favour of the Socialists. But the U-turn was too abrupt to be convincing.

In the parliamentary elections of 14 and 21 June Communist candidates won only 15.27% of the vote on the first ballot, while the Socialists won 38.60%. In spite of this, the Communists were allotted four ministerial posts in the new government. But they had to negotiate their inclusion in the government from a position of extreme weakness, since the single-member constituency system had given the

Socialists an overall majority in the new Assembly and they were therefore not dependent on Communist support. (The number of Communist deputies fell from eighty-six to forty-three, while the Socialists and MRG went up from 116 to 283.) The programme of the new government was to all intents and purposes that of the PS, and the Communists had to commit themselves to support it in all fields of activity—foreign and domestic, political and industrial.

Of course, their agreement to do so was tactical. They calculated that they had a better chance of extending their influence from within government than from outside, and that their chances of profiting when the Socialists began to lose popularity—as any governing party must—would be better if they could show that they had played the game loyally and were not responsible for the government's difficulties. For the time being, however, their position in French politics was strikingly weakened. They had returned to government in a much less influential role than they had enjoyed in their previous experience of it, in 1944–7.

Notes

Chapter 1

1. Jean Fréville, *La Nuit finit à Tours*, Edition du cinquantenaire (Paris, 1970), p. 209.
2. R. Wohl, *French Communism in the Making* (Stanford, 1966), p. 19.
3. Peter Campbell, *French Electoral Systems* (London, 1958), p. 85.
4. Wohl, loc. cit.
5. Ibid., pp. 31–2.
6. Christian Gras, *Alfred Rosmer et le mouvement révolutionnaire international* (Paris, 1971), p. 51.
7. Ibid., pp. 84–5.
8. Jacques Chastenet, *Histoire de la Troisième République*, vol. III (Paris, 1955), p. 332.
9. M. Drachkovitch, *Les socialismes français et allemand et le problème de la guerre 1870–1914* (Geneva, 1954), pp. 80, 150.
10. F. F. Ridley, *Revolutionary Syndicalism in France* (Cambridge, 1970), p. 79.
11. Chastenet, op. cit., p. 332.
12. Ibid., p. 330.
13. Ibid., p. 341.
14. Ibid., vol. IV (1957), pp. 151, 163.
15. A. Kriegel, *Aux Origines du Communisme français* (Paris and The Hague, 1964), vol. I, p. 235.
16. Guesde's remark quoted by Compère-Morel at the Congress of Strasbourg in 1920. See Kriegel, op. cit., vol. I, p. 47.
17. Alexandre Zévaès, *Jules Guesde, 1845–1922* (1929), p. 171.
18. Quoted in Wohl, op. cit., p. 52.
19. See for example the song quoted by Wohl, op. cit., p. 23n.
20. Jouhaux to Dumoulin, 9 December 1914, in the Monatte Archives. Quoted in Kriegel, op. cit., vol. I, p. 61n.
21. Wohl, op. cit., pp. 49–50.
22. See Kriegel, op. cit., p. 59n.

23. Ibid., p. 362.
24. Chastenet, op. cit., vol. IV, pp. 340–2.
25. L.-O. Frossard, *De Jaurès à Léon Blum, Souvenirs d'un militant* (Paris, 1943), p. 116.
26. Both texts in A. Rosmer, *Le Mouvement ouvrier pendant la guerre*, vol. I (Paris, 1936), pp. 377–82, and in *Syndicalisme révolutionnaire et Communisme: les Archives de Pierre Monatte* (Paris, 1968), pp. 183–7.
27. Wohl, op. cit., p. 101.
28. E. H. Carr, *The Bolshevik Revolution 1917–1923*, vol. III (London, 1953), p. 126.
29. André Marty, *La Révolte de la Mer Noire*, vol. I (Paris, 1927), p. 84.
30. Carr, loc. cit.
31. Chastenet, op. cit., vol. V (1960), p. 54.
32. Wohl, op. cit., p. 128.
33. Ibid., p. 117.
34. Kriegel, op. cit., vol. I, p. 277.
35. Marty, op. cit., vol. II (Paris, 1928), p. 33.
36. Ibid., p. 401.
37. Ibid., p. 33.
38. Wohl, op. cit., pp. 85–6.
39. Quoted in Gras, op. cit., pp. 158–9.
40. Rosmer in *La Vie Ouvrière*, 30 April 1919.
41. Monatte, ibid., 5 May 1919.
42. Verdier at the CGT Congress, September 1919. Quoted in Wohl, op. cit., p. 136.
43. Wohl, ibid.
44. Kriegel, op. cit., p. 346.
45. Ibid., p. 544.
46. Ibid., p. 523.

Chapter 2

1. F. Borkenau, *The Communist International* (London 1938), p. 188; E. H. Carr, *The Bolshevik Revolution*

1917–1923, vol. III (London, 1953), p. 168.

2. Quoted in Kriegel, op. cit., vol. I, p. 346.

3. Wohl, op. cit., p. 154.

4. Carr, op. cit., p. 176.

5. Quoted in Kriegel, op. cit., vol. II, p. 607.

6. Quoted in Carr, op. cit., p. 190.

7. Kriegel, op. cit., vol. II, p. 633n.

8. Frossard, 'Mon Journal de voyage en Russie' (1921), Bibliothèque Nationale, Paris. No page numbers. From *L'Internationale*, December 1921.

9. Gras, op. cit., p. 201.

10. Kriegel, op. cit., vol. II, p. 648.

11. Ibid., p. 622.

12. Frossard, *Le P. S. et l'Internationale*, p. 28. Quoted in Kriegel, op. cit., p. 645.

13. *L'Humanité*, 14 August 1920.

14. Ibid., 18 August 1920.

15. Carr, op. cit., vol. III, p. 188.

16. Ibid., p. 212.

17. Jane Degras (ed.), *The Communist International 1919–1943: Documents*, vol. I, 1919–1922 (London, 1956), pp. 166–72.

18. *Le Populaire*, 12 November 1920.

19. Wohl, op. cit., p. 189.

20. Ibid., pp. 192, 483.

21. *Le Populaire*, 23 November 1920.

22. Kriegel, op. cit., p. 856.

23. Ibid., pp. 834–5.

24. Ibid., p. 839.

25. Ibid., p. 837.

26. *La Vague*, 23 December 1920. Quoted in Wohl, op. cit., p. 198n.

27. Letter printed in Léon Trotsky, *Le Mouvement communiste en France (1919–1939)*, Textes choisis et présentés par Pierre Broué (Paris, 1967), pp. 113–15.

28. Ibid., pp. 116–19.

29. Ibid., pp. 120–3.

30. Ibid., pp. 124–30.

31. Quoted in Carr, op. cit., vol. III, p. 385.

32. Trotsky, op. cit., p. 139.

33. A.-P. Donneur, 'Internationale deux-et-demie et Internationale communiste', in *Le Mouvement Social*, January–March 1971, p. 36.

34. Trotsky, op. cit., pp. 187–95.

35. Quoted in Gérard Walter, *Histoire du Parti Communiste Français* (Paris, 1948), p. 100.

36. Ibid., pp. 100–1.

37. Ibid., pp. 109–11.

38. Humbert-Droz to Zinoviev, 30 December 1922: in Jules Humbert-Droz, *De Lénine à Staline: Dix Ans au Service de l'Internationale communiste* (Neuchatel, 1971), p. 133.

39. Ibid., p. 123.

40. Kriegel, 'Le PCF sous la Troisième République', *Revue Française de Science Politique*, 1966, pp. 18–19; A. Ferrat, *Histoire du Parti Communiste Français* (Paris, 1931), p. 143.

41. Humbert-Droz, op. cit., p. 138.

42. Quoted in Carr, op. cit., vol. III, p. 207n.

43. G. Lefranc, *Le Mouvement syndical sous la Troisième République* (Paris, 1967), p. 248, quoting Monatte, *Trois scissions syndicales*, p. 152. See also Kriegel, *Aux Origines du Communisme français*, vol. II, pp. 747–8.

44. Kriegel, op. cit., vol. II, pp. 748–9.

45. Quoted in ibid., p. 750, and in Lefranc, op. cit., p. 251.

46. Antoine Prost, *La CGT à l'époque du Front Populaire 1934–1939* (Paris, 1964), p. 33n.

47. Lefranc, op. cit., p. 254.

48. Wohl, op. cit., p. 242.

49. Gras, op. cit., pp. 227–8; J. Maitron and C. Chambelland (eds.), *Syndicalisme revolutionnaire et Communisme: les Archives de Pierre Monatte* (Paris, 1968) [henceforth cited as *Archives Monatte*], p. 291.

50. Gras, op. cit., pp. 228–31.

51. Quoted in Lefranc, op. cit., p. 256.

52. Ibid., pp. 256–8.

53. Ibid., loc. cit.

54. Ibid., pp. 259ff.

55. Preface to F. Brupbacher, *Socialisme en liberté* (1954). Quoted in *Archives Monatte*, p. 273.

56. *Trois scissions syndicales* (Paris, 1958), p. 152.

57. J. Berlioz, 'La lutte pour l'unité syndicale', *Cahiers du Militant*, no. 9. Quoted in Kriegel, op. cit., vol. II, p. 749n.

58. Lefranc, op. cit., p. 259.
59. Gras, op. cit., p. 245.
60. Lefranc, op. cit., p. 259.
61. M. Chambelland, *Revolution Prolétarienne*, I, 1951.
62. *Archives Monatte*, pp. 334–5.
63. Gras, op. cit., p. 255.
64. G. Monmosseau, preface to V. Lénine, *Du rôle et des tâches des syndicats dans les conditions de la Nouvelle Politique Economique* (Paris, 1949). Quoted in Lefranc, op. cit., pp. 239–40.
65. *Bulletin Communiste*, 11–18 January 1923.
66. *Krasnyi Internatsional Profsoyuzov*, April 1924, p. 294. Quoted in Wohl, op. cit., p. 303.
67. Quoted in Gras, op. cit., p. 267. See also Wohl, op. cit., p. 301.
68. Carr, op. cit., vol. III, p. 455.
69. Wohl, op. cit., p. 344n.
70. *L'Humanité*, 1 July 1923.
71. *La Vie Ouvrière*, 24 August 1923.
72. Humbert-Droz to Zinoviev, 2 January 1924.

Chapter 3

1. Jederman, *La bolchévisation du p.c.f. (1923–1928)* (Paris, 1971), p. 61.
2. *L'Humanité*, 3–10 January 1924.
3. Degras, op. cit., vol. II (London, 1960), p. 80.
4. Ibid., vol. I, p. 260.
5. Ibid., vol. II, p. 80.
6. Jederman, op. cit., p. 24.
7. Degras, op. cit., vol. II, p. 81.
8. Ibid., p. 80.
9. Ibid., pp. 68–78.
10. Humbert-Droz to Zinoviev, 10 and 29 September 1923, 8 December 1923.
11. *L'Humanité*, 26 January 1924.
12. Humbert-Droz, *De Lénine à Staline* (op. cit.), p. 159.
13. Text in *Bulletin Communiste*, 4 April 1924. Reprinted in *Le Mouvement Social*, January–March 1971.
14. Degras, op. cit., vol. II, p. 84.
15. B. Lazitch, 'Two Instruments of Control by the Comintern', in *The Comintern: Historical Highlights*, ed.

Milorad M. Drachkovitch and B. Lazitch (Stanford, California, 1966).
16. *Bulletin Communiste*, 22 February 1924.
17. Ibid., 14 March 1924.
18. Wohl, op. cit., p. 160.
19. Ibid., pp. 377–8.
20. Ibid., p. 349.
21. Carr, *Socialism in One Country*, vol. III (London, 1964), p. 92.
22. See letters of Florimond Bonte to Monatte, 28 March 1924 (in *Archives Monatte*, p. 375) and of Maurice Thorez to Souvarine, 11 April and 2 May, in *Bulletin d'Etudes et d'Informations Politiques et Internationales* [BEIPI], 1–15 May 1950.
23. Carr, op. cit., p. 74.
24. Ibid., p. 147.
25. Jederman, op. cit., p. 38.
26. Degras, op. cit., vol. II, p. 154.
27. Ibid., p. 148.
28. Ibid., pp. 122–3.
29. Ibid., pp. 122–3.
30. Ibid., p. 126.
31. Ibid., p. 155; Jederman, op. cit., p. 28.
32. See A. Kriegel, 'Le PCF sous la Troisième République', in *Revue Française de Science Politique*, February 1966, p. 20.
33. *Cahiers du Bolchévisme*, no. 14, 1 March 1925.
34. Lepetit (Guralsky), 'Courtes remarques sur les défauts de notre travail', in *Cahiers du Bolchévisme*, no. 21, 15 June 1925. See Jederman, op. cit., pp. 38–53.
35. Degras, op. cit., vol. II, pp. 189–99. See also Carr, op. cit., pp. 297–8.
36. Carr, op. cit., pp. 328–9.
37. See the embarrassed comments of Krasin, the Soviet ambassador in Paris, in *Le Temps*, 8 August 1925.
38. See Carr, op. cit., pp. 353–62.
39. Ibid., pp. 362–3.
40. *Cahiers du Bolchévisme*, no. 47, 15 April 1926, pp. 883–6. See Carr, op. cit., pp. 514–17.
41. *Ve congrès du P.C.F.*, séance du 26 juin. Quoted in Jederman, op. cit., p. 56.
42. *Rapport politique du comité central*, quoted by A. Kriegel, *Le pain et les roses*, p. 216.

43. *Cahiers du Bolchévisme*, no. 86, December 1927.
44. Renaud Jean in *L'Humanité*, 22 June 1926.
45. Carr, op. cit., p. 925.
46. Jederman, op. cit., p. 69n.
47. Wohl, op. cit., p. 403. See 'Rapport moral du Sécrétariat général' (special number of *Cahiers du Bolchévisme*, 20 December 1924). One of the sixty-five Bobigny pupils was Jacques Duclos; J. Duclos, *Mémoires*, vol. I (Paris, 1968), p. 229.
48. Wohl, op. cit., pp. 405–6, quoting letter from Souvarine to the Russian opposition, December 1927 (in the Trotsky Archives), and M. Laporte, *Les Mystères du Kremlin* (1928), p. 229.
49. Dieter Wolf, *Doriot* [French translation of *Die Doriot Bewegung*] (Paris, 1969), pp. 32–40.
50. M. Thorez, *Fils du Peuple* (1970 edition), p. 58.
51. Letter from 'Léon' to unknown correspondent, Paris, 12 April 1924 (Rappoport Papers). Quoted in Wohl, op. cit., p. 380.
52. Rosmer, Charbit, Antonini, Godonnèche and Chambelland to Sellier, 23 April 1924 (*Archives Monatte*, p. 386).
53. Bruyère to Souvarine, 15 April 1924 (*Archives Monatte*). Quoted in Wohl, op. cit., p. 383.
54. Bouët to Monatte, 24 May 1924 (*Archives Monatte*).
55. Lazitch, art. cit., pp. 49–50. Guralsky used the pseudonym 'Kleine' in Germany, and 'Lepetit' in France.
56. *L'Humanité*, 2 June 1924.
57. Lazitch, art. cit., p. 50.
58. Reported by Lucie Colliard (*Archives Monatte*). Quoted in Wohl, op. cit., p. 388n.
59. Monatte to Zinoviev, 16 June 1924 (*Archives Monatte*, pp. 388–9). Lozovsky had pointed out to Monatte that 'of all the French communist leaders, you alone have not yet visited the Russia of the Soviets' (ibid., p. 387). Zinoviev had telegraphed a personal summons in

the name of the ECCI presidium (ibid., p. 388).
60. Wohl, op. cit., p. 388.
61. Carr, *Socialism in One Country* (op. cit.), vol. III, p. 146.
62. Rosmer to Monatte, 18 July 1924 (*Archives Monatte*, p. 392). Rosmer comments caustically that among Souvarine's bitterest foes were 'the "syndicalists" Sémard and Monmousseau who found nothing more interesting to do than follow these interesting debates'.
63. Carr, op. cit., pp. 147–8.
64. *L'Humanité*, 23 and 24 September 1924.
65. *Archives Monatte*, p. 402.
66. Ibid., pp. 402–6.
67. Ibid., pp. 407–13.
68. Ibid., pp. 416–17.
69. Ibid., p. 416.
70. Herclet to Monatte, 12 January 1925 (*Archives Monatte*, pp. 423–4).
71. Carr, op. cit., p. 153; Wohl, p. 419.
72. See Rosmer to Monatte, 6 June 1924 (*Archives Monatte*, p. 390).
73. Carr, op. cit., p. 155.
74. Ibid., pp. 349–51; Wohl, op. cit., pp. 424–5.
75. Carr, op. cit., pp. 351–66, 514–17.
76. Humbert-Droz to his wife, June 1926 (in *De Lénine à Staline*, pp. 269–71). Dunois had once described Suzanne Girault as 'a backstairs Catherine the Great, brutal, coarse and ferociously ambitious'. (Letter to Humbert-Droz, 2 February 1924, in Jules Humbert-Droz, *L'oeil de Moscou à Paris*, Paris, 1964, p. 227.)

Chapter 4

1. Kriegel, *Les Communistes français* (1970 edition), p. 161.
2. Jederman, op. cit., p. 97.
3. Humbert-Droz, *L'oeil de Moscou à Paris* (op. cit.), pp. 255–6.
4. Humbert-Droz, *De Lénine à Stáline* (op. cit.), pp. 277–80.
5. Quoted in *Histoire du Parti Communiste Français*, Tome I, *Des Origines à 1940*

(Paris, Editions Veridad, n.d.) [henceforth cited as Unir I], pp. 134–5.

6. Degras, op. cit., vol. II, pp. 401–2.
7. S. V. Gallup, 'Communists and Socialists in the Vaucluse 1920–1939' (unpublished dissertation, UCLA, 1971), pp. 222–3.
8. Ferrat, op. cit., p. 218.
9. Isaac Deutscher, *The Prophet Unarmed* (1970 edition), p. 362.
10. *Cahiers du Bolchévisme*, December 1927.
11. *L'Humanité*, 24 November 1927.
12. Unir I, p. 138.
13. Wolf, op. cit., pp. 61, 66–8, 75.
14. Ibid., pp. 57–8.
15. Humbert-Droz, *De Lénine à Staline* (op. cit.), pp. 295–8.
16. Degras, op. cit., vol. II, pp. 429–30.
17. Humbert-Droz, *De Lénine à Staline* (op. cit.), p. 306.
18. Degras, op. cit., vol. II, p. 485.
19. Ibid., pp. 512–13.
20. Humbert-Droz, op. cit., p. 340.
21. Lazitch, art. cit., p. 59.
22. Humbert-Droz, Statement to the ECCI presidium on the policy of the KPD (autumn 1928): printed in *De Lénine à Staline*, pp. 326–40. The passage quoted is on p. 338.
23. *L'Humanité*, 4 April 1929.
24. Unir I, p. 144.
25. Ibid., p. 254.
26. Kriegel, *Les Communistes français* (1970 edition), pp. 216–17.
27. Ibid., pp. 254–5.
28. *L'Humanité*, 3–4 November 1929.
29. Kriegel, op. cit., p. 140.
30. *Discours . . . au Comite Central du 17 juillet 1930*, pp. 23, 25.
31. Brochure containing the reports of Thorez and Frachon to the Conference, quoted in Unir I, p. 151.
32. Lazitch, art. cit., p. 62.
33. Drachkovitch and Lazitch (eds.), op. cit., p. 390.
34. 'M. Fauvet saisi par la légende', in *Preuves*, February 1965.
35. Brochure *Le Parti Communiste Français devant l'Internationale*, quoted in Walter, op. cit., pp. 221–2.
36. Ferrat, art. cit.
37. 'Pas de Mannequins', in *L'Humanité*, 14 August 1931; reprinted in Thorez, *Oeuvres Choisies* (Paris, 1967), vol. I, pp. 87–9.
38. 'Les Bouches s'ouvrent', in *L'Humanité*, 21 August 1931; reprinted in Thorez, op. cit., pp. 90–4.
39. Ferrat, art. cit.

Chapter 5

1. See F. Castaing, 'Aux Origines des Jeunesses communistes de France', in *Le Mouvement Social*, no. 74 (January–March 1971).
2. Wohl, op. cit., pp. 318–19.
3. Unir I, p. 95.
4. Wohl, op. cit., p. 323, quoting Barbé, 'Souvenirs de militant et de dirigeant communiste' (MS at the Hoover Institution), pp. 19–33.
5. The Communist agitation is not even mentioned, for example, in the chapter 'L'Affaire de la Ruhr' in Jacques Chastenet, *Histoire de la Troisième République*.
6. 'Rapport et résolution sur le communisme et les colonies, adoptés au premier Congrès du parti communiste (Marseille, 25–30 décembre 1921)', *Bulletin Communiste*, 14 February 1922; reprinted in J. Moneta, *Le PCF et la question coloniale* (1920–1965) (Paris, 1971), pp. 21–4.
7. 'Extraits du discours de L. Trotsky, rapporteur au IVe Congrès mondial de l'Internationale communiste sur le parti français devant l'Internationale', *Bulletin Communiste*, no. 2–3, 11–18 January 1923; reprinted in Moneta, op. cit., pp. 28–9.
8. 'Résolution sur la question coloniale, adoptée à l'unanimité par le Conseil national du P. C. les 1 et 2 juin 1924', *Bulletin Communiste*, no. 25, 20 June 1924; reprinted in Moneta, op. cit., pp. 36–7.
9. See J. Spiegler, 'Aspects of Nationalist Thought among French-speaking West Africans

1921–1939' (typed D.Phil. thesis, Oxford, 1968), p. 94n.

10. Wolf, op. cit., p. 42; Unir I, pp. 110–11.

11. Wolf, ibid.

12. 'La guerre du Maroc', *Cahiers du bolchévisme*, no. 19, 15 May 1925; reprinted in Moneta, op. cit., pp. 53–4.

13. Quoted in Unir I, p. 112.

14. Wolf, op. cit., p. 51.

15. Spiegler, op. cit., p. 97.

16. Chastenet, op. cit., vol. V, p. 19.

17. Lenin, *Works* (French edition), vol. XXII, p. 252.

18. E. Bonnefous, *Histoire Politique de la Troisième République*, vol. IV (Paris, 1960), pp. 51–4.

19. Ibid., p. 221n.

20. Ferrat, *Histoire du Parti Communiste Français* (op. cit.), p. 247.

21. *L'Humanité*, 25 December 1929.

22. See Moneta, op. cit., pp. 84–104.

23. See graph in A. Kriegel, 'Le P.C.F. sous la Troisième République', in *Revue Française de Science Politique*, February 1966, p. 35.

24. A. Prost, *La C.G.T. à l'époque du Front Populaire 1934–1939* (Paris, 1964), p. 35.

25. G. Lefranc, *Le Mouvement Syndical sous la Troisième République* (Paris, 1967), p. 271.

26. Prost, op. cit., p. 34.

27. Alfred Sauvy, *Histoire Economique de la France entre les Deux Guerres*, vol. I (Paris, 1965), p. 261.

28. Prost, op. cit., pp. 33–4.

29. Jederman, *La bolchévisation du p.c.f.* (op. cit.), p. 96.

30. Lefranc, op. cit., p. 277.

31. Quoted in Jederman, op. cit., p. 97.

32. Ibid., pp. 97–8.

33. Lefranc, loc. cit.

34. Ibid., p. 278.

35. See Gras, *Alfred Rosmer et le mouvement révolutionnaire international* (op. cit.), pp. 366–7.

36. Ibid., p. 366.

37. Bonnefous, op. cit., vol. V (Paris, 1962), p. 94.

38. Lefranc, op. cit., p. 324.

39. Ibid., pp. 275–6.

40. Jacques Julliard, 'Le Mouvement Syndical', in Sauvy, *Histoire Economique de la France entre les Deux Guerres*, vol. III (Paris, 1972), p. 187.

41. See Prost, op. cit., pp. 51–64.

42. Wohl, op. cit., p. 218.

43. Trotsky, *Le Mouvement Communiste en France* (op. cit.), pp. 155–6.

44. Trotsky, *Kommunisticheskoe dvizhenie vo Frantsii* (Moscow, 1923), pp. 142–3. Quoted in Wohl, op. cit., pp. 331–2.

45 *L'Humanité*, 17 December 1924.

46. See *Le Populaire*, February and March 1924 *passim* (esp. 4 February and 26 March); Wohl, op. cit., pp. 384–5, 501.

47. Jederman, op. cit., p. 100.

48. Wohl, op. cit., p. 385.

49. Gallup, op. cit., pp. 163–6.

50. See, for example, the study of the Puy-de-Dôme by J.-P. Vaudon in *Le Mouvement Social*, January–March 1971, p. 80.

51. Jederman, op. cit., p. 101.

52. François Platone, 'L'Implantation municipale du PCF dans la Seine et sa Conception de l'Administration municipale' (typed *Mémoire*, Fondation Nationale des Sciences Politiques, Paris, 1967), pp. 12–14.

53. *Cahiers du Bolchévisme*, no. 38, 4 February 1926.

54. Ibid., no. 50, 31 May 1926.

55. Jederman, op. cit., pp. 101–2; Bonnefous, op. cit., vol. IV, pp. 201–2.

56. Bonnefous, op. cit., vol. IV, p. 251.

57. See map in Jacques Fauvet, *Histoire du Parti Communiste Français*, vol. I (Paris, 1964), p. 283.

58. Jederman, op. cit., p. 105; Walter, op. cit., p. 192.

59. *L'Humanité*, 5 September 1931.

60. *Cahiers du Bolchévisme*, 1 May 1932, pp. 621–3. See Walter, op. cit., pp. 239–40.

61. Quoted in Annette Vidal, *Henri Barbusse Soldat de la Paix* (Paris, 1953), p. 73.

62. *L'Humanité*, 10 May 1919.

63. D. Caute, *Communism and the French Intellectuals* (London, 1964), p. 43.

64. Vidal, op. cit., p. 126.

65. Caute, op. cit., p. 23.
66. Ibid., p. 76.
67. Vladimir Brett, *Henri Barbusse* (Prague, 1963), pp. 232–3.
68. Quoted in A. Breton, *Entretiens* (Paris, 1952), p. 111.
69. Ibid., pp. 95, 98–9, 111.
70. Quoted in ibid., p. 118.
71. André Thirion, *Révolutionnaires Sans Révolution* (Paris, 1972), p. 126.
72. Breton, op. cit., pp. 126–7.
73. Thirion, op. cit., pp. 285–92.
74. Caute, op. cit., p. 102.
75. Breton, op. cit., pp. 163–4.
76. L. Aragon, *Pour un réalisme socialiste* (Paris, 1935), pp. 16, 54. Quoted in Caute, op. cit., p. 98.
77. Thirion, op. cit., pp. 305–6.
78. Interview with *Les Nouvelles Littéraires*, quoted in A. Ginsbourg, *Nizan* (Paris, 1966), p. 9.
79. Caute, op. cit., p. 270.
80. Ginsbourg, op. cit., pp. 22–3.
81. Vidal, op. cit., p. 241.
82. Text in N. Racine and L. Bodin (eds.), *Le Parti Communiste Français pendant l'Entre-Deux-Guerres* (Paris, 1972), pp. 193–5.
83. Caute, op. cit., p. 108.
84. Thirion, op. cit., p. 329.
85. Ibid., p. 383.
86. Thorez, *Fils du Peuple* (1970 edition), pp. 79–80.
87. Extracts in Vidal, op. cit., pp. 276–7.
88. Ibid., p. 282.
89. See for instance Gallup, *Communists and Socialists in the Vaucluse* (op. cit.), p. 314.

Chapter 6

1. See Alfred Sauvy, *Histoire économique de la France entre les deux guerres*, vol. I (Paris, 1965), pp. 114–27; vol. II (Paris, 1967), pp. 15–137, 151–4, 401–11, 554–6.
2. Speech to the XIth Plenum of ECCI.
3. *Internationale*, December 1931.
4. Kriegel, *Les Communistes Français* (Paris, 1968), p. 154.
5. *Cahiers du Bolchévisme*, 15 October 1932.

6. W. E. Scott, *Alliance Against Hitler* (Durham, North Carolina, 1962), pp. 8–73.
7. Sauvy, op. cit., vol. II, pp. 37–9.
8. Thorez, *Oeuvres Choisies*, vol. I (Paris, 1967), pp. 95–112.
9. See D. Wolf, *Doriot* (op. cit.), pp. 89–96.
10. *L'Humanité*, 6 March 1933.
11. Ibid., 1 April 1933.
12. Fauvet, *Histoire du Parti Communiste Français*, vol. I (Paris, 1964), p. 116.
13. Caute, *Communism and the French Intellectuals* (op. cit.), p. 106.
14. Wolf, op. cit., pp. 94–5.
15. Jane Degras (ed.), *The Communist International 1919–1943: Documents*, vol. III, 1929–1943 (London/New York/Toronto, 1965), p. 303.
16. *International Press Correspondence (Inprecorr)*, 7 May 1934, p. 710. Quoted in Daniel R. Brower, *The New Jacobins* (Ithaca, New York, 1968), pp. 8–9.
17. Degras, op. cit., vol. III, p. 288.
18. Ibid., p. 292.
19. Ibid., p. 291.
20. Quoted in Wolf, op. cit., p. 96.
21. Brower, op. cit., pp. 20–2, quoting personal interview with P.-L. Darnar.
22. Wolf, op. cit., pp. 97–100.
23. Bonnefous, *Histoire de la Troisième République*, vol. V, pp. 206–12.
24. Wolf, op. cit., p. 106.
25. Brower, op. cit., p. 34 (again quoting Darnar).
26. See *L'Humanité*, 25 May 1955, and Jacques Duclos, *Mémoires*, vol. I, p. 401.
27. Wolf, op. cit., pp. 107–8, quoting manuscript account by Barbé of a conversation with Doriot.
28. Vassart, 'Compte-rendu d'une conférence', *La Révolution Prolétarienne*, no. 414, February 1957, p. 23.
29. Bonnefous, op. cit., pp. 220–1.
30. Wolf, op. cit., pp. 110–11.
31. Ibid., p. 112.
32. Ibid., p. 115n.
33. Ibid., p. 114.
34. Brower, op. cit., p. 41.
35. Degras, op. cit., vol. III, p. 315.
36. Ibid., p. 328.

37. Lefranc, *Le Mouvement syndical sous la Troisième République* (op. cit.), pp. 320–1.
38. Wolf, op. cit., pp. 115–17.
39. *Les Communistes de Saint-Denis et les événements du 6 au 12 février. Pour l'Unité d'Action! Lettre ouverte à l'Internationale communiste. Preface de Jacques Doriot* (n.d.). A short extract is printed in N. Racine and L. Bodin (eds.), *Le Parti Communiste Français pendant l'Entre-Deux-Guerres* (op. cit.), pp. 215–17.
40. Wolf, op. cit., p. 118.
41. Célie and Albert Vassart, 'The Moscow Origin of the French Popular Front', in Drachkovitch and Lazitch (eds.), *The Comintern: Historical Highlights* (op. cit.), pp. 234–52.
42. Wolf, op. cit., pp. 118–23.
43. Quoted in Brower, op. cit., p. 49. The unsigned article was translated in *L'Humanité* of 31 May, but the article by Thorez never appeared in it!
44. Wolf, op. cit., p. 124.
45. Ibid., pp. 124–5.
46. *Le Populaire*, 16 June 1934.
47. Ibid., 21 June 1934.
48. C. and A. Vassart, art. cit., pp. 248–51.
49. *L'Humanité*, 29 June 1934. See Brower, op. cit., p. 60; also Ferrat, 'Le Parti Communiste', in *Esprit*, no. 80, May 1939, p. 167, where, however, these events are misdated May 1934. The full text of Thorez's speech is in his *Oeuvres* (Paris, 1950–60), Livre II, Tome 6. Extracts in *Oeuvres Choisies*, vol. I, pp. 121–35.
50. Thirion, *Révolutionnaires Sans Révolution* (op. cit.), pp. 396–8.
51. *Le Populaire*, 31 August 1933.
52. Duclos, op. cit., vol. I, p. 419.
53. See Scott, op. cit., *passim*.

Chapter 7

1. Texts of all three documents (Socialist proposal of 23 June, Communist counter-proposal of 2 July, and text finally adopted on 27 July) in *Cahiers du Bolchévisme*, 1 August 1935, pp. 959–61; reprinted in Racine and Bodin, op. cit., pp. 221–4.
2. See Brower, op. cit., p. 66.
3. Bonnefous, op. cit., vol. v, p. 278.
4. Brower, op. cit., p. 72.
5. *L'Humanité*, 12 October 1934. See Brower, op. cit. pp. 74–5.
6. Bonnefous, op. cit., vol. v, p. 294.
7. *L'Humanité*, 25 October 1934.
8. See Brower, op. cit., pp. 76–8.
9. See Bonnefous, op. cit., vol. v, pp. 298–303.
10. Brower, op. cit., pp. 78–9.
11. *Kommunisticheskii International*, 1 December 1934. Quoted in Brower, op. cit., pp. 80–1.
12. Ibid., 10 January and 1 February 1935. Quoted in Brower, op. cit., p. 83.
13. *Internationale*, 5 March 1935. Quoted in Brower, op. cit., p. 77–8.
14. Branko Lazitch, 'Informations fournies par Albert Vassart sur la Politique du PCF entre 1934 et 1938' (MS in Hoover Institution, Stanford University), p. 17. Quoted in Brower, op. cit., pp. 84–5.
15. Bonnefous, op. cit., vol. v, pp. 320, 325.
16. Scott, op. cit., pp. 230–46.
17. Bonnefous, op. cit., vol. v, p. 328, quoting *L'Ordre* and *Le Temps* of 8 May.
18. G. Dupeux, *Les Elections de 1936 et le Front Populaire* (Paris, 1959), pp. 85–6.
19. Ibid., p. 85; Brower, op. cit., p. 86; Scott, op. cit., p. 251.
20. See F. Platone, 'L'Implantation municipale du PCF dans la Seine et sa Conception de l'Administration municipale' (typed *Mémoire*, Fondation Nationale des Sciences Politiques, Paris, 1967); also Brower, op. cit., p. 87, and Bonnefous, op. cit., vol. v, p. 330.
21. Henri de Kerillis in *L'Echo de Paris*. Quoted in Bonnefous, ibid.
22. *Journal Officiel*, Chambre des Députés, *Débats Parlementaires*

(Paris), 15 March 1935. See
Bonnefous, op. cit., vol. v, pp. 321–2,
and Scott, op. cit., p. 228.

23. Scott, ibid., p. 253; Geoffrey Warner,
Pierre Laval and the Eclipse of France
(London, 1968), pp. 81–2.

24. See *L'Humanité*, 16, 17 and 18 May
1935. Also Unir I, p. 173.

25. *Le Populaire*, 17 May 1935.

26. Brower, op. cit., pp. 91–3.

27. Ibid., pp. 94–5.

28. Bonnefous, op. cit., vol. v, p. 337–41.

29. *Journal Officiel*, Chambre des
Députés, *Débats Parlementaires*, 8 June
1935.

30. Bonnefous, loc. cit.; Dupeux, op. cit.,
pp. 91–2.

31. *Front mondial*, May 1935.

32. *Le Temps*, 9 January 1936.

33. Dupeux, loc. cit.

34. Brower, op. cit., p. 103.

35. *L'Humanité*, 14 July 1933.

36. Brower, op. cit., p. 104.

37. Dupeux, op. cit., p. 93.

38. Bonnefous, op. cit., vol. v, p. 344.

39. Degras, op. cit., vol. III, pp. 364–5.

40. *L'Humanité*, 26 October 1935.

41. Ibid., 12 November 1935.

42. Brower, op. cit., p. 113.

43. Ibid., p. 120.

44. Thorez, *Oeuvres* (op. cit.), Livre III,
Tome 11 (January–March 1936),
pp. 104–6.

45. *Compte rendu . . . du VIIe Congrès*,
p. 378.

46. Brower, op. cit., p. 128.

47. Ibid., p. 131.

48. See ibid., pp. 133–4.

49. See Joel Colton, *Léon Blum: Humanist
in Politics* (New York, 1966), p. 115.

50. This section is based mainly on
Antoine Prost, *La C.G.T. à l'époque du
Front Populaire 1934–1939* (Paris,
1964), chapter VI, 'Croissance
syndicale et force des tendances'. See
also Georges Lefranc, *Le Mouvement
Syndicale sous la Troisième République*
(Paris, 1967), part III, chapters VI and
VII.

51. Lefranc, *Juin 36* (Paris, 1966), p. 55.

52. Lefranc, *Les Expériences Syndicales en
France* (Paris, 1950), p. 365.

53. Ibid., p. 365.

54. For all the above see Georges
Dupeux, *Le Front Populaire et les
Elections de 1936* (Paris, 1958).

55. Brower, op. cit., p. 131.

56. Kriegel, 'Le PCF sous la Troisième
République' (art. cit.), from which
most of these statistics are taken.

57. The figure was given by Léon
Mauvais in his report to the Central
Committee meeting of January
1945. See A. Kriegel, *Les
Communistes Français* (1970 edition),
p. 261.

58. *L'Humanité*, 23 June 1938; Brower,
op. cit., p. 217.

59. Mauvais, loc. cit.

60. In Dupeux, op. cit.

61. Prost, op. cit.

62. Kriegel, loc. cit.

63. Brower, op. cit., p. 197.

64. J. Danos and M. Gibelin, *Juin 36*
(Paris, 1952), pp. 180–1.

65. Unir I, p. 204.

66. Jean Chaintron, in conversation
with the author, 25 November 1971.

67. *Cahiers du Bolchévisme*, 1 August
1935.

68. Degras, op. cit., vol. III, p. 358.

69. Ibid., p. 377.

70. Thorez, *Pour la cause du peuple* (Paris,
1935), p. 78.

71. See Kriegel, *Les Communistes
Français*, pp. 64–6.

72. Speech by Thorez to an assembly of
Parisian Communists, 6 August
1936.

73. Vaillant-Couturier in *L'Humanité*,
19 July 1936. Thorez at Congress of
Arles (December 1937).

74. Quoted in Fauvet, op. cit., vol. I,
p. 216.

75. *Recueil des textes authentiques des
programmes et engagements électoraux des
députés proclamés élus à la Chambre des
députés à la suite des élections générales
de 1936* (Paris, 1939), pp. 22–4.

76. See Caute, op. cit., for a very full
treatment of this subject.

77. A. Prost in *Léon Blum, Chef de
Gouvernement, 1936–1937* (Cahiers de
la Fondation nationale des Sciences
politiques, 155; Paris, 1967), p. 73.

78. *L'Humanité*, 27 June 1936.

79. Quoted by Dupeux in 'Léon Blum et la majorité parlementaire' in *Léon Blum, Chef de Gouvernement* (op. cit.), p. 112.
80. See his *Lettre ouverte aux membres du P.C.*, p. 13.
81. *L'Humanité*, 13 July 1936.
82. Ibid., 30 November and 2 December 1936.
83. For all the above, see Dupeux, art. cit., and Brower, op. cit.
84. See Thorez, *Fils du Peuple*, p. 121; Duclos, *Mémoires*, vol. ii, p. 147.
85. François Billoux, *Quand Nous Etions Ministres* (Paris, 1972), pp. 17–18.
86. Degras, op. cit., vol. iii. p. 392. See also Kriegel, 'Léon Blum et le Parti Communiste', in *Léon Blum, Chef de Gouvernement* (op. cit.).
87. See remarks by André Blumel (Blum's *Directeur de Cabinet*) in 'Les Leçons du Front Populaire', *Democratie Nouvelle*, May 1966.
88. Article in *Le Figaro*, reprinted as 'Dilemme du Chrétien' in *Le Communisme et les Chrétiens* (Paris, Plon, 193?).
89. Speech to assembly of Parisian Communists, printed in *Cahiers du Bolchévisme*, 25 August 1936.

Chapter 8

1. For this period, see especially Daniel R. Brower, *The New Jacobins* (Ithaca, New York, 1968), chapters vi and vii.
2. See Scott, *Alliance Against Hitler* (op. cit.)
3. Brower, op. cit., p. 207. See also Michel Debré, *Une certaine idée de la France* (Paris, 1972), p. 22: 'Peut-être étais-je trop enfermé dans mon milieu ou dans mes affaires. En tout cas je n'avais aucun contact avec des communistes'.
4. *Cahiers de Bolchévisme*, 25 August 1936.
5. *L'Humanité*, 27 August 1936.
6. See for instance his conversation with Bernanos, reported in the latter's *Le Chemin de la Croix-des-Ames*.
7. *Histoire du Parti communiste français (manuel)* (Paris, 1964), p. 332.
8. See Hugh Thomas, *The Spanish Civil War* (London, 1961), pp. 296–304, 637–9.
9. Notably Chaintron, in conversation with the author, 25 November 1971.
10. See Unir i, p. 201.
11. *L'Humanité*, 15 January 1938.
12. Ibid., 16 January 1938.
13. Ibid., 19 January 1938.
14. Joanny Berlioz in *Correspondance Internationale*, 8 April 1938.
15. See Gitton's article in *L'Humanité*, 24 March 1938.
16. Brower, op. cit., pp. 112–13.
17. Joel Colton, *Léon Blum: Humanist in Politics* (New York, 1966), p. 300.
18. *L'Humanité*, 13 April 1938.
19. *Le Populaire*, 22 April 1938.
20. See article by Joanny Berlioz in *Correspondance Internationale*, 30 July 1938.
21. Quoted in *Syndicats*, 28 September 1938.
22. *L'Humanité*, 11 November 1938.
23. *World News and Views*, xviii, 53, p. 1203, 5 November 1938; reprinted in Degras, op. cit., vol. iii, pp. 428–33.
24. *L'Humanité*, 25 November 1938.
25. Lefranc, *Le Mouvement Syndical sous la Troisième République* (op. cit.), p. 385.
26. Fauvet, op. cit., vol. i, pp. 244–5.
27. See Duclos, *Mémoires*, vol. ii, chapter 5.
28. See M. Beloff, *The Foreign Policy of Soviet Russia* (London/New York/Toronto, 1947), vol. ii, p. 269.
29. Ibid., pp. 270–2.
30. Ibid., pp. 271, 272n.
31. *Le Populaire*, 23 August 1939.
32. Quoted in Unir I, p. 230.
33. Quoted in Fauvet, op. cit., vol. i, p. 252.
34. Ibid., p. 260.
35. Auguste Lecoeur, *Le Partisan* (Paris, 1963), pp. 105–7.
36. Quoted in Fauvet, op. cit., vol. i, p. 253.
37. *Gringoire*, 27 August 1939.
38. See Blum in *Le Populaire*, 27 September 1939.
39. Fauvet, op. cit., vol. i, pp. 253–4.

40. See Caute, op. cit., pp. 137, 308–9.
41. See Henri Michel, *La Drôle de Guerre* (Paris, 1971), p. 101.
42. *Le Communisme en France* (BEIPI, no. 126: 1–15 March 1955), p. 7.
43. Unir I, p. 240.
44. *Le Populaire*, 27 September 1939.
45. Ibid., 4 October 1939.
46. *Journal Officiel*, 20 March 1940.
47. Fernand Grenier, *Journal de la Drôle de Guerre* (Paris, 1969), pp. 56, 60, 62, 68.
48. Reproduced in the *Daily Worker*, 4 November 1939, and partially in the clandestine *L'Humanité* of 17 November 1939.
49. *Rapports du Comité Central pour le Xe Congrès National* (Paris, 1945).
50. See Colton, op. cit., pp. 332–3.
51. Thorez, *Oeuvres*, Livre V, Tome 19 (1959), pp. 28–53.
52. *Le Partisan*, p. 139.
53. Quoted in A. Rossi, *Les communistes français pendant la drôle de guerre* (Paris, 1951).
54. Michel, op. cit., p. 202.
55. Quoted in Florimond Bonte, *Le Chemin de l'Honneur* (Paris, 1970), pp. 104–5.
56. *Journal Officiel*, 17 January 1940.
57. Degras, op. cit., vol. III, pp. 465–6.
58. Michel, op. cit., p. 201.
59. Quoted in Grenier, op. cit., p. 219.
60. Louis Aragon, *Les Communistes*, vol. III (Paris, 1951), p. 326.
61. Duclos, *Mémoires*, vol. III, part I, p. 55.
62. *Histoire du Parti Communiste Français*, Tome II, *De 1940 à la Libération* (Paris, Editions Unir, n.d.) [henceforth cited as Unir II], p. 25.
63. Ibid., and Fauvet, op. cit., vol. II, p. 58.
64. Unir II, p. 26.
65. Institut Maurice Thorez, *Le Parti Communiste Français dans la Résistance* (Paris, 1967), p. 73.
66. Auguste Lecoeur, *Le Parti Communiste Français et la Résistance* (Paris, 1968), p. 88.
67. See Duclos, *Mémoires*, vol. III, part I, p. 57; H. Noguères, M. Degliame-Fouché, and J.-L. Viglier, *Histoire de la Résistance en France de 1940*

à *1945*, Tome I: *Le première année, juin 1940–juin 1941* (Paris, 1967), p. 54; Grenier, in Institut Maurice Thorez, *Des Victoires de Hitler au triomphe de la démocratie et du socialisme. Origines et bilan de la deuxième guerre mondiale (1939–1945)* (Paris, 1970), p. 90; Eugène Saint-Sébastien in *La Nation Socialiste*, December 1967; and H. R. Kedward, *Resistance in Vichy France* (Oxford, 1978), p. 50.
68. Full text in Thorez, *Oeuvres Choisies*, vol. II, pp. 193–202.
69. Text of the letter in Unir II, pp. 42–7. Billoux acknowledged writing it in *L'Humanité*, 18 May 1951.
70. Unir II, p. 47.
71. Quoted in ibid., p. 53.
72. *Lettre aux militants communistes* (pamphlet published early in 1941). Quoted in Unir II, p. 57.
73. Clandestine *L'Humanité*, January 1941.
74. Ibid., February 1941.
75. Special number of *L'Humanité*, 18 March 1941.
76. See Unir II, pp. 59–68; A. Rossi, *La Guerre des Papillons*, pp. 47, 50, 51, 58, 87.
77. *Cahiers du Bolchévisme*, 2e et 3e trimestres 1941.
78. Rossi, op. cit., p. 207.
79. Caute, op. cit., p. 144.
80. Grenier, op. cit., chapter VII *passim*.
81. Conversation with the author, 25 November 1971.
82. *La Nation Socialiste*, January 1958. Quoted in Lecoeur, *Le Parti Communiste* (op. cit.), pp. 74–6.
83. Charles Tillon, *Les F.T.P.* (2nd edition, 1967), pp. 24–5.
84. Claude Angeli and Paul Gillet, *Debout, Partisans!* (Paris, 1970), pp. 118–20.
85. Ibid., p. 143.
86. René Gallissot, 'Débuts de la Résistance' in *Le Mouvement Social*, no. 74 (January-March 1971), p. 137.
87. Noguères, op. cit., p. 252n.
88. Evidence, ibid., pp. 124, 252.
89. Unir II, p. 20.
90. Chaintron, conversation with the author, 25 November 1971.

91. H. Rol-Tanguy, in Noguères, op. cit., p. 250.
92. Tillon, op. cit., p. 44; Marcel Paul, in Noguères, op. cit., pp. 272, 350–1.
93. Unir II, pp. 70–4.
94. *Le Partisan*, pp. 172–5.
95. Angeli and Gillet, op. cit., p. 291.

Chapter 9

1. Georgette Elgey, *La République des Illusions* (Paris, 1965), p. 36.
2. *La Vie Ouvrière*, 16 August and 17 October 1941.
3. N. I. Godunov, *The Struggle of the French People against the Hitlerite Occupiers and their Accomplices* (Moscow, 1953), quoted in Alfred J. Rieber, *Stalin and the French Communist Party 1941–1947* (New York and London, 1962), p. 84.
4. General de Gaulle, *Mémoires de la Guerre*, vol. II, *L'Unité 1942–1944* (Livre de Poche edition, Paris, 1956) [henceforth cited as *L'Unité*], pp. 310, 308.
5. De Gaulle, *Mémoires de la Guerre*, vol. III, *Le Salut* (Paris, 1959) [henceforth cited as *Salut*], p. 30.
6. Quoted in Tillon, *Les F.T.P.* (op. cit.), p. 332.
7. See Rieber, op. cit., p. 135.
8. Robert Aron, *Histoire de la Libération de la France* (Paris, 1959) [henceforth cited as *Libération*], pp. 599–633.
9. De Gaulle, *L'Unité*, p. 6.
10. Ibid., pp. 184–5.
11. Unir II, pp. 294–301.
12. Aron, *Histoire de l'Epuration*, vol. I, *De l'indulgence aux massacres, novembre 1942–septembre 1944* (Paris, 1967), p. 222.
13. F. Grenier, *C'Etait Ainsi* (Paris, 1970), pp. 167–8.
14. Fauvet, op. cit., vol. II, p. 116.
15. De Gaulle, *Le Salut*, pp. 173–81.
16. Henri Michel, *Les Courants de Pensée de la Résistance* (Paris, 1962), p. 470.
17. See de Gaulle, *Salut*, p. 9.
18. Aron, *Libération*, p. 594.
19. Ibid., pp. 614–15.

20. Ibid., pp. 620–1.
21. Ibid., p. 118, quoting circular issued by Region R6 on 14 August 1944.
22. Fauvet, op. cit., vol. II, p. 147.
23. De Gaulle, *Salut*, pp. 38–9.
24. Unir II, pp. 246–7.
25. Ibid., p. 220.
26. Aron, *Libération*, p. 605.
27. Ibid., p. 617.
28. Ibid., pp. 621–2.
29. Unir II, pp. 254–5.
30. Ibid., p. 259.
31. See Lecoeur, *Le Partisan* (op. cit.), pp. 206–7.
32. Ibid.
33. Unir II, pp. 260–1.
34. Philip M. Williams, *Crisis and Compromise* (London, 1964), p. 391.
35. Tillon, *Les F.T.P.* (op. cit.), p. 363n.
36. De Gaulle, *Salut*, p. 5.
37. Unir II, pp. 259–60.
38. De Gaulle, *Salut*, p. 100.
39. Unir II, pp. 247–8.
40. *L'Humanité*, 1 December 1944.
41. De Gaulle, *Salut*, p. 63.
42. Ibid., p. 101.
43. *S'unir, combattre, travailler* (pamphlet published by the PCF in January 1945).
44. Tillon, *Les F.T.P.* (op. cit.), p. 363n.
45. Unir II, p. 271.

Chapter 10

1. *S'unir, combattre, travailler* (op. cit.).
2. G. A. Deborin, *International Relations in the Years of the Great Patriotic War, 1941–45* (Moscow and Leningrad, 1948), p. 248. Quoted in Rieber, op. cit., p. 113.
3. Royal Insititute of International Affairs, *The Soviet-Yugoslav Dispute* (London, 1948), p. 51.
4. Robert E. Sherwood, *Roosevelt and Hopkins: An Intimate Biography* (New York, 1949), pp. 785–6.
5. Rieber, op. cit., pp. 209–10.
6. Quoted in Elgey, *La République des Illusions* (op. cit.), p. 18.
7. Ibid., p. 103.
8. Ibid., p. 104.

9. Joseph M. Jones, *The Fifteen Weeks* (New York, 1955), p. 140.
10. Elgey, op. cit., p. 249.
11. Thorez, *Oeuvres Choisies*, vol. ii, pp. 342–3.
12. Ibid., pp. 318, 344.
13. *The Times*, 18 November 1946.
14. Quoted in Elgey, op. cit., p. 22.
15. For this section, see especially Georges Lefranc, *Les Expériences Syndicales en France* (Paris, 1950).
16. See Rieber, op. cit., pp. 179–81.
17. *Carnet d'un captif* (Paris, 1945), p. 49.
18. De Gaulle, *Salut*, pp. 256–7, 267–8.
19. Quoted in Elgey, op. cit., p. 35.
20. Ibid., p. 17.
21. See Jean Schwoebel, *La Presse, Le Pouvoir et l'Argent*.
22. Fauvet, op. cit., vol. ii, p. 178.
23. De Gaulle, *Salut*, pp. 266–7, 269–70.
24. See Jean Ranger, 'Le vote communiste en France depuis 1945', in *Le Communisme en France* (Cahiers de la Fondation Nationale des Sciences Politiques, Paris, 1969), pp. 211–53.
25. Fauvet, op. cit., vol. ii, pp. 166–7.
26. See Rieber, op. cit., pp. 161–3.
27. Williams, op. cit., p. 391.
28. Elgey, op. cit., pp. 20–2.
29. De Gaulle, *Salut*, p. 275.
30. Elgey, op. cit., p. 119.
31. Ibid., p. 19.
32. Kriegel, *Les Communistes français* (1968 edition), p. 57.
33. *S'unir, combattre, travailler* (op. cit.).
34. 'Produire, Faire du Charbon', in *Oeuvres Choisies*, vol. ii, p. 399.
35. Quoted in Lefranc, *Les Expériences Syndicales en France* (op. cit.).
36. Jacques Pruja, 'Le gauchisme, base de manoeuvre de la réaction dans le mouvement ouvrier', in *Servir la France*, October 1946.
37. Lefranc, op. cit., p. 173; Rieber, op. cit., pp. 310–11.
38. Lefranc, op. cit.
39. *Le Partisan*, p. 216.
40. Elgey, op. cit., p. 30.
41. Fajon in the Consultative Assembly, 11 July 1945.
42. Bonte, ibid., 21 November 1944.
43. Henri Lozeré, 'La Question coloniale', in *Cahiers du Communisme*, no. 6 (April 1945), p. 74.
44. *Paris-Saigon* (Saigon), no. 19 (29 May 1946) as quoted in Bernard Fall, 'Tribulations of a Party Line', *Foreign Affairs*, xxxiii, no. 3 (April, 1955), p. 500.
45. See Elgey, op. cit., pp. 30–35.
46. See Rieber, op. cit., chapter xii; Elgey, op. cit., chapters iv, v, vi; Gordon Wright, *The Re-shaping of French Democracy* (New York, 1948).
47. Elgey, op. cit., p. 55.
48. De Gaulle, *Salut*, p. 269.
49. Elgey, op. cit., p. 202; Rieber, op. cit., p. 293.
50. Elgey, op. cit., p. 217.
51. Ibid., p. 64; Rieber, op. cit., pp. 275–8.
52. Elgey, op. cit., pp. 64–89.
53. Ibid., pp. 100–10; Rieber, op. cit., p. 283.
54. Jacques Duclos, *En avant pour la victoire de la République* (report to the Central Committee, 20–1 April 1946) (Paris, 1946).
55. Wright, op. cit., p. 178; Elgey, op. cit., p. 202.
56. See Elgey, ibid., pp. 142–3.
57. Ibid., p. 210.
58. Rieber, op. cit., pp. 300–1.
59. Elgey, op. cit., pp. 231–2; Rieber, op. cit., p. 307.
60. Elgey, op. cit., pp. 232–44; Rieber, op. cit., p. 344.
61. Elgey, op. cit., pp. 288–92.
62. Ibid., p. 292.
63. Quoted in Rieber, op. cit., p. 355.
64. *L'Humanité*, 20 May 1947.
65. Fauvet, op. cit., vol. ii, p. 199.
66. Elgey, op. cit., p. 330.
67. Fauvet, op. cit., vol. ii, pp. 202–3; E. Reale, *Avec Jacques Duclos au banc des accusés* (1958), *passim*.
68. Quoted in Elgey, op. cit., p. 336.
69. Ibid., p. 360.
70. Ibid., pp. 375–6.

Epilogue

1. *Cahiers du Communisme*, November 1974, p. 55.

Notes

2. Kriegel, *Les Communistes Français* (1970 edition), p. 13.
3. Ibid., p. 298.
4. See Caute, op. cit., chapter 6.
5. Fauvet, *Histoire du Parti Communiste Français 1920–1976* (new one-volume edition, 1977), p. 523.
6. Quoted by Jacques Ozouf in *Esprit*, February 1975, p. 187.
7. *Le Monde*, 16 May 1974, p. 44.
8. F. Claudin, *The Communist Movement: From Comintern to Cominform* (English translation, Penguin Books, 1975), pp. 384–5.
9. Institut Maurice Thorez, *La Marche de la France au Socialisme* (Paris, 1966), p. 71.
10. Jean Elleinstein, *Le P.C.* (Paris, 1976), p. 15.
11. Fauvet, op. cit., p. 532.
12. Quoted by W. Rochet, *L Avenir du Parti Communiste Français* (Paris, 1969), p. 117.
13. Parti Communiste Français, *Changer de cap: programme pour un gouvernement démocratique d'union populaire* (Paris, 1971), p. 128.
14. *Le Programme commun de gouvernement* (supplement to *L'Humanité*, 18 June 1972), p. 10.
15. See Jean Montaldo, *Les Finances du P.C.F.* (Paris, 1977).
16. Zhores Medvedev in Bertrand Russell Peace Foundation, *The Case of Nikolai Bukharin* (Nottingham, 1978), pp. 102–3.
17. See Neil McInnes, 'From Komintern to Polycentrism', in Filo Della Torre, E. Mortimer and J. Story (eds.), *Eurocommunism: Myth or Reality* (Milan, 1978; London, 1979).
18. Fauvet, op. cit., p. 523.
19. Ibid., p. 529.
20. Ibid., p. 562.
21. Ibid.; Ronald Tiersky, 'Le PCF et la détente', in *Esprit*, February 1975, p. 224.
22. Tiersky, 'French Communism in 1976', in *Problems of Communism* (1976), p. 41.
23. *L'Humanité*, 15 January 1976.
24. Elleinstein, op. cit., p. 19.
25. *L'Humanité*, 5 February 1976.
26. See *Le Monde*, 5 October 1977: 'M. Poperen (P.S.): l'objectif du P.C.F. est de détruire la social-democratie'.
27. See André Fontaine, 'La main de Moscou?', in *Le Monde*, 25–6 September 1977.
28. Elleinstein, op. cit., p. III.
29. Elleinstein, 'Du XXIIe congrès du P.C.F. à l'échec de la gauche', *Le Monde*, 13–15 April 1978.
30. Elleinstein, in *Maintenant*, no. 9 (7 May 1979), p. 3.
31. *Humanité Dimanche*, Paris regional edition, no. 171 (13 May 1979), p. 4.
32. *Le Monde*, 12 May 1979, p. 12.
33. *L'Humanité*, 10 May 1979, pp. 6, 7.
34. *Le Monde*, 13 May 1981.

Index

411

415

Index

Index

Duclos, Jacques, 223, 285, 294; 1928 election, 162; 1932 election, 178; 1934 crisis, 210, 211; nationalism, 257, 258; on the Radicals, 262; and the 'Clichy affair', 264; right accuses of spying, 284; in German occupation, 298n., 302, 303, 305; and the Liberation, 316, 322 and n., 323; and the constitution, 352; 1947 defeat, 356, 357, 358; 1969 presidential election, 369
Dudilieux, Edouard, 97, 131, 167
Duhamel, Georges, 181
Dumont, Colonel, 271, 296
Dumoulin, Georges, 32, 41, 89, 168, 169
Dunkirk, 162, 285
Dunois, Amédée, 74, 75, 126, 128, 157, 181, 182
Düsseldorf, 71

L'Ecole Emancipée, 121–2
Ehrenburg, Ilya, 260
Einstein, Albert, 192
Eisenhower, Dwight D., 309
elections (general): May 1914, 21, 24; November 1919, 48–9, 158, 171; May 1924, 108, 120, 173–4; April 1928, 133, 136, 138, 160, 162, 176–7; May 1932, 177–8, 200; April/May 1936, 240, 248–9, 251–3, 258, 262; October 1945, 338, 341–2, 351; June 1946, 342, 352; November 1946, 342, 353, 361; November 1958, 361–2, 387; November 1962, 362, 365; March 1967, 368; June 1968, 368–9, 387; March 1973, 370; March 1978, 371, 384–8; June 1981, 362, 394–5
elections (presidential), 365–6; 1965, 366, 367–8; 1969, 369; 1974, 370; 1981, 394
Elleinstein, Jean, 383, 389–90
Eluard, Paul, 184, 185
L'Emancipation nationale, 291
Epstein, Joseph, 306
L'Esprit, 188
Essen, 82, 95, 152–3
Estonia, 203n.
Étudiants communistes, 302
'Eurocommunism', 389, 391, 392–3
'European Anti-fascist Workers' Congress', Paris (1933), 193
'European Committee for the Struggle against Fascism', 193
European Defence Community, 363, 364, 389
European Economic Community (EEC), 367, 374, 378, 389
Executive Committee of the Communist

International (ECCI), 58, 79, 120, 123, 141, 143, 173; split in the Second International, 55–6; meetings with SFIO delegates, 57; Second Comintern Congress, 62, 63; Souvarine elected as representative to, 69; dissolves the Committee for the Third International, 71; and the formation of the PCF, 72; defeat of PCF centre, 73; united front tactic, 76, 204, 205–6; factory cells, 100–2, 108, 111; and the failure of the German revolution, 102; and the British Communist Party, 105; Plenum (1925), 114, 126; and the KPD, 115; Sixth Enlarged Plenum (1926), 116–17, 128, 157; and the power struggle in the PCF, 122, 125–8; and electoral combinations, 133; 'Letter of April 2nd', 133–4; Sacco-Vanzetti strike, 134; Ninth Plenum (1928), 139–40; Tenth Plenum (1929), 146; Eleventh Plenum (1931), 148, 149; and PCF's anti-colonialism, 163; Twelfth Plenum (1932), 200; Thirteenth Plenum (1933), 203, 205–6; anti-fascist movement, 204, 212–13, 275; and the campaign against Doriot, 215; and Spain, 266; May Day manifesto (1940), 288, 291–2

Fabre, Henri, 72, 73, 74, 76
Fabre, Robert, 385
Fajnzylberg, Roger, 391
Fajon, Etienne, 333, 357, 358, 381
Farge, Yves, 317
Farman aircraft factory, 289
fascism, 140, 143, 198–9, 328; 'social fascism', 146, 147, 199, 206; anti-fascist movement, 190–4, 212–14, 218, 221, 226, 237–8, 269–78; Communists' reactions to, 199–200; Comintern opposition to, 204; 1934 demonstrations, 208–9
Faure, Paul, 219; opposition to First World War, 32–3; 1919 election, 48; and the split in the SFIO, 63, 65; government repression, 163; 1932 election, 177; and the united front tactic, 202, 203, 205, 207; 1934 crisis, 211; formation of Popular Front, 237; and appeasement, 269
'Fédération Communiste des Soviets', 52
Fédération de la Gauche Démocrate et Socialiste, 368–9, 370
Fédération des syndicats d'employés catholiques, 25

417

Index

95–6, 97, 101–2; and the Second
International, 49–50; and world
revolution, 55; possibility of
revolution, 56; 'March Action', 73;
Kapp putsch, 83; Locarno Treaty, 115,
159; French occupation of the Ruhr,
152–3; rise of Nazism, 191, 194, 198–9;
Hitler's rise to power, 193, 198, 203,
204, 206, 217, 222; rearmament, 193,
231; 1930s economic crisis, 198;
customs union with Austria, 201; 1932
elections, 202; relations with Soviet
Union, 224; reoccupation of
Rhineland, 239; growing threat, 260,
268, 269; German-Soviet
Non-Aggression pact, 267, 268,
278–83, 285, 290, 294, 303–7, 333; and
Non-Intervention, 269–70; invasion of
Austria, 272; appeasement of, 273,
274–5; invades Poland, 284;
Communist collaborators, 291;
advances on France, 292–3;
occupation of France, 294–306,
307–14; attacks Russia, 300, 305, 306;
defeat in France, 315–16; see also
Kommunistische Partei Deutschlands
Gerö, Ernö, 149
Gestapo, 304
Gide, André, 193, 260
Gide, Charles, 181
Ginzburg, Alexander, 389
Giraud, General Henri, 314–15, 324
Girault, Suzanne, 105, 107, 108, 116–17,
120, 128, 131, 139
Giscard d'Estaing, Valéry, 370, 382, 385,
387–8, 392, 393, 394
Gitton, Marcel, 241, 261, 264, 278, 284,
285 and n., 303
Glassworkers' Federation, 242, 245
Godonnèche, Victor, 87, 88
Goldenberg (student revolutionary), 58,
61
Gomulka, Wladislaw, 381
Gorky, Maxim, 192
Gottwald, Klement, 332
Gouin, Félix, 343, 344, 350n., 351, 352,
353, 355
Grandel (local councillor), 296
Grange-aux-Belles, 216
Greece, 318
Grenier, Fernand, 287, 291, 301, 314,
317, 323, 324, 343
Grimm, Robert, 50
Gringoire, 283, 284
Griot, Alfred see Rosmer, Alfred
'Groupe communiste français de

Moscou', 37, 39, 59, 181
La Guerre Civile, 182
Guesde, Jules, 21, 23, 26, 27, 29, 38, 67
Guesdists, 22, 24, 27, 33
Guigui, Albert, 335
Guilbeaux, Henri, 58–9, 61, 181
Guillot, Marie, 92, 95, 96, 97
Guingouin, Georges, 309–10, 324
Guralsky, August, 114, 122, 123–4
Guterman, Norbert, 189
Guyot, Raymond, 142, 148, 150, 284–5,
332n.

Halle, 64, 65
Hapiot, Julien, 305
Hardy, Thomas, 181
Haut-Rhin, 158, 177
Haute Vienne, 33
Havez, Auguste, 301
Hegel, G. W. F., 184, 185
Heimatbund, 160
Hemingway, Ernest, 271
Herriot, Edouard, 222, 223, 268; and
Alsace-Lorraine, 159; Soviet
non-aggression pact, 201, 233; retains
power, 228–9; and the proposed
Popular Front, 235–6; and outbreak of
war, 286, 287; and German invasion,
301; postwar contacts with
Communists, 340–1
Hervé, Pierre, 324
Hilferding, Rudolf, 61
Hitler, Adolf, 160, 199, 216, 226, 277,
287, 288, 290, 291, 320, 335; rise to
power, 193, 198, 203, 204, 206, 217,
222; becomes Chancellor, 203;
rearmament, 231; Non-Intervention
policy, 270; invasion of Austria, 272;
and appeasement, 274–5;
German-Soviet pact, 279, 281, 282,
303; invades Poland, 284; advances on
France, 292; occupation of France,
297, 301, 326; attacks Russia, 300, 305,
306; and the Resistance, 313
Ho Chi Minh, 154, 349
Hoffmann (German socialist deputy), 33
Holland, 42, 294, 312
Hueber, Charles, 160
L'Humanité, 38, 60, 97, 103, 104, 105, 135,
143, 155, 157, 181, 188, 189–90, 207,
208, 293n., 321, 325, 340, 381, 389;
circulation, 21; Cachin's editorship,
41, 69, 77–8, 80, 81; Trotsky criticizes,
71; purge of staff, 82; international
trade union movement, 85; opposition
to centralization in, 100; and the

419

Index

strikes, 276; and the German-Soviet pact, 281; and postwar electoral system, 337; and Communist takeover of CGT, 338; CGT split, 359–60
Le Journal du Peuple, 72, 76
Journal Officiel, 286, 357
Julien, André, 181
Juquin, Pierre, 392

Kagan, Georges, 149
Kamenev, Lev Borisovich, 102
Kapp Putsch (1920), 56, 83
Kardelj, Edvard, 358
Kautsky, Karl, 61
Ker, Antoine, 75, 78, 79, 80, 95
Kerensky, Alexander, 264
'Kerensky period', 43
Kharkov Congress (1930), 186, 192
Khrushchev, Nikita, 371–2, 375–8
Kienthal conference (1916), 34, 41, 70
Kommunistische Partei Deutschlands (KPD), 107, 110, 224; formation, 44; at Second Comintern Congress, 58; USPD unites with, 65; failure of revolution, 101–2, 105, 108, 109; and struggle for power amongst Russian Communists, 102; united front tactic, 102–3, 216; Comintern criticism of, 115, 127; bureaucratization, 118; and the Stalin/Bukharin struggle, 141; Neumann denounced, 148; and the occupation of the Ruhr, 153; and Hitler's rise to power, 203–4, 217; and the occupation of France, 298
Kosygin, Alexei, 378
Kriegel, Annie, 46, 49n., 112n., 113, 255, 256, 345
Kriegel-Valrimont, Maurice, 324
Krivine, Alain, 369
Kun, Béla, 71
Kuomintang (KMT), 139

Labour Party (Britain), 20, 29, 104–5, 106, 107, 108
Labourbe, Jeanne, 37
Labrousse (anarcho-syndicalist), 90
Labrousse, Ernest, 181
Lacoste, Robert, 330
Lafont, Ernest, 59
Langevin, Paul, 190, 192, 236, 237, 284
Laporte, Maurice, 71, 95, 152
Largo Caballero, Francisco, 266
Larminat, Colonel R. de, 299
La Rocque, Colonel François de, 251n., 257, 259
Lartigue, Joseph, 97

Lattre de Tassigny, General de, 318–19
Laval, Pierre, 175, 198, 220, 223, 231, 232–4, 235, 239, 268, 340
Lazitch, Branko, 148n.
Lebecq (rightist leader), 231–2
Le Brun, Pierre, 338
Lecoeur, Auguste, 289; in Spanish Civil War, 271; and the German-Soviet pact, 282; in German occupation, 296; hostility to Vichy regime, 302n.; miners' strike, 305; and the Liberation, 322–3; 'grande affaire', 324; in postwar government, 343–4; postwar tactics, 348
Lecoin, Louis, 91
Ledebour (German socialist deputy), 33
Lefebvre, Henri, 189
Lefebvre, Raymond, 58, 60, 64, 180, 181
Légitime Défense, 185
Leiciague, Lucie, 71, 76
Leipzig, 50
Lenin, 39, 56, 123, 125, 221; meeting with French syndicalists, 33; meeting with Loriot, 35, 42; world revolution, 54, 55, 60; '*Left-Wing' Communism*, 57, 84; negotiations with SFIO, 64; and the formation of the PCF, 71; 'French Commission', 79; and international trade union movement, 84; interview with Monmousseau and Sémard, 93–4; Bolshevization and, 114–15; and Alsace-Lorraine, 159; the surrealists and, 183, 184
Leningrad, 381
Lepetit, Jules, 58, 83
Leroy, Roland, 392
Lescure, François de, 302
'Letter of April 2nd', 133–4
'Letter of the 250', 127, 128
Liberation, 308–10, 312–13, 322, 334–5, 354, 393; PCF and, 315–19, 322–3, 327; as a revolution, 339
Libération, 339
Libya, 277
Liebknecht, Karl, 49
Liebknecht, Wilhelm, 26
Ligue des droits de l'homme, 80, 132, 172, 190, 192, 236, 238, 260, 284, 337
Ligue Syndicaliste, 166, 168
Limoges, 176, 309–10, 315
Liochon (print union leader), 89
Litvinov, Maxim, 191, 222
Livre jaune français, 290 and n.
Locarno, Treaty of (1925), 115 and n., 159
Lominadze group, 148

421